The English Language in Canada

Status, History and Comparative Analysis

The English Language in Canada examines the current status, history and principal features of Canadian English, focusing on the "standard" variety heard across the country today. The discussion of the status of Canadian English considers the number and distribution of its speakers, its relation to French and other Canadian languages and to American English, its status as the expressive medium of English-Canadian culture and its treatment in previous research. The review of its history concentrates on the historical roots and patterns of English-speaking settlement that established Canadian English and influenced its character in each region of Canada. The analysis of its principal features compares the vocabulary, pronunciation and grammar of Canadian English to standard British and American English. Subsequent chapters examine variation and change in the vocabulary and pronunciation of Canadian English, while a final chapter briefly considers the future of Canadian English.

CHARLES BOBERG is Associate Professor in the Department of Linguistics at McGill University, Montreal.

Already published in this series:

The English Language in Canada

Status, History and Comparative Analysis

CHARLES BOBERG

Department of Linguistics, McGill University

CAMBRIDGE UNIVERSITY PRESS
Cambridge, New York, Melbourne, Madrid, Cape Town, Singapore,
São Paulo, Delhi, Dubai, Tokyo, Mexico City

Cambridge University Press
The Edinburgh Building, Cambridge CB2 8RU, UK

Published in the United States of America by Cambridge University Press,
New York

www.cambridge.org
Information on this title: www.cambridge.org/9780521874328

First published 2010

Printed in the United Kingdom at the University Press, Cambridge

A catalogue record for this publication is available from the British Library

Library of Congress Cataloguing in Publication data
Boberg, Charles.
The English language in Canada : status, history and comparative analysis /
Charles Boberg.
    p.   cm. – (Studies in English language)
Includes bibliographical references and index.
ISBN 978-0-521-87432-8
1. English language – Canada.   2. English language – Canada – History.
3. English language – Variation – Canada.   4. English language – Spoken
English – Canada.   I. Title.   II. Series.
PE3208.B63   2010
427'.971 – dc22   2010018878

ISBN 978-0-521-87432-8 Hardback

For my sons: William James, Thomas George and Henry Matthew

Contents

Figures

ix

Tables

Acknowledgments

I would like to acknowledge the contributions of many people who aided in the production of this book in one way or another. First, I was greatly assisted by many students at McGill University who helped to carry out the research on which it is based. In addition to the several hundred students in my undergraduate sociolinguistics classes who collected responses to the vocabulary survey reported in Chapter 4, these include many who worked for me as research assistants: Robin Anderson, Antonia Aphantitis, Aileen Bach, Krista Byers-Heinlein, Rachel Corber, Leetal Cuperman, Anicka Fast, Deena Fogle, Hillary Ganek, Rebecca Green, Ulana Harasymowicz, Tracy Higgens, Ivana Iulianella, Ellen House Kogut, Katherine Lanman, Erika Lawrance, Tasha Lewis, Jennifer MacDonald, Corrine McCarthy, Jason McDevitt, Ryan Mullins, Kelly O'Connor, Anne Robitaille, Marie-Catherine Savoie, Sam Shooklyn, Carol Sisson, Kristina Supinski, Carolyn Trengrove, Eva Villalba, Michael Wakahe and Eliza Ycas. Among this group, Bach, Fast, Fogle, Kogut, Lawrance, MacDonald, Shooklyn and Wakahe made particularly important contributions as computer consultants, data analysts, lab administrators and participant interviewers. Equally important, of course, were the members of the public, both McGill students and others, who agreed to be interviewed or who filled out questionnaires, thereby providing the data that underlie many of the analyses in this book. Administrative support was also offered by several members of the secretarial staff in the Department of Linguistics, especially Andria De Luca, Connie Digiuseppe, Mercini McCollum, Linda Suen and Lise Vinet, while the book would never have reached publication without the active encouragement, able assistance and expertise of the staff at Cambridge University Press, particularly Helen Barton, David Cox, Sarah Green, Kay McKechnie and Christina Sarigiannidou, as well as the series editor, Merja Kytö.

The research that went into this book received financial support from three granting agencies: the Canadian Foundation for Innovation; the *Fonds québécois pour la recherche en société et culture* (Grant no. 2003-NC-81927); and the Social Sciences and Humanities Research Council of Canada (Standard Research Grants nos. 410–02-1391 and 410–2005-1924).

Next, I would like to thank people who had a less direct but no less important role in making the book possible. These would include Lydia White and Glyne Piggott, who were Chairs of Linguistics at McGill during much of the period in which the research was carried out; Shari Baum, who made her lab available to me for acoustic analysis when I first arrived at McGill; Jack Chambers, who helped me get started in research on Canadian English as a collaborator on his Dialect Topography project; Bill Labov, who, as my doctoral supervisor at the University of Pennsylvania, taught me most of what I know about sociolinguistics, dialectology and North American English; and my parents, Einer and Julia Boberg, who gave me all the instruction, support, encouragement and love any son could want.

Finally, I would like to thank my wife, Myrtis, without whose heroic efforts and selfless dedication as wife and mother my own work would be impossible.

Map 1 Canada

Map 2 Nova Scotia

Map 3 Ontario

1   English in the Canadian context

One of the most notable demolinguistic phenomena of the modern age has been the expansion of the English language, from its roots as a set of West Germanic dialects in early medieval England to its current position as the leading global lingua franca. It now has hundreds of millions of native speakers and an even larger population of non-native speakers, living in every region of the world. This expansion has involved three major phases: the anglicization of Britain's Celtic population; the transfer of English to other continents through emigration from Britain and colonialism; and the adoption of English as an international language by people in non-English-speaking countries beyond the former British Empire (the three diasporas of Kachru, Kachru and Nelson 2006, originally conceived by Kachru 1985). Part of the middle phase of expansion, beginning in the seventeenth century, was the bringing of English to North America by British colonists. These were as much Irish and Scottish as they were English, thereby reflecting the initial phase of expansion. The eventual success of their colonial project drew many more settlers, first from Britain and Europe and then from all over the world. If they did not already speak English, most of these settlers adopted it and most of their children became native speakers, so that English was established as the majority language of two new multi-ethnic nations, the United States and Canada. This book is a study of the English language in Canada: its current status, history and most important characteristics. It will not comprise a detailed survey of every regional, social or ethnic variety of English spoken in Canada: such a survey is beyond its scope and studies of local varieties of Canadian English are available elsewhere. Rather, it will principally examine the main features of what might be called Standard Canadian English, the variety spoken with subtle regional variations by most middle-class and indeed by many working-class people across the country.

This first chapter will describe and discuss the current status of English in Canada: its relationship with French, Canada's other official language; its co-existence with many other non-official languages; its major regional types; its close contact with the United States and with American English; its role as the voice of English-Canadian culture; and the body of research of which

1

it has been the focus. The following chapters will examine other aspects of Canadian English: Chapter 2 will present the history of settlement that created English-speaking Canada; Chapter 3 will compare the main features of Canadian English with those of other standard varieties; Chapters 4 and 5 will analyze regional variation at the lexical and phonetic levels, respectively; while Chapter 6 will present a summary of the foregoing chapters and a brief speculation on the future of Canadian English.

1.1   One of two official languages

1.1.1   The roots of Canadian bilingualism

According to the Census of Canada, there were 17,882,775 mother-tongue speakers of English in Canada in 2006. These account for about 5 percent of the world total of 337 million calculated by Crystal (1997: 60). While this seems a small proportion, Canada is in fact one of the major English-speaking nations of the world, along with the United Kingdom, the United States, Australia and New Zealand, countries with which it shares a special cultural affinity based on a common language and history. Notwithstanding this bond, Canada is distinguished from these other anglophone nations by having two official languages: in Canada, English shares official status with French. This is a result of Canada's binational colonial history, which is examined in greater detail in Chapter 2. In fact, many Canadians would point to official English–French bilingualism as one of the defining features of Canadian nationhood, differentiating Canada from its much more powerful and influential neighbor to the south.

Whatever its value as a national symbol, the relationship between English- and French-speakers in Canada has often been difficult. It developed from open warfare in the eighteenth century to a resentful separation under British domination in the nineteenth. It then flared up again into armed hostilities in the Papineau Rebellion of 1837 and the Riel Rebellion of 1885 before subsiding into an uneasy and unstable co-existence in the twentieth century. In the title of a recent book on bilingualism in Canada, Fraser (2006) labeled Anglo-French relations "the Canadian crisis that won't go away." Ever since the British defeat of France at Quebec in 1759 and the transfer of France's remaining North American colonies to Britain by the Treaty of Paris in 1763, the common thread of this troubled history has been a struggle among French Canadians to avoid marginalization and linguistic and cultural assimilation in an evermore English-speaking continent, a fate that to a large extent has befallen both the Aboriginal cultures that predate the arrival of the British and French in Canada and the successive waves of immigrants from around the world that followed their arrival.

Canada's modern bilingual status originates in two historic developments: the colonization and settlement of the territory that now constitutes Canada by both France and Britain; and the decision of British colonial authorities, following the British conquest, to allow a continuation of French language, culture and institutions in Quebec, rather than attempting the complete assimilation of their French-speaking subjects into an English-speaking and culturally British society (the Quebec Act of 1774). When Canada became an autonomous British dominion in 1867, though extensive English-speaking settlement had already reduced French-speakers to less than a third of the population, the status of French as one of two national languages was protected by the British North America Act, Canada's founding legislation. Section 133 of this act stated that:

> Either the English or the French Language may be used by any Person in the Debates of the Houses of the Parliament of Canada and of the Houses of the Legislature of Quebec; and both those Languages shall be used in the respective Records and Journals of those Houses; and either of those Languages may be used by any Person or in any Pleading or Process in or issuing from any Court of Canada established under this Act, and in or from all or any of the Courts of Quebec. (Canada, Department of Justice, 1983: 45–46)

When Canada revised and updated its constitution in 1982, the new Canadian Charter of Rights and Freedoms included a section on official languages of Canada that confirmed the provisions of the British North America Act, stating plainly in Section 16 (1) that:

> English and French are the official languages of Canada and have equality of status and equal rights and privileges as to their use in all institutions of the Parliament and government of Canada. (Canada, Department of Justice, 1983: 65)

Despite these official guarantees, the practical status of English and French in Canada has never been equal, with English in the ascendant and French struggling to survive outside its main base in Quebec. Even within Quebec, many French Canadians by the mid twentieth century felt their language and culture to be threatened by a large and powerful English-speaking minority and by a steady influx of immigrants who tended to adopt English rather than French as their second language. This situation contributed to the rise of a French-Canadian nationalist movement in the 1960s that posed a serious threat to Canadian unity. The federal government attempted to respond to this threat in 1963 by establishing a Royal Commission on Bilingualism and Biculturalism to study the problem. The commission's findings led, in 1969, to the adoption of the federal Official Languages Act, which sought to promote bilingualism across Canada, both within federal institutions and in Canadian society as a whole, thereby making French Canadians feel more like equal partners in Confederation.

Canada, however, is a federal state, in which administrative prerogatives are divided between the federal government, in Ottawa, and the governments of Canada's ten provinces (the three northern territories are federally administered, with more limited local autonomy). To provincial jurisdiction the British North America Act assigned such crucial legislative domains as healthcare, municipal institutions, natural resources, education and agriculture, thereby creating a decentralized federal state, in which federal power is constitutionally limited. With respect to language, this has meant that the provinces have been free to develop their own policies, as long as the federal Charter rights are respected. In large part, these policies have reflected local demolinguistic reality rather than national bilingual idealism. The reality is that speakers of Canada's two official languages, far from being evenly distributed across the country, are heavily concentrated in certain areas. Tables 1.1a and b show the number of people reporting English, French and non-official languages as their only mother tongue in each province and territory of Canada, first with the proportion of each province or territory's population accounted for by each language group (Table 1.1a), then with the proportion of each language group accounted for by each province or territory (Table 1.1b). In discussions of language use in Canada, these groups are referred to respectively as *anglophones*, *francophones* and *allophones* (*allo-* from the Greek for *other*).

Beyond the general national predominance of English over French (57 vs. 22 percent), Tables 1.1a and b show the uneven territorial distribution of speakers of Canada's two official languages. The large majority of francophones live in Quebec (86 percent), where they constitute the majority of the provincial population (79 percent), while the rest of Canada is mainly English-speaking, with relatively few francophones. New Brunswick, on Quebec's eastern border, is the only other province where francophones constitute more than 5 percent of the population. Indeed, Quebec, New Brunswick and Prince Edward Island, the latter two of which attract very little overseas immigration, are the only provinces or territories where francophones are not outnumbered by speakers of non-official languages as the second-largest linguistic group after English. This has meant that full, official bilingualism at the provincial level is restricted to New Brunswick, where francophones make up a third of the population, while the provincial governments of Ontario and Manitoba provide services in French to their proportionally smaller francophone populations on an as-needed basis. The French Language Services Act introduced by Ontario in 1986, for example, guarantees the right of Franco-Ontarians to receive provincial government services in French in twenty-five designated areas. It is overseen by an Office of Francophone Affairs, which seeks to encourage Ontario's francophones to participate fully in provincial life while maintaining their linguistic and cultural heritage.

Table 1.1a *Mother tongues in Canada, 2006 (single responses by province and territory, with percentage of total populations) (see Map 1 for locations)*

Province	Tot. pop.	English	% of tot.	French	% of tot.	Non-official	% of tot.
BC	4,074,385	2,875,775	70.6	54,740	1.3	1,091,530	26.8
Alberta	3,256,360	2,576,665	79.1	61,225	1.9	583,525	17.9
Sask.	953,845	811,730	85.1	16,055	1.7	118,465	12.4
Manitoba	1,133,515	838,415	74.0	43,960	3.9	236,315	20.8
Ontario	12,028,895	8,230,705	68.4	488,815	4.1	3,134,045	26.1
Quebec	7,435,900	575,560	7.7	5,877,660	79.0	886,280	11.9
NB	719,650	463,190	64.4	232,980	32.4	18,320	2.5
NS	903,090	832,105	92.1	32,540	3.6	34,620	3.8
PEI	134,205	125,265	93.3	5,345	4.0	2,960	2.2
Nfld/Lab.	500,610	488,405	97.6	1,885	0.4	9,540	1.9
Yukon	30,195	25,655	85.0	1,105	3.7	3,180	10.5
NWT	41,055	31,545	76.8	970	2.4	8,160	19.9
Nunavut	29,325	7,765	26.5	370	1.3	20,885	71.2
Canada	31,241,030	17,882,775	57.2	6,817,655	21.8	6,147,840	19.7

Source: Statistics Canada, 2006 Census of Canada.

Table 1.1b *Mother tongues in Canada, 2006 (proportion of total population and of each language group living in each province) (see Map 1 for locations)*

Province	Tot. pop. (%)	English (%)	French (%)	Non-official (%)
BC	13.0	16.1	0.8	17.8
Alberta	10.4	14.4	0.9	9.5
Sask.	3.1	4.5	0.2	1.9
Manitoba	3.6	4.7	0.6	3.8
Ontario	38.5	46.0	7.2	51.0
Quebec	23.8	3.2	86.2	14.4
NB	2.3	2.6	3.4	0.3
NS	2.9	4.7	0.5	0.6
PEI	0.4	0.7	0.1	0.0
Nfld/Lab.	1.6	2.7	0.0	0.2
Yukon	0.1	0.1	0.0	0.1
NWT	0.1	0.2	0.0	0.1
Nunavut	0.1	0.0	0.0	0.3
Canada	100.0	100.0	100.0	100.0

Source: Statistics Canada, 2006 Census of Canada.

1.1.2   English and French in Quebec

The situation of English and French in Quebec deserves special consideration, since it is very different from that in the rest of Canada, having been shaped by a program of massive government intervention designed to prevent a gradual decline in the vitality of French. This program has met with some success and has therefore attracted considerable attention outside Quebec, particularly from those in language-planning circles who are interested in sustaining the viability of minority or traditional languages, or in moderating, stopping or reversing the global expansion of English. Unfortunately, the effort to support French in Quebec has had the secondary effect of damaging Quebec's English-speaking community, a fact that is of less interest to the world's language planners but cannot be ignored by the half million English-speakers who remain in the province. Indeed, while English thrives in the rest of Canada, gaining new speakers every year, in Quebec it has been in retreat during the three decades since Quebec's language laws came into effect. These developments have been highly controversial and have generated a huge body of comment and analysis in both popular and academic circles, from a wide range of perspectives. Here, in keeping with the focus of this book, the author will attempt a summary of the main issues from the perspective of their impact on the English-speaking community, and offer some of his own views of this much debated situation.

In Quebec, the Official Languages Act and the guarantees of linguistic equality in the Federal constitution, referred to in the previous section, were not enough to quell many French Canadians' fears of linguistic attrition and assimilation, while a smaller group believed the only way to secure the future of the French language and francophone culture in North America was political separation from Canada. In fact, following passage of the Official Languages Act, French Canadian nationalism seemed to grow rather than ebb. It came to focus on four perceived threats to the future survival of French: the general decline of francophones as a proportion of the Canadian population; the declining birth rate of francophones in Quebec; freedom of choice in language of schooling; and the dominant position of English in commerce and industry (d'Anglejan 1984: 31–36). To a large extent, these threats were seen to be interrelated.

The most pressing concern of the nationalists was the assimilation of immigrants into anglophone rather than francophone culture, an issue that rose to prominence because of a sharp decline in the birth rate of native Quebec francophones. Until the 1960s, Quebec's francophone population had been not only sustained but increased by a high birth rate, consistent with the Roman Catholic values and traditional family structure of the majority of the population. During the nineteenth century, Quebec women had an average of six children each; the average was as high as eight among rural francophones, which was double the average for anglophones. This produced a large increase in the francophone population known as *la revanche des berceaux*, 'the revenge of the cradles' (Henripin 1989: 31). As late as the 1950s the rate was still close to four children per woman, well above the level required to balance deaths (Henripin 1989: 35, 51). The growing immigrant populations of Canada and Quebec tended to favor English as their adopted language: even in Quebec, transfers to English during the post-war immigrant boom were more than twice as common as transfers to French (Caldwell 1974: 52; Charbonneau and Maheu 1973: 71). Despite this pattern, natural increase of the francophone population balanced immigrant additions to the English-speaking population and maintained traditional proportions of francophones: about a third of Canada and 80 percent of Quebec.

The societal changes that accompanied Quebec's *Quiet Revolution* in the 1960s threatened to alter this balance, however, by causing the proportion of francophones in both Canada and Quebec to shrink. A rebellion against the traditional power and influence of the Church in Quebec society challenged traditional family structures and encouraged the practice of contraception and abortion, while the rise of feminism meant that younger Quebec women were better educated, more independent and less interested in devoting their lives to raising children than their mothers had been. As a result, by 1971 the birth rate was cut in half; over the following decade it dropped further, until it was fewer than two children per woman. This was not enough to sustain the current population, let alone match the continued growth of the increasingly anglophone immigrant population; by the mid 1980s it had reached a low of one and a half children per woman (Henripin 1989: 35). In light of these changes, which seemed unlikely to be reversed, it became clear to language planners that maintaining the historic proportions of francophones would depend on compelling immigrants to speak French rather than English (Henripin 1973). A failure to do so threatened demographic doom, at least in the long term. One demographic projection made in 1969 predicted that by the year 2000, in the absence of corrective governmental intervention, the proportion of francophones would decline from 82 percent to 72 percent in Quebec as a whole and from 66 percent to 53 percent in Montreal (Charbonneau, Henripin and Légaré 1970: 201). Another, similar projection was made for the year 1991 by Charbonneau and Maheu (1973: 292). The cause of this projected decline was not natural increase among Quebec anglophones: their rate of natural increase was also dropping and remained consistently below that of francophones (Charbonneau and Maheu 1973: 279; Paillé 1985: 108). It was the growth of the immigrant population. By the late 1970s, 72 percent of Montreal allophones were transferring to English, compared to only 28 percent transferring to French (Paillé 1985: 55).

The main assimilatory agent causing the transfer of immigrant populations to English was clearly the school system in which immigrant children were educated. In 1969, the Quebec government attempted to address this concern by adopting Bill 63, which respected the right of parents to choose the language of instruction for their children while encouraging immigrant children to attend French schools and ensuring that all children developed an adequate knowledge of French. Unfortunately, far from appeasing nationalist sentiment, Bill 63 aggravated it by appearing to enshrine the principle of free choice: without stricter controls, it was assumed that most immigrants would continue to choose English. Moreover, Bill 63 did nothing to address another systemically related concern, the language of work. One of the reasons that immigrants wanted English-language education for their children, and that many French Canadians themselves felt a need to learn English, was that English was still a necessary language in many workplaces and was strongly associated with upward social mobility. To satisfy these concerns, which were examined by the provincially appointed Gendron Commission from 1968 to 1973 (Government of Quebec 1972), Bill 63 was superseded in 1974 by Bill 22. This more comprehensive law made French the official language of Quebec; implemented a process of *francisation* of the workplace; and abolished freedom of choice in education, restricting English-language education to children with sufficient pre-existing knowledge of English, thereby effectively barring non-English-speaking immigrant children from attendance.

Finally, in the provincial election of 1976, an avowedly separatist group, the Parti Québécois, was elected to office. Its first legislative business was to introduce Bill 101, now Law 101, the controversial Charter of the French Language (1977), which sought to go farther even than Bill 22 in establishing Quebec as an exclusively French-speaking domain. The Charter ended the remaining official use of English in government and law (thereby overturning the bilingual status conferred on Quebec by the British North America Act); made *francisation* mandatory for large businesses; limited access to English education to children whose parents or siblings had been educated in English in Quebec; and introduced what was to become its most iconic measure, a ban on English commercial signage, as part of an intended *francisation* of Montreal itself. Some provisions of the Charter were subsequently challenged successfully in the courts and had to be softened: English education rights were extended to children whose parents had been educated in English anywhere in Canada; and the ban on English signs, declared a violation of Canadians' constitutional right to freedom of expression, was replaced with a requirement that French be predominant over other languages (Bill 178, 1988 and Bill 86, 1993). This predominance was to be measured and enforced by a team of inspectors, derisively called by their detractors the "language police." The inspectors' efforts, particularly when directed at such evidently absurd targets as imported British beer coasters, kosher food products and "authentic" Irish pubs, or against apparently trivial orthographic infringements like apostrophes in business names or the lack of a final <e> on *Tavern*, have frequently attracted scorn and ridicule in Montreal's anglophone community. More seriously, they have often been resented by the affected businesses as harassment and bullying, given the businesses' responsibility for buying and installing new signage and the government's power to levy fines for non-compliance.

Not surprisingly, while it was welcomed by most francophones, the Charter met with overwhelming disapproval among anglophones. Locher (1988: 83) reports a survey showing over 80 percent of anglophones opposed to the law and fewer than 10 percent in favor (see also Levine 1990: 119–120). Among many it was perceived as a direct attack on their rights and on their historic status as one of the founding peoples of modern Quebec (Taylor and Dubé-Simard 1984). Caldwell (1982: 60) presents statistics showing that English Quebeckers have consistently made up about a fifth of the province's population going back to the 1840s; Rudin (1985: 28) shows that they made up 10 percent of the population – more than twice the proportion of francophones in any Canadian province other than Quebec or New Brunswick today – as early as 1812; Provost (1984) documents the already considerable English community of over a thousand people resident in Montreal by the 1770s (see also Levine 1990: 8). In a flagrant denial of this history, the Charter sought to impose a unilingual state on a bilingual society.

The Charter's principal architect, Parti Québécois cabinet minister Camille Laurin, denied any anti-English sentiment in its intent. He insisted that its main goal was "to give the people of Quebec concrete means with which to express their own identity and to make it respected everywhere by all, without committing injustice" and "to assure, in a climate of respect for others, the expansion of the French language in all domains of the social life of Quebec". He emphasized, moreover, that it "was not adopted to stifle the expression of an English culture in Quebec" and that the spirit of its authors was "far from meanness or a spirit of vengeance in regard to the anglophone community." On the contrary, he predicted that "the English community will remain vital in Quebec" and urged that, "if this community undertakes to integrate itself increasingly in the cultural life of Quebec, without ever renouncing its language, identity or institutions, this will enrich Quebec society" (the author's own translation of Laurin 1980: 9).

Nevertheless, to some of its opponents the Charter seemed to be exactly what Laurin claimed it was not: a mean-spirited, vengeful attack on Quebec's English community. William Johnson, a harsh critic of Bill 101, argues that this attack was the culmination of a long history of anglophobia in French Canadian society; a suspicion, resentment and even hatred of "the English" that has deep roots in the intellectual and literary traditions of Quebec, nurtured by a cultural memory of the British Conquest (Johnson 1991; see also Scowen 1991: 143–147). For the Catholic clergy who dominated traditional Quebec society, the English were the main local representatives of Protestantism, in their eyes a dangerous heresy, as well as of secular liberalism, a further threat to the spiritual well-being of their parishioners. For the secular leaders of modern Quebec, the English were the capitalist elite, a convenient scapegoat for the frustrations of the French-Canadian people and a target for the resentment of its working class in particular: fanning that resentment could serve the interests of an aspiring populist politician or union organizer. For their part, some of the English had perhaps encouraged this resentment by an imperious assumption of their own superiority and a refusal to learn or use French: they had behaved like colonial overlords in a conquered land. Of course, most of the English were not members of any elite and bilingualism was higher among Quebec's anglophones (37 percent) than among franco-phones (26 percent) even in 1971 (Termote and Gauvreau 1988: 65), but such facts do not get in the way of ethnic stereotyping. Another factor sometimes alluded to in arguments about language laws is the history of anglophone treatment of francophone minorities in English-speaking provinces, which was not always as generous or nurturing as Ontario's current policy, in some cases ranging from neglect to hostility. Though most anglophones, as is evident in Ontario's current approach, now admit that such treatment was wrong or at least regrettable, its legacy has been to contribute to franco-phones' sense of themselves as a threatened minority and to encourage their resentment of English dominance.

Whether or not the Charter was conceived in a spirit of vengeance, its approach does seem to discount the crucial role that anglophones played in the development of several regions of Quebec, especially the Gaspé, Quebec City, the Ottawa Valley, the Eastern Townships and of course Montreal. It appears to reject the two-centuries-old bilingual culture of Montreal in particular, which was once the most important metropolis of Canada and a symbol of its national bilingual and bicultural identity. Indeed, in the mid nineteenth century, a small majority of Montrealers were anglophones: Levine (1990: 8) says this was true as early as 1831 and that, by 1851, 55 percent of the population of 60,000 was of British ethnic origin (see also Rudin 1985: 36, who points out that even Quebec City was 44 percent anglophone in 1861). It was a comparatively high francophone birth rate (the *revanche des berceaux* discussed above), together with the migration of a surplus rural population into the city to find work (often in businesses established by anglophones), that restored a francophone majority later in the century. But the creation of modern Montreal as a major industrial city in the nineteenth century, and its further development in the twentieth, had relied crucially on the contributions of English-speakers (Baillie and Baillie 2001; Rudin 1985: 69–93, 201–221).

Despite this history, the goal of the francophone nationalist movement, and of the Charter, appeared to be the development of an exclusive equiv-alence between the "national" culture of Quebec and the French language, a blending of civic and ethnic entities through an identification of the state with the language and culture of the majority of its citizens. No longer French Canadians, an ethnolinguistic minority within Canada, these citi-zens would be *québécois*, the people of a francophone state. To that end, the Charter aimed not simply to ensure a place for French alongside English in public life, or even to establish a dominance of French corresponding to its majority status, but to eliminate the use of any other language for any public purpose, thereby symbolically erasing the non-francophone element of Quebec's heritage and identity. The role of non-francophone citizens in this *québécois* national enterprise seemed uncertain; some feared they might become second-class citizens, ruled by a government dedicated not to equal treatment of all but to the cultural interest of the majority.

As if to emphasize the deliberate and officially sanctioned effacement of Montreal's English heritage, where money for new public signs was in short supply, English words like *street* and *road* and *building* and *shopping center* were simply painted over, evidence of which can still be seen in some Montreal neighborhoods today. Even English-language bookstores came under the general law governing commercial signage and were obliged to display their wares under section titles like *romans*, *enfants* and *nouveautés*, though all of the books and, presumably, most of the customers were English. While many American cities now provide Spanish-language signage, tickets and notices on their public transit systems to accommodate minority populations, Montreal's public transit agencies communicate with their riders exclusively in French, even on commuter trains that serve a largely English-speaking clientele; there is more English in the metro systems of many European cities than in Montreal's. The latest insult to non-francophone Quebeckers has been a campaign by the government's French Language Office to distribute stickers to be displayed in the entrances of businesses, bearing the provincial *fleur-de-lys* symbol and proclaiming, "*Ici on commerce en français*" ('Here we do business in French'). In other Canadian cities, painting over minority-language signs or posting notices implying that minority-language customers are not welcome would likely have decidedly racist undertones. For instance, it is difficult to imagine a sign saying "Here we do business in English" being acceptable, much less officially promoted, in a multi-ethnic neighborhood of Toronto, where the city takes pride in the great diversity of languages on its street signs. In Montreal, however, the proponents of these measures feel they are justified by the threatened status of French as a minority language in the continental context, a status that obviously does not apply to English in Toronto.

In the decades following the rise of the nationalist regime, its exclusionary language legislation, together with the political uncertainty arising from the separatist movement, prompted a massive exodus of English-speakers from Quebec, numbering well over 100,000 people. This was the main factor in reducing Montreal's anglophone population by a third, from a high of over 600,000 mother-tongue speakers in 1976 to just over 400,000 in 2001 (Jedwab 2004: 7, 14). Most of these went to other parts of Canada, particularly neighboring Ontario (Jedwab 1996: 43–44), thereby contributing to the increasing polarization of Canada's official language communities in separate parts of the country (Castonguay 1998: 41–43). While some businesses and institutions adapted successfully to francization (Miller 1984), others chose to leave rather than adapt. Joining the general anglophone exodus were therefore many businesses, trades people and professionals, a flight of capital and skills that damaged Montreal's economy, created shortages in certain occupations, depressed property values and aided the rise of Toronto, already underway for other reasons, to replace Montreal as Canada's pre-eminent metropolis. (In the Census of 1971, Montreal was still the largest metropolitan area in Canada, though businesses had been transferring their operations to better-located and faster-growing Toronto for several decades. By the Census of 1981, Montreal had lost even its population advantage, becoming the regional commercial center of Quebec and the cultural center of francophone Canada rather than the metropolis of Canada a whole.) The fact cannot be ignored that some francophones were in a position to benefit from the anglophone exodus, occupying the jobs and houses (at bargain prices) that the anglos left behind. While it would be overly cynical to suggest that this shift of resources was one of the motivations for Bill 101, it was certainly one of its effects. To be fair, other francophones were hurt by the Charter, such as those who want their children to learn more English than is taught in public schools and now have to pay for private schools in order to circumvent the language laws.

On the positive side, Bill 101 appeased the insecurities of the majority of the francophone population, so that once the most resentful anglophones had left, a period of relative linguistic peace and intercultural harmony was achieved – if on largely francophone terms – that lasts to this day. While language transfers of immigrants continued to favor English, transfers to French rose dramatically (Barbaud 1998: 189; Veltman 1996: 223) and the large majority of immigrant children now attend French schools (Barbaud 1998: 192). This has helped the proportion of francophones in Quebec and Montreal to stay well above the dire forecasts of the demographers, as shown by the current data on mother tongues presented above in Tables 1.1 and 1.2. Equally important, barriers to employment and socio-economic advancement for monolingual francophones have been greatly alleviated (Barbaud 1998: 193–194; Bourhis 2001: 125–126; Laporte 1984: 61–67; Veltman 1996: 229). Bilingualism – or at least knowledge of French and willingness to speak it – has increased among Quebec's remaining anglophone population (partly owing to the departure of many monolingual anglophones). By 1981, 53 percent of Montreal anglophones were already bilingual, compared to only 40 percent of Montreal francophones (Termote and Gauvreau 1988: 65); by 2001, the proportion had climbed to 67 percent, compared to 37 percent of francophones (Parenteau, Magnan and Thibault 2008: 15). Most crucially, two subsequent attempts (in 1980 and 1995) by the Parti Québécois to win a referendum giving them a mandate to begin negotiating separation from Canada were defeated, if only by narrow margins dependent on non-francophone votes.

Meanwhile, in some respects the situation for Quebec's English-speakers has not been as grim as some have made out or feared it would become. English-language services continue to be extended on demand to

English-speaking residents by the provincial government and its agencies in a quiet, limited, non-official way, a situation that is in some respects not unlike the treatment of large francophone populations in English-majority provinces. Municipalities that had anglophone majorities at the time the language laws were introduced are permitted to continue serving their populations in both languages; even those not meeting this criterion offer some services and communications in both languages as warranted by demand. Moreover, many anglophone institutions and small and family businesses continue to function primarily in English. These include English-language radio and television stations, a major daily newspaper (the *Gazette*), public school boards, several junior colleges, McGill, Concordia and Bishop's Universities, several major hospitals and the Anglican and United Churches.

Nevertheless, significant problems remain for Quebec's English-speaking minority (Caldwell 1984, 1998; Veltman 1996: 227–233). In rural areas, small anglophone populations face the same pressures of assimilation and out-migration as rural francophone populations in English-majority provinces (Rudin 1985: 175–199). Even in Montreal, where the decline has been less drastic, the viability of many English-language schools has been threatened or defeated by the law cutting them off from sources of new students among the immigrant population (Quebec Ministry of Education 1992; Mallea 1984: 240). Rather than insisting only that non-English-speaking children attend French school, which would have corrected the main source of imbalance in the language transfer pattern, Bill 101 prevents even English-speaking immigrants from attending English schools. This is a strong disincentive against anglophones from other parts of Canada or the world moving to Quebec and makes English schools entirely dependent on the native population of anglophones for their students. Given the rate of natural increase in this group, which, like the native francophone rate, is too low to sustain the population, this policy essentially dooms the English school system to eventual collapse. Between 1970 and 1990, enrolment in Montreal English schools declined by 64 percent (Quebec Ministry of Education 1992; Jedwab 2004: 32), a precipitous drop that seriously hampers the English community's ability to perpetuate itself.

Once they leave school, many Quebec anglophones, even when they speak functional second-language French, face language-based barriers to employment and advancement. This is especially true in Quebec's large public sector, which is disproportionately francophone: of over 57,000 public service employees, fewer than 1 percent are anglophones (Jedwab 2004: 51). Some graduates end up leaving the province to find work, thereby further diminishing the anglophone population and depriving its schools of the next generation of anglophone children. In 1991, a survey of high school and junior college students in Quebec found that 61 percent of anglophones intended to leave Quebec within five years, and that the province's language laws were the most common reason for leaving (Locher 1992: 13, 21). Bourhis (2001:

121) cites a "brain drain" of anglophone university graduates: in the decade following the introduction of the Charter, 26,550 graduates left Quebec, as high as 40 percent of the total. As recently as the late 1990s, another 28,660 anglophones were lost to net interprovincial migration. Anglophones were five times more likely to leave Quebec than the population as a whole, and the age group most likely to leave was those between 15 and 34 years old: young adults starting careers and families (Parenteau, Magnan and Thibault 2008: 26–27).

In light of these problems and a general sense of injustice (Taylor and Dubé-Simard 1984: 162–167), some Quebeckers, especially anglophones, have questioned whether the vitality of French in Quebec was really so threatened as to justify the more extreme measures of Quebec's language legislation, which appear to have sought the promotion of French at least partly through the demotion and suppression of English. While the inferior economic position of francophones relative to anglophones was a demonstrable problem across Canada, established by the Royal Commission on Bilingualism and Biculturalism in the 1960s, the substantial demolinguistic decline of French was a problem restricted largely to Canada outside Quebec: if French needed emergency support, it was in Ontario and western Canada, not in Quebec. The proportions of people speaking English and French in Quebec remained essentially stable at 13–14 percent and 80–83 percent, respectively, over the two decades preceding the imposition of Bill 101 (Castonguay 1998: 42). Both languages showed a very gradual relative decline as the proportion of speakers of non-official languages grew, but the number of people using French at home in 1971 was actually 2,850 more than the 4,870,100 mother-tongue speakers (Castonguay 1998: 42), indicating that a large-scale anglicization of francophones was not underway. On the contrary, the proportion of people of British ethnic origin with French as their mother tongue (16.5 percent) was far higher than the proportion of people of French ethnic origin with English as their mother tongue (0.6 percent, Caldwell 1974: 55). Only 1.5 percent of Quebec mother-tongue francophones spoke English at home in 1971, compared to 6.2 percent of mother-tongue anglophones who spoke French at home (Paillé 1985: 67). Moreover, outside Montreal, the proportion of francophones was over 90 percent, hardly justifying drastic intervention.

Only in Montreal was French competing with other languages spoken by substantial populations, but even in Montreal it was still the majority language. Much of the purported justification for language legislation came not from the contemporary situation but from future projections made by demographers, as discussed above. Even the least favorable models of these projections, however, indicated a moderate diminution of the size of the francophone majority rather than its reduction to a minority, at least in the foreseeable future. The projection of Charbonneau, Henripin and Légaré (1970: 201), that Montreal would be only 53 percent francophone by 2000, is very much in line with the proportion of native English-speakers in Toronto or Vancouver today (Table 1.2). There is no evidence that such a proportion seriously impedes local cultural life, particularly not when backed up by a large hinterland that is virtually monolingual. Another perceived threat was from the high incidence of French–English bilingualism among Montreal francophones (42 percent in 1961, Charbonneau and Maheu 1973: 111). This was seen not as an economic and cultural advantage for the bilinguals but as a dangerous first step in an imagined future transfer to English, which indeed it is for francophones outside Quebec, who in most places lack the critical mass of population to sustain a francophone culture. In Quebec, however, francophone transfers to English were and remain negligible: in 1981, they amounted to only 106,375 people, or 2 percent of the francophone population, which was much lower than the 12 percent of the anglophone population who had transferred to French by that year (Termote and Gauvreau 1988: 131–132).

The demotion and suppression of English in Quebec was evidently predicated on the notion that the position of French was so weak as to prevent its survival in anything other than a unilingual French society; that the attachment of francophones themselves to speaking French was so tenuous as to be abandoned in the face of any temptation to speak English instead. Yet this notion seems at odds with the admirable vitality of contemporary francophone culture in Quebec. In fact, it is difficult to see how the use of English by some people in some districts of Montreal threatens the ability of other people in other districts, or in Quebec City, Saguenay, Sherbrooke or Trois Rivières, to live their lives in French. From a different perspective, the bilingual and multicultural nature of Montreal, so distinct from the rest of Quebec, might have been seen as a valuable resource with the potential to enrich local society, rather than as a dangerous threat to be eliminated through the forcible francization of non-francophones. That it was not seen in this light suggested to some that the true motivation for restrictions on English was simply the pleasure of a newly powerful majority in asserting itself and winning a symbolic victory over its former colonial masters: a latter-day revenge for France's defeat on the Plains of Abraham, or retribution for the arrogance – or ignorance – of clerks in English-owned businesses who had refused to serve francophone customers in French.

Other Quebeckers – even many anglophones – concede that there was an imminent decline in or serious impediment to the vitality of French and that something needed to be done to reverse it, which justified certain limits on personal freedom in deference to societal goals. However, some of these supporters believe that the laws have now accomplished their task and should be loosened or lifted. Quebec's francophones today enjoy a vibrant, well-established local culture that includes celebrated successes in film, literature, popular music and theater, while millions of the province's people live entirely in French, using the language at home, in higher education, at work (regardless of occupational level) and in their recreational activities, watching French-language television and reading French newspapers and magazines. Indeed, many would suggest that it is now the English community that shows signs of decline warranting support (Jedwab 2004: 3–5; Libman 2009): from a demolinguistic perspective, it has certainly suffered a far more alarming erosion than the francophone community. From a high of 25 percent in 1851, Table 1.1a above indicates that the English share of Quebec's population has declined by about two-thirds to today's level of less than 8 percent. In the last three decades alone, it has fallen by a third, a decline far worse than the most pessimistic forecasts of the decline of French, which justified Bill 101. Nonetheless, on the other side of the debate, some francophones, like members of the Mouvement Montréal Français, the Parti Québécois youth wing and the Saint-Jean-Baptiste Society, believe the laws have not yet gone far enough, or are not adequately enforced (Bourhis 2001). They point to lingering use of English in business, where bilingual employees are still preferred over monolingual francophones, and by immigrants, some of whom continue to show a preference for English and fail to integrate into francophone society. They also criticize the loss of francophone students to English colleges and universities, once these students have graduated from high school and are beyond the reach of laws governing the language of education (Barbaud 1998).

Language legislation and the proper status of English in Quebec continue, then, to be a source of controversy, with each person's perspective – as English, French or other; mono- or bi- or trilingual; libertarian, liberal or socialist – influencing his or her opinion (see Bourhis (1984a) for a range of views and approaches; Fishman (1991), Bourhis (2001) and Oakes and Warren (2007) for retrospective assessments of Bill 101; Legault (1992) for a francophone perspective; and Caldwell and Waddell (1982), Levine (1990), Rudin (1985), Scowen (1991) and Stevenson (1999) for some anglophone perspectives). To a large extent, the conflict reflects a basic tension between individual rights, the cornerstone of the Anglo-American liberal tradition, and collective rights, which hold greater importance for many francophones, having historical roots in Roman Catholicism and finding modern secular expression in the social welfare state constructed in Quebec since the 1960s (Arnopoulos and Clift 1984: 35–50; MacMillan 1998: 100–138; Scowen 1991: 88–91).

Moral high ground in the debate seems difficult to establish. The historical primacy invoked by some francophones as a justification for declaring Quebec a French-only state ("we were here first") is clearly falsified by Quebec's Aboriginal peoples, who predate the French by thousands of years, yet few people express equivalent concern for the vitality of Algonquian or Iroquoian languages in Quebec. From the Aboriginal perspective, French and English are both intrusive colonial languages, neither of which has any natural right to predominate. From the European colonial perspective, Britain gained control of New France in a struggle between more or less equally powerful colonial empires: the original French conquerors were conquered themselves. Britain then invested money, resources and people into developing the colony, seemingly securing the right of future English-speakers to enjoy at least an equal place in the society that resulted. From a Canadian perspective, Canada, since its independence from Britain, has further devoted tremendous national resources to the development of Quebec and continues to give it billions of dollars in "equalization payments" from richer provinces, along with other direct investments, federal transfers and subsidies, which help to sustain its economy and infrastructure and the level of services it can offer its citizens. This would seem to justify an expectation that the Canadian principle of equal regard for Canada's two founding cultures and official languages would be respected. From the civil rights perspective, the liberal principle of freedom of choice would seem to favor granting individuals the right to choose the language in which they wish to express themselves or educate their children, thereby leaving the fate of the languages themselves up to the collective weight of individual choices: if French is to survive, it should be up to French-speakers, not others, to save it.

Proponents of language legislation, however, might point out that there is no real freedom of choice if that choice is constrained by social, institutional or economic pressures to choose one language over the other. In this view, continued use of French can be assured only by diminishing or extinguishing local use of English, which enjoys "unfair" advantages stemming from its majority status in North America and its international status as the world's leading global language. If Quebeckers' use of English is therefore to be extinguished, however, it is difficult to see how there is a net gain in language rights, since one person's freedom to use his or her language is preserved only by taking away another's. There is a net gain only in the sense that there are more winners than losers in this scenario, French being the majority language in Quebec. From this democratic perspective, of course, the majority rules, which is perhaps the only principle that really matters in this case: the majority has voted in free and legitimate elections for laws limiting individual freedom of choice. Indeed, after enacting Bill 101, the Parti Québécois was returned to government in the next provincial election. Moreover, people who object to the laws enacted by the majority have had the right to leave, a right many have already exercised.

Nevertheless, one might ask whether, if francophones have a collective right to the survival of their language and culture, the same right extends to Quebec's anglophones. The experience of the last three decades suggests that it does not: Quebec's language laws have clearly sought the protection of the former group at the expense of the latter. Given comparably low birth rates in both communities, which have made them equally dependent on immigration for survival, a law forcing the entire immigrant population to integrate with one community essentially condemns the other to eventual collapse. Quebec's francophones have used their majority to shift what was once their own predicament onto the English community instead. At present, that community has no legal means of sustaining its population, let alone increasing it, short of a miraculous rise in the birth rate of native anglophones, or a massive immigration of anglophones from other provinces, both of which are highly unlikely. In fact, anglophones continue to leave Quebec, thereby deepening the crisis. To some, who see Quebec's English community merely as a local extension of the larger North American community, its possible disappearance is of no great concern: the more important goal is ensuring the continued vitality of French. To others, who see Anglo-Quebec as a unique English community with a legitimate place in Quebec and Canadian society and a long history worth preserving, its probable fate is lamentable.

The evolution of this debate in the decades to come will no doubt have a major effect on the future of English in Quebec. At least for the foreseeable future, its current resolution has established English as a minority language in Quebec in every sense: not just numerically, as before, but now socially and institutionally as well. This unique status, it will be suggested in later chapters, has contributed to the distinctive character of Montreal English and therefore, ironically, to its cultural value in Canada and in the English-speaking world as a whole.

1.1.3   Bilingualism in Canada today

To the extent that Quebec's language legislation did in fact prevent or reverse a decline in Quebec's French-speaking population, it can be seen as contributing to the success of the federal ideal of a bilingual Canada: bilingualism is clearly not served by the gradual extinction of one of the two linguistic communities that constitute it. In a more obvious sense, however, Quebec's language laws demoting English to non-official status represent a significant defeat for the federal ideal: the rejection of official bilingualism in the province with the country's largest minority-language population. As Table 1.1a shows, Ontario's 488,815 and New Brunswick's 232,980 francophones are both smaller populations, in absolute terms, than Quebec's 575,560 anglophones, yet Quebec does not grant English the same official status as French enjoys in New Brunswick, or even the quasi-official status it enjoys in Ontario or Manitoba. Road signs, for instance, are in English and French in Ontario but only in French in Quebec, though francophones represent less than 5 percent of Ontario while anglophones are about 8 percent of Quebec. Despite this non-reciprocity and violation of federal principle, while English rights groups in Quebec have received some assistance from federal agencies, no federal government has found the courage to intervene clearly and decisively on behalf of Quebec's English-speaking population, for fear of offending the powerful contingent of francophone voters in

Quebec (Stevenson 1999: 266). Instead, the fate of Quebec's English-speaking community has been left to provincial governments that can win legislative majorities without its support (Veltman 1996: 231–232).

Canada, then, is really bilingual only in name and in federal officialdom: it is a country with two official languages, not a country in which most individuals actually speak those two languages (Avis 1986: 213). In fact, the number of people who are fully bilingual in the sense of claiming both English and French as their mother tongues was only 109,415 in 2006, a third of 1 percent of the national population. Of course, many more people than this have non-native command of a second official language, ranging from rudimentary to fluent, which they are able to use in vocational, social or other functions. The business of the federal government is conducted in both official languages, a policy that extends beyond the Houses of Parliament and departments of the government itself to federal institutions like the Armed Forces and the Royal Canadian Mounted Police, to crown corporations like Air Canada (now privatized), Canada Post, the Canadian Broadcasting Corporation and VIA Rail, and to domains of federal regulation like airports and commercial product labeling. The latter domain provides the most visible presence of both languages in the daily lives of the majority of the population, being responsible for, among other things, the bilingual milk cartons and cereal boxes on Canadians' breakfast tables. These, together with bilingual safety instructions on Air Canada flights (even where they may seem unnecessary, as on flights between Toronto and Calgary or Vancouver), have become a symbol – celebrated by some, resented by others – of Canada's official language policy.

In most other domains, however, daily life for the majority of the population is monolingual, or involves a second language that is not one of the two official languages. It would be quite impossible to live normally in Quebec City without speaking any French, or to get along outside one's home in Halifax, Calgary or Vancouver without speaking English: one could buy stamps at the post office or talk to a clerk at the federal employment office, but ordinary interaction with the majority of the local population would be extremely difficult. Of Canada's major cities, only two – Montreal and Ottawa – contain large numbers of people who are fluent in both official languages. In a population of 31 million people, according to Canada's 2006 Census, 21 million say they know only English and 4 million say they know only French, leaving 5.5 million who know both (besides half a million immigrants who know neither language). This is just a sixth of the population, or 17 percent: hardly indicative of a generally bilingual nation. Outside Quebec, then, Canada is no less English-speaking than many parts of Great Britain, the United States or Australia. Here, the proportion of single-response mother-tongue English speakers rises to 75 percent, while that of the population claiming to know only English, of Canada's two official languages, is 87 percent, the overwhelming majority.

1.2   One of many home languages

Despite the apparent predominance of English outside Quebec, the difference between the 18 million Canadians who claim English as their only mother tongue, the almost 21 million who claimed English as their most common home language in 2006 and, moreover, the almost 27 million who in 2006 claimed to "know" English (if sometimes in conjunction with French), indicates that there are up to 9 million second-language speakers of English in Canada, of varying proficiency. Even in many parts of the country where French is rarely spoken, then, Canadian English does not exist in a monolingual – much less mono-cultural – environment. On the contrary, for every two or three Canadians who speak native English, there is one who speaks English with a foreign accent, a proportion that does not include the groups of people who speak native but non-Canadian varieties of English, such as many recent immigrants from Britain, the Caribbean or India. English in Canada, at least in the country's most populous regions, is only one of many home languages.

Table 1.1 shows that Canada's 18 million native speakers of English are concentrated overwhelmingly in just three provinces: over three-quarters of them (76.5 percent) live in British Columbia, Alberta and Ontario. These are not, however, the most anglophone parts of the country. That distinction goes to Newfoundland and Labrador, where 98 percent of the population claims English as their only mother tongue. Nova Scotia and Prince Edward Island are similarly homogeneous, with native English-speakers making up over 90 percent of the population. New Brunswick is less anglophone than its Maritime neighbors only because of its francophone population: put together, the two official-language mother-tongue populations make up 97 percent of the province's residents. Of the western provinces, Saskatchewan is easily the most anglophone, with 85 percent of the population reporting English as their only mother tongue. What unites these regions is their lack of appeal to recent immigrants: the fishing economy of the Atlantic seaboard and the largely agricultural economy of Saskatchewan have not provided significant employment opportunities to prospective immigrants, while an absence of large cities in these regions has further discouraged new arrivals, so that their populations are mainly native.

By contrast, British Columbia, Alberta and Ontario, together with Quebec, contain Canada's six largest cities and have been the main centers of growth in the late twentieth-century Canadian economy. Traditionally, this growth has come from natural resource industries in the West, like forestry and mining in British Columbia and oil and gas in Alberta, and from manufacturing industries in central Canada, like steel and automobile plants in Ontario and aerospace, garment and pharmaceutical factories in Quebec. (Forestry and mining have also played important roles in the economy of central Canada and, of course, agriculture remains a key industry in central

Table 1.2 *Number and proportion of mother-tongue anglophones, francophones and allophones in Canada's ten largest metropolitan areas (single responses, 2006) (see Map 1 and 3 for locations)*

Metropolitan area	Total pop.	English (n)	Engl. (%)	French (n)	Fr. (%)	Other (n)	Other (%)
Toronto, ON	5,072,075	2,746,480	54.1	58,590	1.2	2,160,330	42.6
Montreal, QC	3,588,520	425,635	11.9	2,328,400	64.9	760,445	21.2
Vancouver, BC	2,097,960	1,190,555	56.7	24,130	1.2	845,660	40.3
Ottawa, ON/QC	1,117,125	550,260	49.3	360,175	32.2	185,875	16.6
Calgary, AB	1,070,295	797,555	74.5	16,310	1.5	242,895	22.7
Edmonton, AB	1,024,825	785,760	76.7	21,975	2.1	203,990	19.9
Quebec, QC	704,180	10,255	1.5	671,140	95.3	19,415	2.8
Winnipeg, MB	686,035	507,525	74.0	29,025	4.2	139,770	20.4
Hamilton, ON	683,450	516,360	75.6	9,725	1.4	149,695	21.9
London, ON	452,575	363,885	80.4	6,055	1.3	78,805	17.4

Source: Statistics Canada, 2006 Census of Canada.

and western Canada, if not a major source of growth in employment.) More recently, an expanding services sector has spurred significant growth in all of these regions, with industries like banking, communications, consulting, education, engineering, healthcare, insurance and retail creating thousands of jobs, many of which have been highly attractive to immigrants. This is evident in the number and distribution of speakers of non-official languages shown in Table 1.1a. The overwhelming majority of this population – 93 percent – lives in the four provinces just mentioned. In individual provinces, the proportion of allophones ranges from 12 percent in Quebec, where only Montreal has a significant number, to 18 percent in Alberta to over a quarter in Ontario and British Columbia, which have received a large share of recent immigration from Asia. Manitoba, while similar to Saskatchewan in its relative dependence on agriculture, has in Winnipeg a large, cosmopolitan city, which has helped to attract a proportion of allophones similar to Alberta's.

The presence of allophones is particularly evident in the nation's biggest cities, which tend to provide the largest number of jobs and services for immigrants and contain well-established ethnic communities that can ease the cultural and linguistic transition for newcomers. Table 1.2 shows the number and proportion of mother-tongue anglophones, francophones and allophones in Canada's ten largest metropolitan areas, while Table 1.3 shows the number of mother-tongue speakers of individual non-official languages in the six largest cities, indicating more precisely the nature of the multilingual milieu in which urban Canadian English is spoken.

The ten cities listed in Table 1.2 contain 53 percent of the national population (16.5 million people) but 78 percent of the nation's allophones

Table 1.3 *Number of mother-tongue speakers of most common non-official languages in Canada's six largest metropolitan areas (single responses, 2006)*

Lang.	CANADA	Toronto	Montreal	Vancouver	Ottawa	Calgary	Edmonton
Chinese*	989,105	401,540	58,105	315,410	26,050	53,650	37,125
Italian	455,040	185,760	120,145	17,675	10,915	5,670	6,070
German	450,570	40,420	11,205	30,290	7,120	14,885	18,520
Panjabi	367,505	132,745	11,735	116,635	3,135	21,185	13,905
Spanish	345,345	108,380	90,105	26,455	12,710	14,520	9,695
Arabic	261,640	56,155	97,905	7,360	28,410	9,600	8,815
Tagalog	235,620	100,425	11,495	45,830	3,885	14,795	11,460
Hindi/Urdu	224,040	132,125	11,890	28,540	5,675	10,745	8,375
Portuguese	219,275	108,180	29,310	8,435	6,575	2,365	4,285
Polish	211,175	80,095	14,830	12,535	6,160	8,420	10,330
Vietnamese	141,630	45,325	23,235	20,720	6,535	10,890	7,720
Ukrainian	134,500	27,300	4,850	5,300	1,835	3,840	16,150
Farsi	134,080	63,975	12,975	26,760	5,925	4,585	2,620
Russian	133,580	65,205	17,735	11,745	5,060	5,420	2,970
Dutch	128,900	11,290	2,115	9,560	2,865	4,770	5,735
Korean	125,575	47,750	3,755	41,325	1,800	6,370	3,260
Greek	117,285	46,310	40,575	5,475	2,155	1,580	1,185
Tamil	115,880	93,590	11,525	2,925	2,120	765	435

Source: Statistics Canada, 2006 Census of Canada.
*Chinese includes figures for "Chinese not otherwise specified," Cantonese and Mandarin.

(4.8 million). Apart from sharing large populations, however, Canada's ten largest cities differ considerably in their linguistic make-up. One of them clearly stands out from the rest: Quebec City's linguistic composition is no different from that of much smaller cities and towns in Quebec, being overwhelmingly francophone (95 percent). Its once considerable anglophone population has either left or been assimilated and it has attracted very little non-francophone immigration. Of the remaining nine cities, Montreal obviously stands out as being dominantly francophone, but its proportion of allophones, 21 percent, is more like those of other large cities. Nevertheless, this is only half the proportion in comparably sized Toronto and Vancouver, further indicating the general preference of allophone immigrants for English-speaking cities. Ottawa, Canada's national capital, is located on the Ontario side of the Ottawa River, but its metropolitan area includes the Gatineau region of Quebec; the central districts of Ottawa and Hull, Quebec, are closely linked by bridges and by a shared distribution of federal government offices and institutions. This bi-provincial status accounts for the large proportion of francophones in the metropolitan area, much higher than in other Ontario cities. Considered separately, the Ontario portion of metropolitan Ottawa is more like these other cities: of 835,470 people, 514,680 (62 percent) are anglophone, 139,205 (17 percent) francophone and 165,355 (20 percent) allophone.

Among the seven anglophone metropolitan areas, the proportion of allo-phones ranges from about a fifth of the population in mid-sized centers like Winnipeg, Hamilton and London to over 40 percent in Toronto and Vancouver, English Canada's largest cities. In every case the allophone pop-ulation is vastly larger than the proportion of francophones, which ranges from 4.2 percent in Winnipeg, home to a significant historical francophone community, to just over 1 percent in Toronto and Vancouver. To some residents of these regions, this imbalance raises challenging questions about the continued justification of national English–French bilingualism, with its associated costs and privileges: whatever its historical justification and sym-bolic value in maintaining national unity, the modern demographic situation that justifies this policy is clearly restricted to only two major cities, Mon-treal and Ottawa. Among mother tongues, French ranks ninth in number of speakers in Toronto and Vancouver. Anglophones are correspondingly outnumbered by allophones in Montreal, but not by nearly as great a margin as francophones in anglophone cities, being in second place after French-speakers and comprising more than three times the number of speakers of the most populous non-official language. Alberta's two major cities, Calgary and Edmonton, have recently experienced large increases in population owing to the province's booming economy, but appear to have attracted inter-provincial migration from other parts of Canada more than international immigration from abroad: despite a growing allophone presence, their pop-ulations are still dominantly anglophone. It is Toronto and Vancouver alone that present the remarkable situation wherein almost half of the metropolitan population is allophone. In many districts of these cities, given the tendency of allophone groups to cluster in certain neighborhoods, mother-tongue English is a minority language, as in the section of Toronto's Dundas Street West where Chinese joins English on the street signs and predominates over English as the language of pedestrians, shopkeepers and commercial signage.

Of course, allophones are only a coherent group in a statistical sense: no single non-official language enjoys the same demographic prominence as allo-phones taken together. Some are nevertheless more numerically prominent than others. Table 1.3 shows that in 2006 there were eighteen non-official languages claimed by more than 100,000 people across Canada as their only mother tongue. Six of these have more than a quarter of a million speak-ers nationwide. This group includes two European languages, Italian and German, that were dominant among older groups of immigrants arriving before the 1970s, and four other languages that dominate recent and current immigration to Canada. Of the latter, the largest, Chinese, is a combination of two main "dialects," Cantonese and Mandarin, whose status as sepa-rate languages is debatable. The purpose of combining them here is not to take a position on their linguistic status but to give a more accurate indica-tion of their joint numerical importance. Also, the most common Chinese response was "Chinese, not otherwise specified," making it impossible to give meaningful individual tallies for Cantonese and Mandarin, as this response category presumably includes speakers of both. A similar case might have been made for emphasizing the collective numerical importance of a number of closely related Indic languages, but criteria of mutual intelligibility and the absence of a parallel category of "Indic, not otherwise specified" prevent a parallel combination, beyond the obvious case of Urdu (145,805 speakers) and Hindi (78,235); the smaller populations who speak Gujarati (81,465) and Bengali (45,680) do not therefore make it into the table. Even without these combinations, Panjabi, the most commonly spoken Indic language in Canada, occupies fourth place after German. Together, the high rankings of Chinese and Panjabi serve to emphasize the major shift in recent immigration to Canada away from its traditional sources in Europe to new sources in East and South Asia, Latin America, the Middle East and North Africa. The latter three of these regions account for the large populations of speakers of Spanish and Arabic, the last two of the top six non-official languages.

Canadian English finds itself in a unique contact situation in each major city. In Montreal and Ottawa, obviously, the major contact is with Canadian French: the intensity of contact with other languages pales in comparison, though in Montreal, Italian, Arabic and Spanish also have a major presence. Of these groups, only Italians have tended to transfer mostly to English, though even they have tended to be trilingual, originally integrating more closely with the francophone community and only later shifting toward English (Boissevain 1967). Arabic- and Spanish-speakers have integrated more commonly into the francophone community (Jedwab 1996: 71), though 50 percent of Arabic-speakers and 40 percent of Spanish-speakers also claim a knowledge of English (Jedwab: 122). Of Montreal's largest allophone groups, those who have transferred most consistently to English are speakers of Chinese and Greek (Jedwab: 71), as well as, historically, the large population of originally Yiddish-speaking Eastern European Jews, a group that is now overwhelmingly anglophone and represents a significant component of the city's English-speaking community (8 percent in 1981, according to Rudin 1985: 166).

In Toronto and Vancouver, the contact situation is dominated by Asian languages. Toronto's 400,000 speakers of Chinese form Canada's largest allophone community by a considerable margin, though Vancouver's Chinese-speaking community is actually twice as large as a proportion of the metropolitan population (15 percent vs. 8 percent in Toronto). If they were a separate municipality, Toronto's Chinese-speakers would be the thirteenth-largest city in Canada, bigger than St. Catherines, Halifax, Oshawa, Victoria or Windsor. Chinese-speakers, in fact, are the largest linguistic minority in every major anglophone city. Only in bilingual Montreal and Ottawa are they outnumbered by other groups, in Ottawa only very slightly by speakers of Arabic. In Toronto, nevertheless, the contact situation is also significantly enriched by speakers of Italian and of Indic languages, while Edmonton features proportionately large communities of German- and Ukrainian-speakers, groups who generally came earlier than the bulk of the Asian population and whose national prominence has traditionally been rooted in less urban regions.

Canadian English, then, is and has been subject to a range of potential influences from contact with other languages, apart from the obvious cases of French, documented by McArthur (1989) and Boberg (2005b: 36–37), and of early lexical transfers from Aboriginal languages. To date, the observable effects of such influence have been largely restricted to the ethnolects spoken by bilingual members of the allophone groups themselves and perhaps to the speech of their children (as among the ethnic groups in Montreal's anglophone community examined by Boberg (2004b) and in Chapter 5 of this volume). Of course, like all those who came before them, current generations of allophones will no doubt be gradually absorbed into English- or French-speaking society, but even as these groups assimilate, they will be followed by more. Whether the presence of large numbers of speakers of other languages in Canadian cities eventually has a discernible effect on Canadian English will be determined by future immigration trends, as discussed in Chapter 6. For now, we can say no more than that Canadian English is a multi-ethnic language, spoken by people of every color and creed on earth.

1.3   Varieties of Canadian English

Ethnic variation and variation arising from contact with other languages are only two of the sources of variation in Canadian English. Like every national type of English, indeed like every language, Canadian English also displays variation that correlates with region, speech style and a broad range of social categories, including those associated with age, sex and socio-economic class (itself an amalgam of factors like occupation, income, education and residence). It might be asked whether there is truly a single, unified variety of English that can be identified as Canadian.

The most basic definition of Canadian English might be that it is the variety of English spoken by people who acquired their knowledge of English as children exclusively or mostly in Canada. This definition, if somewhat trivial and circular, does at least exclude those varieties of English spoken in Canada that were not acquired in Canada, such as the English of recent immigrants from other English-speaking countries, or of immigrants from non-English-speaking countries who learned their English elsewhere. It is not unusual to hear British, American, Caribbean and other accents in Canadian cities, not to speak of non-native accents, as was shown above: these varieties, then, are not Canadian English, except in the vacuous sense of being spoken by people who happen to live in Canada. Even if we exclude these non-Canadian varieties, however, and concern ourselves only with native varieties of English that were acquired mostly in Canada, we still have to contend with a highly varied object of description.

The most obvious division of native Canadian English is along regional lines (see Maps 1–3 at the beginning of the book for locations). There is one clear regional division that comes first to everyone's mind, linguists and general public alike, and that raises the most serious challenge to the notion of a single, unified Canadian English corresponding in its territorial domain to the modern Canadian state. This is the division between Newfoundland, which only joined Canada in 1949, having been a separate British colony for over 300 years, and the rest of Canada. Newfoundland and mainland Canada were settled at different times by different groups from different places and have had different histories since their founding as English settlements, guaranteeing a wide divergence in speech. The contrast between the heavily Irish-influenced speech of Newfoundland's Avalon Peninsula and the North American speech of Ontario and western Canada is obvious to even the least perceptive listener and has long been celebrated in Canadian popular culture. Indeed, that Newfoundland English is to be considered at all in a study of Canadian English is a result of purely political, not linguistic factors; linguistically, traditional Newfoundland English has more in common with the southwestern English and southeastern Irish varieties from which it is historically derived than with mainland Canadian English. Newfoundland English might, then, be thought of as Canadian in only that vacuous sense of being a variety spoken in Canada, even if in this case it is a variety acquired as a native language within the political borders of modern Canada. Nevertheless, Newfoundland's modern political status as a Canadian province, with the patterns of linguistic influence that that implies, does have linguistic consequences, insofar as young Newfoundlanders, particularly in larger towns, show convergence with many features of mainland Canadian English. In this sense of direction of shift, Newfoundland English can be thought of as a variety of Canadian English: young, upwardly-mobile Newfoundlanders model their speech not on that of Ireland or England but on that of mainland Canada.

Distinctive regional settlement histories, which are discussed in Chapter 2, have also created several smaller, less broadly recognized speech enclaves within Canada, which likewise challenge the notion of a unified Canadian English, if not as starkly as the case of Newfoundland. Today, these are found mostly in Nova Scotia, where they include Cape Breton Island (the northern part of Nova Scotia), settled mostly by Scottish Highlanders; Pictou County, a second center of Highland Scots settlement on the mainland; Lunenburg, a town on the south shore settled largely by Germans; and an African-Canadian community, dispersed among several locations, made up of descendants of the servants who accompanied Loyalist immigrants and of refugees from American slavery.

Beyond Nova Scotia, we find several more distinctive enclaves: on Prince Edward Island, which received more Scottish and less American settlement than other parts of Canada; in Quebec, where English, as we have seen, is a minority language in intimate contact with French; and in the Ottawa Valley of eastern Ontario, where, again, a heavy concentration of immigrants from Scotland and Ireland was responsible for creating a regional speech island. Farther west, originally Low-German-speaking Mennonite settlements in southern Manitoba retain some distinctive features. Armin Wiebe, who comes from that community, deployed many of these to colorful effect in the narrative voice of his comic novel *The Salvation of Yasch Siemens* (1984), which is packed with Low German words as well as German-influenced usage and syntax. In southern Alberta, heavy immigration of American Mormons at the end of the nineteenth century continues to be reflected in some aspects of local speech around Lethbridge.

Today, most of these enclaves – especially those in western and central Canada – are strongly recessive and even the speech islands of eastern Canada now show signs of convergence with mainstream Canadian English. Nonetheless, as long as they continue to exist, the varieties of English found in these enclaves can be thought of as distinct from Canadian English in the sense that they all represent the failure of initially non-Canadian varieties (Scottish English, African American English, etc.) to assimilate fully to the Canadian English spoken in the larger regions around them. They are Canadian varieties in the same sense as is Newfoundland English: it is toward a Canadian English target that they are now shifting.

A final apparently regional division is really more closely related to ethnicity and contact with other languages than with region per se. This is Canada's North: the federal territories of the Yukon, the Northwest Territories and Nunavut, plus the northern halves of all the provinces from British Columbia to Quebec and the Labrador portion of Newfoundland. In northern Canada the European-origin population is relatively small, sparsely distributed and recently arrived from a wide range of origins, so that the Canadian English spoken in this region can be thought of more as a dialect still in formation than as a cohesive, unified regional variety. In many northern regions, people of European origin are outnumbered by Aboriginal people, most of whom speak varieties of English that are influenced to varying degrees by Aboriginal languages; Scollon and Scollon (1979) and Toohey (1985) are studies of two such varieties. Some of these speakers are bilinguals whose proficiency in English ranges from limited to native; others have transferred more or less completely to English, retaining only passive knowledge – if any knowledge at all – of an Aboriginal language but speaking a variety of English nonetheless influenced by an Aboriginal substrate. The isolation of many remote northern communities, in which there are relatively few native Canadian English models at hand, tends to perpetuate the influence of these substrates longer than it would survive in the speech of Aboriginal people in a more urban context. Even in southern urban Canada, Aboriginal-influenced speech can be heard among Aboriginal people who have migrated to the cities from northern regions or from nearby reservations where, as in the North, the ratio of Aboriginal to non-Aboriginal speech is very high.

Many observers have asserted that, apart from the regional enclaves just mentioned, Canadian English, at least at the middle-class level, is largely homogeneous across most of the country, from British Columbia in the west to Ontario in the east, and perhaps even farther. An early statement of this view is found in Bloomfield (1948: 63), who asserts that "one type of English is spread over Canada's 3,000-mile populated belt." A later one comes from Avis (1973: 50–51), who observes that "the speech habits of Canadians, especially educated Canadians, have become remarkably homogeneous, though by no means free from regional variations." He attributes this to the spread of "General Canadian" outward from southern Ontario "through education and modern communications, even to the young in the enclaves formerly characterized by marked regional dialects." Avis' view was most recently echoed by Chambers (2006: 385a), who declares that "Canadian English is remarkably homogeneous across the vast expanse of the country. Except for Newfoundland, urban, middle-class Canadians speak with much the same accent . . . " Chambers emphasizes the early settlement of Ontarians in the West as the main historical root of this transregional similarity. These attributions of homogeneity are largely correct in the comparative sense in which they were surely intended: compared to the regional diversity found in Britain or even the United States, that in Canada is minimal. Nevertheless, it will be shown in Chapters 4 and 5 that some regional differences do exist, even within Standard Canadian English and even between western Canada and Ontario.

In general, ordinary Canadians seem to agree with the professional view that Canadian English shows only limited dialect diversity, though they may be more willing than most linguists to assign normative evaluations to the regional varieties that they do perceive. This subject was explored in an opinion survey that was part of the study of phonetic variation in the speech of McGill undergraduate students from across Canada reported in Chapters 3 and 5. The survey, a two-page written questionnaire filled out by the participants themselves, probed their attitudes about a range of subjects focused on varieties of English and social identities. Answers to the first section of the survey, dealing with varieties of English, help to illuminate Canadians' own views of regional variation in Canadian English. For instance, one question asked, "Apart from Newfoundland, how much regional variation exists in Canadian English?" The majority of respondents, 41 out of 64 (64 percent), said "a little bit," though a smaller group of 22 (34 percent) were prepared to say "a lot." Only one person said "none."

Asked where in Canada they felt the best English was spoken, the respondents' answers were closely linked to the distribution of Canada's

English-speaking population: the largest group identified a variety spoken in Ontario (19, 30 percent), followed by British Columbia (11, 17 percent), followed by the West more generally (4, 6 percent). This distribution was not simply a function of where respondents themselves were from: though few westerners identified central or eastern varieties as superior to their own, some Ontario respondents believed western varieties to be best, while most Quebeckers and Atlantic Canadians identified varieties outside their own regions. Three respondents felt the best Canadian English was to be found in cities in general, regardless of region. Others identified the speech of particular cities as best: the most common responses of this type were Toronto (4) and Ottawa (3). As for the worst variety of Canadian English, the most common responses were not surprisingly "Newfoundland" and "Quebec" (each 17, 27 percent), the latter probably reflecting an evaluation of the second-language English of francophones more than the native English of anglophones. The next most common answers identified varieties spoken in the Maritimes (10, 16 percent), especially Cape Breton, and Ontario (6, 9 percent). Despite the comparative homogeneity of Canadian English, then, to the extent that the student respondents to this survey are representative of the general population, Canadians themselves do have some sense of regional diversity and are prepared to evaluate it.

In addition to regional divisions, Canadian English displays social variation very similar to that found in other English-speaking societies and in other languages. Indeed, as discussed in Chapter 3, this variation involves many of the same variables studied in other varieties: (ing), (-t/-d), double negation, non-standard verb forms and so on. Beyond these variables, the distinctive speech of the traditional enclaves discussed above is more likely to be heard from working-class people with little formal education than from middle-class people with a university degree. Non-standard forms are also more likely to be heard from men than from women, other things being equal. Finally, as in other places, Canadian English also varies with speakers' ages in ways that often signify changes in progress, with younger speakers displaying higher frequencies of innovative forms. Canadian youth, for example, have joined their age peers in other English-speaking nations in adopting *be like* as a quotative verb, used instead of *say* to introduce reported thought or speech, as in, "she was like, 'should I buy this dress?' and I was like, 'no way!'." These sorts of variation, however, while of great interest to sociolinguistics at a broader level, are not a distinctive trait of Canadian English, except to the extent that they sometimes involve uniquely Canadian variants or patterns, as in the Canadian Vowel Shift. In many cases, the sociolinguistic patterns they exhibit are typical of universal social properties of language that are not specifically Canadian and that have been well studied elsewhere. Such patterns will therefore not be a central concern of this book, though some correlations of Canadian lexical and phonetic features with age and sex will be examined in Chapters 4 and 5; Chapter 5 will also examine ethnicity as a factor in the phonetics of Montreal English.

1.4   Canadian English and American English

The greatest present influence on Canadian English, certainly greater than its contact with other languages within Canada, is Canada's geographic situation in the top half of North America, a continent dominated by the United States. In addition to its colonial and post-colonial relations with Britain, Canada has naturally had a close relationship throughout its history with the United States, with which it shares most of the continent, a 3,000-mile (4,500-km) border and a common language. Indeed, as Canada's historical ties to Britain have weakened, those to the United States have become stronger. While Canada's evolution toward independence from Britain was very different from that of the United States, and while many other differences remain between the two countries (Lipset 1990), they are nevertheless broadly similar and closely integrated in many respects. Given the vastly larger population of the United States, the cross-border influence arising from this close integration has always flowed predominantly northward. While Canadians have been self-consciously obsessed with their relationship to the United States and to all things American, an obsession that has evoked emotions ranging from amity to disdain, from respect to envy to fear, the attitude of Americans toward Canada has generally been one of benign ignorance, even in regions close to the international border. Over time, this unidirectional influence has had important consequences for the formation and development of English in almost every region of Canada.

Historically, as will be discussed in greater detail in Chapter 2, American immigrants played an important role in two of the three major periods of Canadian English-speaking settlement: to this extent, the origins of Canadian and American English have been identical. Ever since this seminal influence, but particularly over the course of the later twentieth century and up to the present, northward migration from the United States has involved not people so much as goods, ideas, culture and language. Canadians have generally enjoyed widespread and virtually unrestricted access to American books, magazines, radio, film, recordings and television, not to mention most recently the internet. These media have helped to make American popular culture the dominant influence on Canadian popular culture, pervading Canadian tastes in dress, food, architecture, urban design, entertainment and lifestyle. Indeed, on these levels, overseas visitors find it very difficult to distinguish between Canadians and Americans. Jeans, T-shirts and baseball caps; hamburgers, pizza and beer; office towers, shopping malls and suburban bungalows; television, pop music and Hollywood movies; backyard barbecues, weekends at the lake and beach vacations; Santa Claus, the Easter Bunny, Halloween trick-or-treating and turkey dinner at

Thanksgiving: these constitute a common Anglo-North American culture in which the international border is an almost imperceptible partition. To some degree, moreover, North American geography imposes a trans-border continuity of regional cultures, with Canada's regions forming the northern extensions of the corresponding American ones. The Atlantic and Pacific coasts, the Appalachian and Rocky Mountains and the plains and prairies between them are common to both countries and have engendered not only regional economic patterns but in some respects regional cultures that span the border: prairie folk in Saskatchewan and North Dakota or fishermen in Nova Scotia and Maine may find they have more in common with one another than with their countrymen in Toronto or Chicago, or with the particular cultural enclaves in places like Montreal, Vancouver, San Francisco, New York City or Miami.

American culture diffuses easily into Canada along well-established channels: by 2001, according to Statistics Canada, the Canadian government's official statistical agency, 99 percent of Canadian households had a television, 92 percent a video cassette recorder, 71 percent a compact disc player, 68 percent cable television service, and 50 percent home access to the internet. Canadian homes with cable or satellite television service have access to all of the major American television networks, in addition to the American programs licensed to Canadian networks, which are also available to television owners without cable service. In 2004, Statistics Canada reports that Canadians watched an average of twenty-one hours of television per week, or three hours per day, a pattern established as early as the 1970s; children aged two to eleven years, approximately the period for acquiring language, watched an average of fourteen hours per week, or two hours per day. Almost two-thirds – 63 percent – of Canadian television viewing was of foreign programs, the vast majority of these American. While three-quarters of the news and public affairs programming Canadians watched in 2004 was Canadian, the most popular program category, accounting for 27 percent of the Canadian audience, was drama, which was 81 percent non-Canadian. Ash (2003: 161) lists the most-watched programs on Canadian television in 2001–2002: all of these except two news programs are American. Popular American television dramas like *CSI*, *ER* and *Law and Order* (the top three programs in 2001–2002) have an audience of 1.5 million Canadian viewers each. Among special broadcasts, the American *Academy Awards* drew by far the largest audience, over 4 million people, or two and a half times the number who watched the top-rated Canadian special. The pop music consumed by English-speaking Canadians has been less solidly American than their television, with a strong British presence as well as a surprising number of Canadian stars, but popular film is almost exclusively produced in Hollywood, while American authors garner a large share of the popular fiction market. New York City and Los Angeles are therefore cultural capitals for Canadians almost as much as for Americans.

Travel, too, has brought Canadians into frequent contact with American culture and American English. Whether for business or pleasure, Canadians travel most frequently to the United States and Americans are the most frequent visitors to Canada. Central and eastern Canadians escape Canada's long, harsh winters in Florida (or the Caribbean), while westerners go to Hawaii; New England, New York City, Las Vegas and California are other popular Canadian vacation destinations. Statistics Canada reports that, in 1971, Canadians made 33 million visits to the United States, an average of 1.5 per person. Of these, only 9 million were overnight visits; the remainder were brief day-trips across the border, mostly for business or shopping. By 2004, the number of overnight visits alone had almost doubled to 14 million, about one for every second Canadian. Visits to the United States represented 74 percent of all Canadian overnight travel to foreign countries; the United Kingdom, in second place, received only 754,000 visits, about 5 percent of the American-bound traffic. In the other direction, Americans made 15 million overnight visits to Canada in 2004, balancing the Canadian outflow and accounting for 83 percent of all foreign visitors. The United Kingdom again occupies a distant second place, supplying only 800,000 visitors, 5 percent of the American total. The set of American states most frequently involved in cross-border travel is very similar in both directions: New York, Michigan, Washington and California are four of the top five sources and destinations of visitors. For Canadians visiting the United States, these are naturally joined by Florida, which is slightly behind New York State in number of visits but well ahead in number of nights: Canadians spent 35 million nights in Florida in 2004, six times as many as in any other state. For Americans visiting Canada, the fifth-largest home state is Ohio; Pennsylvania, Massachusetts and Minnesota also contributed over half a million visits each.

Of course, not all Canadians are equally likely to be exposed to American English through travel. Exposure in both directions is likely to be most frequent and intensive where relatively large populations face each other across the border, as in New York State, Ontario and Michigan, or in British Columbia and Washington State, or where the distance to the border is shortest. As it happens, Canada's two largest concentrations of English-speaking population, in southern Ontario and southwestern British Columbia, are located one or two hours' drive from the major American cities of Buffalo, Detroit and Seattle. Some communities are located even closer to the border: the mid-sized city of Windsor, Ontario, looks across a river at downtown Detroit. Other towns only a bridge away from the United States include St. Stephen in New Brunswick and Cornwall, Niagara Falls, Fort Erie and Sault Ste. Marie in Ontario. Wiebe's novel about southern Manitoba describes a youthful stunt in which the narrator illegally crosses "the big ditch that cuts us off from the States" to climb a television tower on the other side, the tower's blinking red lights serving as a potent symbol of American cultural influence, beaming American English into Canadian homes (Wiebe 1984: 1–2, 8). In the village of Rock Island, now part of Stanstead in Quebec's Eastern Townships, the international boundary passes through the municipal library, separating one section of the building from another. The placement of the boundary has created a number of even stranger peculiarities that encourage close international contact, if only of small populations: for instance, residents of Point Roberts, Washington, and Angle Inlet, Minnesota, can reach other parts of the United States only by driving through Canada, or by water. By contrast, residents of Edmonton, Canada's northernmost major city, are six hours' drive from the border, making casual or frequent cross-border travel inaccessible for most of the population. Halifax, too, is well isolated from the United States, while other cities, like Calgary, Regina, Winnipeg and Thunder Bay, are closer to the border but not to large centers of American population. From Winnipeg it is only an hour's drive to the border but a day's drive to Minneapolis–St. Paul, the nearest major city.

Canadians travel to the United States for three principal reasons: business, vacations and shopping. All of these are affected by economic factors: in particular, a strong Canadian dollar encourages pleasure travel and cross-border shopping, while a weak Canadian dollar deters this kind of contact. Apart from winter visits to Florida, many of which are in fact made by French Canadians rather than by English-speakers, business travel is the most frequent and consistent source of cross-border contact between Canadians and Americans. Canadian businesspeople are therefore most likely to be subject to American linguistic influence through interpersonal contact, in addition to the passive contact that they and other Canadians have through the mass media. If the average number of Canadian visits to the United States is one per year for every second person, given that many Canadians travel rarely if at all to the United States, this implies that some Canadians visit the United States very frequently indeed, making them potential conduits of linguistic influence when they return to their home communities in Canada.

This pattern of regular contact arises from a high degree of integration between the Canadian and American economies. Many Canadian industries have significant levels of American ownership, while many Canadian companies have grown by extending their operations to the United States. The major exceptions are industries subject to governmental regulation limiting foreign ownership, like banking, communications and transportation. Outside these sectors, to a large extent the North American economy operates on a continental basis. Canadian post-war economic expansion was driven in large part by subsidiaries of American companies operating in Ontario and Quebec, particularly in the automotive industry, where the Canada–United States Automotive Products Agreement (the "Autopact" of 1965) provided for the integration of Canadian branch plants into a continental production system based in Detroit. The oil and gas industry in western Canada, recently the major source of growth in the Canadian economy, was also developed largely by American oil companies, which continue to play a dominant role, while the pride of Canada's aerospace industry, concentrated in Montreal, was the development of the Canadarm, a remote manipulator system for the American space shuttle. Economic integration was further advanced in 1994, when Canada, the United States and Mexico signed the North American Free Trade Agreement. The United States is Canada's largest trading partner by far: in 2001 it was the source of 73 percent of Canada's imports and the destination for 84 percent of Canada's exports. American retail chains like Best Buy, the Gap, Home Depot, McDonald's, Sears, Starbuck's and Wal-Mart are omnipresent in Canada. The result of all this cross-border commerce is that a small but influential group of Canadians and Americans is regularly exposed to one another's speech patterns through face-to-face communication, thereby facilitating the cross-border transference of linguistic features.

Another important factor in the flow of linguistic influence across the border is Canadians' attitudes about the United States, American culture and American English. People who have a critical, resentful or hostile attitude toward something are presumably less likely to want to imitate it, though this does not of course rule out the possibility of sub-conscious imitation. Moreover, rejecting something based on its association with a given attribute depends on being able to recognize that attribute: for instance, linguistic forms that are associated in people's minds with youth culture in general, rather than with American culture specifically, even if they originate in the United States, may be imitated by people with otherwise anti-American feelings. As one admittedly simple approach to this complex issue, the opinion survey cited in the last section, which was part of the study of phonetic variation reported in Chapters 3 and 5, also included questions about national varieties of English. The answers to these questions shed some light on the nature of the English Canadian linguistic relation to the United States. For instance, out of 64 responses from students from across Canada, 49 (77 percent) admitted that Canadian English is more similar to American than to British English; only 15 (23 percent) maintained that it is more similar to British. Canadian English is therefore understood to be a North American variety, by linguists and non-linguists alike. Nevertheless, asked just how similar American and Canadian English are, most students (44, 69 percent) said they are "slightly different." Only 12 (19 percent) thought they are "quite similar," while 7 (11 percent) asserted that they are "very different"; no one believed them to be "very similar." It is perhaps significant that 80 percent of the students chose to emphasize the distinctness rather than the similarity of Canadian and American English.

Moreover, when it comes to normative evaluation of the varieties, the orientation of the students shifts sharply away from the United States toward Britain, the traditional prestige model for English Canada. Asked which national variety is "more correct," 39 (61 percent) said British English, while

20 (31 percent) said Canadian; only one student thought American English to be more correct. As for which "sounds nicer," British English again came out on top (37, 58 percent), with Canadian English again in second place (26, 41 percent); not a single respondent felt American English to be the nicest-sounding of the three national varieties. Finally, asked about their "general feelings about the United States and American culture," the students showed a fairly even distribution across the evaluative scale, from "very positive" (6, 9 percent) to "slightly positive" (15, 23 percent) to "neutral" (26, 41 percent) to "negative" (17, 27 percent). This distribution reflects the conflicting, inconsistent and ambivalent nature of Canadians' emotional relationship to their larger southern neighbor, referred to above. To the extent that these students' views are representative of the general Canadian population, these data suggest that, while the opportunity for extensive American influence on Canadian English exists in theory, such influence may be tempered in reality by attitudinal obstacles, as proposed by Boberg (2000: 23). An earlier speculation on this factor is offered by Bloomfield (1948: 62), who says, "the continuing influence of the United States [on Canadian English] . . . cannot be ignored," but "Canada's sense of inferiority and pride has generally kept it as slight as possible." (For other empirical studies of Canadian attitudes toward national varieties of English, see Warkentyne 1983 and Richards 2004.)

1.5 Canadian English and Canadian culture

Like any language or variety of a language, Canadian English is not merely a means of practical communication and social identification among Canadians but also the linguistic form and expressive medium of much of English-Canadian culture. The distinctive qualities of Canadian English contribute to the distinctive quality of Canadian culture and it is in the products of that culture as much as in the everyday speech of individuals that we may find evidence of what makes Canadian English distinct. Indeed, given what has just been said about the close similarity of American and Canadian culture at many levels, subtle differences in form of expression – as opposed to content – may take on a heightened importance in distinguishing Canadian from American cultural products. Moreover, the relationship between language and culture can be bidirectional: if Canadian English characterizes and helps to define Canadian cultural achievements, so cultural forms like books, popular songs or films can help to sustain or shape Canadian English, diffusing Canadian words, pronunciations or expressions. While there is also much in English-Canadian culture that is highly distinctive but non-verbal and therefore of no concern here – the paintings of Emily Carr, Tom Thompson and the Group of Seven, for example – the written and recorded forms of Canadian English can provide a rich source of data on what makes Canadian English distinct. Just as literature, journalism, song and film are the permanent record of languages like French, German, Italian or Russian, so they can stand as a monument to the differences among varieties of English. An important aspect of the study of Canadian English is therefore the examination of its use as a medium of cultural expression.

In a frontier society, the great majority of people are necessarily concerned with practical matters, first of survival, then of economic progress, then of nation-building on a broader front. There is typically little concern with cultural expression; "culture," whether folk idioms like popular song or more elaborate products like novels, plays and poetry, is usually something imported from the overseas homelands of immigrants or, as often in the Canadian case, from a larger, more densely settled neighbor. Even the first local cultural products, while sometimes concerning themselves with local matters, tend to reflect a non-local perspective and non-local language, being produced by people who are essentially foreigners, even if long-term residents. This is certainly true of most of the first writing undertaken on future Canadian territory, such as the journals of explorers, traders or colonial officials. It applies even to some of the first well-known works of what is today thought of as Canadian Literature, in both English and French. *Roughing It in the Bush*, an account of Upper Canadian pioneer life by Susanna Moodie (1852), like *Maria Chapdelaine*, the classic novel of French-Canadian pioneer life by Louis Hémon (1914), was written by an immigrant. As Hémon was born in France, coming to Canada only as an adult, Moodie was born in England, along with her sister, Catherine Parr Traill, a botanist and author of *The Backwoods of Canada* (1836), a more scientific report of the Upper Canadian frontier. Moodie and Traill emigrated to Canada with their husbands in 1832, at around 30 years of age, with British linguistic patterns well established. While their writings offer invaluable testimonies of life in nineteenth-century Canada, they cannot be thought of as Canadian from the linguistic point of view: theirs was simply British writing about Canada.

The first truly Canadian writing to attract wide attention appeared at the start of the twentieth century. The best-known Canadian authors from this period are undoubtedly Lucy Maud Montgomery (1874–1942), from Prince Edward Island, whose *Anne of Green Gables* (1908) is an international children's classic about an orphan-girl growing up on a local farm; and Stephen Leacock (1869–1944), from Ontario, a political economist and humorist whose *Sunshine Sketches of a Little Town* (1912) satirizes small-town Ontario characters in Dickensian fashion. (Leacock was actually born in England but grew up in Ontario on a farm near Lake Simcoe and went to school at Upper Canada College in Toronto.) By the 1940s, English Canada had produced a small but respectable group of serious writers whose work offered native perspectives on the Canadian experience, written increasingly in a spare, unadorned prose reflective of ordinary Canadian speech. This is particularly true of Morley Callaghan (1903–1990), from Toronto, whose novels examine moral, philosophical and religious questions in urban settings, and of Sinclair

Ross (1908–1996), from Saskatchewan, whose *As for Me and My House* (1941) portrays the isolation of "cultured" people in a small prairie town, in a vein similar to Sinclair Lewis' great novel of American small-town prairie life, *Main Street* (1912). W. O. Mitchell's (1914–1998) *Who Has Seen the Wind* (1947), also set in Saskatchewan, took a lighter and more positive approach to chronicling life on the Prairies. The conscious promotion of specifically Canadian themes and subject matter in Canadian literature is best exemplified by Hugh MacLennan (1907–1990), from Nova Scotia, whose *Barometer Rising* (1941) is based on the catastrophic explosion of a munitions ship in Halifax Harbor in 1917, and whose *Two Solitudes* (1945) deals with perhaps the ultimate Canadian issue, the relations of French and English Canadians in Quebec. At the same time, the French-Canadian perspective on this issue was powerfully articulated by a Franco-Manitoban, Gabrielle Roy (1909–1983), whose *Bonheur d'occasion* (1945), translated into English as *The Tin Flute*, portrays working-class life in the St-Henri district of Montreal.

It was in the post-war period, however, that serious Canadian literature really blossomed, in both English and French, becoming a source of entertainment, education and enlightenment for a growing popular readership beyond specialist and academic circles, in some cases including a substantial number of non-Canadian readers abroad. Canadian English had now become indisputably a literary language, on a par with its British and American cousins, even if the sparse population and recent settlement of much of Canada meant that the volume of literature produced was small in comparison with that of the more established nations (for a list of better-known titles, both fiction and non-fiction, see Vancouver Public Library 1999). The first post-war literary star to emerge was Mordecai Richler (1931–2001), whose *The Apprenticeship of Duddy Kravitz* (1959) was based on his boyhood in Montreal's Jewish ghetto. In some ways a Canadian equivalent to Philip Roth's *Portnoy's Complaint* (1969), *Duddy Kravitz* was the first major Canadian novel to challenge the Franco-British cultural establishment, presenting a Jewish view of the Canadian experience and a rich store of the Yiddish-influenced variety of Canadian English that has a special prominence in Montreal (see Chapter 5, Section 5.3 for examples). Montreal's Jewish community also produced the poets Irving Layton and Leonard Cohen and the novelist Saul Bellow, though the latter moved with his family to Chicago and is now thought of more as an American writer.

Richler's success was only the first of many that, by the 1970s, were to make "CanLit" a cultural phenomenon attracting international attention. While an explosion of cultural energy associated with Quebec's Quiet Revolution was producing a bumper crop of great French-Canadian writers – the likes of Marie-Claire Blais, Anne Hébert and Michel Tremblay – a cultural maturation in English Canada was engendering a new enthusiasm for literature reflecting the Canadian experience and for home-grown authors. In particular, four great writers were to dominate the Canadian literary scene in the 1970s: Margaret Atwood (b. 1939), Robertson Davies (1913–1995) and Alice Munro (b. 1931), all from Ontario, and Margaret Laurence (1926–1987), from Manitoba. Davies and Laurence are known largely as novelists, though of very different stripe: Davies' *Deptford Trilogy* (1970–1975) and Laurence's *Manawaka* cycle of novels, culminating in *The Diviners* (1974), are among the great achievements of Canadian literature. Munro is known mostly for her short stories, many of which portray life in small-town Ontario, where she grew up. Atwood has turned her hand to poetry, short stories and novels in a wide range of genres and has concerned herself with feminist issues and other philosophical matters, but some of her novels, like *Edible Woman* (1969) and *Life Before Man* (1979), contain vivid portrayals of life in contemporary Toronto, while *Surfacing* (1972) is, among other things, a meditation on Canadian–American relations set in the wilderness of Quebec, where she spent her early childhood before moving to Toronto. Nevertheless it is Laurence and Munro, both from small towns in frontier areas (the former from Neepawa, Manitoba; the latter from Wingham, Ontario), who, arguably, have the strongest personal connection to the experiences of ordinary Canadians (despite Laurence's many years abroad) and whose work presents in its dialog the closest approximation to vernacular Canadian English.

Indeed, many Canadian writers have been exposed to non-Canadian influences. While Munro lived all her life in Ontario and British Columbia and never completed a post-secondary education, Laurence lived for many years in Africa and England, Atwood studied at Harvard and has lived in several countries and Davies studied at Oxford. Of the earlier generations, Callaghan, Mitchell, Montgomery and Ross spent their lives entirely in Canada (Ross retired abroad), but Richler lived for many years in England, Leacock went to the University of Chicago, and MacLennan studied at Oxford and Princeton. Moreover, many of Canada's writers have continued to come from abroad: from Frederick Philip Grove (1879–1948), a German-Canadian equivalent to Willa Cather or Ole Rölvaag with his chronicles of pioneer life in Manitoba, to Carol Shields (1935–2003), an American immigrant to Canada whose brilliant novels of modern life, like *The Stone Diaries* (1993), are often set in Winnipeg. CanLit's brightest contemporary stars also include Anne-Marie MacDonald, born to an armed forces family stationed in Germany; Yann Martel, born to French-Canadian parents in Spain; Rohinton Mistry, from India; and Michael Ondaatje, born in Sri Lanka. It is often difficult to know how much these authors' foreign experiences might have shaped their use of English, not to speak of the potentially non-Canadian influence their editors may have had. Of course, attending a foreign university for a couple of years does not necessarily obscure one's sense of one's native dialect; on the contrary, it may heighten it. Nevertheless, whatever their literary merit or their value as observers of or commentators on Canada and the Canadian experience (which is not at issue here), we cannot look as confidently to these authors for a native representation of Canadian English that is free of other influences.

Fiction is not, of course, the only source of written Canadian English. Canada's first newspapers began during the colonial period; by the early twentieth century there were several daily papers in each big city. During the late twentieth century the Canadian newspaper industry experienced the same trends of declining readership, consolidation and loss of local autonomy as affected the American industry. Despite this contraction, many papers remain today as daily records and diffusers of Canadian English, read by millions of Canadians: the *Globe and Mail* and the *National Post* at the national level and local dailies in each major city, usually including both a broadsheet paper aimed at middle-class readers (among these are the *Halifax Chronicle-Herald*, the *Montreal Gazette*, the *Ottawa Citizen*, the *Toronto Star*, the *Winnipeg Free Press*, the *Calgary Herald*, the *Edmonton Journal*, the *Vancouver Province* and the *Vancouver Sun*) and a tabloid paper aimed at working-class readers. *Maclean's*, a popular weekly news magazine, has been published since 1911 and *Chatelaine*, a women's monthly, since 1928. *Saturday Night*, a more intellectual review of the arts and current events, goes back to 1887 but has often had difficulty maintaining profitability. Unlike newspapers, magazines have to compete with imported titles: though they are available, very few Canadians read American newspapers, whereas many read American magazines. The Canadian government lends Canadian publications a hand through the Publications Assistance Program and Canada Magazine Fund, which help with some of the costs of production and mailing.

The post-war boom in Canadian fiction was matched by growing interest in local non-fiction, from biography to history to politics and a wide range of other subjects. Several Canadian writers rose to prominence in this market: for example, Pierre Berton (b.1920) for his popular histories; Farley Mowat (b.1921) for his politically charged autobiographical writings; and Peter C. Newman (b.1929) for his revelatory studies of Canadian business and political leaders. To these we might add great Canadian-born scholars of international significance, whose writing presumably betrays at least some influences of their Canadian youth: for example, the literary critic Northrop Frye (1912–1991); the economist John Kenneth Galbraith (1908–2006); the sociologist Erving Goffman (1922–1982); the economist and communications theorist Harold Innis (1894–1952); and the communications theorist Marshall McLuhan (1911–1980). The international status of these and other scholars – particularly their acceptance as American by some Americans – raises the question whether Canadian English is in fact a distinct variety at this level, or whether formal, written Canadian English is largely indistinguishable from the American written standard, particularly in non-fiction genres where scientific or technical vocabulary plays a greater part than the lexicon of everyday life. Nevertheless, while much of what makes Canadian English distinct involves phonetic differences not represented in standard orthography, Chapter 3 will examine the occurrence of distinctly Canadian vocabulary in written Canadian English, and particularly in some of the major novels mentioned above.

Of course, one of the most important distinctions for a literary language – such as Canadian English has now become – is the production of a set of formal standards to be applied especially to the written form of the language, which distinguish it from other standards or varieties; in short, dictionaries and usage guides. This is one respect in which Canada seems indeed to occupy a transitional zone between Britain and the United States. In the past, Canadian schools made use of both British and American educational materials and British and American English dictionaries continue to be used for reference by many Canadians, reflecting a national uncertainty about which way to turn in matters of spelling, grammar and style. As the discussion in the previous section implies, some Canadians abhor Americanisms as vulgar and cling desperately to British usage; others see British usage as obsolete or pretentious and happily adopt the American standard that comes in on the tide of the mass media from south of the border. Negotiating a middle way between these opposing forces has been a controversial and difficult task for Canadian writers, editors and lexicographers (as attested by the collection of papers in Lougheed 1986). What seems to have emerged is a compromise: for example, British spelling in *centre*, *cheque* and *colour* – at least in formal contexts – beside American spelling in *program*, *jail*, *curb* and *tire* (for a recent discussion of Canadian spelling, see Pratt 1993).

The first attempt to sort all of this out – at least the first to produce a widely used reference book – was the *Gage Canadian Dictionary*, published in junior and intermediate editions for schools and in a senior edition for adult use, beginning in 1967. Unlike several more or less "canadianized" versions of major non-Canadian dictionaries, the *Gage* was prepared entirely by Canadian scholars and lexicographers. More recently, Oxford University Press published a *Canadian Oxford Dictionary* (*COD*, 1998), edited by Katherine Barber, who asserts in its preface that "it is based on thorough research into the language: five years of work by five Canadian lexicographers examining almost twenty million words of Canadian text held in databases representing over 8,000 different Canadian publications" (viii). This, then, like the *Gage*, is not a superficially modified British or American dictionary, but a truly Canadian document, attempting to set a Canadian standard for spelling, grammar and usage and to define the many uniquely Canadian words and usages that do not appear in non-Canadian dictionaries. Canadians have also produced their own usage guides for writers: the *Canadian Press Stylebook* (1992) establishes standards for journalists, while Fee and McAlpine (1997) addresses a wider audience; other examples are Freelance Editors' Association of Canada (1987), Noad (1932) and Scargill (1974). Together, the *Gage* and the *COD* have helped to legitimize Canadian English as a distinct national variety of English with an independent standard, as subtle as its divergences from other standards may at times appear to be.

Written texts can reflect Canadianisms only at the lexical or grammatical levels; for phonetic variation, we must turn to the spoken language. Beyond literature and the print media, there are many non-written, verbal channels through which English-Canadian culture is expressed, in which we may find evidence of distinctive Canadian pronunciation, as well as grammar and word choice, at least when Canadian-born people are involved in them. The most important of these channels are television, film and popular music. Of course, these are also the media in which it has historically been most difficult to maintain distinctively Canadian content, given the costs involved in their production and the ease with which American cultural products, in partic-ular, are diffused across the border for consumption by Canadians. Perhaps not surprisingly, it is in these media that French-speaking Canada has to some extent fared proportionately better than English-speaking Canada in fostering a local cultural industry (though Barbaud (1998: 196–197) discusses similar challenges in Quebec). While a language barrier at least partly insu-lates French-speaking Canada from American popular culture, encouraging local production of French-language television, film and pop music, the high production costs associated with the modern forms of these industries cre-ate economies of scale that heavily favor American products where there is no language barrier, as in English Canada. Another factor favoring local French-Canadian culture is that France is more distant from Canada than the United States in every sense: geographically, historically, and in terms of its modern global cultural power.

In response to these formidable challenges to the development of an autonomous English-Canadian culture, the Canadian government has sought to nurture and protect Canadian cultural expression through a series of programs that fund or subsidize Canadian productions and require minimal levels of Canadian content in broadcasting. Perhaps the most obvious of these is the Canadian Broadcasting Corporation, or CBC, established in 1936 as a public broadcaster roughly parallel to its British equivalent, the BBC (though it now includes commercial advertising as an additional source of revenue). The CBC not only maintains radio and television channels in both official languages in every part of Canada, but produces content for those channels ranging from news and sports coverage to radio talk shows, television dramas and comedies and documentary films. Shortly after launching the CBC, in 1939 the federal government established the National Film Board, which was to foster the production of films by Canadians about Canada; it became particularly well known for documentaries and for animated films, such as those by Norman McLaren.

In addition to its direct involvement in the production of Canadian radio, television and film, the federal government has more recently sought to encourage such production in the private domain. In the late 1960s, the

Broadcasting Act established the Canadian Radio-television and Telecommunications Commission, or CRTC, which was given responsibility for regulating and supervising all aspects of the Canadian broadcasting and telecommunications industries. Among other things, its subsequent activity included licensing the cable television companies that would carry a steady flow of American programming into Canadian homes, but also the establishment of minimum quotas for Canadian content in television and radio broadcasting, which came to be known familiarly as "CanCon." At the same time, the federal government mandated the Canadian Film Development Corporation, now called Telefilm Canada, with promoting the development of a Canadian feature film industry through grants to independent producers.

Like most instances of government intervention in private markets, these programs have sometimes been controversial, but they have undoubtedly played at least some role in encouraging Canadians to produce and consume Canadian cultural products, particularly in popular music and, to a lesser extent, television. If relatively few Canadians have ever watched any of the productions of the National Film Board, the CanCon regulations have guaranteed Canadian musicians and singers a proportion of airtime on popular radio stations, which has helped a broad public audience to discover and come to appreciate Canadian popular music alongside the American and British products it competes with. Partly as a result, English Canada has produced a succession of popular singers and groups that have won a large domestic following; some have even succeeded beyond Canada (for a list of performers, see Barris and Barris 2001 or Jackson 1994). The Canadian Academy of Recording Arts and Sciences administers an annual program of Juno Awards, which are given to outstanding Canadian performers, as well as a Canadian Music Hall of Fame. A partial list of some past award winners and Hall of Fame inductees that have garnered wide national and even international acclaim includes the groups April Wine, Arcade Fire, Bachman-Turner-Overdrive, the Band, Blue Rodeo, the Guess Who, Loverboy, Kim Mitchell, Nickelback, Rush, Streetheart, the Tragically Hip, Triumph and Trooper; and the singers Bryan Adams, Jann Arden, Michael Bublé, Tom Cochrane, Bruce Cockburn, Leonard Cohen, Burton Cummings, Nelly Furtado, Diana Krall, Gordon Lightfoot, Sarah McLachlan, Murray McLauchlan, Joni Mitchell, Alanis Morissette, Anne Murray, Shania Twain, Gino Vanelli and Neil Young. Of course, Canadian popular musicians were making contributions even before Juno Awards were given out, and even in such intrinsically American genres as country and western music: Wilf Carter (also known as Montana Slim), Stompin' Tom Connors and Hank Snow, all Maritimers by birth, and Tommy Hunter, an Ontarian, played an important role in establishing country music in Canada and even gained some recognition in the United States. Moreover, many successful and popular performers have never won Juno Awards, such as the rock groups Harlequin, Frank Marino & Mahogany Rush, Max Webster or the Pat Travers Band. Along with their award-winning cousins, these bands, though no longer recording, still get regular airplay on Canadian classic rock stations that reach many thousands of listeners, partly thanks to the CanCon regulations.

While the performers just listed, among many others, attest amply to the vitality of the Canadian popular music scene, the extent to which this scene is a lyrical showcase of Canadian English is much less clear. In fact, certain genres of popular music are so symbolically tied to their American roots that singers in those genres tend to adopt elements of the varieties of American English with which they are associated, such as Appalachian English in country and western music, or African American English in rock music, or in the blues music on which rock music is based. Thus, Canadian popular singers can frequently be heard monophthongizing the /ay/ diphthong in words like *my* and *time*, vocalizing postvocalic /r/, or employing double negatives not heard in their own speech varieties, in an effort to sound more authentic; indeed, these and other features have become conventional in popular singing wherever it is performed, much as singers of French still pronounce the mute <e>s that are no longer sounded in speech. Nevertheless, even within these heavily conventionalized performance traditions it is sometimes possible to identify distinctively Canadian forms. For instance, as will be noted in Chapter 3, one of the distinguishing features of Canadian English is its tendency to use the /æ/ vowel of *fat* rather than the /ah/ vowel of *father* in words of foreign origin spelled with the letter <a>, such as *drama* and *llama*, where both British and American English prefer /ah/. Clear instances of Canadian /æ/ in *llama* occur both in *If I Had a Million Dollars*, by Barenaked Ladies, who also pronounce *Picasso* with /æ/ in the same song, and in *Ride My Llama*, by Neil Young, who rhymes *llama* with *Texarkana*. On the lexical level, the former song also includes an instance of the Canadian term *chesterfield*, in its sense of a couch or sofa, as does the song *Good Times Gone* by Nickelback.

The production costs for a successful popular music recording – sometimes a "demo tape" recorded in a band member's basement – need not be large and many musical groups are able to build an initial fan base by playing in local bars and at school dances, having spent a few thousand dollars on instruments and a vehicle. While there is a long and difficult journey between a first successful demo tape and a contract with a major record company, the relatively low costs associated with popular music production have favored the success of many Canadian performers, despite American and British domination of their industry. In television and film, by contrast, production costs are relatively high – often in fact enormous – even at the entry level, except perhaps on the "local access" or "community" cable television channels, which few people watch. While the recent advent of mass-market digital video recording equipment and editing software may start to bring entry costs down, in the past these costs have seriously hampered the development of an English Canadian film and television industry with anything like the commercial success of Canadian popular music. Moreover, many Canadian actors, directors, producers and writers with ambitions in film and television have simply moved south, finding it easier to pursue their careers in Hollywood, where opportunities are greater and where they can pass more or less easily for Americans. Conversely, most of the large-scale commercial feature film production in Canada involves American movies being shot by Hollywood companies, which seek to benefit from lower labor and production costs in locations that can easily be made to look American.

Much of the successful Canadian television programming that has emerged in spite of these challenges has been produced and aired by the CBC. The most obvious and widely successful example is CBC's news and sports programming, which is watched by millions of Canadians on a regular basis. The nightly news program *The National* and the professional ice hockey games broadcast on *Hockey Night in Canada* have been staple viewing for Canadian households for decades. In 2004, according to Statistics Canada, two-thirds of Canadians' news and public affairs viewing and almost half of their sports viewing was of Canadian programs. Producing successful comedy and drama, where the need for local perspective is less pressing, has been more difficult: in the same year, foreign comedy and drama programs were viewed four or five times as often as comparable Canadian programs. Nevertheless, at least a few Canadian-made shows have attracted a considerable audience in each decade: for example, *The Beachcombers* and *King of Kensington* in the 1970s; *Street Legal* in the 1980s; *The Newsroom* and *Da Vinci's Inquest* in the late 1990s; and *This Is Wonderland* in the mid 2000s. The last of these was a courtroom drama set in Toronto that examined social and judicial problems in a multicultural urban environment with acute sensitivity and realism, a unique perspective that clearly separated it from similar American programs without compromising entertainment value, creative quality or production values. Most importantly for present purposes, it was full of Canadian English, spoken by characters ranging along the social spectrum from lawyers and judges to criminals, drug addicts and homeless people, most (though not all) of the actors being Canadian; the Toronto setting was also accurately reflected by a wide variety of allophone speech varieties. While this seemed just the sort of the thing the CBC should be spending its public funding on, the show was unfortunately cancelled after a few seasons: evidently, the appetite of the average Canadian viewer for the slick glamour and unrealistic fantasy of Hollywood dramas had overcome any interest in watching something truly Canadian and more invested in social realism.

A very different type of Canadian television show was *SCTV* (*Second City Television*), a satirical spoof about a local access cable television network and its programs. *SCTV* grew out of comedy routines performed by a group of Canadian comics at Toronto's Second City Theatre. Airing for six seasons, from the late 1970s to the early 1980s, the show was written in Toronto and filmed in Toronto and in Edmonton, where it had a production deal with local cable company ITV. It was then licensed to both the CBC and American networks. Because the CBC had less advertising than the American networks, it required two minutes more programming to fill an hour-long slot and asked the comedy troupe to come up with some distinctly Canadian content to make up the hour. In typically satirical fashion, two of the comics, Rick Moranis and Dave Thomas, responded by creating a series of two-minute segments called *The Great White North*, featuring the characters Bob and Doug McKenzie, a broad parody of various symbols of Canadian identity and of idiotic, inarticulate, beer-swilling Canadian outdoorsmen. The McKenzie brothers – wearing lumberjack shirts, toques and parkas, and seated amid stacked cases of Canadian beer, a map of Canada and a mug in the shape of a Mountie – fry back bacon on a Coleman camp stove, while offering drunken comments in vernacular Canadian accents on a range of absurd topics. This satire of Canadian content became *SCTV*'s most memorable legacy, entertaining American audiences as much as Canadian; the segment's success led to the release of a *Great White North* recording in 1981 and a feature film, *Strange Brew*, in 1983. It popularized several expressions putatively representative of vernacular Canadian speech, such as "how's it goin', eh?"; "have a good day, eh?"; and the dismissive "take off, eh?!", as well as the term *hoser*, which describes dim-witted louts like the McKenzie brothers themselves. A similar theme – bumbling rural outdoorsmen producing low-budget community television about absurd topics – underlies another, more recent series, which also attracted an American audience in addition to its Canadian following: *The Red Green Show*, which ran from 1991 to 2006.

Perhaps the most surprising and promising success in recent Canadian television production came not from the CBC but from CTV, a national commercial network. This was the series *Corner Gas*, a disarming but wittily satirical sitcom about a roadside restaurant and gas station in a small town in Saskatchewan, shot on location in the village of Rouleau, south of Regina, with a backdrop of real grain elevators and freight trains. Focusing on the gentle humor of Brent Butt, a stand-up comedian who actually grew up in a small town in Saskatchewan, the episodes poke fun at a broad range of trends and social types, from Brent's father, a grouchy retiree, to the owner of the restaurant, a recent arrival from Toronto who finds small-town life endlessly baffling, to a pair of very underworked local police officers. One of the police officers and the manager of the local hotel bar are played by Aboriginal actors, lending a realistic tone to the show's ethnic mix, given its Saskatchewan setting. In fact, all of the lead actors, Aboriginal or otherwise, are western Canadians, which ensures an accurate match between speech and setting seldom found on comparable American programs. Finally, the show often features cameo performances by well-known Canadians, from politicians to sports stars to pop singers, making it a veritable festival of Canadiana.

Together, *This Is Wonderland* and *Corner Gas* represent the full range of what English Canadian television can accomplish, beyond the obvious domains of news and sports: one a drama, one a comedy; one urban, one rural; one produced by the publicly funded CBC, one by a private broadcaster; but both brilliantly written and reflective of modern Canadian life and speech. Far from being merely second-rate local imitations of American programming, *This Is Wonderland* and *Corner Gas* were uniquely Canadian products that, in some ways, far surpassed many of their American equivalents, if not in entertainment value then at least in artistic merit. Many Canadian viewers have been thrilled with the qualities of these and other Canadian programs, while the successes of English Canadian television have been celebrated since 1986 at the Gemini Awards, presented annually by the Academy of Canadian Cinema and Television. However, while Canadian English is an important part of what makes these shows Canadian, their capacity as agents of Canadian English, providing models for viewers and instigating new trends, is limited by their relatively small audiences and brief life spans. As long as Canadians watch more American than Canadian programs, television will continue to be primarily a medium of American influence on Canadian English, rather than a medium through which Canadian English diffuses and evolves.

This is still truer of English-Canadian feature films, which have seen even less commercial success than Canadian television. While French-Canadian feature films have included a number of national and even international successes – for example, Claude Jutra's *Mon oncle Antoine* (1971), Denys Arcand's *Le déclin de l'empire américain* (1986) and *Les invasions barbares* (2003) and Jean-François Pouliot's *La grande séduction* (2004), among others – similar successes in English Canada have been lamentably few. It seems that the ready supply of Hollywood films designed to appeal to a continental anglophone market has virtually smothered the English-Canadian domestic industry, confining it to low-budget documentaries and independent features seen by relatively small audiences. It is difficult to compete with Hollywood's mix of huge budgets, new technologies and powerful marketing, the latter involving famous stars, product placement and retail tie-ins. As in television, however, a lack of Hollywood-scale commercial backing and mass audience appeal has not prevented a few cinematic successes from emerging in English Canada (for an encyclopedic list of Canadian films, ranging from the successful to the obscure, see Pratley 2003). Atom Egoyan and Anne Wheeler have established considerable reputations as directors of thoughtful films examining a variety of contemporary social and psychological issues, while *My American Cousin* (Sandy Wilson, 1985) provided a more light-hearted and nostalgic look at a small British Columbia town in the 1950s, addressing aspects of the Canadian relationship with the United States. In the satirical vein of television's McKenzie Brothers but with the accent more on an urban heavy metal music lifestyle than on backwoods buffoonery, Dave Lawrence and Paul Spence created another pair of comical *hosers* in the film *FUBAR* (Michael Dowse, 2002), a mock-documentary about the lives of two headbangers, Terry and Dean, filmed in and around Calgary. Another Calgary-made film, *Waydowntown* (Gary Burns, 2000), takes place entirely in that city's network of office towers joined by enclosed pedestrian overpasses, while *The Delicate Art of Parking* (Trent Carlson, 2004), like *FUBAR*, is a *mockumentary*, in this case examining the tribulations of a parking enforcement officer in Vancouver.

Some of the best English-Canadian films have been based on Canadian novels: Mordecai Richler's *The Apprenticeship of Duddy Kravitz* was filmed by Ted Kotcheff (1974), while an otherwise little-known novel by Max Braithwaite, *Why Shoot the Teacher?* (1965), was given brilliant cinematic treatment by Silvio Narizzano in 1977. Narizzano's film, shot on location near Hanna, Alberta, tells the story of a newly trained schoolteacher who, unable to find a better post during the Great Depression, takes a job in a one-room school on the bald prairie of rural southern Saskatchewan, where he encounters poverty, isolation, regional alienation, blizzards, and austere farm folk more concerned about feeding their families and the price of wheat than about the value of book-learning. The film relates its place and time – an important piece of Canadian history – with realism, sensitivity, passion and humor. However, this and other Canadian feature films sometimes make use of non-Canadian actors, particularly in lead roles, which reduces their value as documents of Canadian English, at least at the phonetic level: both Duddy Kravitz and the teacher of *Why Shoot the Teacher*, for example, are played by American actors (Richard Dreyfuss and Bud Kort, respectively, both from the New York City area). Whatever their merit as records of the Canadian experience, then, Canadian feature films – to the extent that they can be seen at all – can be used only with caution as exemplars of Canadian English.

1.6   Previous studies of Canadian English

Half a century ago, Morton Bloomfield (1948: 59) was justified in remarking that very little serious research had been devoted to Canadian English, especially in comparison to the body of work by then published on American or British English. In particular, the projected *Linguistic Atlas of the United States and Canada*, which had already produced groundbreaking studies of dialect variation along the Atlantic seaboard of the United States, had not yet been extended to Canada, beyond a few scattered informants along the American border, interviewed in connection with studies of neighboring American regions (Allen 1976; Kurath and McDavid 1961). The Linguistic Atlas project never did reach Canada: in fact, it was never completed even for the United States. Instead, shortly after Bloomfield noted its absence, a domestic tradition of Canadian research on Canadian English began to develop, which eventually produced a substantial body of work that is still growing today. In fact, there is now far too much serious research on Canadian English to permit an exhaustive review of all of it to be undertaken here. A more complete enumeration of the studies and articles that appeared up until fairly recently can be found in two published bibliographies: Avis and Kinloch (1978) for the period up to 1975 and Lougheed (1988) for the period from 1976 to 1987. Earlier lists of writings on Canadian English, compiled by Avis, appeared occasionally in the *Journal of the Canadian Linguistic Association*, from volume 7 (1961) known instead as the *Canadian Journal of Linguistics* (see, for example, vol. 15/1 (1969)); a selected bibliography is appended to Avis (1973: 68–73). Here, we will identify some of the most important previous research that addresses the aspects of Canadian English treated in this book.

The body of research on Canadian English with which we are concerned here is focused on six major themes: (1) lexicographic work on Canadian and regional Canadian English; (2) the alternation in Canada among American, British and Canadian words, pronunciations and usage, with an accompanying discussion of the historical origins and development of Canadian English; (3) the documentation of traditional regional speech enclaves; (4) microsociolinguistic studies of variation in urban Canadian English; (5) sociophonetic research on regional and social variation in the articulation of the vowels of Canadian English; and (6) macrosociolinguistic studies of the use of English and other languages in various regions of Canada, particularly Quebec. Chapter-length reviews of several or all of these areas, each with different emphases, have been written by Avis (1973), Bailey (1982), Brinton and Fee (2001), Chambers (1979b, 1991, 1998a, 2006a), Görlach (1991), Priestly (1951) and Stroinska and Checchetto (1999). Chambers (1975a) and Clarke (1993a) are anthologies of articles on various aspects of Canadian English from a wide variety of perspectives, while special issues of journals devoted to Canadian English, containing a similar variety of articles, include volumes 28/1 (1983) and 51/2–3 (2006) of the *Canadian Journal of Linguistics* and volume 19/2 (2008) of *Anglistik*. Orkin (1970) provides a book-length popular account of Canadian English, while McConnell (1979) and Baeyer (1980) are introductions to the subject for use in schools.

First, in the lexicographic tradition, reviewed by Gregg (1993), there are now several dictionaries of both the national and regional varieties of Canadian English. Avis, Crate, Drysdale, Leechman and Scargill (1967), a *Dictionary of Canadianisms on Historical Principles*, is an exhaustive list of Canadian words and of Canadian uses and senses of words that occur elsewhere in other uses or senses. Some of the groundwork for the dictionary was laid by Lovell (1955, 1956, 1958), who examines methodological issues and suggests preliminary materials. More general dictionaries of Canadian English, already mentioned above, are the *Gage Canadian Dictionary*, first produced in 1967 (De Wolf, Gregg, Harris and Scargill 1997), and the *Canadian Oxford Dictionary*, first published in 1998 (Barber 1998). In both of these can be found, in addition to the vocabulary of international English, many of the Canadian words and pronunciations to be discussed in Chapter 3, such as *drama* pronounced with /æ/, *parkade* for a parking garage, or *scribbler* for a student's notebook. At a more popular level, Bill Casselman has compiled several dictionaries of Canadian words and sayings that are both exhaustively researched and highly entertaining (Casselman 1995, 1999–2004).

The same mix of serious and popular work characterizes the lexicography of regional varieties of Canadian English. The most notable product in this field is undoubtedly the *Dictionary of Newfoundland English* (Story, Kirwin and Widdowson 1990), to the extent that Newfoundland English can be considered a regional variety of Canadian English, rather than an autonomous, non-Canadian variety. The *DNE* is a monumental lexicographic achievement, comprising thousands of meticulously detailed entries occupying more than 700 pages, now in its second edition. A smaller but similarly scholarly work is the *Dictionary of Prince Edward Island English* (Pratt 1988), which was followed a decade later by a dictionary of sayings (Pratt and Burke 1998). In addition to these, a wide variety of less academic dictionaries and phrasebooks have been compiled on many other regional varieties of Canadian English, ranging from more to less serious in style. One of the earliest is Sandilands (1912), a *Western Canadian Dictionary and Phrasebook*, which contains some entries whose uniquely Canadian status is dubious, but which nevertheless provides some of the earliest documentation of western Canadianisms like *bluff* (a cluster of trees), *chinook* (a warm winter wind), *coulee* (a ravine or gully) and *saskatoon* (a wild purple berry). More recent contributions in this vein include Parkin (1989) for British Columbia, Higinbotham (1962) and Thain (1987) for the Prairies, Trivisonno (1998) for Italian Montreal English, Poteet (1992) for Quebec's Eastern Townships, Underhill (1996) for New Brunswick's Miramichi Valley and Poteet (1988) for the South Shore of Nova Scotia.

One of the general characteristics of Canadian English that emerges from a close inspection of some of the lexicographic materials just mentioned is its mixture of British, American and Canadian words, pronunciations and grammatical forms. Alternation among these three major sources of linguistic influence in Canada has been the subject of what has become perhaps the central tradition of research on Canadian English. The earliest efforts in this domain often amount to little more than brief, anecdotal observations, whose primary value is historical. These include Ahrend (1934), Ayearst (1939), McLay (1930) and Munroe (1929). More systematic study of Canadian English began in the 1950s, stimulated in part by a debate about its historical origins that was articulated by Bloomfield (1948), Avis (1954) and Scargill (1957). In Bloomfield's view, "Canadian English . . . is to all intents and purposes General American with a few modified sounds" (1948: 62), owing to its origins in American Loyalist settlement, while Avis (1954: 13–14) suggests that "Canada is an extension of the northern speech area of the

United States" and that what is not American about Ontario English is British (15). By contrast, Scargill protested that Bloomfield's "loyalist theory" was "built on shaky foundations" (1957: 612), ignoring the important subsequent influence of British settlement, and that Avis' characterization "seems to deny any independent development of Canadian English" (610), which might have produced unique Canadian forms found neither in American nor in British English (see also Scargill 1977). Avis later clarified his view, agreeing that Canadian English is a mixture of American, British and uniquely Canadian elements (1973: 50; 1983: 7).

Serious study of just what forms were to be found in Canadian English, involving dialect questionnaires and usage surveys distributed to large numbers of respondents, was pioneered by Avis (1954, 1955, 1956), who examined speech differences along Ontario's border with the United States. Hamilton (1958) launched a similar investigation of Montreal's English-speaking community. Farther west, Allen (1959) extended Avis' interest in the international border as a linguistic division to northwestern Ontario and the Prairies (see also Kinloch 1995), while Scargill (1954, 1955) reported on a pilot study of Alberta speech. Following its initiation in the 1950s, the questionnaire tradition of research on Canadian English reached its zenith in a first national survey, the *Survey of Canadian English*, which involved over 14,000 schoolchildren and their parents in every province of Canada. The results are reported in Scargill and Warkentyne (1972); a summary and analysis of the data was produced by Warkentyne (1973) and a book-length analysis, in German, by Bähr (1981). Rodman (1974) examines the survey data from British Columbia in greater detail.

Following the appearance of the *Survey of Canadian English*, the questionnaire tradition continued to be practiced in smaller studies, such as a survey of Saskatchewan English by Nylvek (1992, 1993) and a study of the United States–Canada border by Zeller (1993), but the majority of research on Canadian English over the next two decades turned to other methods of research. It was fully reprised in the 1990s by J. K. Chambers, who developed an updated approach to it that he called *Dialect Topography*, making use of computerization and of sociolinguistic methods of representative sampling and quantitative correlational analysis. Chambers himself conducted the first Dialect Topography survey, which examined the "Golden Horseshoe" region around the western end of Lake Ontario, focused on Greater Toronto. The results of the Golden Horseshoe survey have been featured in several articles (Chambers 1994, 1995b, 1998b, 1998c, 2000). Chambers then recruited collaborators to implement the survey in other regions. Data from Montreal are analyzed in Boberg (2004b, 2004d), while those from the small English-speaking population of Quebec City appear in Chambers and Heisler (1999) and Chambers (2000); Burnett (2006) uses Dialect Topography data to examine the linguistic status of the border between New Brunswick and Maine. The results of another new dialect questionnaire examining regional differences in vocabulary usage, the *North American Regional Vocabulary Survey*, are reported by Boberg (2005b, 2008b), as well as in Chapters 3 and 4 of the present book.

Though many of the studies just mentioned took their data from restricted regions of Canada, most of them were conceived not as regional studies per se but as investigations of Canadian English at a more general level, examining regional differences from a comparative perspective in an effort to describe national usage. Detailed investigation of the various traditional regional speech enclaves enumerated above began with Emeneau's description of the features of the German-influenced dialect of Lunenberg, Nova Scotia (1935). A wide variety of studies of Nova Scotia English, including Emeneau's, are anthologized in Falk and Harry (1999), while the speech of Nova Scotia's African-Canadian community, of special interest because of the evidence it offers of earlier stages of African American English, is examined by Poplack and Tagliamonte (1991) and Walker (2001, 2005). As might be expected, however, the greatest share of regional attention has been devoted to Newfoundland English. A detailed survey of such work is beyond the scope of the present discussion, but, apart from the dictionary already mentioned, important descriptive accounts are given by Drysdale (1959), Porter (1966) and Paddock (1981), while Clarke (1991, 1993b, 2006), D'Arcy (2005) and Hollett (2006) report on sociolinguistic studies of the phonology of St. John's English; Kirwin (1960) is a more narrowly focused but nonetheless interesting analysis of variation in the pronunciation of the place names *Labrador, St. John's* and *Newfoundland*. More general summaries of the distinctive characteristics of Newfoundland speech can be found in Clarke (2004a, 2004b, 2008), Hickey (2002), Kirwin (2001, 2003), Siemund and Haselow (2008), Story (1982) and Wells (1982: 498–501). Beyond the Atlantic enclaves, investigations have also been made of the distinctive varieties of Canadian English in Quebec or Montreal (Boberg 2004c; McArthur 1989; Poplack 2008; Poplack, Walker and Malcolmson 2006; Walker 2007) and in the Ottawa Valley (Chambers 1975b; Pringle, Jones and Padolsky 1981; Pringle and Padolsky 1983). The Mormon enclave in southern Alberta has been studied by Meechan (1998, 1999).

As already mentioned, after the initial drive to produce surveys of Canadian English using traditional written dialect questionnaires, many researchers turned their attention to other methods and approaches. This was in response to wider trends in linguistic research outside Canada, particularly those methods that had come to dominate modern sociolinguistics. Microsociolinguistic analyses of Newfoundland speech were identified above; mainland Canadian English, particularly in its urban varieties, was also subjected to quantitative analyses of correlations between social categories and linguistic variation, beginning in the late 1970s. The largest urban sociolinguistic studies to undertake such analyses, examining a wide range of linguistic variables, were that of Vancouver, with 240 participants, directed by R. J. Gregg, and that of Ottawa, with 100 participants, directed by Howard Woods. Results of the Vancouver study are presented in Gregg (1984, 1992, 1995), De Wolf (1993), De Wolf, Fee and McAlpine (2004) and Esling and Warkentyne (1993). The Ottawa study is reported in Woods (1991, 1993, 1999). The two studies are compared by De Wolf (1983, 1988, 1989, 1990, 1992, 1996, 2004). While De Wolf identifies a number of regional differences between the two cities, they both display sociolinguistic variation very much in line with that observed in other urban communities: "educated usage is on the side of the traditional [variants], while women, especially the mature, are generally the most conservative group in maintaining standard values. Young women, however, often lead a shift in progress" (1992: 150–151). In addition to these general surveys, there have been many sociolinguistic studies of individual linguistic variables, including the discourse markers and grammatical variables analyzed by D'Arcy (2004, 2008), Tagliamonte (2006) and Tagliamonte and D'Arcy (2004, 2007a, b); the existential constructions studied by Meechan and Foley (1994) and Walker (2007); and the verbs of quotation mentioned above (*be like* as a quotative), analyzed by Tagliamonte and D'Arcy (2004, 2007a) and Tagliamonte and Hudson (1999). Also in the sociolinguistic tradition, Owens and Baker (1984) examine the social correlates of linguistic security with a number of traditional variables in Winnipeg.

Within the larger context of microsociolinguistic analysis, an important research tradition in recent North American sociolinguistics has been socio-phonetic analyses of sound changes in progress, particularly those involving the structure of vowel systems: changes in the phonemic status of vowels (mergers and splits) and in the phonetic realization of vowel phonemes (chain shifts). This approach, normally employing computerized acoustic phonetic analysis, stems from the work of William Labov and his colleagues (e.g., Labov, Yaeger and Steiner 1972), recently culminating in the *Atlas of North American English: Phonetics, Phonology and Sound Change* (Labov, Ash and Boberg 2006). The *Atlas* includes substantial coverage of variation and change in the vowels of Canadian English (especially in chapter 15: 216–224), providing, in fact, the first national view of the phonetics of Canadian English.

The first studies of Canadian vowel pronunciation, however, predate Labov's earliest work and use neither acoustic analysis nor sociolinguistic sampling. They follow instead the older tradition of structuralist phonemics, often relying on limited, anecdotal observation or even on introspection rather than on empirical investigation. The first observer to notice one of the main phonological features of Canadian English, the failure to distinguish words like *cot* from words like *caught* (the "low-back merger"), was Scott (1939). Another prominent feature, the "Canadian Raising" of the vocalic nuclei of the diphthongs in words like *house* and *tight*, was first noted by Ahrend (1934) and first analyzed by Joos (1942). Gregg (1957a, 1957b) produced the pioneering study of the pronunciation of Canadian English in a more general sense, as spoken in Vancouver. This was followed shortly by Lehn's description of vowel contrasts in Saskatchewan English (1959), then by Avis (1972) and Walker (1975) on Canadian English as pronounced in Edmonton and Kinloch (1983) and Kinloch and Avis (1989) on central Canadian English (the Prairies and Ontario); general descriptions of Canadian vowel pronunciation are given in Wells (1982: 490–497) and Boberg (2004a, 2008a). Canadian Raising became a major subject of interest in its own right, following its analysis in a generative phonological framework by Chambers (1973): further research on this and related variables is reported in Gregg (1973), Picard (1977), Paradis (1980), Chambers and Hardwick (1986), Chambers (1989), Thomas (1991), Hung, Davison and Chambers (1993), Murdoch (2004), Chambers (2006b), Hagiwara (2006), Idsardi (2006) and Labov, Ash and Boberg (2006: 114–115, 221–222). A variety of other, small-scale phonetic studies of Toronto English, relying on instrumental analysis, are compiled in Léon and Martin (1979).

A new phase in sociophonetic research on Canadian English was initiated by Clarke, Elms and Youssef (1995), who first identified a coordinated set of changes in the quality of the short front vowels of Wells' (1982) KIT, DRESS and TRAP lexical sets, which they labeled the *Canadian Shift*: the TRAP vowel appeared to be retracting from the low-front into the low-central region of the vowel space (a change first noted in Vancouver English by Esling and Warkentyne 1993), while the DRESS and KIT vowels were descending toward the low-front space vacated by TRAP. Since its initial identification, the Canadian Shift has been examined in Montreal English by Boberg (2005a), in Winnipeg by Hagiwara (2006), in St. John's English by D'Arcy (2005) and Hollett (2006) and across Canada by Labov, Ash and Boberg (2006: 78–83, 130, 219–221). Further sociophonetic studies of Canadian English appear in Boberg (2000, 2008a, 2009) and Esling (1991).

The final domain of research on Canadian English to be considered here is macro- rather than microsociolinguistic, specifically the subject of language use, particularly in Quebec, as considered above in Section 1.1. Brief general discussions of English in the Canadian context are offered by Avis (1983, 1986), while anthologies of articles examining language use in each province of Canada, including English, French and Aboriginal languages, have been edited by Chambers (1979a) and Edwards (1998). Given what has already been said about the minority status of English in Quebec, language use in that province has been a subject of particular interest, generating a large and diverse set of studies that cannot all be mentioned here. Among them are profiles of the Quebec English-speaking community by Arnopoulos and Clift (1984), Caldwell (1974, 1984, 1998), Caldwell and Waddell (1982), Levine (1990), Locher (1988), Morrison, Reimer and Shaver (1991), Rudin (1985), Scowen (1991) and Veltman (1996); demolinguistic analyses of English, French and other languages by Castonguay (1998), Charbonneau and Maheu

(1973), Jedwab (1996, 2000, 2004), Paillé (1985, 1989) and Termote and Gauvreau (1988); studies of language and ethnicity by Lieberson (1970, 1981); reports on factors affecting language choice in Montreal by Heller (1982) and Bourhis (1984b); and assessments of the social evaluation of English and French as competing languages in a bilingual context by Lambert (1967) and Giles, Taylor and Bourhis (1973).

Of course, research on Canadian English is not limited to the six domains just outlined. For instance, Dollinger (2006, 2008, forthcoming), following Chambers (1993), has recently turned to historical written materials for evidence of earlier stages of Canadian English, and has examined aspects of the modal auxiliary verb system of Canadian English, producing an innovative body of work in several respects that falls outside the main traditions of work on Canadian English while relating to them in interesting ways. Regardless of how it is classified, the quantity of published research reviewed here demonstrates clearly that, in the half-century since Bloomfield (1948) commented on the paucity of academic work on Canadian English, a strong and diverse tradition of such work has developed. This has made Canadian English today one of the best-studied varieties of English, especially considering the relative size of its population of speakers. The contributions of Avis, Chambers, Clarke, De Wolf, Gregg, Scargill, Warkentyne, Woods and others have made the basic features, historical development and current status of Canadian English well known both in Canada and abroad, and have linked the study of Canadian English to internationally based traditions of linguistic research. The present book cannot hope to give adequate consideration to every part of this large body of research, nor is that its intent, for the work of these other scholars is well represented in the many publications just cited. Rather, while acknowledging the importance of previous work for the view of Canadian English presented here, the greater part of this book will be devoted to presenting new data on Canadian English collected and analyzed by the author, drawing on previous research by others only were necessary or for purposes of comparison. It is hoped that this presentation will thereby add to, rather than merely summarize or reformulate, the current body of knowledge of Canadian English.

2 The establishment and growth of Canada's English-speaking population

An indispensable part of understanding the present form of Canadian English is understanding the historical forces that gave rise to Canada's English-speaking population and promoted its expansion. Apart from being responsible for the very existence of Canadian English, these external, non-linguistic forces have played just as important a role as internal, linguistic forces in determining its modern characteristics. Given Canada's relative youth (at least from the European point of view), the current form of Canadian English is closely bound up with the history of immigration: who first established English in Canada and where they came from; how this initial settlement was built upon, with which people in which proportions; and, finally, where today's speakers of Canadian English come from. To address these questions, this chapter will examine the history of the establishment and further growth of Canada's English-speaking population. It begins with a chronological description of several phases in the settlement of Canada in order to establish the historical roots of Canadian English, then considers the possible origins of important features of modern Canadian English in light of that history. Readers less familiar with the geography of Canada may find it helpful to consult the maps at the front of the book for locations of places discussed in this chapter.

2.1 Origins: fishermen, fur traders and soldiers

The English language is a relative newcomer to Canada. Before European colonization, the land now called Canada was home to a wide array of Aboriginal cultures and their languages: from the Salishan and Wakashan-speaking cultures of Vancouver Island on the west coast, to the Beothuk on the island of Newfoundland in the east; from the Inuit of the Arctic to the Iroquoian culture of southern Ontario. The name *Canada* is in fact an Iroquoian word, *kanata*, meaning a village or settlement. The 2001 Canadian Census shows that Canada is still home to almost a million Aboriginal people, accounting for about 3 percent of the national population, but their languages and cultures have suffered considerable erosion since the arrival of European settlers.

Some Aboriginal languages retain fairly large numbers of speakers, most notably Cree, an Algonquian language spoken as a mother tongue by almost 73,000 people. Comprising several dialects, its territory covers a vast interior region extending from Alberta to Quebec. The next most spoken is Inuktitut, with 29,000 speakers, almost all in the northern territory of Nunavut and in northern Quebec. Nonetheless, many other languages and dialects have been lost, while still others are in the last stages of decline. Most Aboriginal people today are fluent in English, a capacity that facilitates their participation in mainstream Canadian life but further threatens the survival of the languages that remain. Indeed, most Aboriginal people now speak only English, and many more have only an imperfect command of their ancestral languages, depending on English or French for most of their communicative needs. The 2001 Census reports that, of the 976,305 Aboriginal people in Canada, slightly under a quarter (235,065) have "knowledge of" an Aboriginal language and only 18.4 percent still speak an Aboriginal language at home, while two-thirds (639,450) have knowledge of English only. Linguistic assimilation of Aboriginal people to the English-speaking population, combined with recent immigration patterns, has reduced Aboriginal languages to relative obscurity in the Canadian language picture: even Cree and Inuktitut are the sixteenth and seventeenth most commonly spoken mother tongues in Canada today (there are over ten times more native speakers of Chinese than of Cree).

While the first major European settlements in Canada were French, the history of European settlement in what is today Canada actually begins with the Vikings. Norse sagas preserve a largely oral history of Scandinavian voyages to North America around the end of the tenth century, originating from the Norse or Icelandic settlements in Greenland. According to this history, Bjarni Herjolfsson was probably the first European to set eyes on North America and Leif Eiriksson the first to set foot on North American soil. Modern archeological excavations at L'Anse-aux-Meadows on the tip of the Great Northern Peninsula of Newfoundland – thought to be the *Vinland* of the Norse sagas – have discovered the remains of a Norse settlement there, now a Canadian National Historic Site. The sagas claim the settlement was established by Thorfinn Karlsefni, whose son, Snorri Karlsefnisson, was the first European born in North America. That most Canadians do not today speak a Scandinavian language we owe to a number of factors: the primitive state of tenth-century technology; the remoteness of Thorfinn's settlement from sources of supply and new colonists; the small size of the Scandinavian population; the hostility of the local Aboriginal people, whom the Norsemen called *Skrælings*; and very likely also disease, bad weather and a barren landscape. For a combination of these reasons, the *Vinland* settlement appears to have been abandoned after a few years.

A more successful and enduring phase in the European colonization of Canada began with the sixteenth-century voyages of the French explorer

Jacques Cartier. In 1535 he discovered the St. Lawrence River and followed it upstream to an Aboriginal village called Hochelaga, on the modern site of Montreal, claiming the region for France. Permanent French settlement did not begin until the early seventeenth century. Samuel de Champlain founded Port-Royal in Acadia (now Annapolis Royal in Nova Scotia) in 1605 and Quebec, the future capital of New France, in 1608. Montreal was established in 1642 by a group of colonists led by Paul de Chomedey, Sieur de Maisonneuve. Unfortunately for the future of French colonial interests in North America, this was about the same time as Britain was establishing its own settlements farther south, at Jamestown, Virginia, in 1607 and at Boston in 1620. Nevertheless, by the early eighteenth century, French possessions in North America extended in a vast arc from Acadia through several fur-trading outposts in the Great Lakes region to the Mississippi delta in Louisiana, completely encircling the major British presence along the Atlantic seaboard. The nucleus of these possessions, New France, was a well-established concentration of continuous agricultural settlement along the St. Lawrence River in the modern province of Quebec, with several thousand people at each of Montreal and Quebec City.

It was not long, however, before French and British interests in North America began to conflict. Several British expeditions – those of Martin Frobisher from 1576 to 1578, John Davis from 1585 to 1587 and the ill-fated Henry Hudson in 1610–1611 – had brought back early reports of Canada's northern regions, including the giant bay that would be named for Hudson. Hudson Bay did not satisfy Britain's desire for a northwest passage to the Orient, but did provide marine access to the interior of the continent, with its rich opportunities for trade in fur with Aboriginal peoples. In 1670, Britain chartered the Hudson's Bay Company to develop its own fur trade around the bay, competing with the French presence along the Great Lakes and the St. Lawrence River. Tiny British trading-post settlements were established at the mouths of the major rivers flowing into Hudson and James Bays in the late seventeenth century: at Fort Rupert in Quebec, Moose Factory in Ontario and York Factory in Manitoba. More crucially, during the eighteenth century the British settlements along the Atlantic seaboard began to expand inland, as colonists searched for more land and resources. The British presence in North America quickly outstripped the French, reflecting both the generally superior climate and resources available in the British sector and the greater supply of new emigrants. French emigration to North America amounted to no more than 10,000–15,000 people over the 150-year history of New France; natural increase was the main factor in raising the colony's population to around 70,000 by 1760 (Charbonneau, Desjardins, Légaré and Denis 2000: 104, 106). By contrast, Britain's American colonies received over 300,000 immigrants over the same period, helping to raise their population to well over a million by 1760 (Gemery 2000: 171).

The inevitable clash of French and British colonial aims, not to speak of Aboriginal interests, led to what are known in the American historical tradition as the French and Indian Wars, a series of skirmishes, battles and border wars between the two colonial powers and their respective Aboriginal allies that lasted several decades. The most important of these was the North American part of the global conflict known as the Seven Years' War (1756–1763). After some initial French successes in this war, Britain gained the advantage, decisively defeating the French in 1759 on the Plains of Abraham, outside Quebec City. After the French surrender at Montreal in 1760, the war was formally ended by the Treaty of Paris (1763), by which France ceded to Britain its possessions in what is now Canada. The British victory had several important consequences: it cut off further French emigration to Canada; it opened the way for northward expansion of English-speaking settlement into Canada; and it thereby initiated the long struggle of France's former colonists to survive as a French-speaking culture in the midst of an increasingly English-speaking continent (the most recent phase of which is described in Chapter 1, Section 1.1).

Despite French dominance of Canada's early colonial history, English-speaking settlement actually began in a small way before the British victory in the Seven Years' War. The earliest British contact with Canada was instigated by King Henry VII, who commissioned the Venetian mariner Giovanni Caboto – John Cabot – to explore North America on behalf of England. Cabot discovered the eastern coast of Canada in 1497, anticipating Cartier by several decades and prompting England to take an early interest in establishing colonies in the Americas. By the sixteenth century, the rich fishing grounds of Newfoundland's Grand Banks were regularly attracting Portuguese, Spanish, Basque, French and English fleets. In 1583, Sir Humphrey Gilbert received a charter from Queen Elizabeth I to establish a North American colony and claimed the region around St. John's, Newfoundland, for England. Permanent settlement, however, was discouraged and even forbidden, in order to protect the commercial interests of an English fishing industry that wanted no colonial competition for its own operations. A few small English settlements were established by special royal permission beginning in 1610, but these had to compete both with the often violent opposition of the British fishing monopoly and with French counterclaims to the island. They were periodically destroyed and abandoned for over a century, so that the English-speaking population never rose much above a thousand inhabitants (Belcher 1924: 58; Handcock 1977: 16–18, 21; Rothney 1973: 14). Settlement was further limited by the barren terrain of rock and forest, which hindered agricultural development and favored continued dependence on the fishery.

Despite these challenges, a few hamlets of English settlers, mostly fishermen from the English West Country, persisted along with a small group of Irish emigrants (the main group of Irish was to arrive later). In the 1690s Fort

William was constructed and garrisoned to reinforce Britain's claim to the Avalon Peninsula, but this fell to French attackers in 1708. French claims to Newfoundland were only settled by the Treaty of Utrecht in 1713, whereby France ceded the island and peninsular Nova Scotia to Britain, retaining Cape Breton and Prince Edward Island. The treaty put an end to the War of the Spanish Succession, which was the larger context of the Anglo-French conflict, but not to the struggle for control of North America. When British title was again contested in the Seven Years' War, the Treaty of Paris finally returned Newfoundland and the Maritimes (Acadia) to Britain, this time with the smaller islands into the bargain. As Britain took firm possession, if English-speaking settlement was still scarce, probably amounting to no more than a few thousand people (Handcock 1977: 21), it had nevertheless already existed tenuously for 150 years.

The factors leading to the initial English-speaking settlement of peninsular Nova Scotia are examined by Hansen (1940: 23–37) and MacNutt (1965: 1–72). Like Newfoundland, Nova Scotia possessed rich stocks of offshore codfish and timber. It also occupied a strategically important position, lying between the Gulf of St. Lawrence and the American coast, the closest part of the mainland to Europe (other than the barren Labrador coast). The Treaty of Utrecht had established a new British province in Nova Scotia without a British population: European settlement consisted mostly of the French-speaking Acadian population, though both English and New England fishing fleets regularly made seasonal visits to coastal regions. Finding themselves under alien authority, the Acadians declared themselves to be neutral in the Anglo-French conflict, but the British suspected them of continued allegiance to France. Moreover, following the Treaty of Utrecht, France had constructed a massive fortress at Louisbourg, on the northern tip of Cape Breton, suggesting that the French had not entirely abandoned their designs on Acadia. In this context, the establishment of an English-speaking (or at least non-French) population in Nova Scotia became an urgent matter of British imperial strategy.

The initial British response to Louisbourg, apart from successfully attacking it in 1745 and then returning it to France three years later in the Treaty of Aix-la-Chapelle, was the founding of Halifax in 1749. This was accomplished by a group of around 2,500 mostly English settlers led by Col. Edward Cornwallis. Halifax served well as a military counterweight to the French presence at Louisbourg and as a fishing port, but its prospects as an agricultural region, and consequently for large-scale settlement, were limited; inland expansion was further discouraged by the hostility of both the French and Aboriginal populations. There was only modest enthusiasm in England for emigration to Nova Scotia, so recruiting was extended to Europe. This program brought 1,500 Germans and Swiss to Halifax, but they failed to thrive there and were transferred in 1753 to a more promising location farther south, the new township of Lunenburg, where they continued to require government subsidies. The initial drive to settle Nova Scotia also attracted about a thousand New Englanders, who, with their greater experience of the challenges of North American pioneer life, were comparatively successful in establishing themselves. It became apparent that New England, rather than Britain or Europe, would be the most promising source of new settlers for Nova Scotia.

The main obstacle to the expansion of New England agricultural settlement northward into Nova Scotia was the Acadian population, which had already occupied most of the best land in a generally rocky and barren territory. In 1755, mounting Anglo-French tensions and the need of land for new settlement culminated in a decision to expel the Acadian population and resettle their lands with English-speaking colonists. The unfortunate Acadians were dispersed to a wide variety of locations from Quebec to Louisiana, the latter group becoming the Cajuns that are still an important part of the cultural fabric of New Orleans; many others were absorbed into the English-speaking populations of the American colonies. In 1758, the Governor of Nova Scotia issued a proclamation inviting American colonists to settle in the province. This was answered in 1760 by the first fleet of transports carrying new pioneers, mostly from the eastern sections of Massachusetts, Connecticut and Rhode Island and the coastal islands of New England. The northward migration continued through the 1760s, totaling about 7,000 people by 1776 (Harris and Warkentin 1974: 182; MacNutt 1965: 61), but was eventually slowed by the opening of the much more fertile Ohio territory for settlement in 1768. Indeed, some of those who had arrived looking for good land in Nova Scotia moved on to the Ohio territory after 1768. By this time, however, the English-speaking population of Nova Scotia had been well established, mostly by former New Englanders.

Thus, even as Britain first took possession of its new imperial lands in British North America following the Seven Years' War, English-speaking settlement in at least a few regions of those territories had already begun on a modest scale: a small concentration in Nova Scotia, a smaller concentration in Newfoundland and a scattering of outposts around Hudson Bay. As the title of this section suggested, these first English-speakers were overwhelmingly fishermen, fur traders and soldiers, along with some farmers and their families in Nova Scotia.

2.2   The United Empire Loyalists (and others)

Previous English-speaking settlement of present Canadian territory was nevertheless limited in scale when compared to the first major wave of English-speaking migration to Canada, which came two decades after the Treaty of Paris: the arrival of the United Empire Loyalists. This rather grand term designates those American colonists who remained loyal to the crown in the American Revolution and emigrated during and immediately after it to the remaining loyal British provinces in what is today Canada. By no means all American colonists approved of the Revolution: independence from Britain was one of many options that were hotly debated as solutions to colonial grievances. As in the modern controversy over proposals to separate Quebec from Canada, independence seemed to some the only and obvious course, while to others it was an unthinkable act of treason or a grave error that seemed likely to end in political chaos and economic ruin; the opinions of still others fell somewhere in between these camps. Unfortunately, once the independence camp prevailed, for all its noble dedication to liberty and democracy, American revolutionary fervor also included abusive treatment of its ideological opponents, who were branded traitors and *Tories*. Maltreatment ranged from confiscation of position and property to social ostracism and public humiliation to physical violence; suffice it to say that many Loyalists felt they could no longer remain in the places where they or their ancestors had settled. Others simply preferred to live under the protection of the British crown, or feared unfavorable economic or political conditions in the aftermath of the Revolution.

For several years during the course of the Revolutionary War (1775–1783), it was not clear which side would ultimately claim victory, or what the ensuing settlement would be. Small numbers of Loyalists left the American colonies throughout the war, particularly members of the social elite who returned directly to Britain, but the bulk of the Loyalist population, most of whom could not afford passage to Britain and had no prospects there, tended to congregate behind British lines awaiting the outcome of the war. After the British evacuation of Boston in 1776 and of Philadelphia in 1778, New York City became the main British stronghold throughout the remainder of the war and the principal refuge of the Loyalist population. Even a few Loyalists from the southern colonies made their way there, though most southern Loyalists fled instead to the British colonies in the Caribbean, where they could live in the plantation society to which they had become accustomed. The bulk of the New York refugee population comprised former residents of the middle and New England colonies: farmers, tradesmen, merchants, soldiers and administrators from Virginia, Maryland, Pennsylvania, New Jersey, New York, Connecticut, Rhode Island and Massachusetts, accompanied by their families and in some cases by servants or slaves.

By 1782, Britain was increasingly desperate to cut its losses and find a quick settlement of the American conflict. In treaty negotiations with the revolutionaries, the full independence of the new republic was recognized, territorial concessions were made even beyond what the revolutionary armies had won, and any serious effort to prevent prejudicial treatment of the Loyalists was abandoned: mild treatment was recommended to state legislatures but impossible to enforce. This dismayed the Loyalists, many of whom had hoped for some sort of compromise between the two sides, with restoration of their property and a guarantee of protection from the revenge of their former countrymen. Once the terms of the treaty became known, the thousands of Loyalists in New York City began forming themselves into associations that drew up plans to emigrate. To atone for having abandoned the Loyalists in the peace treaty, Britain offered them passage on ships to its remaining North American colonies. This operation was overseen by Sir Guy Carleton, the British commander-in-chief at New York, who refused to evacuate the city until the Loyalists had been given safe passage out of it.

The most natural place of refuge for those of the New York-based Loyalists who could not or would not go to Britain was Nova Scotia, being contiguous with the American colonies and directly accessible by means of one or two weeks' sail up the Atlantic coast. The British province then included three regions: peninsular Nova Scotia, Cape Breton Island and present-day New Brunswick. The first party of several hundred Loyalists left New York in the fall of 1782 to assess the prospects for resettlement in these regions. Members of this advance party returned to New York with positive reports of two sites that seemed to them well suited: the area around the present town of Shelburne (then called Port Roseway), an inlet on the southeastern coast of peninsular Nova Scotia; and the region around the mouth and lower course of the Saint John River in present-day New Brunswick, the site of the modern cities of Saint John and Fredericton. As hostilities ceased and the British prepared to evacuate New York in the spring of 1783, the major emigration of New York Loyalists began, continuing until the winter of 1783–1784.

The consensus of historians of these events (Bradley 1932: 122; Brown and Senior 1984: 38; Moore 1984: 125–126; Wallace 1964: 63) is that the Loyalist emigration of 1783 brought approximately 35,000 new settlers to Atlantic Canada: about 20,000 to Nova Scotia and 15,000 to New Brunswick. Brown and Senior (1984: 38–40) describe the distribution of settlement in some detail. In Nova Scotia, the largest single group, approximately 4,000 people, went to Shelburne, but smaller settlements were found throughout the province, including at Halifax and among the older, pre-Loyalist New England settlers in and around the Annapolis Valley. In addition, about 400 went to Cape Breton and 800 to Prince Edward Island; a few families even found their way to Newfoundland. Many of the refugees did not remain where they initially landed: some went on to Britain; some returned to their former American homes once anti-Tory sentiment had subsided; still others went farther west in Canada as new settlements were opened. Brown and Senior (1984: 50–51) estimate that, while 85 percent of the Saint John Valley settlers stayed on to become the foundation of modern New Brunswick, up to two-thirds of the migrants to Nova Scotia may have left after a few years. This pattern was most dramatically evident at Shelburne, which grew quickly into a boomtown of 10,000 people shortly after its establishment in 1783, surpassing Halifax, then shrank just as rapidly to a village of 1,600 as its colonists discovered that the initial survey party had been mistaken about the advantages of its site: despite a fine harbor, prospects for agriculture, fishing and forestry turned out to be poor (Brown and Senior 1984: 39). Notwithstanding these losses, many of which were made up for by continued, post-Loyalist immigration in subsequent years, the arrival of 35,000 Loyalists in 1783 provided the first substantial English-speaking population of New Brunswick and greatly increased that of Nova Scotia. Indeed, it was the arrival of such large numbers of Loyalists that led to the establishment of New Brunswick as a separate province the following year.

A second stream of Loyalist refugees moved northward not by sea but overland, a longer and more arduous journey, from the American interior into present-day Quebec and, to a lesser extent, Ontario. Lake Champlain, dividing modern Vermont and New York State, along with the Hudson and Richelieu Rivers, provided a natural escape route for Loyalists from the inland frontier regions of New England, New York, New Jersey and Pennsylvania. Use of this route rose dramatically after the British defeat at the Battle of Saratoga in 1777. By the war's end, the historians agree that there were about 7,000–8,000 Loyalists temporarily stationed at various sites around Quebec, most of them members of colonial military regiments (Bradley 1932: 132; Brown and Senior 1984: 50; Hansen 1940: 64; Moore 1984: 172; Wallace 1964: 93). It was the job of Sir Frederick Haldimand, the British governor of the province, to determine where to settle them more permanently. Moore (1984: 134) describes Haldimand's view of the various options. Many of the Loyalists themselves wanted to stay put, preferring to settle in the Richelieu or St. Lawrence valleys, near British garrisons that could ensure their safety. Fearing that the settlement of so many English-men among the French Canadian population would upset the delicate colo-nial peace that had been established since the British conquest, Haldimand rejected this proposal. The relatively empty region below the St. Lawrence valley in southern Quebec was also rejected, being too close to the American frontier, which Haldimand wanted to maintain as a buffer zone in case of future hostilities. Instead, he sent parties of surveyors westward, up the St. Lawrence, to assess the possibility of settlement in present-day Ontario.

By the spring of 1784, a string of townships had been marked out in a line extending west of the Ottawa River, along the north shore of the St. Lawrence to its source at Lake Ontario: eight Royal Townships, from Coteau-du-Lac, just west of Montreal, to Brockville; and eight Cataraqui Townships, from Kingston to the Bay of Quinte, near Belleville (Brown and Senior 1984: 49). By the summer of 1784, the great majority of Quebec's Loyalists, around 6,000, had been resettled in present-day Ontario; only about 2,000 remained east of the Ottawa River in Quebec, including only about 300 in Montreal (Brown and Senior 1984: 50). In Ontario, those transferred from Quebec joined smaller groups that had found their way there more directly, establishing small settlements in the Niagara Peninsula and across the river from Detroit. These initial groups were later augmented by some of the Maritime Loyalists, who had been disappointed by their prospects in Nova Scotia or New Brunswick and decided to try their luck farther west.

While the original English-speaking settlement of Ontario by true Loyalists during and immediately after the American Revolution probably brought no more than 7,000–8,000 people to the future province, this pioneering effort nevertheless opened the way for further, post-Loyalist settlement, which soon greatly outnumbered the initial group. The reasons for post-Loyalist American emigration to Canada varied, but while in some cases loyalty to the crown was a factor, most post-Loyalist emigrants were more interested in good, cheap land than in politics. As the supply of fertile, unclaimed farmland dwindled in New Jersey, New York, Pennsylvania and even Ohio, southern Ontario became an attractive frontier for agricultural settlement. By 1791, the European population was large enough to justify the division of Quebec, or Canada, into two provinces, Upper and Lower Canada, the forerunners of Ontario and Quebec, respectively.

Upper Canada's first lieutenant governor, John Graves Simcoe, encouraged further immigration by initiating a program of land grants to American settlers. In 1793, he established the village of York on the north shore of Lake Ontario, which would become the city of Toronto in 1834. Upper Canada's population grew even larger over the next two decades as post-Loyalist immigration continued and immigration from Britain began. By 1812, the date of the last military conflict between Britain and the United States, settlement extended all the way from Windsor to Cornwall along the northern shores of Lake Erie, Lake Ontario and the St. Lawrence River (Harris and Warkentin 1974: 117). The population had reached approximately 100,000, the large majority of whom (up to 80 percent) had arrived from the former American colonies. Only a fifth to a fourth of them were Loyalists or their direct descendants; the remainder had come after 1788 (Brown and Senior 1984: 51; Hansen 1940: 90; Harris and Warkentin 1974: 116).

Post-Loyalist immigration was also largely responsible for the establishment of the small English-speaking population of southern Quebec, a region that came to be called the Eastern Townships, to differentiate them from the Western Townships in Upper Canada. This area had been almost entirely neglected during the French regime, so that its first effective European population consisted of migrants from New England, who rushed in once the government of Lower Canada lifted its ban on settlement near the American border in 1791. As in Upper Canada, this was a land rush rather than a political phenomenon; it was part of the same search for new land that had led to the founding of the state of Vermont south of the border in 1791. By 1817, approximately 20,000 people had settled in the Eastern Townships, virtually all of them from northern New England, establishing communities like Granby, Lennoxville, Magog and Sherbrooke. These were economically and culturally an extension of Vermont, despite being politically a part of

Lower Canada (Harris and Warkentin 1974: 93). It was only in the second half of the nineteenth century, once significant French Canadian migration to the Eastern Townships was underway, that the English-speaking character of the region began to change; today it is almost entirely French-speaking (Morrison, Reimer and Shaver 1991).

While the Loyalists and post-Loyalists and their children provided the largest single contribution to the English-speaking population of Canada up to the War of 1812, direct immigration from Britain, particularly from Scotland (Campey 2000a, 2003, 2005; MacNutt 1965: 117–118), had also begun on a small scale before the war. This started as early as 1773, when around 200 Scottish Highlanders arrived at Pictou, Nova Scotia, but became more common in the 1790s: McInnis (2000a: 377) suggests that 16,000–18,000 Scots arrived in Nova Scotia between 1791 and 1811 and a further 2,000 or 3,000 in Prince Edward Island. Campey (2004: 9) offers a more conservative figure of 6,500 emigrant Scots to Nova Scotia (including Cape Breton) between 1773 and 1815 and at least 4,000 to Prince Edward Island, but admits that large gaps in the records make it likely the actual number was higher. The first direct Scottish immigration to Cape Breton was of 340 settlers in 1802 (Campey 2004: 11). In eastern Ontario, a group of Loyalist Highlanders who settled at Lancaster in 1784 were soon joined by immigrants directly from Scotland. While British subjects, however, these Highland immigrants were not necessarily English-speaking: most of them spoke Gaelic. Significant non-Loyalist immigration to New Brunswick began after 1800, when growing British demand for ships' masts and other timber products stimulated that province's forestry industry, attracting settlers from several parts of Britain.

The late eighteenth and early nineteenth centuries were also the peak period of English and Irish emigration to Newfoundland, with tens of thousands of people arriving over several decades. They were attracted by opportunities in the fishery, which by the early nineteenth century was benefiting from a boom in the demand for salt cod and making the transition from a seasonal, migratory industry to a permanent, resident fishery. In the first three decades of the nineteenth century, Newfoundland's population almost quadrupled, from 19,000 to 75,000 people, primarily as a result of immigration (Mannion 1977b: 6, 13). During this period, records indicate about 45,000 passengers on British ships bound for Newfoundland, of whom three-quarters were Irish, and most of the remainder English (Mannion 1997b: 6–7). The English, who came mostly from the southwestern counties of Devon and Dorset and to a lesser extent Somerset and Hampshire, settled all over Newfoundland but were concentrated mostly in the southeast, in St. John's, Conception Bay and Trinity Bay (Handcock 1977: 27). The Irish, most of whom came from a small region around Waterford in southeastern Ireland, specifically parts of Wexford, Kilkenny, Tipperary, Cork and Waterford (Mannion 1977b: 8), were more heavily concentrated in St. John's. By the end of the period of high immigration, Newfoundland's population was about half English and half Irish (Mannion 1977b: 7), though in St. John's the Irish element predominated: statistics from 1857 indicate about four times as many Irish-born as English-born immigrants among the non-native population (Staveley 1977: 54). Like the Scottish Highlanders, many of the Irish were not English-speaking when they arrived.

As Loyalist and post-Loyalist settlement was peopling what would become Canada's historical centers from the Maritimes to Ontario in the late eighteenth and early nineteenth centuries, settlement from different sources was at least beginning, if not yet flourishing, in most of the rest of what would become the populated areas of Dominion of Canada in 1867. The fur trade had initiated European settlement as far inland as Alberta, first explored by Anthony Henday, who set out from York Factory with Aboriginal companions in 1754. Henry Kelsey had explored Saskatchewan as far as Prince Albert as early as 1690. Further exploration and development had followed: Peter Pond built the first European residence in Alberta on the Athabasca River in 1778; Alexander Mackenzie descended the Mackenzie River in 1789 and ascended the Peace River in 1793; and David Thompson crossed the Rocky Mountains to descend the Columbia River in 1807. Most of the major lakes and rivers of Alberta were known to Europeans by the end of the eighteenth century and the fur trade was developing rapidly (MacGregor 1972: 39); trading posts already dotted the rivers of the region that would become Saskatchewan and Manitoba. In Alberta, the North West Company, a competitor of the Hudson's Bay Company based in Montreal, established a post at Fort Chipewyan on Lake Athabasca in 1788 and the North West and Hudson's Bay Companies established rival posts, Fort Augustus and Edmonton House respectively, near the present site of Edmonton in 1795. Continuous European settlement in Alberta was initiated at Fort Chipewyan in 1803 and at Edmonton in 1813 (MacGregor 1972: 43). In Manitoba, Thomas Douglas, the Fifth Earl of Selkirk, established western Canada's first significant agricultural colony on the Red River in 1811. The first Red River colonists were about 280 Scottish and Irish immigrants (Harris and Warkentin 1974: 247–248; Campey 2003). British Columbia, lying on the far side of the continental divide, was initially less accessible to Europeans, but Spanish and English traders had begun to compete for furs along the Pacific Coast by the 1770s. James Cook made the first British landing in 1778 and the exploratory voyages of George Vancouver in the 1790s helped to secure the territory for Britain, though the permanent settlement of what would be the cities of Victoria and Vancouver did not begin until later.

As the nineteenth century began, then, English-speaking settlement in British North America was widely and firmly if sparsely established: from a sprinkling of lonely fur traders at remote outposts of the Hudson's Bay and North West Companies throughout the northwestern interior; to the predominantly ex-American population of the growing towns of Upper Canada,

New Brunswick and Nova Scotia; to the administrative and commercial elites of Quebec and Montreal; to the tiny fishing communities dotting the coasts of Nova Scotia and Newfoundland. By 1811, the European population of British North America stood at over half a million people: about 135,000 in the Maritimes and about 375,000 in Canada (McInnis 2000a: 373), of which around 100,000 were in southern Ontario (Harris and Warkentin 1974: 116). Apart from the 200,000 French Canadians in Lower Canada (Charbonneau *et al.* 2000: 105) and a few thousand speakers of Gaelic and German, the majority of the remaining 300,000 would have been English-speaking. In addition to these, there were nearly 20,000 people in Newfoundland (Harris and Warkentin 1974: 182), a number that was growing quickly as the main Irish immigration was underway at this time; Mannion (1977b: 13) gives a higher figure of almost 26,000 people in 1811. Canada was poised for its first century of rapid growth.

2.3   A growing majority: British settlement in the nineteenth century

If the foundation of Canada's English-speaking population was accomplished in the eighteenth century largely by Loyalist refugees from what would become the United States, its establishment as the dominant culture of modern Canada was assured in the nineteenth century by a more or less constant flow of direct immigration from Britain and Ireland. The nineteenth-century immigrants were refugees not from political upheaval and war but from poverty, social dislocation and lack of economic opportunity.

During the eighteenth and nineteenth centuries, Great Britain became the most powerful nation on earth and the ruler of a global empire, by means of science, naval power, commercial ambition and an industrial revolution that completely transformed British society. A people who had been largely rural became increasingly urban; an economy that had been primarily agricultural became increasingly industrial, engaged in railway construction, coal mining and the mass production of steel, ceramic ware and textiles. The Industrial Revolution brought many benefits to large numbers of people and even enriched a few, but much of the population had great difficulty adjusting to the changes it wrought. Small farmers lost their land and livelihood as agricultural operations consolidated and became more efficient. In the infamous Highland Clearances, many of the peasants or "crofters" of the Scottish Highlands were forcibly removed from their traditional lands to make room for intensive sheep farming. Traditional craftspeople in cottage industries found they could not compete with mechanization and large-scale, industrial production; the introduction of power looms in textile mills, for instance, threw thousands of weavers out of work.

Many displaced farmers and craftspeople and their families moved to Britain's growing cities to find work in factories, often in much less profitable and salubrious conditions than those they had left. Urban industry could absorb only some of their number, however, and was subject to periodic contractions in a cycle of growth and recession. To make matters worse, the advance of medical knowledge and a general improvement in sanitation and living standards, while beneficial in some respects, meant that the historical check on population growth – relatively high infant mortality – was less and less effective, so that the population began to expand rapidly. From about 13 million in 1780, the population of the United Kingdom almost doubled, to 24 million, by 1831 (Morgan 1984: 477). Population growth was particularly problematic in regions where the potato had been introduced as a new staple food, replacing grain, which could not support as dense a population. Even at periods of peak industrial employment, these factors produced a surplus of people. In periods of recession, the slums of Britain's growing cities were crowded by millions of unemployed and displaced citizens, many of them living in conditions of miserable poverty and spiritual despair.

During the Napoleonic Wars, much of the excess population, which had not yet grown as large as it later would, was engaged either in direct military employment or in the production of goods to support the war effort. Death in combat provided a further check on population growth and a demand for more manpower. When Napoleon was finally vanquished at Waterloo in 1815, Britain's century of imperial glory lay before her, but the end of hostilities in Europe caused population pressures to mount at home. Some among Britain's leadership saw one of these developments as the best solution to the other: Britain's growing empire, if it was to be maintained, strengthened and expanded, would require people to settle and defend it, to implant British institutions and develop British commercial interests in each colony. In India, a huge native population and highly sophisticated native culture meant that British settlement would be confined to a small elite of military, administrative and commercial personnel. In Australia, New Zealand and British North America, by contrast, the relatively sparse Aboriginal populations and their less advanced stages of cultural development, together with the availability of vast tracts of undeveloped land, appeared to legitimize and even demand large-scale British settlement, eventually leading to the establishment of new British nations in these territories. In British North America in particular, the Anglo–American hostilities of the War of 1812 had posed a demonstrable threat to British colonial interests. If the United States were to be prevented from expanding northward to absorb Britain's remaining colonies, those colonies would require a large population of loyal British subjects. Britain's own surplus of people seemed the natural source of this population.

Thus, in 1815, as a post-war economic recession set in, the first major period of British and Irish emigration to Britain's overseas dominions began. The causes and progress of this vast migration are studied in great detail in several historical accounts, e.g. Belcher (1924), Carrothers (1929/1969),

Cowan (1961) and Johnson (1913). Campey (2003, 2004, 2005) examines Scottish immigration in particular. Elliott (1988) and Houston and Smyth (1990) take different approaches to studying the prominent role of immigrants from Ireland, the former a detailed qualitative study of the migration of Protestant families from Tipperary to Upper Canada, the latter a broader, more quantitative study of Irish migration to Canada as a whole. While a detailed discussion of immigration history is beyond the scope of this book, it may be generally remarked that the British government encouraged emigration to relieve pressure on its towns and parishes for relief of the poor, while colonial administrations encouraged immigration to provide much needed manpower for agriculture, industry, administration and defense.

The emigrants, often miserably poor and unable to afford even the sea passage, let alone the costs of establishing themselves in the New World, were frequently assisted financially and otherwise by both governments and charitable individuals or organizations. Others paid their own way with their savings or with the proceeds from the sale of their farms or businesses. Not all were poor: a small minority were second or third sons of the upper classes excluded from inheritance by rules of primogeniture, or wealthy people who had fallen into debt or social scandal and sought anonymity and a fresh start in the New World. A few emigration impresarios, motivated by profit or idealism or a mixture of both, undertook to manage the process themselves, buying up tracts of land, recruiting companies of emigrants, hiring ships and resettling their charges in the wilderness or in remote villages thousands of miles from home. Some of the settlements were successful; others failed. Most emigrants faced crushing hardships of one kind or another, from malnutrition, disease and death during the three-month passage on crowded emigrant ships, to difficult, hostile and often dangerous conditions in their new homes, for which they were often completely unprepared.

Notwithstanding these troubles, the stream of emigrants continued more or less unbroken, with several peaks and lulls, until the 1860s. It was encouraged by the promise of new opportunity abroad, by news of emigrants who had succeeded, by governmental and commercial propaganda and by limited opportunities and even worse conditions in Britain for those who had not prospered in the Industrial Revolution. In the 1860s, British immigration declined, while emigration of Canadians to the United States began to rise, owing to economic troubles in Canada and greater economic prospects south of the border. As a result, Canada experienced a net loss of population from international migration during the later nineteenth century (Urquhart and Buckley 1965: 22; McInnis 2000a: 422). Population growth during this period depended on the natural increase of the Canadian-born population. At the end of the century immigration revived, initiating a second major period of British immigration that lasted until the middle of the twentieth century. As Canada's English-speaking population was well established in most parts of the country by this time, the most important period from the point of view of studying the origins of Canadian English was the first, from the end of the Napoleonic Wars to Canada's confederation in 1867.

Estimating even the approximate size of the first great British emigration to Canada is difficult, as there are many sources of error in the available data. Canadian statistics only began to be collected with any reliability in 1829, the year after the British government appointed an immigration agent to supervise and register arrivals at the port of Quebec. British statistics on emigrant departures for Canadian ports go back before this, but are subject to even grosser inaccuracies. These arise from a number of sources, the greatest of which was the tendency of many emigrants to sail to Canadian ports on their way to the United States, the passage to Canada being cheaper. Despite the hostilities of the American Revolution and the War of 1812, the United States were an attractive destination for British emigrants throughout the nineteenth century; considerably more attractive for much of it than Canada, judging by the greater number of emigrants with American destinations. While emigrants bound for British North America generally exceeded those bound for the United States in the first decades of the century, from 1835 the reverse was true, so that by the 1850s American-bound passengers vastly outnumbered those bound for British North America. Even many of the latter – particularly the Irish, who generally had no great love of England or of life under the British crown – left for the United States shortly after arriving in Canada.

By way of illustration, the peak of emigration occurred in 1847, during the Irish potato famine (1845–1849). In this year, the British statistics record 109,680 emigrant departures from British ports to British North America, along with 142,154 to the United States (Cowan 1961: 288), a massive exodus. Of those destined for Canada, about 16,000 passengers died of "emigrant fever," either during the voyage or upon their arrival (McInnis 2000a: 382); Carrothers (1929/1969: 192) reports an even higher figure of 17,445 deaths. Unfortunately, the Quebec immigration agent was himself suffering from emigrant fever and made no report for this momentous year, making the Canadian data even less reliable than usual. Carrothers (1929/1969: 192) cites a figure of 84,445 arrivals at Quebec and Montreal, of whom 70,065 were Irish. Houston and Smyth (1990: 26) estimate 70,000 Irish arrivals at Quebec and half that number at Saint John. Cowan (1961: 289) cites 89,562 arrivals at Quebec, including 54,310 Irish. McInnis (2000a: 380–381) estimates that 54,562 immigrants were actually retained, once immediate departures to the United States are accounted for, amounting to only half of the recorded British departures.

A further source of error in the British statistics on emigrant departures is that they only began to distinguish between British and non-British passengers in 1853. By this time thousands of Europeans, particularly Germans, were emigrating to North America via British ports. Carrothers (1929/1969:

214) specifies that non-British emigration through Britain became an important trend in 1846, when parties of Germans arrived in London on their way to the United States. In 1853, 30,000 non-British emigrants sailed from British ports, about a tenth of the total of British for that year; thereafter, this number tended to grow. The records of the immigration agent at Quebec, who attempted to distinguish between British and non-British immigrants and to record how many of the arrivals left immediately for the United States, are therefore the best guide to the size of the British immigration to Canada. Canada (that is, Quebec and Ontario) received the large majority of immigration to British North America and Quebec City was Canada's main port of entry, prior to the deepening of the river channel between Quebec City and Montreal in the 1850s, which allowed ocean-going vessels to ascend the St. Lawrence as far as Montreal.

McInnis (2000a: 380–381) provides a revised series of immigration statistics that attempts to account for the main sources of error in the data on arrivals at Quebec and adds an estimate of arrivals at Maritime ports, giving perhaps the best available approximation to the actual number of British subjects who settled in British North America between 1829 and 1860. For the period before 1829, however, he resorts to British emigration statistics. Elliott (2004: 62) provides data on Quebec arrivals for most of this earlier period, 1815–1824, based on harbor-masters' registers and contemporary newspaper reports, which reduce the British figure of 119,762 departures to 77,469 arrivals, probably a more accurate figure. Combining Elliot's estimates for 1815–1824 with McInnis' for 1825–1860, we arrive at a British immigration of 823,251 people. Despite its apparent precision, this number is of course a gross approximation, and may still be too high, not taking account of the many arrivals – again, particularly Irish immigrants – who left for the United States after spending a few years in Canada.

Notwithstanding its imprecision, this seems at first an astonishing figure, being more than twenty times as great as the Loyalist migration, which was exceeded in the first five years of British immigration alone, and considerably greater than the entire European population of British North America in 1811. It was undeniably an enormous addition to Canada's population that could only have had a correspondingly important impact on the early development of the culture and language of English Canada. However, it must be kept in mind that these hundreds of thousands of British immigrants arrived over the course of more than four decades, not all at once, and were dispersed over a very large territory. In fact, given the relatively high fertility rates of the time, natural increase was a more important component of Canada's early nineteenth-century population growth than immigration. McInnis (2000a: 379) estimates that 84 percent of the increase in Canada's population between the censuses of 1811 and 1861 could be accounted for by an annual rate of natural increase of 3 percent, which he suggests is a reasonable assumption (he cites 3.7 percent as the actual rate for this period (2000a: 373)). Early

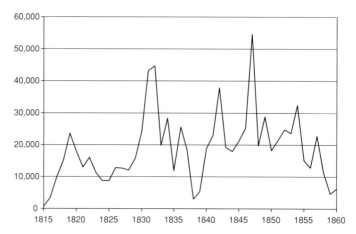

Figure 2.1 Retained British immigration to Canada, 1815–1860
Source: revised data from McInnis (2000a: 380–381)

census data from the various colonies indicate that British immigrants never attained majority status in any of them, peaking at around one-third following the Irish famine influx. In Upper Canada, the proportion of the population born in Britain declined from 36 percent in 1848 to 29 percent in 1861. In Lower Canada, as a proportion of the non-French population, it declined from 35 percent in 1851 to 29 percent in 1861. British-born proportions for the Atlantic provinces, which received and retained fewer immigrants, are even lower: 16 percent in New Brunswick and Prince Edward Island in 1861 and 9 percent in Nova Scotia (1861) and Newfoundland (1857). By 1871, the first national census of Canada records half a million British-born residents in a population of almost 3.5 million, only 14 percent; 83 percent of Canadians were Canadian-born. These data indicate that, while the British-born population may have been particularly concentrated in some places, it did not in general overwhelm the Canadian-born population, at least on a national or even regional basis.

Nevertheless, something over 800,000 immigrants between 1815 and 1860 makes an average of over 15,000 per year, a dramatic influx. Of course, this is only an average: the actual number fluctuated widely between a low of under 3,000 arrivals in 1838 and the peak of 54,562 in 1847 (McInnis 2000a: 380). It was subject to the vicissitudes of the British and Canadian economies and a number of other factors: the Crimean War (1853–1856) and the Indian Mutiny (1857–1858), for example, increased the demand for manpower in Britain, thereby reducing the flow of emigrants. The annual fluctuation in McInnis' estimate of British immigration to Canada is presented in Figure 2.1. The peaks in the early 1830s and early and late 1840s are clearly discernible, as are the lulls in the 1820s, late 1830s and late 1850s. The influx helped to raise the population of British North America to over 3 million by

1861, just before the confederation of Ontario, Quebec, New Brunswick and Nova Scotia as the Dominion of Canada in 1867.

From the point of view of the origins of Canadian English, it is important to examine more precisely where the British immigrants originated. The historical accounts of the British immigration offer a mass of detail about small groups of people who came from particular locations in the British Isles and settled in particular locations in Canada, but we will be concerned here with broader generalizations that can be distinguished amid the mass of individual facts, which may have some importance in understanding the creation and development of Canadian English. The British immigrants came from all four nations of nineteenth-century Britain – England, Wales, Scotland and Ireland – and from virtually every region of these. Determining the proportion of immigrants from each nation or region is beset by the same difficulties as determining the total number of immigrants and is subject to the additional complication of Scottish and Irish emigrants who sailed from English ports, sometimes after spending many years trying to improve their lot in England. Despite these difficulties, it is clear that the first great period of British immigration to Canada was dominated by the Irish, with English immigrants in second place and Scottish in third. The Welsh are usually not distinguished in the available analyses from the English, Wales having been joined to England much earlier (1536) than the Acts of Union subsuming Scotland (1707) and Ireland (1801) and having also a smaller population than those nations; however, all indications are that the number of Welsh immigrants was generally very small in comparison to the other three groups, consistently running a distant fourth.

Data on the earliest period, the decade following 1815, are cited by Elliot (2004: 62, table 1). At this time, Irish emigration appears to be strongly dominant, accounting for 58 percent of the more than 77,000 recorded arrivals at Quebec between 1816 and 1824. Arrivals from England, by contrast, account for only 13 percent, with the remaining 30 percent coming mostly from Scotland. Cowan (1961: 289) provides statistics on arrivals at Quebec from 1829 to 1859, covering the period she calls "the Great Migrations." Table II of her appendix B shows a total of 275,501 English, 467,413 Irish, and 104,977 Scottish arrivals over these three decades, yielding proportions of 30, 51 and 11 percent, respectively (the small remainder comprising arrivals from Europe and the Maritime provinces). While Irish immigrants still dominate overall, an anglicization of immigration is already evident. For the first years of the period, Irish immigration is triple that of English, which is in turn double that of Scottish. Irish arrivals peak at over 54,000 in 1847, then decline sharply and level off, to drop even further in later decades. Annual English immigration first exceeds Irish in 1854 and is as much as ten times greater by the end of the period, as Irish immigration trails off dramatically. Another remarkable trend is the rapid rise in European arrivals, beginning in the late 1840s. Europeans account for a third of all arrivals by the mid

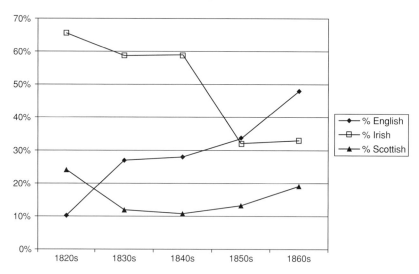

Figure 2.2 Ethnic composition of retained British immigration to Canada, 1815–1860
Source: adapted from Elliott (2004: 62, table 1) and Cowan (1961: 289)

1850s, surpassing all but the English in importance, and total over 60,000 for the period. This was, of course, only the start of a much larger trend toward European immigration in the late nineteenth century, which continued until the middle of the twentieth.

If we combine Elliott's data for 1815–1824 with Cowan's proportions applied to McInnis' estimates for 1825–1860, we arrive at approximate ethnic proportions for the entire first period of British immigration: 56 percent Irish (almost half a million people); 30 percent English (a quarter of a million); and 14 percent Scottish (over a hundred thousand). The change in these proportions over the period is shown in Figure 2.2: Scots are in second place at the beginning of the period but then take third place behind the English; Irish immigration dominates for most of the period but gives way to English dominance at the end. The effect of these proportions is evident in the statistics on ethnic origin in the Canadian Census of 1871 (Urquhart and Buckley 1965: 18): of 3,485,761 people in the new dominion, 24 percent claimed Irish origin; 20 percent English; and 16 percent Scottish. These figures amount to 40, 33 and 26 percent, respectively, of the British-origin population. A further 31 percent of Canadians claimed French origin: though still the largest single ethnic group in Canada, French Canadians were already a minority of the national population by this time, outnumbered two-to-one by British Canadians. The only other significant ethnic group in the 1871 statistics were those of German origin, who accounted for nearly 6 percent

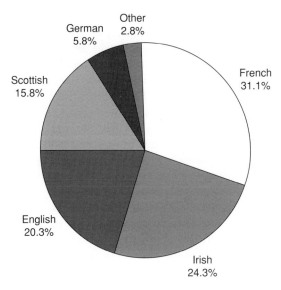

Figure 2.3 Ethnic origin of the Canadian population in 1871 (original four provinces of Ontario, Quebec, New Brunswick and Nova Scotia) Source: Urquhart and Buckley (1965: 18)

of the population (though it is likely that the less than 1 percent listed as Aboriginals were undercounted). These data are shown in Figure 2.3.

Of the 61 percent of the population who were of British origin, then, the Irish, not the English, formed the largest ethnic group. In addition to the large group in Newfoundland, which was not yet part of Canada, the Irish were particularly concentrated in Halifax, in New Brunswick, in eastern Ontario and northwest of Toronto up to Lake Huron. According to Houston and Smyth (1990: 204), they formed more than half the population in five areas: along the south coast of New Brunswick, including Saint John, the most Irish city in Canada; along the Rideau River in eastern Ontario between Ottawa and Kingston, centered on the region of Smith Falls, where immigration impresario Peter Robinson had settled a group of southern Irish at Almonte in 1823; along both sides of the Ottawa River upstream from Ottawa; in the region around Peterborough, Ontario, a town named after Robinson, who had settled another 2,000 Southern Irish there in 1825; and in parts of Simcoe, Dufferin, Grey and Middlesex counties northwest of Toronto, where another immigration impresario, Thomas Talbot, settled 172 Protestant Ulstermen near London in 1818. While Houston and Smyth suggest that Irish immigrants were considerably less prevalent in Quebec and Nova Scotia (outside Halifax), where they generally formed less than 20 percent of the population (1990: 190, 208), Rudin (1985: 116) cites Census data indicating that in Montreal, the nation's largest city, the Irish made up half the English-speaking population in 1871; the other half was divided equally between English and Scottish. The Irish were an even larger proportion of the English-speaking populations of Quebec City and the Ottawa Valley.

Until its partition in 1922, Ireland was a single province of Great Britain. In accordance with this status, statistics on Irish immigration and ethnic origin throughout the first major period of British immigration to British North America generally make no distinction between the two regions of Ireland that we are accustomed to think of today: the largely Roman Catholic South, now the independent Republic of Ireland; and the religiously divided North, or Ulster, which remains part of the United Kingdom. The dialects of these regions have some pan-Irish features in common, but are also easily distinguished (Hickey 2004; 2007: 11–16), so that making at least a general division between northern and southern Irish immigrants, if not among more specific regional origins, is of some importance in determining the origins of Canadian English. Just as British immigration shifted gradually from Irish to English over the first half of the nineteenth century, the source of Irish immigration shifted gradually from Ulster to the Catholic South. A majority of those who came in the first great wave of the 1830s were Protestant Scotch-Irish from Ulster; a majority of those who came in the famine period of the 1840s were Catholic. By 1871, Protestants dominated in the areas of heaviest Irish immigration, forming over two-thirds of Ontario's Irish-origin population and over half of that in New Brunswick; Harris and Warkentin (1974: 118) estimate that three-eighths of Ontarians were of Scotch-Irish origin by Confederation, outnumbering by 50 percent the quarter of Ontarians who claimed English origin. Only in Quebec did Catholics dominate the Irish-origin population, forming over 60 percent; in Nova Scotia the two groups were evenly balanced (data from Gordon Darroch and Michael Ornstein cited by Houston and Smyth 1990: 229). Newfoundland's 50,000 people of Irish-origin were overwhelmingly Catholic (Houston and Smyth 1990: 227).

Another facet of the denominational divide was that Protestants tended to pursue pioneer farming in frontier areas, whereas Catholics tended to pursue urban occupations, mostly as laborers, in the port cities where they landed. In 1871, this was true both of Ontario, where the Irish were two-thirds Protestant, and of Quebec, where they were two-thirds Catholic. The highest proportion of Protestant Ulstermen was therefore found in rural Ontario (72 percent), while that of Catholic southern Irish was found in urban Quebec (84 percent; Houston and Smyth 1990: 227).

Like the Catholic Irish, the English tended to prefer the older, settled areas to the frontier: in Ontario, they were concentrated along the shore of Lake Ontario, especially near Toronto, and in the Thames River Valley in a region stretching south to Lake Erie, including the city of London (Harris and Warkentin 1974: 118; Elliott 2004: 77). Determining the more specific regional origin of Canada's English settlers is even more important than determining the regional origin of Irish immigrants, given the wide disparity among the dialects of southeastern, southwestern and northern England, yet the lack of a clear regional cultural cleavage equivalent to that between northern and southern Ireland makes this task more difficult than the Irish case. Cowan's table IV in appendix B (1961: 291–293) lists arrivals at Quebec from individual British ports from 1831 to 1860. These data make it clear that some ports predominated among the departure points of British emigrants destined for Canada, sending forth far greater numbers than others. Particularly important among the English ports over the entire period were Hull, Liverpool, London and Plymouth. Unfortunately, it is immediately apparent that these ports cover virtually the whole of England rather than indicating more specific regions of origin. A similar set of data on English ports provided by Elliott (2004: 64, table 5) for the period 1815–1854 suggests a prevalence of arrivals at Quebec and Montreal from northern ports until the early 1830s, giving way to a prevalence of arrivals from Liverpool from the late 1830s to the early 1850s, though there is also a sudden surge of departures from East Anglia in the late 1830s and a solid contribution from West Country ports from the 1840s on. Again, these data indicate departures from virtually every region of England: northeast, northwest, southeast and southwest. Moreover, information on ports of departure is of only limited use in establishing where the emigrants actually came from, since many of them would have traveled some distance from home to reach a suitable port.

Elliott attempts to bring more precision to this question by examining data from oaths of allegiance, land grants, obituaries and Toronto-region gravestones, where these sources indicate the county of origin of the person concerned (2004: tables 2–3 on pp. 58–59; appendices 3–4 on pp. 78–79). Keeping in mind their limitations and selective character, all of these sources show a large plurality of Yorkshire origins. The obituaries (which are from Methodist newspapers) show smaller concentrations of Cornwall, Devon, Lincolnshire and London origins, in that order; the gravestones (which are in Peel, Halton and York Counties in Ontario) show secondary concentrations of Devon, Lincolnshire and Cumbrian origins. It must be concluded that, while immigration from northern England was certainly an important element in the English settlement of Ontario, perhaps the most important element, it would be an oversimplification to suggest that the North of England was the only or even the main source of settlement; on the contrary, English settlers appear to have come from all over the country. On the other hand, when settlement from northern and western England is combined with that from Scotland and Ireland, it is immediately clear that settlement from southeastern England – the London region – was a very small proportion of the British migration to Canada. This fact is symbolized even today by the annual St. Patrick's Day parades in many Canadian cities, including that of Montreal, the oldest in North America, and by the appearance of kilted Scottish pipers at ceremonial occasions like graduations and memorial services. Montreal's flag bears a shamrock and thistle in addition to its English rose and French *fleur-de-lys*, and Canada's former national anthem sang of "the thistle, shamrock, rose entwined; the maple leaf forever."

Scottish immigration also showed a shift over the course of the nineteenth century, from a predominance of Gaelic-speaking Highlanders in the early nineteenth century as the effects of the Highland Clearances were felt, to a predominance of English-speaking Lowlanders by mid-century. The Scots went proportionately more to Nova Scotia and Prince Edward Island, which in 1871 were 38 and 45 percent Scottish, respectively, than to New Brunswick and Ontario, which were 14 and 20 percent Scottish, or to Quebec, where the small Scottish population of about 4 percent was mostly restricted to Montreal. Notwithstanding this distribution, the Scots were an important element in most regions of nineteenth-century Canada, playing a crucial role in the lumber camps of New Brunswick, the commercial and industrial development of Montreal, the pioneer farming regions of southwestern Ontario up to the shores of Lake Huron, and the fur trade of the northwestern interior.

Indeed, while the Scots were the least numerous of the three main groups of British immigrants to Canada, their vigor and ambition as adventurers, pioneers, settlers and entrepreneurs gave them a disproportionately large influence on early Canadian life (a point also made by Avis 1973: 50). Among the many leading figures of eighteenth- and nineteenth-century Canada born in Scotland can be counted the explorer Alexander Mackenzie; the fur traders William McGillivray, Simon McTavish and George Simpson; the journalist-politicians George Brown and William Lyon Mackenzie; the colonizer Thomas Douglas, Lord Selkirk; the Anglican bishop and educator John Strachan, a leader of elite Toronto society; the businessmen Robert Dunsmuir, Sandford Fleming, Henry Morgan, John Redpath, Robert Gillespie Reid, James Ross, Donald Smith and George Stephen, who were developers of coal mines, department stores, sugar refineries, bridges, banks and railroads; and Canada's first two prime ministers, John A. Macdonald and a second Alexander Mackenzie. The prominence of Scots should not be overstated: among the explorers of western Canada the Scot Mackenzie shares fame with the Englishmen John Franklin, Anthony Henday and David Thompson, the Irishman John Palliser and two New Englanders, Simon Fraser and Peter Pond; many of Canada's first governors and administrators were of course English, including Isaac Brock and John Graves Simcoe, Anglican bishop Jacob Mountain and the first chief justice William Osgoode; and among the country's greatest early businessmen were the Englishmen Alexander Galt and John Molson, the American William Van Horne and the Irishmen Timothy Eaton, John Labatt, William McMaster and Eugene O'Keefe. Nevertheless, in relation to their numbers, Scottish immigrants played a remarkable role in the development of Canada, as documented by

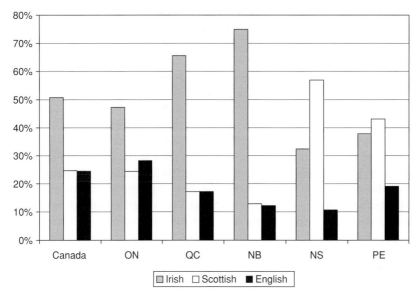

Figure 2.4 Ethnic origin of British-born population by province, 1860
Source: Provincial censuses of 1860–1861

Shaw (2003); the names just listed reveal that even some of the English and Irish-born figures in Canadian history had Scottish ancestry, as did many leading figures born in Canada. The best-known Scottish Canadian is undoubtedly Alexander Graham Bell, who emigrated from Scotland to Brantford, Ontario, as a young man in 1870, making the world's first long-distance telephone call from Brantford to nearby Paris, Ontario, in 1876. Though, like many enterprising Canadians, he later went to the United States to pursue further opportunities, he returned regularly to Canada and eventually retired to Nova Scotia.

To summarize this discussion of ethnic groups in various parts of Canada, Figure 2.4 shows the proportion of Irish and Scots and English in the British-born population of each British North American province in 1860, compiled from the provincial census records of that year. In comparing this with previous figures, the high proportion of people born in Scotland, which here equals the English proportion, is surprising. Some of the discrepancy can be explained by a further decade of predominantly English immigration between 1860 and the first national census of 1871. This would cause the Scottish proportion to drop and the English to rise. The other obvious difference is that Figure 2.4 includes heavily Scottish Prince Edward Island, which is not included in the national census data in Figure 2.3, since Prince Edward Island was not yet a Canadian province. Nevertheless, a certain degree of uncertainty surrounds these data, which can only be assumed to reflect the problematic nature of nineteenth-century record-keeping. What Figure 2.4

makes clear is that the relative proportions of the three major British ethnic groups varied significantly from one province to another.

Regardless of its ethnic composition, the British migration of the nineteenth century helped to transform the older British North American provinces from a frontier society of pioneers into a settled dominion of well-established towns and industries. Indeed, the settlement of the Maritimes was more or less completed by this migration: the vast majority of post-Confederation immigration went to central and western Canada, with future population growth in the Atlantic region depending almost exclusively on natural increase. If the arrival of the Loyalists in the eighteenth century had confirmed Britain's territorial gains under the Treaty of Paris and justified the creation of New Brunswick and Ontario, the enormous influx of British immigrants in the nineteenth helped to create the modern nation of Canada in 1867. British immigration had contributed to a vast increase in the populations of all of Canada's provinces by the time of Confederation: in 1871, New Brunswick had almost 300,000 people, Nova Scotia almost 400,000, Quebec over a million and Ontario one and a half million. Prince Edward Island, which did not join Confederation until 1873, had almost 100,000. Even Manitoba, which joined in 1870 as a small square of territory grown from the seed of Lord Selkirk's Red River settlement, registered 25,000 residents in the 1871 Census. Settlement was also getting underway farther west, though the major development of western Canada would have to await the completion of the Canadian Pacific Railway in 1885: the Northwest Territories, then including the future provinces of Saskatchewan and Alberta, counted 48,000 people, while British Columbia, which became Canada's sixth province in 1871, had 36,000 people in that year. The western numbers in particular can only represent very rough estimates, given the limited development of administrative capability at this early date. The regional distribution of Canada's population in the 1871 Census is shown in Table 2.1, together with the percentage of each province and territory that had been born in Britain. Table 2.2 shows the ten largest cities, with their populations.

Canada was still a mainly rural country at this point: only 20 percent of the population lived in incorporated towns and cities of any size and only one city, Montreal, had over 100,000 people. However, while the majority of Canadians still lived on farms or in small towns and villages, the British influx had nevertheless established the beginnings of urban Canada. Apart from Montreal's 115,000 people, Quebec City, Toronto and Saint John each had around 50,000 people; Halifax, Hamilton and Ottawa 25,000–30,000; and London and Kingston about 15,000. At mid-century, Lower Canada's cities had large British-origin, English-speaking populations: people of French origin represented only 58 percent of Quebec City and 45 percent of Montreal in 1851. Montreal's large English-speaking population in particular included a wealthy and influential merchant class, with a heavy concentration of Scots

Table 2.1 *Population of Canada by province and territory, 1871, with proportion of British-born*

Province/Terr.	Population	% of total	% British-born*
British Columbia	36,247	1.0	11.7
Northwest Terr. (AB, SK)	48,000	1.3	0.5
Manitoba	25,228	0.7	12.4
Ontario	1,620,851	43.9	22.7
Quebec	1,191,516	32.3	5.0
New Brunswick	285,594	7.7	11.3
Prince Edward Is.	94,021	2.5	7.4
Nova Scotia	387,800	10.5	7.0
Canada	3,689,257		13.9

Source: Urquhart and Buckley (1965: 14); Government of Canada (1912: 14–23).
*Proportion of British-born for original four provinces (ON, QC, NB, NS) in 1871; that for others is 1881 Census.

Table 2.2 *Population of Canada's ten largest cities, 1871*

City	Population
Montreal, QC	115,000
Quebec, QC	59,699
Toronto, ON	59,000
Saint John, NB	41,325
Halifax, NS	29,582
Hamilton, ON	26,880
Ottawa, ON	24,141
London, ON	18,000
Kingston, ON	12,407
Charlottetown, PEI	8,807

Source: Government of Canada (1912: 7–9).

(Levine 1990: 8). This elite directed Canada's commercial and industrial development from offices on St. James Street (now *rue St-Jacques*), Canada's original equivalent of Wall Street (now superseded by Bay Street in Toronto), and occupied elegant, stately homes in a district on the northwestern edge of downtown known as the "Golden Square Mile," a Canadian equivalent of New York's Fifth Avenue during the same period (Rudin 1985: 203–208). A larger population of Montreal English-speakers, with a heavy concentration of Irish, represented the opposite end of the urban social spectrum. They endured crowded, squalid conditions in working-class neighborhoods near the Lachine Canal, which had opened in 1825. The canal allowed ships to bypass the Lachine Rapids, a major obstacle on the water route to the North

American interior, and was soon lined with factories, warehouses, mills and rail yards, becoming the center of Canada's own industrial revolution.

Apart from the large French-Canadian population in Quebec and neighboring regions, mid nineteenth-century Canada had become an almost entirely British land. There were 230,000 Germans and Dutch, 23,000 recorded Aboriginals (most likely a substantial undercount) and about 20,000 people of African descent. The latter were concentrated in parts of the Maritimes, where they were the descendants of African Americans who had arrived with the Loyalists or after the War of 1812, and in parts of Ontario, where they were ex-slaves who had arrived from the United States more recently by way of the Underground Railroad. However, notwithstanding these groups, the total number of people of origins other than British and French was less than 300,000, only about 8 percent of the population. At its birth, the Dominion of Canada was therefore very much a joining of French and British peoples, a fact that came to play a dominant role in its early national identity. The non-French population was almost entirely a mix of Scotch-Irish, English, Irish and Scots in varying proportions. Figure 2.4 shows that Prince Edward Island and Nova Scotia were proportionately more Scottish, while Newfoundland, New Brunswick and Ontario were proportionately more Irish, with the Scotch-Irish particularly dominant in parts of Ontario. Most towns, however, featured a blend of all of these groups, a diversity still reflected in their churches. These were built to serve Roman Catholics, Methodists, Presbyterians, Anglicans, Baptists and Lutherans, affiliations that together accounted for 94 percent of the population in 1871: the largest were Roman Catholics, with about 40 percent, and Methodists, Presbyterians and Anglicans with about 15 percent each; there were only about a thousand Jews in Canada at this time. Of course, this denominational diversity was a mere foreshadowing of what was to come in the twentieth century, but later groups of immigrants, increasingly non-English-speaking, would have much less influence on the basic nature of Canadian English. Local speech patterns would have been well established in Canada's original four provinces by the 1860s, able to absorb millions of new speakers – thousands in each large community – without changing their essential character. The major exception to this state of affairs was the western half of the country, most of which had yet to experience the establishment of its first substantial European population. The opening and settlement of the Canadian West was the main event in the next major period of immigration to Canada.

2.4   The Land Boom: the peopling of the West

It was said above that the late nineteenth century, following the first great period of British immigration to Canada, was characterized by a net loss of people through international migration: the volume of emigrants leaving

Canada, principally for the United States, was greater than the volume of immigrants arriving in Canada. This was a function of both a rise in departures, encouraged by economic problems in post-Confederation Canada, and a decline in arrivals from the high levels of the 1830s to the 1850s, which Carrothers (1929/1969: 207–224) attributes to improved economic conditions in Britain. Nonetheless, immigration continued throughout this period and began to increase dramatically in the 1870s, eventually reaching yearly levels apparently exceeding even those of the Irish famine by the 1880s. The Canadian government's annual tally of immigrant arrivals first topped 100,000 in 1882, the beginning of a sustained period of high immigration lasting until 1891. McInnis (2000a: 421–424) cautions that the government data overstate considerably the real level of immigration, owing to double-counting and through-traffic destined for the United States: while some of the emigrating Canadians were natives and long-term residents, others had arrived very recently in Canada to be counted misleadingly as immigrants. However, even McInnis' revised figures, calculated to eliminate these errors, indicate a continuous inflow, reaching a peak of 50,000 in 1883, equal to the famine influx, and secondary peaks of around 30,000 in 1887 and 1891; his annual figures never drop below 20,000 throughout the 1880s and 1890s (2000a: 423). In all, perhaps another 200,000–300,000 new Canadians arrived during the late nineteenth century, not an insignificant number. Rather than adding to the population in terms of sheer numbers, these immigrants replaced a part of it that had left.

A major feature of late nineteenth-century immigration to Canada was its English character: the anglicization of immigration that had begun in the 1850s was completed during this period. The lack of reliable statistics on immigration in general also complicates the estimation of ethnic proportions, but the British data on emigrant departures to Canada provided by Johnson for 1861–1900 (1913: 347–348) show proportions of 72 percent English, 15 percent Irish and 13 percent Scottish, a dramatic reversal of the earlier pattern. Scottish emigration actually exceeds Irish in the 1890s, while English becomes even more dominant, accounting for over 80 percent of British emigrants. The effect of this anglicization can be seen in the Canadian Census of 1901, both in the ethnic origins of the population in general and in the ethnic origins of the British-born immigrant population in particular. This was the first census in which Canadians of English origin outnumbered those of Irish origin: there were one million Irish (18 percent of the population of 5.4 million) and a million and a quarter English (23 percent). Among the British-born population of 1901, who provide a good measure of retained immigration in the late nineteenth century, English outnumbered Irish two-to-one: of over 400,000 British-born residents, 48 percent were born in England and Wales, 24 percent in Ireland and 20 percent in Scotland.

The major factor responsible for the revival of immigration at the end of the nineteenth century was the opening of Canada's vast western region for settlement. By 1867, the first great period of British immigration had more or less exhausted the supply of new agricultural land in the older, central and eastern provinces. The economy had stagnated and Canadians were leaving in droves for the United States. If the young dominion was to prosper, new sources of growth would have to be found: more settlers attracted and new markets developed for manufactured goods. The example of the United States suggested that westward expansion was the answer. The American frontier was moving rapidly westward at this time, from the Midwest (the old "Northwest") across the Great Plains to the Rocky Mountains, attracting both internal migration from the East and international immigration from Europe. The eastern half of the American Midwest grew in population from 1.5 million people in 1830 (14 percent of the national population) to almost 7 million by 1860 (26 percent); the western half, or Great Plains, grew from 2 million (8 percent) in 1860 to almost 9 million (16 percent) by 1890 (Haines 2000: 318).

Though the 49th parallel had been agreed upon as the western portion of the international boundary in 1846, American westward expansion was so vigorous that some in Canada saw it as a potential threat to Canadian sovereignty over the territory north and west of Lake Huron, which was still largely empty. Rupert's Land, as it was then called, had been granted in 1670 by King Charles II to the Hudson's Bay Company (HBC), for development of the fur trade. By 1867 it still consisted mostly of an almost endless wilderness of rocks, lakes and trees, sparsely populated by nomadic Aboriginal peoples and by a few thousand European and mixed-blood (or *métis*) trappers and fur traders. The HBC, based in London, had had to compete in this territory first with French traders, then with the rival North West Company, a consortium run mostly by Scottish Highlanders based in Montreal. In 1821, the HBC absorbed the North West Company, ending their fierce competition. After the merger, the company employed 2,000–3,000 men, from chief factors, clerks, surgeons and postmasters to servants and tripmen, many of them Highland Scots (Harris and Warkentin 1974: 245). Fort Edmonton became a major center of the trade, collecting furs from all over northwestern North America for river shipment to the company's export posts on Hudson Bay. By 1862 there were fifty men at Edmonton (Harris and Warkentin 1974: 245), but agricultural development had not yet taken place, other than limited activities to sustain this small, temporary population and others like it at posts throughout the region. Yet Edmonton lay at the northwestern edge of an immense northern extension of the American Great Plains, a region that promised to support agricultural development of the type that was already occurring south of the border, in the Dakota Territory and Nebraska. The westward expansion of agricultural development over this southwestern section of Rupert's Land therefore seemed the key to the continued growth and prosperity of Canada.

In 1870, the Canadian government purchased Rupert's Land from the HBC, calling it the North-West Territories. In 1872, the Dominion Lands Act was passed. Similar to its American equivalent, this legislation granted 160 acres of free land – a quarter of a mile-square section – to settlers willing to undertake the enormous challenges of pioneer life: clearing the land of rocks, trees and shrubs; breaking the sod and planting crops; fighting weeds, pests and bad weather; and building houses, sheds and barns, sometimes of sod for lack of wood, all without mechanization or well-developed supply channels. In 1873, the North-West Mounted Police were organized as a paramilitary force and sent out to patrol the new territory, in an effort to avoid the lawlessness and violent conflict with Aboriginal peoples that had often accompanied American westward expansion. The next year, police detachments reached what would become Alberta, establishing Fort Saskatchewan and Fort Macleod in 1874 and Fort Calgary and Fort Walsh (in modern Saskatchewan) in 1875. The police suppressed a destructive illegal whisky trade and established friendly relations with Aboriginal groups, who were encouraged to sign treaties freeing up land for peaceful settlement. By this time, as discussed above, European settlement had already begun on the margins of western Canada, both in Manitoba and in British Columbia, where gold rushes had initiated European interest in the 1850s and 1860s and where Victoria had already become a town of several thousand people. The intervening region, however, remained largely remote and inaccessible, separated from the Pacific Ocean by formidable mountain ranges and from the settled parts of Ontario by a thousand miles of barren rock and rugged bush known as the Canadian Shield, a challenge that American westward expansion did not have to contend with once the Appalachians had been crossed. River transportation, using the natural waterways that drained the Canadian prairies into Hudson Bay, had served the fur trade well enough, but would clearly be inadequate for large-scale agricultural development.

In the United States, frontier expansion and economic growth had been facilitated largely by the westward extension of the railroads. Trains carried immigrants and manufactured goods to the west and returned to the east laden with agricultural products. In 1869, the Union Pacific line, building westward from Chicago, and the Central Pacific line, laying track eastward from San Francisco, met in Utah, creating the first transcontinental railroad. A similar project, linking the North-West Territories and the new provinces of British Columbia and Manitoba with the population and industrial centers of Ontario and Quebec, was seen in Canada as the best way to encourage western growth and assert Canada's claim to its western domains; British Columbia, in fact, had made the completion of a railroad link to the east a condition of its joining Confederation in 1871. The Canadian Pacific Railway was incorporated in 1881 and construction undertaken along a southern route from Winnipeg through Regina and Calgary to Vancouver. The last spike was driven in British Columbia in 1885 and the first Canadian transcontinental train left Montreal in 1886, arriving at Vancouver six days later. By the early twentieth century, a second transcontinental system, the predecessor of the Canadian National Railway, had been developed along a northern route from Winnipeg through Saskatoon and Edmonton to Prince Rupert. With an efficient transportation network in place, the European settlement of the Canadian West could proceed.

Encouraged by the government's offer of free land and enabled by the railroads, settlers poured onto the Canadian Prairies in an immigration boom unprecedented in Canadian history. In the official figures, the annual influx surpassed 100,000 in 1903 and peaked at over 400,000 in 1913, just before World War I slowed arrivals from overseas. Immigration picked up again after the war, in most years reaching over 100,000, until it was drastically cut by the onset of the Depression in 1931. As before, the official data exaggerate the influx: McInnis (2000b: 534–535) reviews the usual sources of error and provides a revised set of data (556) that indicate a total immigration between 1901 and 1931 of 2.8 million people, an average of 100,000 arrivals per year. After accounting for emigration, he estimates a net immigration of just over 1 million people. While only a quarter of the total indicated by the official immigration data, this is still a huge number, even larger than the great British migration of the early nineteenth century and achieved in half the time. It represents 10 percent of the population of 1931, which had doubled since 1901, surpassing 10 million. By 1931, almost a quarter of Canadians were foreign-born.

The largest beneficiary of the immigration boom was western Canada. It began there in the 1880s as an immediate response to the completion of the railway, which had reached Alberta by 1883. While the rest of Canada was still experiencing negative migration, official figures indicate positive net migration in Manitoba, the North-West Territories and British Columbia from 1881 to 1901 (Urquhart and Buckley 1965: 22). These gains, while modest compared to what was still to come, justified the creation of the new provinces of Alberta and Saskatchewan out of the southern portion of the North-West Territories in 1905. Over the next decade, migration to the West continued to grow. By World War I, of the 1.7 million immigrants who had arrived in Canada during the peak immigration period of 1901–1914, two-thirds lived in the West, while only a quarter lived in Ontario, with even smaller fractions in Quebec and the Maritimes (McInnis 2000b: 538).

The massive immigration, together with internal migration, caused a dramatic westward shift in the distribution of Canada's population. In 1881 there had been fewer than 200,000 people in the Canadian West, about 4 percent of the national population. By 1931, the four western provinces had over 3 million people, representing 29 percent of the national total, a striking increase. Vancouver and Winnipeg became the third and fourth largest cities in the country by 1911 and had almost a quarter of a million

Table 2.3 *Population of Canada by province and territory, 1931, with proportion of foreign-born (including British-born)*

Province/terr.	Population	% of total	% foreign-born
British Columbia	694,263	6.7	46.0
Alberta	731,605	7.1	41.8
Saskatchewan	921,785	8.9	34.6
Manitoba	700,139	6.7	33.8
Ontario	3,431,683	33.1	23.4
Quebec	2,874,662	27.7	8.8
New Brunswick	408,219	3.9	6.0
Prince Edward Is.	88,038	0.8	3.2
Nova Scotia	512,846	4.9	8.2
Yukon	4,230	0.0	37.2
Northwest Territories	9,316	0.1	1.4
Canada	10,376,786		22.2

Source: Urquhart and Buckley (1965: 14).

Table 2.4 *Populations of Canada's ten largest cities, 1931*

City	Population
Montreal, QC	818,577
Toronto, ON	631,207
Vancouver, BC	246,593
Winnipeg, MB	218,785
Hamilton, ON	155,547
Quebec, QC	130,594
Ottawa, ON	126,872
Calgary, AB	83,761
Edmonton, AB	79,197
London, ON	71,148

Source: Canada. Dominion Bureau of Statistics, General Statistics Branch (1933: 133).

people each by 1931, vaulting past every eastern city except Montreal and Toronto. Edmonton and Calgary were also among the nation's ten largest cities by this date, having had only 4,000 people each as late as 1901. Tables 2.3 and 2.4 show the populations of Canada's provinces and ten largest cities in 1931; Table 2.3 also shows the proportion of the population of each province that was foreign-born. By 1921, the Canadian cities with the largest proportions of immigrants were all in the West: immigrants accounted for 54 percent of people in Victoria, 51 percent in Vancouver, 48 percent in Winnipeg and Calgary and 45 percent in Edmonton, compared to only 38 percent in Toronto and 19 percent in Montreal. East of Montreal, Canada's oldest population centers were now attracting virtually no immigration: immigrants accounted for only 16 percent of the population of Halifax, 7 percent in Saint John and 2 percent in Quebec City (McInnis 2000b: 541).

Within the West, the immigrants' chief destination shifted steadily westward over the period as the earliest-settled districts filled up: Manitoba received the most net migration in the 1880s, Saskatchewan in the 1890s and 1900s, Alberta in the 1910s and British Columbia in the 1920s. By the 1920s, Saskatchewan and Manitoba were already experiencing net out-migration and Ontario had reasserted its traditional position as Canada's leading destination for immigrants (Urquhart and Buckley 1965: 22). In the 1930s, the Depression would cause a more dramatic reversal, with all three prairie provinces losing people through migration; only British Columbia would continue to gain. Saskatchewan would suffer the largest loss, exceeding even the rate of natural increase, so that the province's population would shrink by 25,000 people by 1941. By the census of 1911, however, Saskatchewan had taken over from Manitoba as the most populous province in western Canada and remained so even in 1941.

Apart from its Aboriginal population and earlier sprinkling of fur traders, the peopling of western Canada was accomplished by four main groups: internal Canadian migrants, mostly from Ontario; and immigrants from Britain, Europe and the United States. Official data on interprovincial migration indicate that the number of people born in central or eastern Canada living in the West peaked in 1921 at almost 400,000. Of these, three-quarters were from Ontario, 14 percent from Quebec and the small remainder from the Maritimes. They were distributed more or less evenly among the four western provinces: 34 percent of them were in Saskatchewan, 25 percent in Alberta, 22 percent in Manitoba and 19 percent in British Columbia, accounting for between 14 and 18 percent – about a sixth – of the 1921 populations of these provinces. Given the ethnic character of Ontario at this period, the Ontario migration to the West would largely have involved people of British origin, though many if not most of them would have been thoroughly Canadian in their speech and culture (some may have been British immigrants who had spent some time in Ontario before moving west). As Chambers contends (1991: 91; 2006a: 385), Ontario migrants were crucial in establishing the basic character of the Canadian West as English-speaking and Protestant, a sort of greatly expanded version of rural and small-town Ontario, and in transplanting Ontario speech westward. Most of the leading political and commercial figures of the early Prairie West were Ontarians, and several large agricultural settlements of Ontarians, such as the Methodists from London who settled near Red Deer and the 300 farmers from Parry Sound who homesteaded near Fort Saskatchewan, ensured a strong Ontario element in popular speech as well (Palmer 1990: 61–68).

Direct immigration from Britain also played an important role in settling the West, having revived after its lull in the late nineteenth century. Official figures show a peak of 120,000 arrivals from the United Kingdom in

1908, followed by a sustained period of up to 150,000 per year from 1911 to 1914, producing a British-born population of over a million people by 1931, at the end of the immigration boom. British immigrants, however, continued to favor central Canada relative to other groups. In 1931, 44 percent of British-born Canadians lived in Ontario, far more than in any other province, compared to only 25 percent of non-British foreign-born Canadians, a greater proportion of whom lived in Quebec and the West. Notwithstanding this preference for Ontario, large numbers of British immigrants did find their way to the West, and particularly to British Columbia. By 1931, there were almost 200,000 British-born immigrants living in British Columbia, representing 27 percent of the population, a proportion established as early as 1911. The British presence on the Prairies was smaller but still significant, having reached about 100,000 in each province by 1931, representing 15 percent of the population of Manitoba and Alberta and 11 percent of Saskatchewan.

British immigration to Canada during the immigration boom was still largely English in ethnicity, but with a growing Scottish component: data on British departures for the years 1901–1911 (from Johnson 1913: 347–348) indicate 75 percent English, 21 percent Scottish and 4 percent Irish; official records of arrivals for the years 1916–1923 indicate 66 percent English, 25 percent Scottish and 8 percent Irish. Welsh immigrants, tallied separately from English for the first time, make up no more than 1 percent in either period. Data on ethnic origins indicate that people of Scottish ancestry outnumbered people of Irish ancestry in all four western provinces in 1921 and 1931, by as much as two-to-one in British Columbia. People of English origin, however, were predominant everywhere, generally being as numerous as the Scottish- and Irish-origin populations combined. (Since these data indicate ethnic origin rather than birthplace, they give only an approximate sense of the mixture of British dialects spoken on the Prairies: many of these English, Scottish and Irish people would in fact have been Canadian or American by birth.)

Immigration from continental Europe – the third group of western settlers – had played a relatively minor role in the settlement of Canada in the nineteenth century. During the western land boom, its importance increased dramatically. Aware that Britain, the preferred source of immigrants, could not possibly supply all of the settlers needed in the West, the government began recruiting in central and eastern Europe, eventually attracting thousands of Germans and Ukrainians, along with several smaller groups. Ukrainians, while not desirable immigrants according to the anglocentric ideology of the day, were nevertheless encouraged to immigrate because they were thought likely to succeed in the harsh conditions of northern prairie agriculture, which were totally foreign to Englishmen. To oppressed and landless east European peasants, of course, the offer of free land in unimaginable quantities would have been particularly attractive.

In the official data, the volume of immigration from countries other than Great Britain and the United States first matched British immigration in 1898, surpassing it until 1902 and again during the late 1920s. By 1931, there were over 800,000 foreign-born people in Canada from countries other than Britain and the United States, representing 7.5 percent of the population. As a result, the representation of the "founding cultures" of Canada declined from 61 percent British and 31 percent French in 1871 (92 percent combined) to 52 percent British and 28 percent French in 1931 (80 percent combined). Unlike British arrivals, these "foreign" immigrants went predominantly to western Canada. Two-thirds of Canada's European-born residents lived in the four western provinces in 1911, with the largest single group (over 90,000 people) in Saskatchewan: they actually outnumbered British-born settlers in Saskatchewan and nearly equaled them in Alberta and Manitoba. By 1931, official data on the ethnic origins of the Canadian population indicate that the largest non-British, non-French ethnic groups in Canada were Germans, Ukrainians, Jews, Dutch and Poles, in that order, all of these groups being larger than the recorded population of Aboriginal people. If Danes, Icelanders, Norwegians and Swedes had all been counted as Scandinavians, they would have been more numerous than Ukrainians, second-only to Germans; if Czechs, Poles, Russians, Slovaks and Ukrainians had all been counted as Slavs, they would have equaled the Germans and Austrians. There were sizeable populations of all of these groups in Canada by 1931, plus substantial numbers of Finns, Hungarians, Italians and Romanians, as well.

Of the 473,544 Germans, by far the largest single group (over half a million if Austrians are included), the largest proportions lived in Ontario (37 percent), Saskatchewan (27 percent) and Alberta (16 percent), with a small majority (55 percent) living in the West as a whole. They reached their highest proportion of the population in Saskatchewan, accounting for 14 percent of the people in that province. Like the Germans, a large proportion of Canada's 150,000 Dutch lived in Ontario (40 percent), but a slightly larger number (47 percent) were in the West. The 146,000 Poles in Canada showed a stronger proclivity to settle in the West: 63 percent were located there, with a particular strength in Manitoba, compared to only 29 percent in Ontario. Canada's 225,000 Ukrainians were overwhelmingly concentrated on the Prairies: 86 percent of them lived in Manitoba, Saskatchewan and Alberta, where they made up about 10 percent of the population. Scandinavians, too, were heavily concentrated in the West, with 87 percent of their population of 228,000 in the four western provinces, where they accounted for an average of 6 percent of the population (8 percent in Saskatchewan and Alberta): 34,000 Danes went most commonly to Alberta (33 percent), 19,000 Icelanders almost exclusively to Manitoba (69 percent), 93,000 Norwegians mostly to Saskatchewan (43 percent) with a smaller contingent in Alberta (29 percent), and 81,000 Swedes more or less equally to Saskatchewan (28 percent), Alberta (24 percent) and British Columbia (20 percent).

The western land boom also initiated large-scale Chinese immigration to Canada, as laborers were brought from China to help build the railroads, thereby founding western Canada's first substantial non-Aboriginal, non-European population. By 1911, there were over 40,000 Asians in Canada, two-thirds of them in British Columbia. By 1931, virtually every prairie town had a Chinese restaurant and laundry (Palmer 1990: 73), though over half of Canada's 47,000 Chinese immigrants continued to live in British Columbia, along with a smaller group of 23,000 Japanese, almost entirely concentrated there. In 1921, the Chinese and Japanese were respectively the largest and second-largest non-British ethnic groups in Vancouver, together representing 9 percent of the population.

Of the largest European immigrant groups, only the Jews were not concentrated in the West: apart from a small community in Manitoba, 78 percent of the 157,000 people identified as "Hebrews" in the Census of 1931 lived in Ontario and Quebec. Italians, though not yet among the largest groups, showed a similar preference for central Canada, with 77 percent of the 98,000 living in Ontario and Quebec, concentrated particularly in Ontario. While Ukrainians and Scandinavians came to Canada mostly to farm, Jews and Italians filled bustling immigrant neighborhoods in the cities, most notably Montreal's Jewish ghetto, between Park Avenue and St-Laurent Boulevard, which divided the city's west-end English and east-end French populations (discussed further in Chapter 5, Section 5.3). By 1921, Jews were by far the largest non-British ethnic group in Canada's three largest cities, excluding the French in Montreal: there were 43,000 in Montreal, 35,000 in Toronto, and 14,000 in Winnipeg. By 1941, there were 130,000 native speakers of Yiddish in Canada, including over 50,000 in each of Quebec and Ontario. In Montreal, where the English-speaking community of the time comprised only 149,000 people of British origin, the Jews were a particularly significant group, representing 19 percent of the non-French population. To this day, Montreal's best-known English-language writers have been Jewish and the local foods that most typify Montreal in particular – as opposed to Quebec in general – are not French-Canadian pea soup and *tourtière* (meat pie), but bagels and pastrami, the latter served on rye bread with mustard and known locally as *smoked meat*. Italians were still a smaller group than Jews in 1921, numbering 14,000 in Montreal and 8,000 in Toronto, but were already the largest non-British ethnic group in Hamilton. The major Italian migration to Canada, along with those of other southern European groups, would come after World War II. Though relatively few Jews and Italians lived in the West, their arrival was nevertheless connected indirectly with the western land boom, since the opening of the West was partly responsible for the growth of industry in central Canada. Ukrainian and Scandinavian farmers in western Canada perused their Eaton's mail-order catalogs for goods made by Jewish and Italian factory workers in Ontario and Quebec, who consumed food made with western grain.

Finally, the western land boom caused a resumption of American immigration to Canada, the first since the similarly motivated migrations of the post-Loyalists a century earlier. After the War of 1812, the government had closed the border to further American immigration, fearing that additions to the already predominantly American population of Upper Canada would endanger Canadian security in another armed conflict with the United States. With that fear put to rest, the border was reopened and migration across it, which for most of the nineteenth century had mostly involved an outflow of Canadians to the United States, turned once again in Canada's favor as American westward expansion spilled over into Canada. American immigration to Canada, examined in detail by Hansen and Brebner (1940: 219–263) and by Harvey (1991), increased dramatically in 1903 and continued to grow until it exceeded 100,000 people per year from 1910 to 1914. Over the whole land boom period of 1901–1930, over 1.5 million American arrivals are recorded in the official figures, an average of more than 50,000 per year. Most of this influx went to western Canada: in the peak years of 1910–1914, the West was the intended destination of 78 percent of American immigrants, of whom over 80 percent went to the Prairies (Harvey 1991: 359).

Of course, immigration numbers do not tell the whole story: many of the American immigrants to Canada during this period were in fact repatriated Canadians who had emigrated in the nineteenth century and a majority of the American arrivals were not retained, returning to the United States after spending several years in Canada (Harvey 1991: 264). A large proportion of them were not Americans at all but European immigrants arriving in Canada via the United States. For instance, while the Mormon pioneers who settled near Lethbridge, Alberta, were old-stock Americans, many of Alberta's Danes came not directly from Denmark but from Danish immigrant communities in the American Midwest (Palmer 1990: 87; among these was the author's grandfather, Søren Bovbjerg, who homesteaded in 1917 at Dalum, near Drumheller, having arrived via the United States). Even among the American-born United States immigrants, only two-thirds were native speakers of English in 1931: 14 percent were French-speaking, that is, unassimilated French Canadians who had returned to Canada; 7 percent spoke German and another 7 percent a Scandinavian language (Harvey 1991: 381). About half of the Germans and Scandinavians on the Canadian Prairies in 1921 were American-born (Harvey 1991: 237). Given that many communities of immigrants on the rural frontier were effectively isolated from native English-speaking populations, it is not clear what mixture of American and foreign features would have characterized the speech of these people. On the other hand, many American arrivals in the earliest period were probably not recorded, as little account could have been kept of settlers' wagons crossing open prairie from North Dakota or Montana into Canada; border facilities would have been scarce and primitive.

Perhaps the surest guide to the actual size of the American immigration to Canada is the segment of the Canadian population born in the United States, as recorded in the Census: this rose from 81,000 in 1891 to 374,000 in 1921, an increase of almost 300,000 people, or almost 10,000 per year; it then declined slightly to 345,000 in 1931. This is much less than the data on arrivals would suggest and only a third the size of Canada's British-born population in 1921, which was over a million. It is nonetheless a substantial American population, particularly since, as the immigration data have already indicated, it was heavily concentrated in western Canada, where the Canadian-born population base was smaller. By 1911, two-thirds of Canada's American-born residents lived in the West, with the largest groups in Alberta and Saskatchewan, together accounting for half the national total. In Alberta, American-born settlers actually outnumbered British-born, reversing the relation between these groups that held in the rest of the country. Expressed as a proportion of provincial populations, American-born settlers were 22 percent in Alberta, 14 percent in Saskatchewan and 10 percent in British Columbia, but only 3.5 percent – less than the national average – in Manitoba. Though most of the American migrants came to farm or ranch (Harvey 1991: 395), many joined the population of the West's growing towns and cities, especially in southern and central Alberta and southwestern Saskatchewan, the main areas of American settlement. In 1911, American-born residents represented 21 percent of Moose Jaw, 22 percent of Fort Macleod, 24 percent of Strathcona (which in 1912 became the south side of Edmonton), 31 percent of Red Deer and 33 percent of Medicine Hat; in Regina, Saskatoon, Calgary and Edmonton they were 13–14 percent of the population (Harvey 1991: 375–376).

As a result of the immigration patterns just discussed, the formative period of Canadian English in the western provinces, particularly the prairie provinces, was characterized by a diverse mixture of native languages in addition to the blend of regional dialects of British and American English that characterized the formative period of central and eastern Canada a century earlier. Furthermore, while the four western provinces had many things in common in their early development, each also had its distinctive features. This was especially true of British Columbia, whose Pacific coastline and mountainous geography both isolated and distinguished it from the prairie provinces to its east, but also of the prairie provinces, which can be differentiated in subtle ways despite the obvious artificiality of the straight, longitudinal lines that were devised as the borders between them. These differences involved not only variation in agricultural activities and age of settlement imposed by geographical and climatic factors, but also variation in ethnic mixture. By 1911, for instance, Manitoba had the highest proportion of Canadian-born residents, Saskatchewan of European-born, Alberta

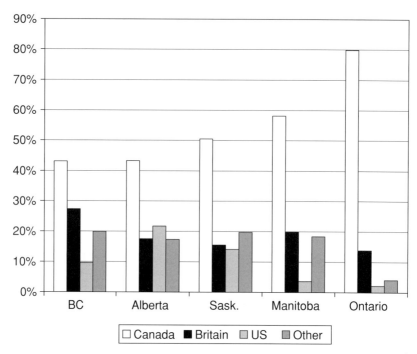

Figure 2.5 Birthplaces of the populations of the western provinces and Ontario in 1911
Source: Census of Canada, 1911, reported in Government of Canada (1914: 64–65)

of American-born and British Columbia of British-born, even if there were at least some of all of these groups in each province.

To summarize the immigration patterns discussed in this section, Figure 2.5 shows the proportions of birthplaces in the western provinces and Ontario in 1911, while Figure 2.6 shows the proportions of ethnic origins in Canada's regions in 1931, after the immigration boom had come to an end. Figure 2.5 emphasizes the differences among the western provinces' formative populations in the first census taken after the creation of the provinces of Alberta and Saskatchewan in 1905, while contrasting the large non-Canadian population of the West as a whole with the overwhelmingly Canadian-born population of Ontario. Figure 2.6 shows the disparities in ethnic composition that were already apparent among Canada's regions by 1931, challenging the earlier conception of Canada as a union of British and French cultures: this was true only of Quebec and the Maritimes. Even Ontario had more people of other European origins than people of French origin, while in western Canada these other origins were far more important than French origin, challenging even the dominance of British origins in the prairie provinces.

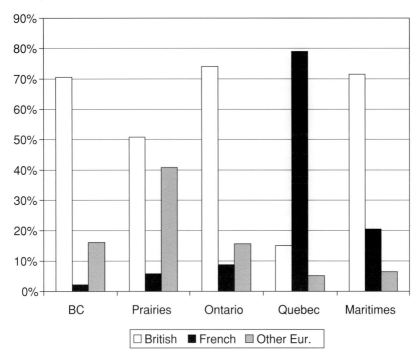

Figure 2.6 Ethnic origin of the populations of Canada's regions in 1931
Source: Census of Canada, 1931, reported in Canada, Dominion Bureau
of Statistics, General Statistics Branch (1933: 120–121)

2.5   The world comes to Canada: modern Canadian English as a multi-ethnic language in a multilingual setting

The great immigration boom of the early twentieth century had initiated a diversification of Canada's ethnic character, introducing the first substantial populations of neither Aboriginal nor British or French ancestry (other than small groups of Germans). The proportion of the Canadian population claiming British ethnic origin declined gradually from 61 percent in 1871 to 57 percent in 1901 to 52 percent in 1931. The French component, while growing rapidly through natural increase, was also declining slowly in proportional terms, from 31 percent in 1871 to 28 percent in 1931. The proportion of other ethnic origins climbed rapidly during this period, from 8 percent in 1871 to 20 percent in 1931: a fifth of Canadians were already excluded by the founding conception of Canada as a Franco-British amalgam. Following World War II, this traditional conception became even more outdated, as millions of immigrants were added to Canada's population, first from all over Europe, then increasingly from non-European sources,

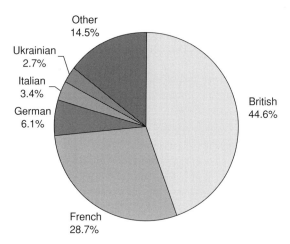

Figure 2.7 Ethnic origin of the Canadian population in 1971
Source: Government of Canada (1974: 167)

especially Asia. Canada would become a multicultural society, and Canadian English a multi-ethnic language.

Late twentieth-century immigration is measured in the millions: about 1.5 million immigrants arrived in Canada in each decade from the end of World War II to the 1970s, an average of 150,000 people per year. About a third of this quantity was lost through emigration, leaving about a million people gained through net migration in each decade. The post-war influx peaked at almost 300,000 in 1957 and at over 200,000 in 1967 and 1974 (McInnis 2000b: 583, 595). Since the 1990s, the annual average has grown closer to 200,000 arrivals while the rate of natural increase among the native population has declined, so that the immigrant proportion of the Canadian population has started to rise once again from a low of 15 percent in 1951. In 2001, it stood at 18 percent, or 5.5 million people out of a population of almost 30 million.

During the immediate post-war period through the 1960s, 87 percent of the immigrants continued to come from the traditional sources of the early twentieth century, but immigration from Britain (24 percent) was overwhelmed by that from Europe (56 percent). Northern Europe was the largest single source of immigrants in the first decade after World War II (30 percent), giving way to southern Europe from the mid 1950s through the 1960s (27 percent; McInnis 2000b: 585). By 1971, following the great European influx, Canada had 21.6 million people, of whom only 45 percent were of British and 29 percent of French ethnicity; 23 percent were now of other European origins, including 1.3 million Germans, 731,000 Italians, 581,000 Ukrainians, 426,000 Dutch, 316,000 Poles and 297,000 Jews, the six largest non-Franco-British ethnic groups. The ethnic composition of the Canadian population in 1971 is shown in Figure 2.7.

After the 1960s, immigration came increasingly from non-traditional sources, particularly Asia, but also the Caribbean, the Middle East, Latin America and elsewhere, as indicated by the discussion of non-official languages in Chapter 1. By 2001, there were over 2 million people of pure or partly Asian descent in Canada, almost 8 percent of the population, including over 700,000 who claimed pure or partly East Indian heritage and over a million who claimed pure or partly Chinese heritage. That said, the analysis of ethnicity became considerably more complex by the new millennium. For one thing, intermarriage created increasing numbers of people with more than one ethnicity, so that the statistics are now divided among single and multiple responses, the total of these being substantially greater than Canada's population; the number of respondents claiming multiple or blended ethnic identities is now considerably greater than the number claiming a single identity. Intermarriage has nearly obliterated some ethnic groups in Canada, while leaving others almost unaffected. If ethnic purity is measured as the proportion of people reporting a single ethnic affiliation out of the total number of people reporting either single or partial affiliations with that ethnic group, the groups with the highest rates of assimilation are Welsh, Americans, Swedes, Norwegians, Irish, Scots and Danes; those with the lowest rates of assimilation are Chinese, East Indians, Filipinos, Vietnamese, Portuguese, Greeks and Jamaicans. To take the extreme cases, only 8 percent of Canadians reporting Welsh ancestry consider themselves to be purely Welsh, whereas 86 percent of Chinese Canadians claim no other ethnic identification than Chinese. East Indians are 82 percent "pure," while Swedes are 89 percent mixed. British and Scandinavian Canadians in particular have intermarried freely with one another, thereby creating a large northwest-European ethnic continuum and greatly reducing their ethnic distinctiveness. By contrast, Asians and southern Europeans have tended to hold themselves apart, strongly resisting or being excluded from intermarriage, thereby retaining stronger ethnic identities. This difference may be mostly a matter of time, the more distinct groups having arrived more recently, but undoubtedly also reflects degrees of physical and cultural difference between the groups involved and the majority of the Canadian population. (The failure of some groups to integrate with the larger population is an important facet of the discussion of ethnophonetic differences in Chapter 5, Section 5.3.)

Another complication in the measurement of ethnicity stems from Statistics Canada's introduction of a new category, "Canadian", which is a subjective, cultural category rather than an objective, ethnic category and is difficult to integrate with an ethnic analysis. The "Canadian" responses can be assumed to be mostly from Franco-British Canadians of old stock, rather than from more recently arrived people who still identify with other ethnic groups. Moreover, they may reflect a genuine feeling among some respondents that they are now simply Canadian rather than British or French or something else, particularly if their ancestors arrived several generations ago from different places. Nevertheless, promotion of national feeling aside, the new response category has introduced an element of uncertainty in the study of ethnicity in Canada, beyond that necessarily connected with multiple identities.

A comparison of ethnic and language data gives ample evidence of the gradual linguistic assimilation of Canada's non-Franco-British ethnic groups into the country's two official-language communities, providing millions of new speakers of Canadian English and, to a lesser degree, French. The rates of assimilation for the various groups closely reflect not only their relative time of arrival but also the differing rates of intermarriage already discussed. All three of these processes are of course tightly linked: the passage of the generations leads to intermarriage, which in turn accelerates cultural assimilation and heritage language loss. For example, Canada's 850,000 native speakers of Chinese represent 91 percent of its population of pure Chinese ethnic origin; very few pure Chinese Canadians have lost their heritage language. By contrast, the large European groups who came in the post-war years have begun to experience considerable heritage language erosion. Even when people of mixed ethnicity are excluded from the analysis, the proportion of native speakers is now only two-thirds of the pure German and Italian populations. Among those of partly German or Italian ethnicity, heritage language retention is rare. Even Canada's large Ashkenazi Jewish population, which continues to be religiously and culturally distinct from the population at large, has nearly lost its linguistic distinctiveness: native speakers of Yiddish are now a small minority. A similar fate has befallen the other major linguistic communities of the pre-war migrations: native speakers of Ukrainian, Polish, Dutch and the Scandinavian languages are now comparatively rare, except among the much smaller numbers of new immigrants from the countries where those languages are spoken.

The process of assimilation is inexorable, gradually defeating the best efforts of those in the minority communities who try to prevent it among their children; the most that can be achieved is a slight delay of one or two generations. Indeed, the very concept of pure ethnolinguistic communities surviving beyond one or two generations in the liberal, pluralistic, egalitarian context of modern Canada's cities is essentially absurd: prolonged survival could only be effected by a rigid ethnic separatism, which would be perceived by most people today as narrow-minded or even bigoted, much as it might appeal to the more traditional values of some immigrant communities. Even official sponsorship in the form of a federal ministry of multiculturalism (now subsumed in a Department of Canadian Heritage) has had little effect on long-term assimilation, despite millions of dollars spent. It has achieved little more than symbolic value in a propaganda campaign designed to establish a multicultural "mosaic" as the basis of Canadian national identity, in self-conscious contrast to the "melting pot" ideology that prevails (or used to prevail) in the United States.

Notwithstanding the beliefs of Canadian nationalists, cultural and linguistic assimilation has followed similar paths in the two countries. Even the major exceptions to it are broadly parallel: the fishing communities of Newfoundland and North Carolina's Outer Banks; the Hassidic Jews of Montreal and New York City; the German-speaking agricultural communities of the Amish in Pennsylvania and the Mennonites in Manitoba; the Aboriginal communities in Canada's North and the American Southwest; the large Chinese communities of Vancouver and San Francisco. Moreover, Canada's official linguistic duality is becoming less of a distinguishing feature as the Spanish-speaking community in the United States grows in numbers and influence. This has generated, if not an official, at least a de facto bilingualism in some American cities exceeding that in many Canadian ones: there is much more Spanish spoken in Los Angeles, San Antonio and Miami (or even New York and Chicago) than French in Vancouver, Calgary and Halifax.

At a general level, multiculturalism in both countries is a function not of national culture or government sponsorship but of recent immigration patterns: New York City is no less multicultural than Toronto, while Newfoundland and Saskatchewan are no more so than Maine and North Dakota. Multicultural diversity is perpetuated not by the segregation and non-assimilation of older immigrant groups, but by the constant renewal of the immigrant population by newly arrived groups, who modify its character. For the older groups, assimilation is the rule: especially for the majority of Canadian-born children of immigrants, the lure of an English-speaking North American popular culture is irresistible. Nevertheless, a by-product of linguistic assimilation in areas where the concentration of particular ethnic groups is strongest has been the development of ethnic varieties of native English that differ from majority speech in subtle ways, like the Montreal example discussed in Chapter 5, Section 5.3. These have perpetuated at least a vestige of linguistic distinctiveness for the groups concerned and have greatly enriched the character of the affected varieties of English.

2.6 Immigration history and the development of Canadian English

So far, it has been asserted that Canadian English owes its very existence to three of the most important historical events in the rise of the modern world: the British victory in the Seven Years' War; the American Revolution; and the Industrial Revolution in Britain. The first of these secured Canada as a British possession, while the second two peopled it with American and British immigrants, respectively. It remains to be seen how the sources of this immigration determined the linguistic character of Canadian English.

In the case of Newfoundland English, this relation is quite clear. As discussed above, the source regions of British and Irish immigration to Newfoundland were very specific: the great majority of settlement came from southwestern England and southeastern Ireland within a relatively short period of about half a century. Moreover, Newfoundland itself is fairly small and its communities have remained comparatively isolated from any subsequent changes that might have been introduced by successive phases of settlement, which has made the problem of tracing the origins of Newfoundland speech less complex that it might otherwise be. Many features of contemporary speech in St. John's bear an obvious relation to features of contemporary southern Irish English: for example, the relatively retracted and rounded quality of the vowel in STRUT; the relatively open, low-central quality of the vowel in LOT; the relatively front and raised quality of the vowel in START; the use of dental stops in place of interdental fricatives in THIN and THIS; and the occurrence of fricativized final /t/ in GET (Hickey 2007: 328–332). That said, it was argued in Chapter 1 that traditional Newfoundland English cannot be considered a Canadian variety in any meaningful sense, so that extensive discussion of it will be left to other works with a specific Newfoundland focus. For an examination of Irish influence on Newfoundland speech, the reader is therefore referred to Clarke (2004c), Hickey (2002, 2007: 407–409) or Kirwin (1993).

Explaining the origins of features of mainland Canadian English in terms of immigration history and settlement patterns is much more difficult than the case of Newfoundland. Perhaps the dominant view of this question can be referred to as the Loyalist Theory, discussed in Section 1.6 of Chapter 1. Bloomfield (1948) and Avis (1954), in trying to explain the largely North American character of Canadian English, appealed to the history of Loyalist settlement discussed above in Section 2.2, suggesting that this established a basic pattern for Canadian English that was only superficially altered by subsequent immigration from Britain, in accordance with the doctrine of first effective settlement put forward by Zelinsky (1973). Scargill (1957) took issue with this view, arguing that it oversimplified the origins of Canadian English, giving too much weight to the Loyalist contribution and too little to other factors, particularly the British immigration of the nineteenth century.

There can be no question that the arrival of the Loyalists had a huge impact on the future of Canada: they contributed substantially to the settlement of Nova Scotia and their large settlements in present-day New Brunswick and Ontario led directly to the creation of those provinces. Their conservative culture of loyalty to the British crown and mistrust of revolutionary republicanism was arguably the seminal influence on what was to become the Canadian national identity, even if that identity emphasizes somewhat different values today. For many decades after their arrival, leading Loyalist families formed the governing elites in several Canadian communities, founded institutions and established social patterns. However, it is less certain what impact the Loyalist immigration had on the formation of Canadian English, because comparatively little is known about exactly where the settlers came from or how they mixed with each other in new communities, much less how they spoke when they arrived.

To begin with, the fact that most of the Maritime settlers arrived from New York City says very little about their speech, since Loyalists from all over the American colonies had found shelter there. Brown and Senior (1984: 30–31) offer a regional breakdown of the refugees arriving in each Canadian region. In New Brunswick, 70 percent came from the middle colonies (40 percent from New York and 22 percent from New Jersey), 22 percent from New England (13 percent from Connecticut and 6 percent from Massachusetts) and only 7 percent from the southern colonies. In Nova Scotia, 50 percent came from the middle colonies, 30 percent from the southern colonies and the remaining 20 percent from New England. In Quebec, the initial point of entry for many of those who later went to Ontario, the "vast majority" came from New York, with much smaller numbers from Vermont, New Hampshire, New Jersey and Pennsylvania. Those who went directly to Ontario could be assumed to have originated mostly from the middle colonies rather than from eastern New England or the South, as suggested by Avis (1954: 15, 1973: 46) and Chambers (2006a: 388–389). The middle colonies – New York, New Jersey and Pennsylvania – were then the predominant source of early Canadian English, but not to the exclusion of other regions. Moreover, even if we assume a predominance of immigrants from the middle colonies, the Mid-Atlantic region today is home to several distinct dialects of American English: in fact, the North–Midland boundary between New York and Pennsylvania, which cuts it in half and divides northern from southern New Jersey, is perhaps the best-known product of American dialectology (Kurath 1949: Figures 3 and 5a; Kurath and McDavid 1961: map 2).

A further difficulty is that, even if it can be established that refugees from one former colony or another predominated in some section of British North America, this information is still of limited use in establishing the roots of Canadian English. While the majority of the Loyalists were of English ethnic origin, there were also many Scots and Germans, as well as several thousand Aboriginal people and African Americans. The ethnic diversity of the refugees is demonstrated by the fact that the Upper Canadian townships were segregated by ethnic and religious affiliation. The first five Royal Townships, granted to former members of the King's Royal Regiment of New York, were settled by Catholic Highlanders, Scottish Presbyterians, German Calvinists, German Lutherans and Anglicans, respectively (Brown and Senior 1984: 49). Though most of the Loyalists were American-born (up to 90 percent in New Brunswick, somewhat less in Nova Scotia (Brown and Senior 1984: 31)), it is far from clear what sort of English any of these groups might have spoken, if they spoke English natively at all. Even many of the American-born may have been first-generation Americans living in isolated frontier communities that had little or no exposure to the linguistic norms of Boston, New York or Philadelphia.

Notwithstanding these difficulties, we can agree with Chambers (2006a: 383) that the basic difference between the types of English heard today in the former British colonies of Australia and New Zealand and in the former North American colonies is due in large part to the different histories of British emigration to the southern and northern hemispheres. It reflects in particular the fact that the southern hemisphere colonies were settled mainly in the nineteenth century, after certain changes had taken place that now characterize Standard Southern British English (Trudgill 2004), whereas the northern hemisphere colonies were first settled in the seventeenth and eighteenth centuries, before those changes had taken place. This accounts for two of the major differences between Standard British, Australian and New Zealand English, on the one hand, and most dialects of North American English, on the other: the split of Middle English short /a/ into short and lengthened classes with backing of the lengthened vowel to /ah/ (e.g. *staff*, *bath*, *pass* and *cast*); and the vocalization of /r/ in non-prevocalic contexts, such as *dark* and *four* (see Chapter 3, Section 3.2, for an explanation of the pronunciation features discussed here). These features became general in southeastern British English after the initial settlement of North America: Lass (2006: 89) suggests /a/ was lengthened in the eighteenth century and backed to modern /ah/ in the nineteenth (though Wyld (1925: 203) suggests an earlier date), while general loss of /r/ became common in the eighteenth century (Lass 2006: 92). The influence of American Loyalists on the foundation of Canadian English probably established the earlier forms – an unretracted vowel in *staff* and constricted /r/ in *dark*, etc. – as the future standard of Canadian English. Other important features of Canadian English may also have their roots in Loyalist settlement, to the extent that some regions of the United States from which Loyalists emigrated exhibit those features today. For instance, the low-back merger (see Chapter 3, Section 3.2.1) is found in eastern New England and western Pennsylvania (Labov, Ash and Boberg 2006: 58–65), while "Canadian" raising of /ay/ and /aw/ (Section 3.2.3) is found on Martha's Vineyard, off the Massachusetts coast (Labov 1963; 1972: 1–42), and raising of /aw/ in eastern Virginia (Kurath and McDavid 1961: map 29). These correspondences do not, however, rule out the possibility of later, independent developments on each side of the border. Indeed, the prevalence of unmerged low-back vowels and unraised /aw/ in many of the places the Loyalists came from, including New York City and Philadelphia, argues for later, independent developments.

An important difficulty in attributing features of modern Canadian English to Loyalist settlement was pointed out by Scargill (1957: 611): many of the features we now think of as North American in Canadian English might just as well have descended from various regional types of British English, not via American colonial populations but directly, either in the speech of the earliest British immigrants to Canada, a few of whom predated the Loyalists, or in the speech of the first great British migration of the nineteenth century, which so greatly outnumbered the Loyalists. The discussion in Section 2.3 made it clear that only a minority of the British migrants to Canada would have spoken the southeastern dialects on which the modern British standard is based, and which have so close an affinity with the speech of Australia and New Zealand. Most British immigrants came instead from northern and western England, Scotland and Ireland, regions whose speech, to this day, has more in common with Canadian English (and many varieties of American English) than the speech of the London region.

If we examine the distribution of the four Canadian features just mentioned – unsplit /æ/, retained postvocalic /r/, the low-back merger and raised /aw/ – in the regional dialects of modern British English as described by Wells (1982), we find that unsplit /æ/ (TRAP = BATH) is shared with northern England, Scotland and Ireland; retained postvocalic /r/ (in START, NORTH, etc.) with southwestern England, Scotland and Ireland; the low-back merger (LOT = THOUGHT) with Scotland and parts of northern Ireland (though Chambers (2008: 11–13) argues against this derivation); and raised /aw/ (MOUTH), though not the allophonic pattern of Canadian Raising, with Scotland. The possible origin of Canadian Raising in British input dialects has been dismissed, at least in the case of /ay/, by Gregg (1973: 142), who denies Scottish or Scots Irish influence, but Trudgill (1986: 159) suggests that raised forms of /ay/ spoken by Scottish and other immigrants to Canada may have been mixed with unraised forms spoken by immigrants from other regions, so that new generations of Canadian children resolved the conflict by developing an allophonic alternation between the competing forms (Britain 1997 suggests a similar origin in dialect mixture for Canadian Raising in East Anglia). A fifth defining feature of Canadian English identified by Labov, Ash and Boberg (2006: 224) is monophthongal or peripheral variants of /ey/ and /ow/: Wells indicates such pronunciations of FACE and GOAT in Yorkshire, Scotland and Ireland.

It must be admitted that the representation of vowels in the British dialects discussed here has been oversimplified (see, for instance, Beal 2004, Stuart-Smith 2004 and Hickey 2004 for more detailed discussions of the vowels of northern England, Scotland and Ireland, respectively). Furthermore, it is somewhat simplistic to assume that modern British dialects are the same in these respects as the dialects of nineteenth-century emigrants from these regions that might have influenced Canadian English. Nonetheless, it may not be coincidental that most of the distinctive features of Canadian English are also found, to some extent, in some or all of the regions of the British Isles from which most British immigrants to Canada came in the nineteenth century. Affording an equal place in the formation of Canadian English to British regional inputs would also accord with its mixed lexical character, which shows American and British influences as well as unique Canadian forms, as discussed in Chapter 3 (Section 3.1).

Whatever might have been the mixture of American and British influences in the establishment of the basic sound pattern of Canadian English, it seems likely that this pattern was firmly in place in most of Ontario and parts of the Maritimes by the middle of the nineteenth century. In this position, it came to be identified with English Canadian culture. Over the course of the following decades, it expanded with that culture to most of the remaining regions of the country, in some cases through the migration of Ontarians themselves to new regions, like the Prairie West, in other cases through less direct channels, like schools and other institutions. Though it was pointed out in Section 2.4 that Ontarians and other Canadians were only one of four groups in the mass migration that peopled western Canada, they may have had a greater role than the other groups in establishing local speech patterns by virtue of their identification with English Canadian culture, a kind of domestic standard to which groups with lesser local social status might have assimilated. In the emerging West, American and British speech would have been perceived as foreign in a way that Ontario English was not. If Chambers (2006a: 385) states the case for Ontario influence somewhat more strongly than it is stated here, the spread of Ontario English to western Canada during the Land Boom must have had an important part to play in the development of the comparative pan-regional homogeneity that characterizes Canadian English today, at least between Vancouver and Ottawa (see also Trudgill 1986: 146).

Nevertheless, as with the earlier case of Loyalist influence, it should be emphasized that many of the features of western Canadian English might just as well have originated in the regional dialects brought to the West by British and American immigrants. Indeed, in addition to the similarities between Canadian and regional British English mentioned above, Labov, Ash and Boberg (2006: 146–147) find that Canada and the American Midland and West form a group of highly similar dialects of North American English that are difficult to separate in clear-cut ways: a principal components analysis of twenty-one vowel measures finds these three regions to be directly adjacent in a scattergram. Ontario influence can hardly be adduced as an explanation for these similarities. Rather, it seems likely that the whole of Canada and the western United States form a broad zone of dialect leveling, in which features of various Atlantic American and – at least originally – British regional dialects were intermingled by mixed groups of settlers under similar circumstances, with a great deal of cross-pollination caused by inter-regional migration. Trudgill (1986: 146) discusses this type of leveling as a historical influence on Canadian English, while Kerswill and Williams (2000) and Kerswill (2003) show how it can lead to homogenization even in older dialect areas, like England. Some of the features of western Canadian English, then, might just as well have crossed the border with immigrants from very similar-sounding regions of the western United States, or crossed the ocean with Scottish immigrants, as come from Ontario on the Canadian Pacific Railway. It seems most likely that both sources had at least some influence in shaping the speech of the half of the country that was settled following Canadian Confederation.

Once Canada had been settled from Victoria to Halifax, it seems safe to suppose that future arrivals of new immigrants, however numerous, would have had relatively little influence on Canadian speech, especially as these immigrants came increasingly from non-English-speaking lands. Their children, once they started school, acquired local speech patterns that were by then firmly established as the majority dialect of each community, just as they do today. Any substrate effects in their parents' second-language English, or foreign features in non-Canadian native varieties of English, would have been lost within one or two generations. The massive scale of immigration in modern Canada, filling entire neighborhoods with people who speak languages other than English and French, raises the possibility that future developments in Canadian English may indeed reflect the multi-ethnic and multilingual character of urban Canada, beyond the obvious level of loanwords for ethnic foods and other cultural phenomena. Nevertheless, it should be recalled that, as noted in Sections 2.3 and 2.4, the proportion of immigrants in Canada's cities and in the country as a whole was even higher in the 1920s and 1930s than it is today, yet these huge foreign-born populations apparently had little influence on the development of Canadian English. Their descendants today are linguistically indistinguishable from those of the Loyalists and earlier British immigrants. So it may be for present and future generations of Canadians with non-Canadian origins, however numerous they may be, but a strong upward shift in levels of immigration could alter this forecast, as suggested in Chapter 6.

3   The principal features of Canadian English in comparative perspective

Few people would question the assertion that there are now two widely recognized standard varieties of English in the world: British and American (Trudgill and Hannah 1985: 1–3). This duality arose from the political separation of the United States from Britain in the eighteenth century, together with the barrier to communication presented by the Atlantic Ocean, in an age before jet travel, satellite beams and the internet. Over four centuries, these factors have produced a substantial set of differences between the types of English spoken in Britain and America, aside from the variation found within each of them. Some of these national differences are older forms preserved in American English that have been altered or abandoned in later stages of British English; others are innovations in American English that never spread to Britain. Whatever their origin, these differences led Noah Webster to publish an *American Dictionary of the English Language* as early as 1812 and John Russell Bartlett to produce a *Dictionary of Americanisms* in 1849. In 1919, H. L. Mencken published the first edition of his encyclopedic study of American English, which he significantly called *The American Language*, emphasizing its distinctness from the "language" of Britain. In 1944, John S. Kenyon and Thomas A. Knott put forth a *Pronouncing Dictionary of American English*, which became the standard account of American English pronunciation. Together, these works and others acknowledge that British and American English are different enough to justify separate lexicographic traditions and different standards of usage. The growing power and influence of the United States over the course of the twentieth century and the corresponding decline of Britain following World War I have gradually encouraged international recognition of American English as a second global standard, which may indeed largely supplant the British standard in the twenty-first century, given the larger population and greater influence of the United States.

With respect to the barrier formed by the Atlantic Ocean, if not also to political evolution, Canada shares the North American situation of the United States. Until quite recently, the flow of communication and linguistic influence across the land border between Canada and the United States has generally been easier than communication across the ocean with Britain.

106

Moreover, as argued in Chapter 1 (Section 1.4), Canada has experienced relatively close relations with the United States throughout its history, from the settlement patterns discussed in Chapter 2 to the more recent economic and cultural relations described in Chapter 1. Nevertheless, the history of English-Canadian settlement discussed in Chapter 2 leads us to expect that Canadian English will share many features by way of inheritance with varieties of both American and British English. At the same time, the existence of Canadian English in at least partial isolation from speakers of these non-Canadian varieties for two centuries suggests that we may also find features that have evolved independently in Canada, thereby serving to distinguish Canadian English from other varieties. On the other hand, the continued contact with varieties of American English discussed in Chapter 1, which has arguably intensified in recent decades, has caused Canadian English to adopt some new American features that reflect relatively recent trans-border diffusion, rather than common inheritance.

This chapter describes the principal features of Canadian English in comparative perspective, examining the outcomes of the various patterns of influence just mentioned: what does Canadian English share with other major varieties of English, particularly Standard British and American English, and what differentiates it from those varieties? This examination will begin at the most obvious and easily comprehended level of analysis – vocabulary – and will then turn to more technically complex analyses of pronunciation and grammar. Since the purpose of this chapter is comparison with non-Canadian varieties, it will assume a uniform type of Canadian English spoken over most of the country by the majority of anglophone Canadians, setting aside the less representative minority varieties identified in Section 1.3 of Chapter 1 (for studies of these varieties, including those of Newfoundland, see the previous research cited in Section 1.6). This uniform variety will be labeled *Standard Canadian English*: a variety whose geographic range hypothetically extends from Victoria, British Columbia, in the west to Halifax, Nova Scotia, in the east, and whose social range hypothetically includes the country's social majority, from upper working class to upper middle class. This group is defined educationally as people with at least some post-secondary education, who comprise 12.2 million, or 51 percent, of the 23.9 million Canadians aged 15 and over, according to Statistics Canada's Census of 2001. They comprise an even larger proportion of the population aged 18 and over, since most 15–17-year-olds will also obtain some education beyond high school; in fact, a full quarter of Canadians over 15 had a university education in 2001. While social variation will receive a limited treatment here, particularly in the discussion of grammar, the analysis of regional variation in the lexicon and pronunciation of Canadian English will be reserved for Chapters 4 and 5, respectively.

The data on which the following comparative description is based come from a wide range of sources, which will be identified individually in the text, as appropriate. These sources include the standard dictionaries and previous studies of Canadian English enumerated in Chapter 1 (Section 1.6), particularly the work of Avis (1954–1956), Clarke, Elms and Youssef (1995), Gregg (1957a, b, 2004), Joos (1942), Labov, Ash and Boberg (2006), Scargill and Warkentyne (1972) and Woods (1999). They also comprise the author's own research, as reported especially in Boberg (2005b, 2008a, 2009). A further source of data is the literary texts of Canadian English identified in Chapter 1 (Section 1.5), which will provide evidence of grammar and vocabulary. Finally, the following description also reflects the author's personal experience of Canadian English, based on having spent most of his life in several regions of Canada, including Edmonton, Toronto and Montreal.

Before proceeding to the analysis, it should perhaps be observed that Standard Canadian English is, in most important respects, very similar to other standard varieties of English, to the point where substantial passages of written Canadian English, in particular, might not be recognizably different – at least to many readers – from parallel passages of written British or American English. It seems safe to say, for instance, that the large majority of syntactic constructions that are grammatically acceptable in British or American English are equally so in Canadian, which is true also of ungrammatical constructions and of most aspects of morphology, phonology, usage and vocabulary. No attempt will therefore be made to present here a general account of Canadian English as though it were an independent language: such an account would be largely redundant with material already available in many standard grammars of English. There is no need to point out that *John gave Mary the book* is grammatical in Canadian English, or that Canadian English contains the phoneme /s/ or the word *tree*. Instead, the focus of this chapter will be on those aspects of Canadian English that do differentiate it from other varieties of English, however subtly. This may seem an obvious point, but it is worth remembering as a way of keeping the discussion of differences in proper perspective.

3.1   Canadian English vocabulary

The most readily accessible example of the divergence between British and American English concerns daily vocabulary: the existence of different words for the same things, or different senses or uses of the same words, in Britain and the United States. Many of these differences are well known. Lists of British–American lexical correspondences have long been a commonplace of both histories of English and synchronic descriptions of global English; Moore (1989) and Schur (1987) are examples of book-length lists intended for a popular readership, while Algeo (2006) and Trudgill and Hannah (1985: 75–81) are more academic analyses of the many ways in which the British and American lexicons differ. Most transatlantic travelers, even many ordinary

Table 3.1 *Some lexical correspondences between Standard British and American English*

British English	American English
bonnet (of car)	hood (of car)
boot (of car)	trunk (of car)
chemist	drugstore
chest of drawers	dresser
chips	(French) fries
corn	grain
crisps	chips
(baby's) dummy	pacifier
dustman	garbage man
filling station	gas station
flat	apartment
football	soccer
goods wagon (of train)	freight car
jumper	sweater
letter box	mailbox
lift	elevator
lorry	truck
nappy	diaper
pavement	sidewalk
petrol	gas(oline)
rubbish	garbage/trash
spanner	wrench
sweets	candy
torch	flashlight
washing-up	(dirty) dishes

people who watch television programs or movies produced on the other side of the ocean, can supply a less exhaustive list of lexical differences. A selection from the author's own list of some of the more common differences appears in Table 3.1.

The twenty-five correspondences in Table 3.1 cover a wide range of semantic domains that have witnessed independent technical and cultural development on either side of the Atlantic Ocean since the eighteenth century. The most obvious is transportation: the vehicles, equipment and infrastructure of rail and road transportation have changed beyond recognition since the establishment of English-speaking colonies in North America, a development that has taken place in environments dominated by separate sets of manufacturers and government transportation agencies. Other domains represented in Table 3.1 include architectural features, childcare, clothing, food, furniture, public services, retail, sports and tools: all important facets of daily life. From the Canadian point of view, the significant fact about Table 3.1 is that Canadian English is aligned with American rather than British English in every single case.

Canadian automobile and motoring vocabulary, for example, is thoroughly American: in addition to the instances given in Table 3.1, Canadians use the

American terms *detour, divided highway, fender, license plate, muffler, rental car, rest area, turn signal* and *windshield* rather than their British equivalents *diversion, dual carriageway, mudguard, number plate, silencer, hire car, lay-by, indicator* and *windscreen*. This is perhaps not surprising, given the close integration of the Canadian and American automobile industries discussed in Chapter 1. The same might be said of clothing and fashion, another industry with a high degree of continental integration: for Canadians, as for Americans, *pants* means a man's trousers, not his underpants, as in Britain; a woman's underpants are her *panties*, not her *knickers*; a *vest* is part of a three-piece suit (a British *waistcoat*), not an undershirt; a *jumper* is a dress worn over a blouse (a British *pinafore dress*), not a sweater. However, American influence is seen even in domains where its explanation is less obvious. Canadian musicians, for instance, use the American terms for note values, such as *eighth note, quarter note, half note* and *whole note*, rather than the British equivalents *quaver, crotchet, minim* and *semibreve*, despite the potential for British influence exercised through formal institutional channels like school and church during the colonial period.

The alien character of British vocabulary for most modern Canadians is underscored by the Canadian Broadcasting Corporation's publication of a dictionary of British words and phrases for Canadian viewers of the British soap opera *Coronation Street* (Miller 1986). This guide contains not only standard vocabulary of the sort featured in Table 3.1, but also many of the colloquialisms and slang used by the program's mainly working-class characters. An equivalent guide to the language of an American soap opera would be inconceivable. The recent Canadian television series, *Corner Gas* (see Chapter 1, Section 1.5), used this aspect of Canadian linguistic culture as a source of comedy in Episode 2 of Season 6 ("Bend it like Brent"). The story has one of the characters, Davis, starting up a town soccer team, which, in an incongruous fit of anglophilia, he calls a *football* team. When he asks the gas station owner, Brent, to sponsor the team, the following exchange occurs:

Davis: Hey Brent! Who's your favorite football team?
Brent: The Riders: duh! [The Saskatchewan Roughriders]
Davis: No, not Canadian football.
Brent: Oh, then the, uh, Minnesota Vikings.
Davis: No, out on the pitch!
Brent: Whaddaya mean, soccer? Well then it's a tie between the Manchester
        I-don't-give-a-craps and the London Not-a-real-sports.

The dialog is a humorous illustration not only of the ambiguity of the term *football*, which Brent naturally interprets in its North American sense (the Canadian and American versions of the game are only slightly different), but also of the strongly North American cultural orientation of most native

Canadians: despite the efforts and enthusiasm of a growing North American soccer community, most North Americans still think of soccer as a game that schoolchildren play, not a professional sport watched by adults. Shortly after this exchange, once Brent has agreed to sponsor the team, he mocks Davis' use of British forms like *football* and *pitch* by exclaiming, "Well that's it, then, blokes: let's celebrate with some bangers and mash and ring up our mobiles, or my name isn't Sir Aluminium Boot-Bonnet!" This miscellaneous jumble of British forms is full of playful jabs at an essentially foreign British culture: British food (*bangers and mash*), aristocratic titles, and of course British words that do not occur in North America – *blokes* instead of *guys*, *ring up* a *mobile* instead of *call* a *cell phone*, *boot* and *bonnet* instead of *trunk* and *hood* and the British pronunciation (and spelling) of *aluminum* with a second <i>.

Despite the generally American character of the Canadian English vocabulary, counterexamples of British vocabulary in Canada do exist. The most iconic of these, insisted upon by many Canadians who do not wish to appear American, is the name of the last letter of the alphabet, *zed*, rather than the American *zee*. Another is the use of *tap* rather than *faucet* to designate the device that controls the flow of water into a sink. Still others are British *icing* against American *frosting* for the top layer of a cake; British *chocolate bar* against American *candy bar* for a snack bar of chocolate or chocolate-coated nuts, nougat, caramel, etc.; British *bill* against American *check* for the tally of charges in a restaurant; British *cutlery* against American *silverware* for knives, forks and spoons; and for at least some Canadians the use of British *bum* and *mum* rather than American *butt* and *mom*. (Avis' examples of Canadian British forms are *blind*, *tap*, *serviette*, *braces* and *porridge* where an American would say *shade*, *faucet*, *napkin*, *suspenders* and *oatmeal* (1973: 63; 1983: 6).) Unlike the Americanisms in Table 3.1, however, most of these British forms have only variable currency in Canada.

As discussed in Chapter 1 (Section 1.6), variation among American, British and Canadian forms is the subject of one of the main traditions of research on Canadian English, traditionally carried out with written questionnaires. Proportions of the British and American variants for *zed*, *tap* and *icing* from two nationwide surveys are reproduced in Table 3.2. The *Survey of Canadian English* (Scargill and Warkentyne 1972) is a survey of over 14,000 grade nine students and their parents reflecting the usage of two generations of Canadians in the early 1970s. *NARVS* is the *North American Regional Vocabulary Survey*, a study of lexical variation carried out by the author from 1999 to 2007, with about 2,000 respondents from a broad age range, which is presented in greater detail in Chapter 4. As the data in Table 3.2 demonstrate, while a majority of Canadians report using the British forms *zed*, *tap* and *icing*, a minority report using the corresponding American forms. By contrast, most of the British forms in Table 3.1 would virtually never occur in Canada. (For further data on *zed*, see Avis 1956: 50; Chambers 1993: 12–13; Gregg 2004: 57; Nylvek 1992: 274; Woods 1999: 251; and Zeller 1993:

Table 3.2 *Proportions of British and American variants of three lexical variables in Canada, from two nationwide surveys: the* Survey of Canadian English *(SCE: Scargill and Warkentyne 1972) and the* North American Regional Vocabulary Survey *(NARVS: Boberg 2005b)*

	SCE[a]		*NARVS*	
Variable	% British	% American	% British	% American
zed/zee	72–79	11–15	70	28
tap/faucet	89–93	6–9	74	22
icing/frosting	69–75[b]	23–28	83	13

[a] *SCE* data are ranges encompassing frequencies associated with four respondent categories: male and female parents and male and female students.
[b] Scargill and Warkentyne (1972: 88) distinguish between hard and soft cake coverings; data cited here are for the former, which elicited a higher proportion of *icing* responses. *Icing* also occurs in American English, particularly in the Midland and South, according to a regional analysis of American responses to *NARVS*.

194. For *tap*, see Avis 1954: 18; Chambers 2008: 17–19; De Wolf 1996: 133; Gregg 2004: 78; Woods 1999: 249; and Zeller 1993: 186.)

Beyond being predominantly American, the vocabulary of Canadian English tends to be aligned most often with that of the North of the United States, rather than with that of the Midland and South. This fact led Avis to assert that "Canada is an extension of the northern speech area of the United States" (1954: 13–14), while admitting that the diverse background of the Loyalist settlers of Ontario had also introduced some Midland terms (15). One prominent example of this concerns generic terms for carbonated beverages, which are called *soda* in the northeastern and southwestern United States and *coke* in the South. As will be discussed further in Chapter 4, most Canadians use a third word, *pop*, which appears to have entered Canada from the Inland North of the United States, the only other place it is found. According to the *NARVS* data, *pop* is now the dominant term everywhere in Canada except Quebec and Manitoba, where *soft drink* is preferred (see also Chambers 2000: 190–193). Another example is words for the article that holds water for washing the floor or the car. Though the Midland word *bucket* has recently become strongly prevalent in Canada, the *NARVS* data show that less urbanized areas like Saskatchewan and northwestern Ontario still show a predominance of the northern *pail*. Finally, when Canadians cook food over a grill in the back yard, 99 percent of them speak, like most northern Americans, of *barbecuing*, not of *grilling out*, the word more southerly Americans use to avoid confusion with their more specific sense of *barbecue*, which entails a special preparation of meat with barbecue sauce.

While the combination of the Americanisms of Table 3.1 and the British forms of Table 3.2 could be thought of as uniquely Canadian, Scargill (1957:

612) argues that Canadian English should not be thought of merely as a particular combination of American and British elements. Rather, in a variety of English spoken for two centuries in a place as big as Canada, one should expect to find some distinctly Canadian forms. This is as true of vocabulary as of other levels of language. Though one might disagree with Scargill's assessment of the data in Table 3.1 as "trivial," and while his own examples are needlessly obscure (*Manitoba wave*, *Digby chicken*, *Athens of Canada*, *splake*, *aboiteau* and *droke* are unknown to most Canadians today), his general point is valid. It can be demonstrated with a large set of words or senses of words that are associated primarily with Canadian English, as attested by the *Dictionary of Canadianisms on Historical Principles* (Avis et al. 1967), or by the smaller lists in Lovell (1958), Avis (1973: 65–67; 1983: 11–13) and Woods (1999: 40–49). Avis ultimately agreed with Scargill: despite his earlier statement about Canada being an extension of the northern United States, he later admits that, "Taken as a whole, the English spoken in Canada is neither British nor American: it is distinctively Canadian" (1973: 50); and, still later, that "Canadian English, then, is a dialect which resembles American English in some respects and British English in others and includes, at the same time, a great deal that is significantly Canadian" (1983: 7).

To begin with, like American, Australian and New Zealand English, Canadian English has borrowed many words from Aboriginal languages, mostly to label aspects of the North American natural world or of Aboriginal cultures that were not familiar to Europeans when first encountered. Since natural features and Aboriginal cultures often straddled the present international boundary, many of these words also occur in American English, or at least in adjacent regions of the United States, just as some Aboriginal-origin words associated mainly with American English, like *canoe*, *moccasin*, *mukluk*, *raccoon*, *skunk* and *teepee*, also occur in Canada. A selection of lexical transfers from Aboriginal languages into Canadian English appears in Table 3.3, with sources and definitions based on entries in the *Canadian Oxford Dictionary* (*COD*). In addition to these common nouns, many Canadian place names are of Aboriginal origin, including the names of several major cities (e.g. Mississauga, Ottawa, Saskatoon, Toronto, Winnipeg), of six provinces and territories (Manitoba, Nunavut, Ontario, Quebec, Saskatchewan and Yukon) and of Canada itself. Further Aboriginal lexical influence can be seen in words borrowed from Chinook Jargon, a pidgin combining elements of English, French and Aboriginal languages that arose on the northwest coast of North America during the initial contact period. Though confined largely to the English of British Columbia, these words include *saltchuck*, 'ocean,' and *skookum*, a rare example of a transferred adjective, which means 'strong' or 'brave' (Gregg 1983: 18–19; 1995: 185–186; 2004: 68–69; for more Chinook Jargon see these articles and Harris 1983).

While the Aboriginal component of Canadian English is highly distinctive, particularly in contrast to British English, most words of Aboriginal origin

Table 3.3 *A selection of lexical transfers from Aboriginal languages to Canadian (and American) English, with sources and definitions based on those of the* Canadian Oxford Dictionary

Word	Source	Definition
caribou	Mi'kmaq	North American reindeer
chinook	Salishan	warm winter wind
chipmunk	Ojibwa	striped ground squirrel
coho	Salishan	silver North Pacific salmon
husky	Algonquian	arctic sled dog
igloo	Inuktitut	dome-shaped dwelling of ice blocks
inukshuk	Inuktitut	human form made of large stacked stones
kayak	Inuktitut	one-man canoe with closed top
moose	Abenaki	largest member of deer family
muskeg	Cree	moss-covered swamp or bog
powwow	Algonquian	festive gathering
saskatoon	Cree	wild purple berry
sockeye	Salishan	blue-backed Pacific salmon
toboggan	Mi'kmaq	long narrow sled without runners
wapiti	Cree	North American elk
wigwam	Ojibwa/Algonquin	dome-shaped dwelling of bark over sapling frame

other than place names denote objects or concepts explicitly connected with the natural world or with Aboriginal culture and are not therefore part of the daily vocabulary of most Canadians. There are exceptions to this general rule, many of which appear in Table 3.3; some of these are supported by occurrences in the works of English Canadian fiction mentioned in Chapter 1. Some people do go kayaking and tobogganing for pleasure or own husky dogs (see MacLennan 1941: 216 for *tobogganing*); many eat coho or sockeye salmon and some consume pie, jelly, syrup or even wine made with saskatoons (see Mitchell (1947: 283, 304) for pie and Babiak (2006: 206) for wine); many in western Canada enjoy the mid-winter arrival of a chinook (Mitchell 1947: 115); inukshuks have become fashionable garden ornaments; and Margaret Atwood, in *The Edible Woman*, makes a valiant effort at a figurative use of *muskeg*: "Ainsley's floor is covered by a treacherous muskeg of used clothes . . . " (1969: 8). Some Canadians even use *powwow* in a more general sense to denote a non-Aboriginal gathering, meeting or party, according to the *COD*. Few people, however, have any reason to speak of caribou, igloos, wapiti or wigwams, and the metaphorical use of *muskeg* has yet to catch on.

Moreover, most aspects of the Canadian natural world and even of Aboriginal cultures – such as arrows, bows, buffalo jumps, calumets (peace pipes), dogsleds, dream catchers, harpoons, headdresses, longhouses, masks, medicine men, sun dances, sweat lodges, totem poles and tribal councils – are referred to in Canadian English not by their Aboriginal names but by European names transferred and adapted to the North American context.

Thus, while the species may in some cases differ biologically and bear different scientific names, there is no linguistic distinction in common parlance between the North American and non–North American versions of many animals, plants and features of the landscape. Examples of pre-existing English words transferred to the Canadian context are abundant. Among words for land animals, they include *badger, bear, beaver, bison/buffalo, deer, elk, fox, hare, lynx, mink, mole, mouse, otter, squirrel* and *wolf* (*coyote, gopher, pronghorn* and *rattlesnake* are Americanisms transferred to the Canadian Prairies); among aquatic animals they include *bass, clam, cod, crab, herring, lobster, minnow, mussel, perch, pickerel, pike, salmon, sardine, seal, trout* and *whale*; among birds they include *crow, duck, eagle, goose, grouse, gull, heron, jay, loon, magpie, puffin, robin, sparrow, swallow* and *woodpecker* (a *loon* is called a *diver* in Britain, but the word is Old Norse, not Aboriginal); among lesser animals they include *ant, bee, beetle, cricket, fly, frog, grasshopper, mosquito, snake, spider* and *worm*; among trees they include *ash, birch, cedar, fir, maple, oak, pine, poplar, spruce* and *willow*; and among landscape features they include *badlands, forest, glacier, iceberg, hill, lake, mountain, plain, prairie, rapid, river, stream, valley* and *waterfall*. To the extent that the Aboriginal equivalents of these words survive at all in Canadian English, it is in place names, where they go largely unrecognized. Few people know that *Saskatchewan* means 'swift current,' *Winnipeg* 'murky water,' *Toronto* 'trees standing in water' and *Quebec* 'where the river narrows' (all as given in the *COD*). *Ontario* means simply 'lake,' making the English name *Lake Ontario* redundant. In short, while Canada's Aboriginal languages have contributed a few distinctive words to Canadian English, their impact on the daily language of most Canadians – beyond place names – has been small.

If we wish to build a strong case for the status of Canadian English as a unique dialect at the lexical level, it must be based on words in general usage that do not refer simply to objects or cultural phenomena found only or mostly in Canada. It will not do to rely too much on words like *point blanket*, a blanket produced by the Hudson's Bay Company during the fur trade and still available as a luxury item in their department stores, marked with "points" to indicate its thickness and value. If speakers of other dialects wished to refer to such an item, they would no doubt also call it a Hudson's Bay point blanket, since no alternative term exists in other dialects. To this extent, ironically, the word *point blanket* is not particularly Canadian; it is the artifact, not the word, that is found only in Canada. Equivalent examples from Australia are *boomerang, didgeridoo, kangaroo* and *koala bear*: these words are Australianisms in one sense, but part of World English in another, since there are no other words for them in other dialects of English; indeed, these words are well known, if not often used, in Canadian English. Uniquely Canadian objects or phenomena are a testimony to the distinctiveness of Canadian culture and history, or of the Canadian natural environment, not of Canadian English. If, by contrast, objects or cultural phenomena can be identified

Table 3.4 *Canadianisms in the* NARVS *questionnaire, with nationwide frequencies of use and non-Canadian equivalents*

Canadianism	NARVS freq. (%)	American	British
bachelor apartment	62	studio apartment	studio flat, bed-sitting room
bank machine	55	ATM	cash dispenser
chesterfield	15	couch, sofa	settee, sofa
eavestroughs	55	gutters	gutters
grade one (etc.)	85	first grade	first form
parkade	33	parking garage	car park
runners	26	sneakers, tennis shoes	trainers, plimsolls
running shoes	28	sneakers, tennis shoes	trainers, plimsolls
scribbler	31	notebook	exercise book
washroom	50	bathroom, restroom	cloakroom, lavatory, loo, toilet, WC

that exist throughout the English-speaking world but have different names in Canada, these will better support the status of Canadian English as an autonomous variety, since Canadian words for things that have different names in other dialects presumably never occur outside Canada. Several lexical variables meeting this criterion were investigated by the *NARVS* questionnaire mentioned above. These are shown with their frequencies in the nationwide *NARVS* sample, together with their most common American and British equivalents, in Table 3.4. Some of them have also been investigated in previous studies, to which references will be made in the following discussion.

The ten words listed in Table 3.4, far from naming things found only in Canada, refer to objects or aspects of daily life all over the world. They denote not the sort of obscure, specialized or obsolete vocabulary that tends to fill the notebooks of traditional dialectology but common features of ordinary, contemporary experience for the majority of the population. Nonetheless, they are mostly uniquely Canadian, being heard frequently in Canada but rarely in other countries; the *NARVS* data on current popular usage can in most cases be supported by citations in Canadian literature. That said, while the words in Table 3.4 do not generally occur outside Canada, few of them have exclusive domain within Canada. The one that comes closest to exclusive currency is *grade one* (Hollingshead 1995: 31, 134, 145; Laurence 1974: 31, 44, 53, 62; Mitchell 1947: 83, 87, 101, 103, 158), referring to the first year of elementary education, a usage that receives institutional support from the school system (the second year is *grade two*, etc.). *Bachelor apartment, bank machine, chesterfield, eavestroughs, parkade, runners, running shoes, scribbler* and *washroom* all compete with other words, in most cases including the terms listed in Table 3.4 as American. Of these non-exclusive Canadianisms, the most robust appear to be *bachelor apartment* (a small apartment without a separate bedroom), *bank machine* (an automated teller machine), *eavestroughs* (gutters along the roof of a house, also examined by Scargill and Warkentyne (1972: 99) and Zeller (1993: 191–192)) and *washroom* (toilet facilities, usually in a public place; at home, usage generally shifts to *bathroom*). The remaining words in Table 3.4 enjoy only minority usage, for various reasons.

Chesterfield, an upholstered piece of furniture that seats three people, is in the last stages of decline, as documented in detail by Chambers (1995b; 1998c: 7–11) in the Toronto region, as well as by Gregg (2004: 80) and Woods (1999: 245–255) in Vancouver and Ottawa, respectively. Half a century ago, Avis (1954: 13) cited the example of *chesterfield* as an introduction to his study of speech differences along the Ontario–United States border, presenting it as a Canadianism incomprehensible to Americans. It was still the majority term in the *Survey of Canadian English* (Scargill and Warkentyne 1972: 86) and occurs widely in Canadian fiction writing. It is the dominant term in MacLennan's *Barometer Rising* (1941: 31–38, 106, 109, 122, 146), in Atwood's *Edible Woman* (1969: 30, 35, 71, 87, 158, 163, 165, 184, 223, 284, 291), in Laurence's *The Diviners* (1974: 41, 124, 215, 221, 245) and even in some more recent books, like Babiak's novel *The Garneau Block* (2006: 273, 275, 277, 341, 365, 366). It also occurs in Mitchell's *Who Has Seen the Wind* (1947: 229) and Munro's *Selected Stories* (1996: 108), though these authors also use its main competitor, *couch* (Mitchell 1947: 29, 262, 282; Munro 1996: 334), as does Babiak (2006: 283, 374, 395). Hollingshead's collection of short stories, *The Roaring Girl* (1995), features all three of the main terms, which alternate in different stories, emphasizing their semantic equivalence: *chesterfield* (26, 52, 63, 64, 69, 155, 159); *couch* (95, 105, 133); and *sofa* (79, 109, 111, 166). *Couch* also appears in Watson's *The Double Hook* (1959: 105).

In fact, competitors to *chesterfield* have a long history in Canada: most notably, the dominant term in Montgomery's *Anne of Green Gables* is *sofa* (1908: 96, 140, 141, 154, 157, 203). Laurence (1974), who mixes *chesterfield* and *sofa* and seems to reserve *couch* for something that converts to a bed (364), offers an explicit comment on the changing status of these terms when she describes an apartment as "furnished with Danish Modern, long teak coffee tables, svelte things to sit on (you could not call them *sofas* or *chesterfields*, both words having unseemly old-fashioned connotations)" (245). This suggests that *chesterfield* was going out of fashion by the 1970s, a decline that led eventually to its poor showing in the recent *NARVS* data. The profile of this decline in apparent time, analyzed by Chambers (1995b: 162; 1998c: 10), is dramatic: there is a sudden drop from majority status beginning with respondents then in their fifties, which is completed among respondents in their twenties, suggesting that it occurred over four decades from the 1950s to the 1980s, at least in the Golden Horseshoe region around Toronto. As use of *chesterfield* falls off, use of *couch*, the dominant American term, replaces it (see also Figure 4.1 in Chapter 4).

The other minority-usage Canadianisms suffer not from decline so much as from regional restrictions: they occur only in some parts of the country. There are, in fact, many more Canadianisms in the *NARVS* data that are restricted to a single region, such as those associated with Montreal English, but discussion of these will be reserved for Chapter 4. Those included in Table 3.4 occur frequently in more than one region but not across the whole country, thereby diminishing their prominence in terms of nationwide frequency. Two of these are *parkade*, the normal western Canadian term for a multi-storey parking garage (also used in South Africa), and *scribbler*, a Maritime Canadian word for a book of lined paper that students use in school. *Parkade*, which the *Gage Canadian Dictionary* suggests is a blend of *park* and *arcade*, may have originated as a commercial term used by the Hudson's Bay Company to designate the parking garages attached to its downtown department stores, which were called *the Bay Parkade*. In any case, *parkade* is the majority term for a parking garage from Vancouver to Thunder Bay and on Prince Edward Island, though it is less popular in Manitoba than in the other prairie provinces; it is also the second-most frequent term in Nova Scotia. *Scribbler* is the majority term only in the Maritime provinces, but was also chosen by a quarter to a third of *NARVS* respondents on the Prairies, being particularly strong in Manitoba. In Canadian novels, it occurs frequently in Laurence's *The Diviners* (1974: 32, 51, 79, 86–87), which is set in Manitoba, as well as in Mitchell's *Who Has Seen the Wind* (1947: 99, 239) and McGillis' *A Tourist's Guide to Glengarry* (2002: 112), also set on the Prairies, and in MacLennan's *Barometer Rising* (1941: 128), set in Nova Scotia.

The final pair of minority-usage Canadianisms, *runners* and *running shoes*, suffer from being competing Canadian terms for the same thing: athletic shoes worn as casual attire. Combined, they account for a majority (54 percent) of Canadian responses in the *NARVS* data. They show a clear regional cleavage, with *runners* (also an Irish term) predominant throughout western Canada from Vancouver to Thunder Bay and *running shoes* predominant throughout central Canada from southern Ontario to Montreal (see also Chambers 2000: 185–189; Zeller 1993: 185); Atlantic Canada shows almost exclusive use of the main American term, *sneakers*. Appropriately, we find *runners* in McGillis' novel about Edmonton, *A Tourist's Guide to Glengarry* (2002: 44), but we also find other variants in western Canadian novels, possibly suggesting editorial influence: Watson's *The Double Hook*, written in Calgary by a Vancouverite and set in interior British Columbia, has *sneakers* (1959: 23).

The set of Canadianisms examined by the *NARVS* questionnaire is of course only a small sample of the total number, as is made clear by the *Dictionary of Canadianisms on Historical Principles* (Avis *et al.* 1967), Woods (1999: 40–49), Barber (2008) or Casselman (1995). For instance, there are many compounds involving the words *bush*, *ice* and *snow*, which suggest the influence of Canada's sparsely populated northern landscape on its lexicon. These include *bush pilot*, one who flies small *bush planes* into remote areas; *ice bridge* or *ice road*, a seasonal transportation link across a frozen body of water; *snowbird*, a person who spends winters in Florida; *snow route*, a road designated for priority snow clearance; and *snowmobile*, a kind of tracked motorcycle used for transportation over snow. The latter is also called a *Ski-Doo*, the commercial name used by the machine's inventor, Quebec's Bombardier company. By rough count, the *COD* in fact lists over sixty compounds containing the word *snow*, though only some of these are Canadian; by contrast, the American *Merriam-Webster's Collegiate Dictionary* lists something over fifty, while the British *Concise Oxford English Dictionary* has something over thirty. Nevertheless, snow and ice are common to both Canadian and American experience, making many of the words connected with a cold climate generally North American rather than exclusively Canadian. The American *snowbelt*, from North Dakota to New England (not to speak of Alaska), receives as much snow as anywhere in the populous parts of Canada (and considerably more than English Canada's second largest city, Vancouver): this makes snow blowers, snow fences, snowmobiles, snow plows, snowsuits and snow tires features of regional American life and vocabulary as much as of Canadian. Still, it is hard to imagine a more Canadian literary image than Atwood's "the sidewalks were crowded with furred Saturday ladies trudging as inexorably as icebreakers through the slush" (1969: 270), even if *icebreaker* is not strictly speaking a Canadianism.

Cold Canadian winters also encouraged the development of the game of ice hockey, which first became an organized sport at McGill University in the late nineteenth century, though the professional *National Hockey League* is now dominated by American teams, some of which play in such incongruously un-icy places as California, Texas and Florida. Given the popularity of hockey among Canadians, some of its vocabulary has moved off the *rink* and into common parlance, as when people speak of *stickhandling* their way around a problem, referring to the way hockey players use their sticks to maintain possession of the *puck* while skating. A further lexical product of the northern climate is the word *toque*, also spelled *tuque* (Casselman 1995: 55) and pronounced to rhyme with *spook*, which was borrowed from French to refer to a closely fitting, knitted head-covering that others might call a ski hat. Canadian cold-weather gear might also include *Kamiks*: heavy, waterproof, felt-lined winter boots extending halfway to the knee. Like *Ski-Doo*, in southern Canada this is a commercial name, but it is derived from the Inuktitut word *kamik*, which refers to a traditional Inuit boot made of seal or caribou skin.

Canadians may share with Americans and Australians the use of *dollar* as a unit of currency, but when Canada recently replaced bills of small denomination with coins, Canadians evolved their own terms for the coins, which have become two of the most frequently used Canadianisms. The one-dollar coin, which Americans call a *silver dollar*, bore the image of a loon on its "tails"-side and came to be known in popular speech as a *loonie*. Canadian newspapers now speak of how the loonie is doing against the dollar in foreign exchange. Shortly after the one-dollar coin was introduced, a two-dollar coin followed, which bore the image of a polar bear; by analogy and blending, this became not a *bearie* but a *toonie*. While Canadians have adopted the popular

American words for smaller coins – nickels, dimes and quarters – as well as the slang term *buck* for *dollar*, loonies and toonies are uniquely Canadian.

If Canadian cuisine is far from renowned, many Canadianisms nevertheless relate to food and drink. Perhaps the most frequently used is *canola*, a blend of *Canada* and *-ola*, from Latin *oleum*, 'oil,' which is a type of rapeseed low in erucic acid that is used mainly to produce canola oil, a cooking oil valued for its health benefits (Casselman 1995: 70–71). American dictionaries include *canola* but give its origin as "a former certification mark" (*Merriam-Webster*), rather than as a Canadian blend; British dictionaries give only *rapeseed*. Another Canadian food term is *brown bread*, meaning bread made from wholewheat flour. When ordering a sandwich, a Canadian restaurant customer might be asked, "on white or brown?", where "white or wheat?" would be more common in an American restaurant. The British would refer to *wholemeal* bread, which does not occur in Canada, though the British *Oxford English Dictionary* also gives *brown* in the sense of bread made from wholewheat flour. Other Canadianisms in this semantic category have considerably less nutritional value than canola oil and brown bread. According to the *COD*, *back bacon*, called *Canadian bacon* by Americans, is "round, lean bacon cut from the eye of a pork loin"; a *butter tart* is "a tart with a filling of butter, eggs, brown sugar, and usually raisins"; a *Nanaimo bar*, named after a city in British Columbia, is "a dessert consisting of a crust of chocolate and cookie crumbs, usually also including coconut and nuts, covered with a usually vanilla buttercream filling and a chocolate glaze, served cut into squares"; and *poutine* (pronounced *poo-TEEN*), borrowed from Canadian French and originally a Quebec specialty but recently diffused to other parts of Canada, is "a dish of French fries topped with cheese curds and a sauce, usually gravy" (French *poutine*, in turn, was adapted from English *pudding*).

Turning to drink, Canada's most popular adult beverage, a type of lager beer based on central European models but stronger than its American counterpart, was traditionally sold in a short, fat bottle (a "squat brown bottle" – Atwood 1969: 159) known as a *stubby*, which was replaced in the 1980s by the slimmer, long-necked bottle used by American brewers. This has not stopped the stubby from retaining an iconic status for some Canadians, perhaps all the more poignant in that it represents a lost token of Canadian identity; for instance, it takes pride of place on the front cover of Douglas Coupland's photographic tribute to artifacts of Canadiana, *Souvenir of Canada* (2002; for his discussion of it, see p. 104). Back in the time of stubbies, beer might have been consumed in a *beer parlour* or *beverage room*, now largely obsolete Canadianisms that typically referred to the bar-room of a hotel. *Beer parlour* occurs widely in fiction, for instance in Atwood (1969: 262), Laurence (1974: 117), Mitchell (1947: 95, 96, 129), Watson (1959: 87, 90) and Wiebe (1984: 48, 106, 163); Atwood distinguishes between *beer parlour* and *tavern*, the latter presumably having a less specific meaning; *beer parlour* and *beverage room* appear as synonyms in Wiebe (1984: 111). A stronger and more distinctive Canadian alcoholic product is whisky: where the Scots and Irish make their whisky from barley and the Americans distill their bourbon mostly from corn, Canadian whisky, introduced to American customers by smugglers during the Prohibition period, is made from rye. In Canada, this whisky is simply called *rye*: popular mixed drinks for those who do not like their whisky straight are known as *rye and coke* and *rye and ginger (ale)*. In everyday Canadian speech, the word *rye* refers more often to the liquor than to the grain from which it is made, though, as in American English, it may also refer in a different context to bread (a sandwich *on rye*).

Some Canadianisms have arisen in particular regions of Canada, such as the Prairies, and continue to occur mostly in those regions. For instance, western Canadian farmers use the word *bluff*, which elsewhere means a steep bank or cliff, to refer to a grove or clump of trees (Nylvek 1993: 218–220; Scargill and Warkentyne 1972: 98). Margaret Laurence, writing about Manitoba, comments directly on this regionalism in *The Diviners*: "The small bluffs of scrub oak and poplar. In Ontario, bluff means something else – a ravine, a small precipice?" (1974: 282). The word *coulee*, which elsewhere means a flow of lava, was borrowed from Canadian French to refer in western North America to a deep ravine with steep sides, as throughout W. O. Mitchell's *Who Has Seen the Wind* (1947: 4, 33, 94, 117). Rain or melt water for irrigating crops or watering livestock is collected in a large, excavated pit called a *dugout* (Mitchell 1974: 257). A related word is *slough* (Mitchell 1947: 67, 287; Watson 1959: 45), which elsewhere means a marsh, but on the Canadian Prairies means a temporary pond of rain or melt water in a natural rather than excavated depression, which disappears during dry periods. It is pronounced to rhyme with *who* rather than with *how*, as it does elsewhere. Urban Prairie dwellers in Calgary walk between downtown office towers through a network of enclosed pedestrian overpasses called *plus-15s*, because of their location at 15 feet (4.5 m) above street-level. The model for such a network came from Minneapolis, another "winter city," but there they are called *skyways* or *skywalks*. Downtown Edmonton features a similar network that has both above- and underground components, called *pedways*, while pedestrians in Toronto and Montreal escape the winter cold and summer heat in vast underground tunnel networks, collectively known as the *PATH* in Toronto and the *Underground City*, a translation of French *Ville Souterraine*, in Montreal.

Ontario features another set of regional Canadianisms, such as *concession*, a tract of surveyed farmland, with its related forms *concession line* and *concession road*. *Hydro*, meaning *electricity* (as in *hydro bill* or *hydro lines*), is based on the use of hydroelectric power generation by the provincial power company, which is called Ontario Hydro (a similar usage occurs in other provinces, like Quebec, Manitoba and British Columbia, for the same reason). *Public school* can mean simply *elementary school* in Ontario, but also refers to the publicly funded non-denominational (originally Protestant) school system, as opposed to the publicly funded system for Roman Catholic students. The latter is called by another Canadianism, the *separate school* system. In Alberta and Saskatchewan, a *separate school* is one for students of the religious minority in a given district, whether Protestant or Catholic.

While some of the words just discussed belong to the most notable type of Canadianism – *beer parlour, bluff, brown bread, coulee, dugout, plus-15, stickhandling* (in its figurative sense) and *toque* are Canadian words for things that have other names in other dialects – others fall into the less notable category of words for things that are found only or mostly in Canada, for which other dialects have no equivalent term. As argued previously, *Nanaimo bars, poutine, snowbirds* and *toonies* are distinctly Canadian things more than distinctly Canadian words. The same might be said of a number of words connected with Canadian history and no longer in general use, like *coureurs de bois, voyageurs, York boats, Red River carts* and *Bennett buggies*; or of things named after Canada, like the *Canada goose, Canada jay, Canada lynx* or *Canada thistle*; or of words associated with Canadian institutions, like the *United Church*, Canada's largest Protestant denomination, formed in 1925 by a merger of Methodists, Congregationalists and most Presbyterians, or the Royal Canadian Mounted Police, whose officers are informally called *Mounties*. Other words are Canadian by virtue of the things they describe having been invented or developed in Canada, like the *McIntosh apple*, the *Robertson* square-slotted screw head or the *snowmobile*; Casselman (1995) gives several further examples, like the Anik communications satellite, the Imax™ film projection system, insulin, kerosene and the Wonderbra™ brassiere (17–22, 56).

Finally, there are some expressions, phrases and discourse particles that are typically or distinctly Canadian, such as the greeting, *how's it goin'?*, roughly equivalent to the American *how ya doin'?* or the Australian *g'day*. Another vernacular Canadian phrase, featured prominently in the movie *FUBAR*, is *give 'er*, meaning to make a sincere and enthusiastic effort at something, possibly a shortening of *give 'er what you got*, or *give 'er your best shot*, etc., with the sense of *her* employed by workmen referring to things they are working on. *He was just givin' 'er* means he was going full out or trying his hardest. However, by far the best-known nationally characteristic phrase in Canadian English, having reached the status of a stereotype among Americans, is the tag *eh?*, added to the end of a sentence (Woods 1999: 187–189; Gregg 2004: 100–103; Gold and Tremblay 2006; Gold 2008). While many dialects outside Canada use *eh?* to solicit the addressee's agreement with what was said, as in *that's too bad, eh?*, or *looks like rain, eh?*, its use in Canada extends to soliciting confirmation of the addressee's having understood what was said, as in giving explanations, instructions or directions: *I have to go now or I'm gonna miss my bus, eh?*; *move the table over there, eh?, so people can get by*; *go two blocks south and turn left at the lights, eh?, then you'll see the gas station on your right*; etc. This type of *eh?*, which might correspond to *okay?* or *right?* or *yuh?* or *you know?* or *know what I mean?* in other dialects, occurs throughout Margaret Laurence's *The Diviners* (1974: 60, 170, 175, 322, 341, 366); for example, "Now listen here, Catherine, don't bug me today, eh?" (170); "if I'd known before I was married what I know now, I'd have had some fun, eh?" (175); and "Listen, Jules, just don't tell me what to do, eh?" (341).

To summarize the comparative status of the vocabulary of Canadian English, it may be said that, where British and American English differ, Canadian English inclines usually toward American forms; that the language brought by American and British settlers was transferred to Canada largely intact, without a significant degree of differentiation caused by contact with Canadian Aboriginal languages (or with French); and that the number of true Canadianisms, which is to say Canadian words for things that have other names in other dialects, is small, but nonetheless adequate for asserting the status of Canadian English as an identifiable dialect at the lexical level – a distinct type of North American English.

3.2   Canadian English pronunciation

This section will treat three distinct types of variation in pronunciation:

(a) variation in phonemic inventory, or in the number and nature of phonemic distinctions made in a dialect;
(b) variation in phonemic incidence, or in the phonemes that occur in phonetically defined sets of words (systematic variation) or in particular words (lexically specific variation);
(c) variation in the phonetic realization of phonemes.

Since the first two types of variation can generally be effectively represented in conventional orthography, they have been extensively investigated in the past with written dialect questionnaires. A questionnaire respondent can be asked whether two words, such as *cot* and *caught*, sound the same or different, the answer indicating the presence or absence of a phonemic distinction; or whether a word like *shone* rhymes with *gone* or *bone*, the answer indicating which phoneme occurs in the word of interest. Data from previous surveys of Canadian English will therefore be referred to in the discussions of phonemic inventory and phonemic incidence, along with data from acoustic phonetic studies that bear on phonemic inventory. The third type of variation cannot be effectively studied with written questionnaires, since phonetic variation, by its very nature, cannot be represented in conventional orthography: it requires instead a set of phonetic symbols unknown to non-linguists. Data on phonetic variation will therefore come from impressionistic and acoustic phonetic studies, a separate body of research from the tradition of written questionnaires.

As in the previous section, comparisons will be made between Standard Canadian, Standard British and Standard American English (SCE, SBE and SAE, respectively); comparisons with non-standard regional dialects of British and American English will be made only where appropriate. The identity of SCE was discussed above, while that of SBE is straightforward, being the variety known as Received Pronunciation, which is based historically on the regional variety of southeastern England, particularly London. The identity of SAE is more complex and problematic, as it is not explicitly codified in the same way as Received Pronunciation. For purposes of this analysis, it will be taken to comprise the varieties of American English not generally associated by most Americans with specific regions or groups. It therefore excludes the traditional dialects associated with eastern New England (Boston), New York City, the South and the African American population. SAE pronunciation is generally associated instead with the Midland and western regions of the United States: from west of the Appalachians and north of the Ohio River all the way to the Pacific coast (Labov, Ash and Boberg 2006: 148). An important exception to this regional identification is the area immediately adjacent to the Great Lakes, known as the Inland North, from Rochester and Buffalo, New York, in the east, through Cleveland and Detroit, to Chicago and Milwaukee in the west. Though less prominent than other regions in the popular construal of American regional speech, the pronunciation of the Inland North is characterized by the Northern Cities Shift, a set of changes in the pronunciation of vowels that differentiates it just as sharply from SAE as other "regional" dialects (Labov, Yaeger and Steiner 1972; Labov 1991: 14–20; Eckert 1989; Labov, Ash and Boberg 2006: 187–212). For purposes of comparison, then, we will treat SAE as the variety most often heard among the European-American residents of cities like Columbus, Cincinnati, Indianapolis, St. Louis, Kansas City, Denver, Phoenix, Seattle, San Francisco and Los Angeles, as well as Orlando, Tampa and Miami. Increasingly, this type of English can also be heard among many younger and middle-class residents of other regions, from Dallas, Houston and Atlanta to Washington, New York City, Philadelphia and Boston, as strongly marked regional varieties give way to SAE at higher social levels. Since the intent of the present discussion is a comparative analysis of Canadian English, not an examination of regional differences in American speech, regional and social varieties of American English other than SAE will be set aside, except in specific instances.

3.2.1　*Variation in phonemic inventory*

Differentiation of national varieties of English in terms of phonemic inventory mainly concerns vowels rather than consonants: there are no systematic differences between the consonant inventory of SCE and that of either SBE or SAE. The most important variable of phonemic inventory in the modern English consonant system is (wh), the contrast between voiced and voiceless /w/, or /w/ and /hw/, in pairs like *weather* and *whether*, *wine* and *whine* or *witch* and *which*. All three of the standard dialects under consideration here have lost this distinction, having voiced /w/ in both members of each pair; the contrast survives only among a conservative minority of speakers in the United States and Canada (Labov, Ash and Boberg 2006: 50; see also Table 3.16 below), as well as in some regional British dialects. While Avis found the contrast still slightly predominant half a century ago in Ontario (1956: 53), three decades later he commented on its regression among younger speakers (1983: 13). Gregg (1957a: 26; 2004: 49) noted its loss in Vancouver and Chambers (1998c: 26), Scargill and Warkentye (1972: 71) and Woods (1991: 142–143; 1993: 169; 1999: 138) report mergers for the majority of their participants, with the frequency advancing in apparent time. Woods (1991: 142) suggests that heavy Scottish and Irish settlement in the Ottawa region may account for unusually frequent retention of the contrast in his data. Clarke (2004a: 378; 2008: 101) indicates a merger in Newfoundland.

Turning to vowel contrasts, four major inventory variables serve to differentiate regional varieties within Britain and North America. Of these, three distinguish SCE and SAE from SBE. Using the standard lexical sets of Wells (1982) and the broad phonemic transcription of Labov, Ash and Boberg (2006), the four variables can be identified as follows:

Wells (1982)	Labov, Ash and Boberg (2006)
FOOT VS. STRUT	/u/ vs. /ʌ/
TRAP VS. BATH	/æ/ vs. /æh/
LOT VS. THOUGHT	/o/ vs. /oh/
PALM VS. LOT	/ah/ vs. /o/

The first variable involves the historical split of Middle English short /u/, whereby some tokens of /u/ were lowered and unrounded to modern /ʌ/ (Wells' STRUT class), while others remained in non-peripheral high-back position, retaining /u/ (Wells' FOOT class). This change was complete in southern British English by the mid seventeenth century (Wyld 1925: 232), but it never affected northern British English, in which both FOOT and STRUT retain /u/, so that *look* and *luck*, or *book* and *buck*, are homophones. Its relatively early date meant that the split of /u/ was transferred to North America (as to Australia and New Zealand) with initial English-speaking settlement. It has since spread across the continent: despite the heavy emigration from northern Britain to Canada discussed in Chapter 2 (Section 2.3), SCE shares the FOOT–STRUT split with both SAE and SBE.

The second variable concerns the split of another Middle English vowel, short /a/. Like the split of /u/, this occurred only in southern Britain, but it happened somewhat later. As discussed in Chapter 2 (Section 2.6), short /a/ was lengthened before voiceless fricatives (BATH) in the eighteenth century and then retracted to modern /ah/ in the nineteenth (Lass 2006: 89), while the remaining short /a/ (TRAP) stayed in low-front position, having been fronted to modern /æ/ in the mid seventeenth century (Lass 2006: 86). Thus, in modern SBE, TRAP has /æ/ while BATH has /ah/. While the fronting of TRAP to /æ/ was early enough to have been exported with the initial settlement of all of the new English-speaking societies, the lengthening and backing of BATH was not, being generally adopted only in the southern hemisphere. In North America, the split and lengthening affected the older dialects along the eastern seaboard but never penetrated inland to the expanding frontier of English-speaking settlement. In coastal New England, the lengthened vowel remained in low-front position, [ba:θ], while in the Mid-Atlantic region, rather than moving back to /ah/, as in London, it was raised to mid-front position, developing an inglide, /æh/. Thus, in New York City and Philadelphia, TRAP has /æ/ while BATH has /æh/, the latter having a phonetic value something like [ɛə] (the split and its phonetic consequences are examined in detail by Labov (1972: 73–77; 1994: 334–335)). Labov, Ash and Boberg (2006: 223) found traces of this Mid-Atlantic feature in Maritime Canada, where it may be a survival of the Loyalist speech brought to that region in the eighteenth century (see also Chapter 5). Beyond the Atlantic coast, the split gives way to a single phoneme. In the Inland North, this phoneme is /æh/: both TRAP and BATH have a lengthened, raised and ingliding pronunciation. In the remaining inland regions (the domain of SAE), both sets have /æ/, a short, low-front vowel, with raising restricted to certain phonetic environments, especially before nasal consonants. SCE therefore shares with SAE the lack of a distinction between TRAP and BATH, which differentiates both varieties from SBE (but not from northern British English). Canadian /æ/ in the BATH class is reported in Vancouver by Gregg (1957a: 22), on the Prairies and in northwestern Ontario by Allen (1976: vol. 3, 39–41, 156–157), in southern Ontario by Avis (1956: 52), in Montreal by Hamilton (1958: 75) and in Newfoundland by Drysdale (1959: 32) and Clarke (2004a: 370; 2008: 95–96).

The third variable of phonemic inventory concerns not a split but a merger. By the mid seventeenth century, Middle English short /o/ (the LOT class) had descended to low-back position, [ɒ] (Lass 2006: 86). In southern England, short /o/ advanced farther into low-central position with associated unrounding, [ɑ̈] (Wyld 1925: 240), a pronunciation that became established in colonial North American English. In the eighteenth century, SBE reverted to a more conservative, fully rounded, lower-mid-back variant (Wyld 1925: 242), which was exported to Australia and New Zealand; in Britain, the low-central unrounded variant is now confined to southwestern regional speech. In its new lowered position, short /o/ had to be distinguished from a long vowel, /oh/ (THOUGHT), in the same quadrant of the vowel space. This was derived from monophthongization of Middle English /aw/ (hawk, saw, etc.) in the fifteenth century (Wyld 1925: 252), some of which came from diphthongization of /a/ before /l/ (hall, ball, etc.; Wyld 1925: 201), and from an earlier loss of Middle English /h/ before /t/ (*caught*, *thought*, etc.; Wyld 1925: 305). These subclasses formed the core of the modern THOUGHT class, which had a phonetic value something like [ɔ:]. To them were later added words with short /o/ before voiceless fricatives (Wells' CLOTH set), which tended to lengthen, in parallel with the development of short /a/ in the same environment. These transfers from /o/ to /oh/ – words like *cost*, *cough* and *froth* (Wyld 1925: 257) – became standard in American English but were reversed or never took hold in SBE, which retains short /o/ in the CLOTH class, the variant that was exported to Australia and New Zealand.

Given the proximity of /o/ and /oh/ in the low-back quadrant of the vowel space and the tendency of North American English to rely on quality rather than quantity as the basis for vowel distinctions, the two vowels have tended to merge in many dialects. In Britain, as discussed in Chapter 2, this has happened only in Scotland and parts of northern Ireland, but in North America the low-back merger has been more widespread. In the tradition of structural dialectology, Labov, Ash and Boberg (2006: 123), following Labov (1991), show that many of the most salient phonetic differences among English dialects can be understood as stemming from different strategies for resisting the low-back merger. It is avoided in SBE and in Mid-Atlantic varieties of American English by raising /oh/ to mid-back position, where it develops an inglide and contrasts clearly with /o/. In the southern United States, where /aw/ MOUTH is fronted to /æw/, the low-back merger is avoided by diphthongizing /oh/ to /aw/, with a back upglide. In the Inland North, where /æ/ has been lengthened and raised to /æh/, the merger is avoided by fronting /o/ to low-central or even low-front position, [a], where it contrasts with a lowered and unrounded but low-back /oh/ (the Northern Cities Shift). Where it has not been prevented by one of these three developments, the low-back merger has occurred: in eastern New England, western Pennsylvania, the American West and Canada. It is also now in progress in many of the remaining areas, wherever resistance to it is not structurally reinforced: in western New England, Florida, Texas and the American Midland (Labov, Ash and Boberg 2006: 61). This suggests that SCE and SAE can be characterized as sharing the low-back merger of /o/ and /oh/, or LOT and THOUGHT, in contrast with the retention of this distinction in some American regional dialects and in SBE. In SCE, then, pairs of words like *cot* and *caught*, *stock* and *stalk*, *Don* and *dawn*, and *collar* and *caller*, are homophones.

The final variable of phonemic inventory involves another merger. As Early Modern English short /o/ descended, advanced and unrounded, it came very close to /ah/ (PALM), a long, low-central, unrounded vowel. Because most Middle English long /a:/ had been raised to modern /ey/ (FACE) in the Great Vowel Shift, only a small and irregular class remained in low position as /ah/, including the word *father* and old short /a/ before /-lm/ (*balm*, *calm*, *palm*, *psalm*), which lengthened as /l/ was vocalized, plus a few others. In SBE, this marginal class was greatly supplemented by the lengthening of short /a/: the BATH class is now added to the PALM class, thereby alleviating its marginal character. It later received a further supplement from vocalization of /r/ in the START class (*farther* = *father*), making SBE /ah/ a large class indeed. Its independence from short /o/ was assured when the lower-mid-back, rounded articulation of that vowel was restored, making LOT and PALM/BATH/START clearly different in SBE, in both quantity and quality. In North America, where the advancement and unrounding of /o/ was not reversed and the marginality of the PALM class was not overcome by the addition of BATH words, the two vowels tended to merge. Today, /o/ and /ah/ (*bomb* and *balm*; *bother* and *father*) are merged for most North Americans, including most Canadians. The only place where the merger was systematically avoided was eastern New England, where BATH words joined the PALM class as in SBE, but where /o/ is merged instead with /oh/. Thus, we can say that SCE and SAE share the merger of /o/ and /ah/, or LOT and PALM, in contrast to the retention of this distinction in SBE, even if the phonetic position of the /o-ah/ merger varies widely across North America, from low-central in the Inland North to low-back in Canada. This phonetic variation reflects the presence or absence of the merger of /o/ and /oh/. In the Inland North and Mid-Atlantic regions of the United States, /o/ and /ah/ are merged in low-central position but both are distinct from /oh/ in lower-mid-back position. In Canada, as in some parts of the United States, all three vowels are merged in the low-back quadrant, with more retracted qualities in Canada and more advanced qualities in the American West. This double-merger can be labeled /ah-o-oh/.

The low-back merger was well established, at least in many parts of Canada, by the mid twentieth century. It was noted at that time in Ontario English by Joos (1942: 141), in Vancouver by Gregg (1957a: 21–22) and in Saskatchewan by Lehn (1959: 93). The observations of Ahrend (1934: 137–138) on the distribution of rounded and unrounded low-back vowels in Ontario English imply a merger in the early twentieth century, though the question is not addressed directly; further evidence of merger in this period comes from Scott (1939). In fact, Chambers (1993: 11–12; 2008: 11–13) cites textual evidence that suggests it was established as early as the mid nineteenth century in Ontario and may indeed have been brought to Canada by Loyalists from merged areas of the United States (see also Dollinger forthcoming). However that may be (an alternative possibility of importation from Scotland and northern Ireland was discussed in Chapter 2), Allen's records for five speakers in rural parts of northwestern Ontario, Manitoba and Saskatchewan, collected in 1949–1950, suggest the merger was still incomplete in some areas at mid-century. In the phonetic transcriptions given in his synopses (1976: vol. 3, 39–41, 156–157), the word *crop*, in the LOT class, is usually transcribed with [ɑ], whereas *daughter* and *law*, in the THOUGHT class, have [ɒ] or [ɔ]. Kurath and McDavid's records from southern and eastern Ontario, collected around the same time, also suggest a distinction, with unrounded, low-back to low-central vowels for *oxen* (LOT) in map 15 against rounded, low-back to lower-mid-back vowels for *law* in map 22 (1961). However, apart from the difficulty of making inferences about phonemic status from purely phonetic data on only one word for each vowel, the accuracy of Kurath and McDavid's records is questionable, given that they generally show the same vowel qualities for Ontario and western New York, two regions that show very wide phonetic divergence today, as will be shown below. Indeed, the Toronto woman analyzed by Thomas (2001: 60), born in 1927, shows a merger, while Kurath and McDavid's own data on *daughter* (map 129), for which they show low, unrounded vowels in Ontario, indicate the same quality as in *oxen*.

A generation after its initial observation by linguists, Avis (1973: 64) suggests the merger is found nationwide, while Scargill and Warkentyne (1972: 64) report that *cot* and *caught* rhyme all across Canada, with the exception of Newfoundland. There, a minority of survey respondents (24–33%) claimed to make a distinction. This variation probably reflects the unstable situation described earlier by Drysdale (1959: 32), who found a near-merger, in which "Some speakers are unaware that they distinguish between [/oh/ and /o/], though the difference is clearly audible"; Drysdale further says that /oh/ is distinguished from /o/ by "greater length (though this may not be distinctive) and a closer and tenser tongue position, though rounding remains slight." Thomas (2001: 62) suggests a similarly marginal distinction for the single Newfoundlander he analyzes, showing separate means for the two vowels but noting that they are distinguished "mainly by length." Kirwin (1993: 74–75) reports a merger for the Irish-influenced speech of the Avalon Peninsula, as does Clarke (2004a: 371; 2008: 95–96) for Newfoundland English generally. A similar situation of merger in progress was observed by Pringle, Jones and Padolsky (1981: 173) in the rural region around Ottawa, though Ottawa itself showed a completed merger. In the *Atlas of North American English*, all of Canada except Newfoundland lies within the isogloss enclosing the main continental area of low-back merger (Labov, Ash and Boberg 2006: 60–61). Of the individual vowel systems analyzed by the author and presented at the end of Chapter 5, those from Newfoundland and Nova Scotia show a residual phonemic distinction between /o/ and /oh/, while those from central and western Canada show completed mergers.

The merger of /o/ and /ah/ is less clearly attested in earlier accounts. While Joos claims that *bomb* and *balm* are "identical" in Ontario (1942: 79), Gregg describes *balm* and *father* in Vancouver English as having an "open back vowel" that is distinguished from the /o/ of *bomb* and *bother* (also, confusingly, an "open back vowel") by an absence of lip-rounding, which is nevertheless qualified as "slight" in the latter case (1957a: 22). In the *Survey of Canadian English*, Scargill and Warkentyne report that only 55–63 percent of Canadians claimed that *father* is "pronounced like" *bother*,

Table 3.5 *Status of five phonemic distinctions in Standard British, American and Canadian English. Parentheses indicate dialect variation*

Distinction	SBE	SAE	SCE
/hw/ ≠ /w/ (*whine* ≠ *wine*)	NO	NO	NO
FOOT /u/ ≠ STRUT /ʌ/	YES	YES	YES
TRAP /æ/ ≠ BATH /ah, æh/	YES	NO	NO
LOT /o/ ≠ THOUGHT /oh/	YES	(NO)	NO
PALM /ah/ ≠ LOT /o/	YES	NO	NO

though it is far from clear how well the remainder distinguished between the vowel of *bother* and that of *farm*, the main alternative (1972: 59). When asked about *calm*, 54–77 percent said it is pronounced like *bomb*, with the apparent-time pattern in favor of the merger. Allen's phonetic transcriptions, perhaps more reliable than self-report data though without explicit reference to phonemic contrast, show the same vowel, [ɑ], in *father* and *crop* for his five western Canadian subjects (1976: vol. 3, 39–41, 156–157). As will be shown below, acoustic analysis of the speech of today's young Canadians suggests a complete merger.

There is, however, a further complication in the case of the PALM class in Canadian English. Though this class has /ah/ in all modern standard dialects, in some non-standard dialects it followed the regular development of short /a/, with fronting to /æ/ and subsequent loss of /l/. As shown in map 77 of Kurath and McDavid (1961), /kæm/ and /pæm/ for *calm* and *palm* did occur among some speakers in the American Midland and South and in Canada. Avis (1956: 52) suggested it was found only among "uneducated" speakers in Ontario but it may once have been more general there, as implied by Kinloch and Avis (1989: 411) and by Scargill and Warkentyne (1972: 59), who report that 20–28 percent of parents but only 12–16 percent of children likened the pronunciation of *calm* more to that of *Sam* than to that of *farm* or *bomb*. Allen (1976) shows [æ] for three of the four western Canadian subjects for whom he transcribed the word *palm*. It is also well attested in Newfoundland English (Drysdale 1959: 32; Kirwin 1993: 74; Clarke 2004a: 372; Clarke 2008: 96). Nonetheless, as will be seen below, there is no evidence of this in SCE today, which shows the PALM class merged with LOT and THOUGHT, not with TRAP.

The discussion in this section can be summarized by presenting the five variables of phonemic inventory in Table 3.5, with indications of their status in the three standard dialects under consideration. It is immediately apparent that, as in the lexical domain, SCE shares more with SAE than with SBE, being essentially identical to SAE in terms of the major phonemic distinctions examined here: SAE and SCE are lacking three phonemic distinctions found in SBE. The complete inventory of fourteen stressed SCE vowels is given

Table 3.6 *The fourteen stressed vowel phonemes of Standard Canadian English, with subclasses and broad transcriptional symbols of Labov, Ash and Boberg (2006) and lexical sets of Wells (1982)*

| | Long vowels (Vx) | | |
Short vowels (V)	Front upglides (Vy)	Back upglides (Vw)	Monophthongs (Vh)
/i/ KIT	/iy/ FLEECE	/iw/ *few*	/ah-o-oh/ PALM,
/e/ DRESS	/ey/ FACE	/uw/ GOOSE	LOT, CLOTH,
/æ/ TRAP, BATH	/ay/ PRICE	/ow/ GOAT	THOUGHT
/ʌ/ STRUT	/oy/ VOICE	/aw/ MOUTH	
/u/ PUT			

in Table 3.6, using both the subclasses and broad transcriptional practice of Labov, Ash and Boberg (2006) and the lexical sets of Wells (1982). The reduction under tertiary stress of all vowels to a mid-central quality, [ə], as in Wells' keyword *comm*A, characterizes all English dialects and will not be considered here; its status as a fifteenth phoneme is debatable. Vowels before /r/, which in a strict phonemic analysis can all be considered sequences of one of the phonemes in Table 3.6 followed by an /r/, will be examined below. The vowel of *few*, *new*, *due* and *cube*, in contrast to that of *food*, *noon*, *do* and *goose*, is analyzed here (as in Labov, Ash and Boberg 2006: 12) as a separate phoneme, /iw/, normally pronounced [ju], which will also be discussed further below. It is not so analyzed by Wells, who uses the keyword CURE to represent both words like *cure* and words like *poor*. The example *few* is therefore used instead in Table 3.6.

3.2.2 Variation in phonemic incidence: systematic variables

Two types of variation in phonemic incidence will be considered here: systematic variation caused by conditioned mergers, in which phonemic contrasts are neutralized in certain phonetic environments, affecting large sets of words; and variation of a more miscellaneous character, reflecting nothing more than differential distribution of phonemes in particular words, without any phonological significance. Several variables of the former type are linked to what is undoubtedly the most salient difference in phonemic incidence among varieties of English: the presence or absence of non-prevocalic or coda /r/. The tendency of coda /r/ to weaken or be vocalized or lost has a long and complex history in English, beginning in the fifteenth century (Wyld 1925: 298) but not completed until the nineteenth (Lass 2006: 92) and then only in certain areas, including southeastern England, the regional basis of SBE. The details of this history are of no concern here: suffice it to say that, like the split of short /a/, this change was too late to establish itself in the initial development of American English. By the time it entered the fashionable speech of the cities along the Atlantic seaboard, the older, *r*-ful pattern had

Table 3.7 *Prerhotic vowel mergers in Standard Canadian English, with broad transcriptional symbols of Labov, Ash and Boberg (2006), words exemplifying vowels before intervocalic /r/ from Wells (1982: 289) and lexical sets of Wells (1982)*

Vowel	Example	Merged with	Lexical set
/ir-/	spirit	/iyr/	NEAR
/er-/	herald	/eyr/	SQUARE
/ær-/	carrot	/eyr/	SQUARE
/or-/	sorry	/owr/	NORTH, FORCE
/ʌr-/	hurry	/ɝ/	NURSE

already spread inland, including into Canada with the Loyalist migration. There it awaited its eventual triumph in the twentieth century, following World War II, as the social evaluation of *r*-less speech was reversed (Labov 1972: 136, 145): no longer fashionable, it became associated with stereotypes of snobby Boston, grubby Brooklyn, or Old South gentility. The new American standard was decidedly *r*-ful, in marked contrast to SBE. This applied equally to Canada, which had never had any significant degree of (r) deletion in popular speech to begin with, except in a few enclaves (see Emeneau (1935: 143–144) for Lunenburg, Nova Scotia, and Clarke (2004a: 377; 2008: 102) for Newfoundland). Preservation of coda /r/, then, is one more feature that unites SCE and SAE.

While /r/ vocalization in SBE creates homophones like *father–farther* and *saw–sore*, /r/ retention in SCE has had similarly important consequences for its phonology, since the tongue position required for /r/-constriction tends to limit the number of possible vowel contrasts that can be maintained before the /r/. *R*-fulness has caused several conditioned mergers that have a significant effect on the sound of both SCE and SAE, in contrast to *r*-less dialects of American and British English (Trudgill and Hannah 1985: 37–38). These are listed in Table 3.7, using the transcriptional system of Labov, Ash and Boberg (2006) and the lexical sets of Wells (1982), plus the words used by Wells (1982: 289) to exemplify vowels before intervocalic /r/. The affected environments are before what is best analyzed as an ambisyllabic /r/, which occupies both the coda of the preceding syllable and the onset of the following syllable. In *r*-less dialects, the preceding vowel is not prerhotic, since the coda /r/ is not constricted, allowing a full range of vowel contrasts to be maintained before the onset /r/ of the following syllable. In *r*-ful dialects, the coda /r/ is constricted, introducing the same constraints on the occurrence of vowels before intervocalic /r/ as apply before final /r/, essentially excluding the short vowels. Most of these mergers require qualification and comment.

The merger of /ir/ and /iyr/ in *spirit* and *spear* or *mirror* and *nearer* is variable: some Canadians maintain this contrast, but Gregg (1957a: 22) reports a merger in Vancouver. That of the mid and low front vowels is less variable, at least in the part of Canada where it applies. While all of Canada shows a merger of /er/ and /eyr/, or *ferry* and *fairy*, Montreal and Newfoundland are striking exceptions to the merger of /ær/ and /er-eyr/, or *marry* and *merry/Mary*. These regions retain the vowel sound of *mat* and *cat* in *marry* and *carrot*, etc. (For Montreal, see Boberg (2004c: 550–551) and Figure 5.8 in Chapter 5; for Newfoundland, see Clarke (2004a: 375; 2008: 100); for both regions, see Boberg (2008: 142–143) and Labov, Ash and Boberg (2006: 56, 219).) Not too long ago, the *marry–merry* merger may have been less general in Canada: while Kurath and McDavid (1961: map 51) show /er/ in *married* in Ontario (also recorded by Ahrend 1934: 137), Allen (1976: 39–41, 156–157) indicates distinct vowels in *marry* and *merry* for all five of his speakers farther west; Gregg (1957a: 22) reports the merger only among "some speakers" in Vancouver; Woods (1993: 168; 1999: 126–131) shows an equal split of merged and distinct participants in Ottawa, though with the distinction losing ground among younger participants; and Pringle, Jones and Padolsky (1981: 172) found the rural areas around Ottawa to be following the urban lead toward the merger. Avis (1983: 13) notes the merger as an age difference between his own generation and the next.

The merger of /or/ and /owr/ in *sorry* and *sore* is virtually complete in Canada: few Canadians retain the normal quality of /o/, LOT, before intervocalic /r/, as confirmed in Ottawa by Woods (1999: 148–151). Nor do most speakers of SAE, except in a small set of words that have resisted the merger, like *sorry*, *borrow* and *tomorrow* (for *tomorrow*, see Kurath and McDavid 1961: map 53). Other words in the same lexical set, like *forest*, *horrible* and *orange*, remain distinct only in *r*-less dialects (for *orange*, see Kurath and McDavid 1961: map 54). The extension in SCE of the merger even to the exceptional class is remarkable to American listeners: saying *sore-ry* for *sorry* is a true Canadianism, first noted by Ahrend (1934: 138). In respect of /owr/, it should be mentioned that SCE shares with both SAE and SBE the loss of the distinction between /ohr/ and /owr/, or *horse* and *hoarse, for* and *four* (Wells' NORTH and FORCE sets).

Finally, while it has attracted little notice in previous studies, most Canadians have also lost the distinction between /ʌr-/, in *hurry*, and /ɝ/, in *her*: where speakers of *r*-less dialects retain the lower and more open vowel of *hut* in *hurry*, Canadians have the fully centralized and *r*-colored vowel of *her*. The consequence of all of these mergers is that SCE has the inventory of six prerhotic vowels shown in Table 3.8.

Table 3.8 also requires some clarification. In a strict phonemic analysis, all of the prerhotic vowels it contains can be seen as sequences of one of the fourteen vowels of Table 3.6 followed by /r/, with only allophonic differences in sound: these are not additional phonemes. Despite the transcriptional symbols used, /ɝ/ (NURSE, hurry) can be seen as the prerhotic allophone of /ʌ/, even if its phonetic value is closer to [ɝ] than to [ʌɹ], while /ahr/ is the prerhotic allophone of the double-merger low-back phoneme, /ah-o-oh/, even if START and LOT words have different vowel sounds in SCE. The latter

Table 3.8 *The six prerhotic vowels of Standard Canadian English, with broad transcriptional symbols of Labov, Ash and Boberg (2006), lexical sets of Wells (1982) and words exemplifying vowels before intervocalic /r/ from Wells (1982: 289)*

	Front	Central	Back
High	/iyr/ NEAR, spirit		(/uwr/ poor)
Mid	/eyr/ SQUARE, herald, carrot	/ɝ/ NURSE, hurry	/owr/ NORTH, FORCE, sorry
Low		/ahr/ START	

classification reflects the fact that the historic instances of /o–oh/ before /r/ are now associated with /owr/ in SCE, as shown in Table 3.7, while /ahr/ is implicated in the more general merger of /ah/ and /o/. Though most START words are derived historically from a lowering of Middle English /er/, in American English they have become identified with /or/. That is, American dialects that retain /or/ in *forest, orange, sorry* but have a merger of /o/ and /ah/ have the same vowel in *sorry* words as in START words: *forest* has the same vowel as *far*, and *sorry* and *sari*, the Indian garment, are homophones. While Canadian /ah-o-oh/ is phonetically lower and farther back than /ahr/, the allophonic relation still applies. The parentheses around /uwr/, *poor*, are intended to convey variability: some Canadians maintain a distinction between /uwr/ in *boor, poor, tour* and sometimes also *cure, pure, sure* and /owr/ in *bore, pour, tore, core* and *shore*. Others have /owr/ in *boor, poor* and *tour*, so that *poor* sounds the same as *pour*, and /ɝ/ in *cure, pure* and *sure*, which rhyme with *her*, though these are not necessarily the same people; still others have /owr/ in all of these words. The lowering of /uwr/ to merge with /owr/ is most characteristic of Atlantic Canada, particularly Newfoundland, as noted by Clarke (2004a: 374–375; 2008: 100).

Another systematic variable of phonemic incidence that reflects a conditioned merger and governs the sound of a large set of words in SCE is the neutralization of the distinction between /iw/ and /uw/ after the coronal consonants /t/, /d/ and /n/, so that *dew, due* and *do* all sound the same, and words like *new, student* and *Tuesday* have the same vowel as *noon, stool* and *tooth*. As the spelling of these words suggests, this variable involves two historically different sounds: /iw/, now pronounced [ju], is the reflex both of Middle English /ew/ and related classes (*dew, new, Tuesday*) and of the foreign vowel /y/ in words borrowed from French or Latin (*due, nuisance, student*), while /uw/ is the reflex of Middle English long /oː/, raised to [uː] in the Great English Vowel Shift. While speakers of all standard English dialects distinguish these vowels after labials and velars (*beauty* ≠ *boot*; *cute* ≠ *coot*), most have lost the contrast after /l/, /r/ and /s/ (*lute* = *loot*; *rude* = *rood*; *super* = *soup*) and many have lost it also after the remaining coronals, /t/, /d/ and /n/. The last group excludes speakers of SBE, who retain /iw/ in *new*, *student* and *Tuesday*, but includes most speakers of North American varieties of English, especially outside the South (Labov, Ash and Boberg 2006: 53–55; see also Table 3.16 below), thereby establishing another common, continental feature of North American English.

The conditioned merger of /iw/ and /uw/ after coronals, also called *yod-dropping* (Chambers 1998c: 17–19) or *palatal glide usage* (Clarke 1993b), has been widely studied in Canada. Avis describes Ontario usage as "very much divided and unsettled," with a majority of his participants preserving /iw/ in *Tuesday*, *news* and *dew*, but only half retaining it in *duke*, *tune*, *due* and *student* (1956: 48). This divided usage was confirmed in many later studies: by Gregg (2004: 46–48) in Vancouver; Nylvek (1992: 273–275) in Saskatchewan; Chambers (1998b: 235–244; 1998c: 17–19) in greater Toronto; Woods (1991: 140–141; 1993: 158–159; 1999: 93–96) in Ottawa; Hamilton (1958: 75) and Boberg (2004d: 264) in Montreal; Clarke (1993b, 2006) in St. John's; and Scargill and Warkentyne (1972: 51–52) across Canada.

Nonetheless, if Canadian usage was still divided in the mid to late twentieth century, it was equally clear in all of these studies that the direction of change was toward the more North American pronunciation with /uw/. Chambers (1998b: 242; 1998c: 19) shows the frequency of /uw/ to be 50–60 percent among his oldest participants but 90 percent among his youngest. These data suggest that, in the absence of a sudden reversal, /iw/ will be obsolete after coronals in SCE, as in SAE, within two generations. Where it is retained, /iw/ sometimes causes affrication of the preceding coronal stop in SCE, so that the first syllable of *Tuesday* sounds like *choose* and *dual* and *jewel* are homophones. The unglided North American variant actually has a longer history in Canada than some might suspect: a century ago, when Stephen Leacock, in *Sunshine Sketches of a Little Town*, wanted to portray Josh Smith, the owner of a hotel in a small Ontario town, as a burly and somewhat intimidating yet popular local type, he had him say, "just wait till I get the license renood . . . " (1912: 17) and "Take them signs . . . out of the bar. Put up noo ones . . . ," indicating that he was not the sort to be troubled with the fussy business of distinguishing /iw/ from /uw/.

A final systematic variable of phonemic incidence concerns a consonant rather than a vowel: this is the phonetic process known as *flapping*, or lenition of post-tonic, intervocalic and postrhotic /t/, which has been widely studied as a characteristic feature of North American English, distinguishing it from SBE. Flapping will be treated in this section because, though primarily a phonetic process, it can have phonological consequences to the extent that its output is phonetically indistinguishable from /d/, thereby causing a conditioned merger of /t/ and /d/. Some North American speakers report that pairs of words like *shutter* and *shudder*, *plotted* and *plodded*, or *hurtle* and *hurdle* are homophones, both having either [d] or [ɾ], while others insist they maintain a difference, with [ɾ] for /t/ and [d] for /d/. In their humorous account of Canadian speech, Orkin and Bickerstaff indicate a full merger with respellings like *Albirda* for *Alberta*, *Briddish* for *British* and *Oddawa* for *Ottawa* (1997: 16, 29, 99). In any case, if not altogether neutralized, the voicing distinction between /t/ and /d/ is greatly reduced in post-tonic intervocalic or postrhotic position in normal North American speech. For some North Americans, this also applies after /n/ (*center*, *twenty*, *printer*), where it can result in complete deletion rather than flapping of the /t/, so that *winter* and *winner* are homophones (Orkin and Bickerstaff (1997: 105, 128, 136) spell *plenty*, *Toronto* and *winter* as *plenny*, *Tirana*, *winner*), and after /l/ (*salty*, *bolted*, *ultimate*). As shown below in Table 3.16, it is less regular when the /t/ occurs two syllables rather than immediately after the main word stress, as in *monitor*, *relative* or *sanity*. Before syllabic /n/, as in *button*, *cotton* and *mitten*, /t/ is glottalized rather than flapped in most varieties of North American English, including SCE, though some speakers flap in this environment, too.

Given its phonetic origin in casual speech, flapping is not easily studied with written surveys. Avis (1956: 54–55) discusses this problem and admits that his data on flapping, indicating that only about half of Ontarians were doing it in the 1950s, are suspect. A generation later, Scargill and Warkentyne (1972: 58) asked whether the *tt* of *butter* sounded like the *dd* of *shudder* and got a positive response from only 38–41 percent of their parents and 60–61 percent of their students: while this suggests an increase in flapping, it may simply represent an increase in willingness to admit to flapping; in any case, both proportions are dubious. More trustworthy is the observation of Gregg (1957a: 25) that "the distinction between post-tonic, intervocalic [t] and [d] has been lost in natural Vancouver speech", so that *matter* and *madder*, and *hit it* and *hid it*, are homophones. He notes further that /t/ after /n/, in *twenty*, *plenty*, *winter*, *center*, *interview* and even *Toronto*, has been deleted. Nonetheless, in his subsequent sociolinguistic study of Vancouver, Gregg (2004: 17–40) presents a thorough analysis of medial /t/ that shows it to be still an active variable in Canadian English, a fact confirmed in Ottawa by Woods (1991: 136–138; 1993: 155–156; 1999: 78–86). Both Gregg (2004: 33) and Woods (1999: 81) find flapping to be a change in progress, led by young, working-class males and resisted by older, middle-class females. Like the retreat of /iw/ after coronals, the generalization of flapping indicates the gradual convergence of SCE with SAE (Woods 1993: 172). Indeed, the close similarity between SCE and SAE in terms of systematic variables of phonemic incidence is shown in Table 3.9, which summarizes the patterns discussed so far.

Before leaving the subject of conditioned mergers, it should also be stated that SCE shares with SAE the retention of /e/ before nasals in words like *pen* and *hem*, thereby maintaining the contrast with /i/ in the same environment in words like *pin* and *him*, a distinction that is not maintained in the southern United States. Also, SCE shares with SAE the full range

Table 3.9 *Status of six variables of phonemic incidence involving conditioned neutralizations in Standard British, American and Canadian English*

Distributional variant	SBE	SAE	SCE
/r/ retained in syllable coda	NO	YES	YES
/æ/ retained before /rV/	YES	NO	NO
/o/ retained before /rV/	YES	NO	NO
/ʌ/ retained before /rV/	YES	NO	NO
/iw/ retained after /t, d, n/	YES	NO	NO
/t/ retained medially as [t]	YES	NO	NO

of phonemic distinctions before coda /l/. The conditioned mergers that collapse pairs like *peel* and *pill*, *sale* and *sell*, *fool* and *full*, or *goal* and *gull* in some regional dialects of American English – including some varieties in the Midland region that was associated above with SAE – do not occur in Canada.

3.2.3 *Variation in phonemic incidence: lexically specific variables*

Beyond the systematic, phonetically conditioned variables of phonemic incidence listed in Table 3.9, many other phonemic incidence variables have been studied in Canadian English which operate less systematically, involving not positional neutralizations of phonemic contrast but variation in lexical representation. Some of these nonetheless involve large sets of words. The largest set in English generally, not just in Canadian English, is that of words transferred from other languages in which the stressed vowel is spelled – either in the source language or in its English transliteration – with the letter <a>. Known as *foreign (a) words*, these number in the thousands, particularly if early transfers from Latin and French into Old and Middle English and proper nouns like personal and place names are included. Typical examples are *potato*, *tobacco* and *spa*. As these examples illustrate, the variation reflects the three main phonemic values of the English grapheme <a>: the FACE, TRAP and PALM classes, or /ey/, /æ/ and /ah/.

Variation in assignment of foreign (a) words to these classes – called *foreign (a) nativization* – was first examined in detail by Boberg (1997). A brief description by Shapiro (1997) appeared the same year and phonological aspects of the nativization of foreign /a/ and other vowels were examined earlier by Lindsey (1990). The major British–American difference in assignment was described briefly by Wells (1982: 122, 142–144), Trudgill and Hannah (1985: 34) and Gramley and Pätzold (1992: 342). Boberg's survey of the variation found that nativization of foreign (a) with /ey/, as in *potato*, is no longer a productive pattern, being largely the result of application of the Great Vowel Shift to loanwords that originally had long /a:/. Modern nativization patterns, applying to words first attested in English after 1700, involve variation between /æ/ and /ah/. Boberg (1997: 60) determined that, while SBE and SAE agree on 72 percent of modern assignments, most of the disagreements (21 percent of the total) showed a greater preference for /æ/ in SBE, with either /ah/ or variation between /æ/ and /ah/ in SAE. This pattern is exemplified by words like *macho*, *pasta* and *Scarlatti*, all of which have /æ/ in SBE but /ah/ in SAE (Boberg 1997: 7).

Foreign (a) nativization in Canadian English was first studied in detail by Boberg (2000), though less systematic references to it can be found in some earlier, more general accounts of Canadian English pronunciation. Avis (1956: 52), for example, includes the originally foreign word *drama* among those for which he analyzes alternation between /æ/ and /ah/, while he later mentions "widespread use of /æ/ in such words as 'Vietnam' and 'Yugoslavia'" as an "apparent Canadianism" (Avis 1973: 65); Trudgill and Hannah mention /æ/ rather than /ah/ in "a number of foreign words" as a Canadian feature (1985: 41), though the only example they give is *pasta*. Several studies have surveyed the pronunciation of a few individual foreign (a) words, without considering the wider context: for *garage*, see Avis (1956: 59), Gregg (2004: 53–54) and Woods (1999: 216); for *khaki*, see Avis (1956: 43–44), Gregg (2004: 61), Hamilton (1958: 77) and Woods (1999: 220); for *vase*, see Avis (1956: 43), Gregg (2004: 53), Hamilton (1958: 77), Scargill and Warkentyne (1972: 54) and Woods (1999: 241); all three of these are also discussed by Avis (1973: 65). Other foreign (a) words considered in these and other studies are *apricot*, *caramel*, *guarantee* and *tomato*. However, three of these are in fact atypical of the more general pattern of foreign (a) variation, in that they include a variant with /ey/ (*apricot*, *tomato*, *vase*), the outcome that is now largely obsolete. Others are unusual for other reasons. *Caramel* and *guarantee* feature the variable vowel before intervocalic /r/, where it becomes confused with the variation in prerhotic vowels discussed above. *Khaki*, too, was often pronounced like *car key* in traditional varieties of Canadian English, with an intrusive /r/. This was probably derived by analogy with other British *r*-less pronunciations, perhaps by Canadian soldiers who heard the word in British military circles.

The main Canadian foreign (a) nativization pattern, alluded to by Avis (1973: 65) and Trudgill and Hannah (1985: 41) and revealed in greater detail by Boberg (2000: 17; 2009), is a general preference for /æ/ except where /ah/ is required by phonological constraints. Thus, most Canadians have /æ/ not only in words like *pasta*, where SAE has /ah/ but SBE also has /æ/, but in words like *drama*, *lava* and *Slavic*, where both SAE and SBE agree on /ah/. Traditionally, /ah/ was heard in Canada only in words like *bra* and *spa*, where /æ/ cannot occur, and then it was merged with the /oh/ of *paw*, *raw*, *saw*, etc. Today, presumably as a result of American influence, many younger Canadians also use /ah/ in words like *avocado*, *lasagna*, *llama*, *macho, mafia, Picasso* and *taco*, though the traditional pronunciations with /æ/ survive among older speakers. (SBE has /ah/ in *avocado* and *llama*, variation in *lasagna* and *taco*, and /æ/ in *macho, mafia* and *Picasso*; SAE has /ah/ in all of these.)

A phonological consequence of the increased use of /ah/, or rejection of /æ/, by younger Canadians was examined by Boberg (2009). Acoustic analysis revealed some Canadian foreign (a) productions to be extraphonemic, with a phonetic value between those of the native phonemes /æ/ and /ah-o-oh/. The word *façade*, for instance, was often pronounced so that it rhymed with neither *sad*, with [æ], nor *sod/sawed*, with [ɒ], but had a quality closer to the original French sound, [a]; *taco* was sometimes identifiable with neither *tack* nor *talk*. The existence of this intermediate vowel quality raises the possibility of SCE having three rather than two low vowels (excluding the diphthongs /ay/ and /aw/), calling into question the merger of /ah/ and /o/ indicated in Tables 3.5 and 3.6. As discussed above, this possibility was first addressed by Gregg (1957a: 22), who suggests that, as in SBE, *balm* and *father* have a different vowel in Vancouver English from either TRAP or LOT. To the extent that this is true, non-front nativizations of foreign (a) words may be supplementing this marginal, low-central PALM class, rather than the low-back LOT-THOUGHT class, thereby helping to secure its separate status in the vowel system of SCE. Boberg (2009) suggests that extraphonemic productions arise as a Canadian response to the American model of non-front nativization in the absence of a phonetically appropriate native phoneme, since Canadian /ah-o-oh/ is farther back than /ah-o/ in many American dialects, where it has a low-central articulation similar to the /a/ of the source languages. Whatever its phonological consequences, the Canadian foreign (a) nativization pattern distinguishes SCE from both SBE and SAE.

A selection of twenty foreign (a) words from Boberg (2009) is adapted here as Table 3.10. This shows Canadian and American frequencies of nativization with /ah/, as opposed to /æ/ or extraphonemic values, based on a sample of 62 Canadian and 23 American English speakers from dialect regions across North America, all undergraduate students at McGill University. The data were analyzed acoustically, with the phonetic region between /æ/ and /ah-o/ divided into thirds: foreign (a) tokens with F_2 values in the front third or higher were assigned to /æ/; those with F_2 values in the lowest third, or lower, were assigned to /ah-o/; and those in the middle third were considered indeterminate or extraphonemic (for a more detailed methodological discussion, see Boberg 2009). In the table, the words are ranked according to the size of the difference between the Canadian and American response frequencies. The main pattern is clear: in every case where there is a substantial national difference, Canadian frequency of /ah/ is much lower than American. Only a minority of the Canadian participants have /ah/ in *pasta, lava, plaza, Slavic, drama* and *avocado*, whereas the Americans virtually all have /ah/ in these words. The national divide for

Table 3.10 *Foreign (a) words in Canadian and American English.*
Frequency of /ah/ nativizations by word, in descending order of size
of national difference (results of acoustic analysis, from Boberg 2009)

Word	Canadian (%)	US (%)	US–Can. diff. (%)
pasta	13	91	78
lava	19	91	72
plaza	18	86	68
Slavic	24	91	67
drama	36	95	59
avocado	33	86	54
llama	49	95	46
Picasso	33	77	45
Colorado	22	64	42
pajamas	2	41	39
façade	56	86	30
taco	49	73	24
lasagna	62	82	20
lager	76	91	15
mafia	82	91	9
Iraq	11	18	7
macho	84	91	7
soprano	11	14	3
Pakistani	2	0	2
panorama	4	5	1

other words is less dramatic, but the pattern is consistent. Even where most Canadians do use /ah/, as in *lasagna, lager, mafia* and *macho*, Canadian use is lower than American. On the other hand, Canadians and Americans agree that *Iraq, soprano, Pakistani* and *panorama* have /æ/. Another facet of this variable is that the Canadian pattern displays much more variation than the American. American usage is more or less evenly divided in only two cases: *pajamas* and *Colorado*. The other eighteen words show a general consensus around one vowel or the other, which often approaches complete uniformity. The Canadian pattern, by contrast, includes seven words with frequencies between 33 and 66 percent: *drama, avocado, llama, Picasso, façade, taco* and *lasagna*. This suggests that Canadian nativization of foreign (a) is less stable than American, most likely reflecting the increase in /ah/ nativizations among younger Canadians first noted by Boberg (2000: 18).

Other variables of phonemic incidence, examined by Avis (1956: 45–50) and in several subsequent studies, involve not thousands of words, like foreign (a), but small sets of morphologically related words. One of these is nouns that start with <pro->, like *process, produce* and *progress*. SBE has /ow/ in *process* and *progress* but /o/ in *produce*; SAE has /o/ in *progress* and variation in *process* and *produce*. According to Avis (1956: 45), Ontario English follows the British pattern where it differs from the American, with almost all respondents using /ow/ in *process* and two-thirds favoring /ow/ in *progress*, but 71 percent using /o/ in *produce*. Another variable set of words is adjectives and nouns in <-*ile*, like *fertile*, *futile* and *missile*, which have /-ayl/ in SBE, as in *profile*, but /-əl/ in SAE, so that *futile* sounds like *feudal* and *missile* rhymes with *thistle*. In this set, Ontario usage tends again to follow the British model, with the full vowel in *docile*, *futile*, *senile* and *virile*, but diverges in the case of *fertile*, with a small majority favoring the American form (Avis 1956: 46). A similar divergence is recorded by Scargill and Warkentyne (1972: 64), Nylvek (1992: 272) and Woods (1999: 226), who show a large majority using the American form of *missile*, which may reflect the dominant place of American English in the semantic domain of war and weaponry in the late twentieth century. Otherwise, Woods' data on Ottawa English tend to show more British influence than those of Avis, with almost exclusive use of the British form of *futile* (1999: 214) and with a majority, which actually increases in apparent time, favoring the British form in *fertile* (1999: 213). A third group of words examined by Avis is the combining forms *anti-*, *multi-* and *semi-*, which have /iy/ in the second syllable in SBE but can have either /iy/ or /ay/ in SAE, depending partly on the word they are combined with. Both Avis (1956: 47) and Woods (1999: 201, 228, 236) show British /iy/ to be the strongly dominant form in Canada.

It is in variables of phonemic incidence, then, rather than in variables of phonemic inventory, that British influence can be seen in Canadian English. This is possibly the result of American forms having been deliberately discouraged by anglophile school teachers and textbooks, at a superficial level of grammar where the difference between the competing forms could be readily understood by the general public, but it may also reflect heavy British settlement in Canada during the nineteenth century, as discussed in Chapter 2. Whatever its cause, British influence on phonemic incidence in Canadian English has been selective and inconsistent, as demonstrated by the further examples in Table 3.11, which presents a sample of the remaining miscellany of phonemic incidence variables examined in successive surveys of Canadian English. Data from four of these studies are compared in the table; some of the variables have also been included in Chambers' Dialect Topography project and in the Canadian Index of Linguistic Insecurity of Owens and Baker (1984: 341), among other studies. Most of the variables involve single words, being essentially random and unsystematic and therefore of little interest to theoretical linguists. They are not, however, without iconic value or sociolinguistic import: they reflect the shifting and uncertain allegiances of English-speaking Canadians to the two main historical influences on their language and culture.

The first thing to observe about the data set in Table 3.11 is that it contains relatively few cases of clear, categorical differences between British and American English: often, British forms are given by American dictionaries as acceptable alternatives, presumably indicating their use by at least a minority

Table 3.11 *Ten miscellaneous variables of phonemic incidence in Canadian English, with their usual variants in Standard British and American English and their status (where available) in four surveys: Avis (1956), Scargill and Warkentyne (1972: 51–71), Gregg (2004: 50–64) and Woods (1999: 199–244). The variable portion of each word is underlined; alternative variants are given in order of preference or frequency. Majority responses are shown for the Canadian surveys, in some cases even where usage is fairly evenly divided;* split *indicates an even split between two variants.*

Word	SBE	SAE	Avis	S&W	Gregg	Woods
ag<u>ai</u>n	/e/, /ey/	/e/, /i/, /ey/	/ey/	/ey/	split	/e/
<u>au</u>nt	/ah/	/æ/, /ah/	/æ/	/æ/	n/a	/æ/
<u>ei</u>ther	/ay/, /iy/	/iy/, /ay/	/iy/	/iy/	/iy/	/iy/
gen<u>ui</u>ne	/ay/	/ə/, /i/, /ay/	/i/	/ay/	/i/	split
l<u>ei</u>sure	/e/	/iy/, /e/, /ey/	/e/	/iy/	/e/	n/a
l<u>ie</u>utenant	/ef/	/uw/	n/a	/uw/	/uw/	/uw/
r<u>ou</u>te	/uw/	/uw/, /aw/	n/a	/uw/	n/a	/uw/
<u>sch</u>edule	/ʃ/, /sk/	/sk/	/sk/	/sk/	/sk/	/sk/
v<u>a</u>se	/ahz/	/eys/, /eyz/, /ahz/	/eyz/	/eyz/	/ahz/	split

of Americans. Only in the case of *lieutenant* is there a categorical difference, and in this case the majority of Canadians favor the American term, despite the long military association between Canada and Britain. In fact, this seems to be the general pattern: while there are a few instances of Canadian usage following a British model in individual surveys, like Gregg's report of *leisure* with /e/ rather than /iy/, most of the variables display a Canadian propensity to adopt American rather than British pronunciations, like the consistent finding of *either* with /iy/ rather than /ay/ as the majority form. However, other cases might be adduced to show the opposite alignment, such as the strong past form of *shine*: *shone* rhymes with *bone* in SAE but with *gone* in both SBE and SCE (Avis 1956: 50; Zeller 1993: 184; Chambers 1994: 45–46). Moreover, some American regional variants are rarely heard in Canada, such as *route* with /aw/, from Table 3.11, or *roof* and *root* with short /u/ rather than long /uw/ (Avis 1956: 50).

To the variables of phonemic incidence already discussed might be added the evidence of several more variables that show the alignment of Canadian English with American rather than British phonology. One is the set of words in <-ary>, like *library*, *secondary* and *secretary*, or in <-ory>, like *circulatory*, *laboratory* and *mandatory*, which have reduced or deleted vowels before <-ry> in SBE but full vowels in SAE and in SCE. Another variable is stress assignment in loans from French, like *ballet*, *cachet*, *café*, *frontier*, *garage*, *massage*, *pâté* and *souvenir*, as well as in women's names in /-iyn/, like *Christine*, *Colleen*, *Eileen*, *Kathleen*, *Maureen* and *Pauline*. These words all have initial stress in SBE but final stress in SAE and SCE (see also Trudgill and Hannah 1985: 42–43). On the other hand, Latin-derived verbs in <-ate>, like *frustrate*, *rotate* and *vibrate*, tend to have final stress in SBE but initial stress in SAE and SCE; though the stress pattern is different, the dialect division is the same.

3.2.4 Phonetic variation

As important as the variables in Table 3.11 may be as targets for the corrective efforts of schoolteachers or as matters of concern for Canadian cultural nationalists, in practical terms they have only a minor influence on the sound of Canadian English, since the chance of their occurring in any particular sample of speech is fairly small. Like variation in the actual words people use (*couch* vs. *chesterfield* or *sofa*), variation in the sounds that occur in particular words (*route* being homophonous with *root* or *rout*) loses its symbolic value for both speaker and audience if the relevant words do not happen to arise in conversation. By contrast, phonetic variation, which will be defined here as systematic variation in the sounds of phonemes independent of their lexical context, plays a powerful role – perhaps the most crucial role of all – in allowing speakers to project their regional identities and audiences to assess and react to those identities. What matters for regional identification in everyday speech, then, is not so much whether one says *couch* or *chesterfield*, or whether one has the vowel /aw/ in *route*, but how one pronounces the vowel /aw/, or some other vowel, in the entire set of words that contain it. (As was already mentioned in connection with variation in phonemic inventory in Section 3.2.1, regional differences in the phonetics of North American English mostly involve vowels rather than consonants.)

While many studies of phonetic variation have made effective use of auditory impressionistic analysis, recording and conveying the analyst's impression of vowel quality with detailed phonetic symbols, standard practice in the study of regional and social variation in vowel production has now shifted to computerized acoustic analysis, as in Labov, Ash and Boberg (2006). This will be the method adopted here. It is based on the demonstration by Peterson and Barney (1952) that the quality of English vowels can be accurately and precisely represented by measuring the frequency in Hertz of the first two formants in the acoustic spectrum associated with vowel production. In particular, they showed that the first formant (F1) is inversely correlated with vowel height and the second (F2) directly correlated with vowel advancement (see also Hillenbrand, Getty, Clark and Wheeler 1995). These principles were first applied to the large-scale analysis of dialect differences and ongoing change in vowel production by Labov, Yaeger and Steiner (1972). Since acoustic phonetic analysis is now a standard procedure, it does not warrant further explanation here; readers who are unfamiliar with this method are referred to an introductory phonetics textbook for the requisite background knowledge.

An acoustic study called the *Phonetics of Canadian English* (identified hereafter as *PCE*) was undertaken by the author at McGill University between

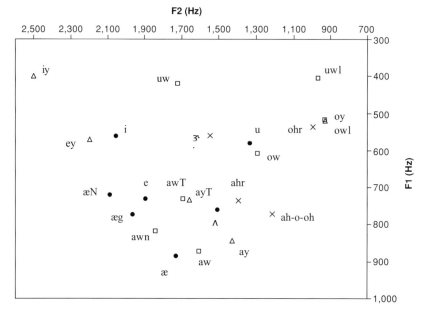

Figure 3.1 Mean F1 and F2 measurements for vowels and allophones of Standard Canadian English. (Interregional mean based on 86 participants in eight regions.) For key to vowel notation, see Table 3.12.

1999 and 2005. Its results were reported in Boberg (2005a; 2008a), which can be consulted for full methodological details. It involved sociolinguistic interviews with 108 McGill undergraduate students from across North America, selected to represent the major dialect regions identified by Labov, Ash and Boberg (2006), as well as the traditional historical and cultural regional divisions of Canada. The regional sample will be used here to develop a nationwide view of SCE in contrast to American varieties, with references to regional differences only where they complicate the national view; detailed discussion of regional differences will be reserved for Chapter 5. The *PCE* participants provided demographic data about themselves, then read a list of 180 words, then carried on spontaneous conversation with the interviewer, a fellow student, for 30–45 minutes.

The *PCE* interviews were recorded on cassette tape, then digitized at a sampling rate of 22 kHz and analyzed acoustically, using both spectrographic analysis and linear predictive coding (LPC), in the CSL 4400 program produced by Kay Elemetrics, the same used by Labov, Ash and Boberg (2006). The method of acoustic measurement was also the same as that of the *Atlas of North American English*, a correspondence guaranteed by the principal analyst in the two projects having been one and the same person: the author. With the aid of the LPC values, a single point of measurement was chosen

Table 3.12 *Data for Figure 3.1: mean F1 and F2 measurements (and standard deviations) for vowels and allophones of Standard Canadian English (interregional mean of 86 participants from eight Canadian regions)*

Vowel	Keyword	F1 (Hz)	F2 (Hz)
/i/	KIT	563 (41)	2,051 (92)
/e/	DRESS	732 (44)	1,891 (89)
/æ/	TRAP, BATH	885 (65)	1,727 (97)
/æg/	*bag*	775 (87)	1,962 (137)
/æN/	*band, ham*	721 (85)	2,085 (151)
/ʌ/	STRUT	761 (54)	1,504 (70)
/u/	PUT	581 (47)	1,333 (91)
/iy/	FLEECE	400 (36)	2,501 (120)
/ey/	FACE	571 (35)	2,198 (100)
/ay/	*tie*	843 (58)	1,428 (88)
/ayT/	*tight*	733 (51)	1,657 (93)
/oy/	VOICE	519 (53)	929 (83)
/uw/	GOOSE	421 (28)	1,720 (197)
/uwl/	*pool*	405 (39)	967 (142)
/ow/	GOAT	608 (52)	1,291 (110)
/owl/	*cold*	517 (47)	932 (78)
/aw/	*cow*	874 (69)	1,604 (73)
/awn/	*down*	817 (90)	1,838 (133)
/awT/	*house*	732 (70)	1,692 (109)
/ah-o-oh/	PALM, LOT, THOUGHT	771 (54)	1,214 (71)
/ahr/	START	735 (49)	1,396 (120)
/or-ohr-owr/	*sorry*, NORTH, FORCE	537 (107)	996 (209)
/ɝ/	NURSE	560 (40)	1,548 (84)

within the nucleus of each vowel. This was the maximum value of the first formant (F1) in the case of vowels whose central tendency is vertical aperture, or a point of inflection in the second formant (F2) in the case of vowels whose central tendency is the movement of the tongue toward, then away from, the front or rear periphery of the vowel space (such as ingliding vowels). Where the nucleus featured a protracted steady state in the values of both formants, a measurement was made within that steady state. The measurements thus obtained were then normalized using the additive point system of Nearey (1978), again as in Labov, Ash and Boberg (2006), in order to eliminate sex-related differences in formant values due to variation in vocal tract size. The data on vowel production presented here are taken from the 145 items on the word list that were selected to represent the normal phonetic range of all of the vowel phonemes of English, with extra representation of allophonic contexts of particular interest. The means for each vowel and allophone are given in Table 3.12 and displayed graphically in Figure 3.1.

Figure 3.1 and Table 3.12 present a balanced, interregional mean of eight regional means: those for British Columbia, the Prairies and northwestern Ontario, southern Ontario, Greater Toronto, eastern Ontario, Quebec, the Maritimes and Newfoundland. An interregional mean, in which each region has equal weight, prevents the national picture from being skewed by the number of participants from each region. Each regional mean is in turn a mean of the individual mean measurements from each participant in the region, with an average of ten participants per region, or eighty-six Canadian participants in total (the regional sample is discussed further in Chapter 5). Formant values for each participant are means of the values of all of the words chosen to represent each vowel or allophone (an average of six words per vowel or allophone). Figure 3.1 and Table 3.12 are therefore an abstraction developed for comparative purposes. While many aspects of this vowel system are common to most speakers of SCE, this is not the vowel system of any single region of Canada, much less of any individual (for examples of individual vowel systems, see Chapter 5, Section 5.5). It serves instead as a national average against which the systems of particular regions or individuals can be compared and which can itself be compared to the vowel systems of SBE and SAE, which is the aim of this section.

The vowel system in Figure 3.1 and Table 3.12 contains all of the vocalic phonemes of SCE listed in Table 3.6, except for /iw/, which has nuclear formant values similar to /uw/, being distinguished by its preceding palatal glide rather than by its nuclear quality. The double low-back merger indicated in the system was confirmed by t-tests of differences between the mean F_1 and F_2 values for each pair of vowels for each speaker. The system also contains three of the prerhotic vowels listed in Table 3.8; the others are omitted, since they involve regional variation in the application of conditioned mergers. Finally, it shows several important allophones as separate analytical categories: /æ/ before front nasals (N) and /g/; /ay/ and /aw/ before voiceless obstruents (T) and elsewhere; /aw/ before /n/; and /uw/ and /ow/ before /l/ and elsewhere. As can be seen in the chart, these allophones are phonetically distinct from the more general qualities of their respective phonemes and are analyzed separately so as to prevent skewing of the main distribution. The short vowels in Figure 3.1 are indicated with black circles, the front upgliding vowels with triangles, the back upgliding vowels with squares and the long monophthongs with Xs. As before, keywords from Wells (1982) are given in Table 3.12 except where allophonic distinctions not made in Wells need to be indicated.

Figure 3.1 displays most of the phonetic characteristics used by Labov, Ash and Boberg to establish "Inland Canada" – from Edmonton to Toronto – as a distinct dialect of North American English (2006: 224, map 15.7). The first of these, also extending to Vancouver in the west and to Montreal in the east, is the Canadian Shift, a lowering and retraction of the front short vowels /i/, /e/ and /æ/ first identified by Clarke, Elms and Youssef (1995). The Canadian Shift appears to be initiated by the retraction of /æ/, first described in Vancouver English by Esling and Warkentyne (1993), which is in turn activated by the low-back merger of /o/ and /oh/, a well-established feature of Canadian English listed among the variables of phonemic inventory in Table 3.5. As /æ/ shifts down and back into the low-central space made available by the merger, /i/ and /e/ shift down and inward in parallel fashion. The original formulation of Clarke, Elms and Youssef emphasized lowering of /i/ and /e/ to fill the space created by the retraction of /æ/, a classic chain shift, while a subsequent study of the shift in Montreal English by Boberg (2005a) emphasized parallel retraction, finding the F2 of /e/ to be the variable that showed the strongest movement in apparent time. Labov, Ash and Boberg (2006: 221) and the apparent-time analysis presented here in Chapter 5 (Figure 5.3 and Table 5.12) find significant effects of speaker age on both the F1 and F2 of /e/, suggesting that the shift involves both lowering and retraction of that vowel.

In keeping with the latter view, Figure 3.1 shows /i/ in upper-mid position opposite /ey/; /e/ in lower-mid position near the raised allophones of /æ/; and /æ/ approaching low-central position, [a̠], well separated from the /ah-o-oh/ double merger in the low-back quadrant. The mean formant values for these vowels in Table 3.12 all conform to the thresholds established by Labov, Ash and Boberg (2006: 219) for the shift: the F1 of /e/ is greater than 650 Hz; the F2 of /æ/ is less than 1,825 Hz; and the F2 of /o/ is less than 1,275 Hz. It is the Canadian Shift, more than any other feature of Canadian English, that supports the identification of Inland Canada as a separate dialect region in the *Atlas of North American English* (Labov, Ash and Boberg 2006: 130). This is particularly true along the border between southern Ontario and the American Inland North, where the phonemic status of /o/ and /oh/ is in direct contrast (Zeller 1993: 188), motivating opposite developments of the low vowels /æ/ and /o/ (Boberg 2000). In the Inland North, the tensing and raising of the entire old short /a/ class as /æh/ – the initiating phase of the Northern Cities Shift – allows the distinction between /o/ and /oh/ to be maintained through the advancement of /o/ into the low-central space. In Ontario, the merger of /o/ and /oh/ allows /æ/ to retract into the same space that is occupied by /o/ across the border. As a result, the phonetic quality [a] corresponds to different phonemes in each country: to /o/ in Detroit and Buffalo, where LOT is pronounced [lat]; but to /æ/ in Toronto, where TRAP and BATH are pronounced with [a]. In southeastern Michigan and western New York, [hat] is the opposite of *cold*; in Ontario it is something you wear on your head. The Michigander's pronunciation of *solid* sounds like *salad* to Canadians, while the Canadian's rendering of *rack* sounds like *rock* to the Michigander (see Willis 1972 for an experimental investigation of dialect differences in perception of /e/, /æ/ and /o/ along the Ontario–New York border).

The next two defining features of Inland Canada in the *Atlas* concern the mid upgliding vowels /ey/ and /ow/: these are relatively more peripheral and less diphthongal in Canada than in most American dialects. The *PCE* data in Table 3.12 almost satisfy the *Atlas* criterion for peripheral /ey/, that the F2 of /ey/ be greater than 2,200 Hz, but fall well short of meeting the threshold for peripheral /ow/, that the F2 of /ow/ be less than 1,100 Hz. The mean of 1,291 Hz in Table 3.12 is well below those of the regions that show centralized /ow/ in the *Atlas* (145), but is aligned more closely with the moderate centralization of the American West than with the almost monophthongal values of the Upper Midwest and Inland North, as in the *Atlas* (105). Part of this discrepancy may arise from the particular words used to establish the F2 of /ow/. In the *Atlas*, which did not control carefully for lexical factors, basing its analysis mostly on spontaneous speech, some speakers did not produce many of the emphatic, post-coronal and syllable-final tokens of /ow/ that tend to encourage centralization of the vocalic nucleus; many tokens of /ow/ were from the word *home*, for example, which is notably conservative with respect to centralization. The *PCE* data, by contrast, are based on word list productions, which are all fully emphatic and include tokens of *go*, *stone* and *toe* for each participant, thereby raising the mean F2 measurement. In any case, relative to SBE and the dialects of the Midland and southern United States, it is safe to say that SCE has a conservative, peripheral realization of /ey/ and only moderate centralization of /ow/, though this pattern is more evident in some regions, like the Prairies, than in others, like Greater Toronto (as shown in Section 5.5 of Chapter 5). Centralization of /ow/ in SCE is blocked by a following /l/: the distance in Figure 3.1 between the main distribution of /ow/ and its allophone before /l/, which is on the rear periphery overlapping /oy/, is a good measure of the extent of centralization.

The same could be said of the relative advancement of /aw/. The mean F2 value in Table 3.12, 1,604 Hz, is not within the threshold of less than 1,550 Hz established by the *Atlas* for Inland Canada, but is within the second quartile of continental F2 values (107), aligning Canada clearly with the North and West of the United States in this respect, rather than with the Midland and South, which show advanced fronting of /aw/. Though Chambers and Hardwick (1986) found evidence of general fronting of /aw/ among young speakers in Toronto and Vancouver, fronting of /aw/ in SCE, comparatively speaking, is mainly restricted to the allophone before /n/ (represented on the *PCE* word list by *down*, *gown* and *town*), as shown in Figure 3.1. On the other hand, the relative position of the two low diphthongs, /aw/ and /ay/, is aligned with that of the Midland and South, with /aw/ farther front than /ay/; the opposite relation holds in the Inland North and eastern New England (Labov, Ash and Boberg 2006: 188). In this respect, the *PCE* data partially contradict the view of the *Atlas*, which shows the Prairies to be within the isogloss delimiting the region where /aw/ is farther back than /ay/, but the rest of Canada to be outside it. Of eighty-six *PCE* participants, there are only three who have /aw/ farther back than /ay/ and they are not concentrated on the Prairies: one is from Manitoba but the others are from Toronto and Montreal. Given what was just said about the absence of advanced fronting of /aw/ in Canada, its relative position in front of /ay/ reflects instead the comparatively retracted position of /ay/.

The more important aspect of /aw/ in Canada is its involvement in Canadian Raising, the last of the features associated in the *Atlas* with Inland Canada. This is the pattern whereby the low monophthongs, /aw/ and /ay/, have non-low nuclei before voiceless obstruents. Thus, raised nuclei in *lout* and *house* contrast with unraised nuclei in *loud* and *houses*; raised nuclei in *tight* and *rice* contrast with unraised nuclei in *tide* and *rise*. This allophonic variation is clearly visible in Figure 3.1: the raised allophone /awT/ (based on the words *doubt, house, shout* and *south*) is 142 Hz higher than the unraised allophone /aw/ (*cow, foul, loud, proud, sour*), while raised /ayT/ (*fight, sight, spice, tight, writer*) is 110 Hz higher than unraised /ay/ (*file, rider, side, sign, tide, tie, tire*). Raising of /ay/ also entails movement in the F2 dimension: /ayT/ is 229 Hz farther forward than /ay/. In the national average of Figure 3.1, the raised nuclei of /awT/ and /ayT/ occur very close to one another, halfway between /e/ and /ʌ/, in lower-mid central position. As will be shown in Chapter 5, however, the position of /awT/ is an important regional indicator in SCE, being farther back in the West and farther forward in Ontario.

Canadian Raising has been extensively studied. It figures in some of the earliest accounts of Canadian English (Ahrend 1934: 136, 138; Ayearst 1939: 231–232; Emeneau 1935: 142–143), suggesting an early origin. Thomas (1991: 152), on the basis of phonetic transcriptions of the speech of Canadians interviewed in connection with the American Linguistic Atlas projects, demonstrates that it was established in Ontario by 1880, while a study of the Elizabethan origins of "raised" (or unlowered) /ay/ is presented by Gregg (1973). Kurath and McDavid (1961) show raised nuclei in Ontario for *twice* (map 27) and *out* (map 29); Allen (1976: 39–41, 156–157) transcribes a mid-central nucleus in *out* in contrast to a low-central nucleus for *down* and *flower* for all five of his Canadian informants; and Gregg (1957a: 24) notes raising of /aw/ and /ay/ in Vancouver English. The status of Canadian Raising as a central concern of linguists working on Canadian English began with Joos (1942). Joos noticed that raising interacts with the flapping of /t/ in words like *writer* (which he treats as voicing) to produce two variants: one in which raising precedes flapping, so that raising applies before flapping eliminates the environment for it; and one in which the opposite order of application prevents raising, which does not occur before voiced consonants. Thus, some Canadians had the same raised vowels in both syllables of *typewriter*, while others had a raised vowel in *type* but an unraised vowel in *writer*, which sounded like *rider*. The first group could be analyzed as having two additional phonemes, since raising before flapping creates a phonemic contrast between raised and unraised vowels in minimal pairs like *writer* and *rider*.

Joos' analysis was elaborated, expanded and related to generative phonological theory by Chambers (1973), who asserted that the rule ordering that favored maximal raising – raising before flapping – had become ubiquitous since Joos' study, while the ordering that blocked it with flapping – flapping before raising – had disappeared (122). While further phonological analysis was pursued by Picard (1977), Paradis (1980) and Idsardi (2006), Chambers subsequently collaborated with other researchers to examine variation and change in Canadian Raising in several Canadian cities (Chambers and Hardwick 1986; Hung, Davison and Chambers 1993). Canadian Raising was also included as a variable in both of the major Canadian sociolinguistic surveys, which found it to be the norm: in Vancouver (Gregg 2004: 40–43; Murdoch 2004) and in Ottawa (Woods 1993: 159–167; 1999: 106–122).

The general consensus of this considerable body of work – recently reviewed by Chambers (2006b) – is that Canadian Raising was well established in Canada as early as the late nineteenth century and certainly by the mid twentieth century, but had begun a gradual recession in some areas by the end of the century. Gregg (2004: 42) finds raising to be a uniform and consistent feature of Vancouver speech with no evidence of recession. He confirms, moreover, Chambers' observation that raising is not blocked by flapping in words like *writer* and *shouted*. Chambers and Hardwick (1986: 36), however, report a substantial increase in non-raising among 12-year-old girls in Vancouver, while Hung, Davison and Chambers (1993: 264) make the same observation in Montreal. Similarly, Woods (1993: 161, 164; 1999: 111, 119) finds young women leading a trend away from raising in Ottawa. Boberg (2004c: 564) discovered that raising, as a native Canadian feature, is not adopted equally by all ethnic groups in Montreal's English-speaking community: Jewish speakers appeared to have acquired raising of /awT/ to the same extent as British-origin speakers, but some of the Italian-origin speakers, a newer addition to the community than the Jews, used the same low vowel for /aw/ and /awT/, as one would in Italian (see also Section 5.3, Chapter 5). Both Kirwin (1993: 75) and Clarke (2004a: 373–374; 2008: 98–99) have noted the general absence of Canadian Raising in Newfoundland, also reflected here in Figure 5.10 of Chapter 5.

Canadian Raising is not, then, a completely uniform or invariant feature of Canadian English. It is also not exclusively Canadian: many studies have noted its presence, especially with respect to /ay/, in several dialects of American English, including those in the north central and northeastern United States along the border with Canada (Kurath and McDavid 1961: map 27; Labov 1963; Vance 1987; Allen 1989; Thomas 1991; Dailey-O'Cain 1997; Niedzielski 1999; Labov, Ash and Boberg 2006: 205–206; Roberts 2007). These facts led Labov, Ash and Boberg (2006: 130, 221) to conclude that Canadian Raising is indeed common in Canada, but is neither consistent nor exclusive enough to define Canada as a dialect region. This view differs from that of Chambers and Hardwick, who regard raising of /aw/, at least, as "the most identifiable trait of CanE, and the one that most readily distinguishes it from other varieties of NAmE" (1986: 28). As already noted, Labov, Ash and Boberg confer this status instead on the Canadian Shift. Whatever its relative importance, the *PCE* data indicate that raising of both /ay/ and /aw/ continues to be a reliable characteristic of Canadian English, even among the young, university-educated *PCE* informants. Of this sample, 88 percent produced a difference between the mean F1 measures of /aw/ and /awT/ greater than the threshold of 60 Hz established for Canadian Raising by Labov, Ash and Boberg (2006: 222), while 81 percent met the same criterion for /ay/. Most of the non-raisers are from Vancouver, Montreal and Newfoundland, a distribution consistent with the findings of Chambers and Hardwick (1986), Hung, Davison and Chambers (1993) and Kirwin (1993: 75), respectively, and with Labov, Ash and Boberg (2006: 222).

While the phonetic characteristics discussed so far are those that best identify SCE as a unique variety in the North American context, other phonetic patterns have an equally important role in shaping the sound of SCE, if not quite so distinctively. One of these, immediately visible in Figure 3.1, is the shift of /uw/ from the high-back quadrant into the high-central region of the vowel space, directly above /æ/. This shift, shared with all dialects of North American English (Labov, Ash and Boberg 2006: 153), is surprisingly advanced in Canada, given the relatively moderate centralization of /ow/ discussed above. Advanced fronting of /uw/ with only moderate fronting of /ow/ is a combination that Canada shares with New York City and the American West, differentiating these dialects from the Midland and South, which show advanced fronting of both vowels, and from the Inland North and eastern New England, which show comparatively little fronting of either (Labov, Ash and Boberg 2006: 145).

Like the centralization of /ow/, centralization or fronting of /uw/ in SCE is blocked by a following /l/ and strongly affected in other environments by phonetic factors. For instance, Labov, Ash and Boberg (2006: 101, 103) reveal that Canada is among the North American regions with the highest values for the F2 of /uw/ after coronals (*soon*, *too*, *do*, etc.), comparable with the Midland and southern United States rather than with the more conservative North, but aligns more closely with the North in the non-post-coronal environment (*boot*, *move*, etc.), which shows advanced fronting only in the Midland and South. In fact, the *PCE* data show that the position of /uw/ is affected more than that of any other vowel by the presence and nature of surrounding segments, with a distribution extending over the entire top region of the vowel space. Table 3.13 shows the ten tokens of /uw/ from the *PCE* word list with their mean F1 and F2 values, averaged across the eighty-six Canadian participants, ranked from furthest back to furthest front. There is a clear break between the tokens before liquids and elsewhere, the former being the only part of the /uw/ set that remains in high-back position, the latter being over 200 Hz farther front. Within the latter set, there is a second break between *boots* and *food*, with initial labials, which show only moderate centralization, and the remainder, with initial coronals,

Table 3.13 *Phonetic effects on the advancement of /uw/*
in SCE: mean F1 and F2 measurements of ten tokens of
/uw/ from the PCE *word list for 86 Canadian*
participants, ranked in descending order of backness

Word	F1	F2
cool	387	866
fool	394	921
tour	434	973
tool	413	1,092
boots	399	1,343
food	417	1,397
tooth	388	1,648
too	402	1,702
soon	450	1,749
do	409	1,973

which show advancement into the high-front quadrant of the vowel space. The most extreme fronting is seen after /d/ in *do*, where the F2 of /uw/ approximates the position of /i/, though with a lower F1.

Another vowel that shows strong effects of phonetic conditioning is /u/. The position of this vowel in Figure 3.1 indicates a fairly lowered and centralized pronunciation very close to the nucleus of /ow/. In fact, as with /uw/, the mean value of /u/ represents a wide range of allophones spread across the F2 dimension of the upper-back quadrant of the vowel space. The *PCE* word list contains only three tokens of /u/. While the F1 of these tokens is relatively constant (537–562 Hz), the F2 ranges from a low of 1,059 Hz before /l/ in *full*, to 1,279 Hz after the labial in *foot*, to 1,630 Hz, a mid-central articulation, after the coronal in *stood*. Both Clarke, Elms and Youssef (1995: 213) and Boberg (2005a) found /u/ to be advancing in apparent time, as does the apparent-time analysis of Table 5.12 in Chapter 5.

As can be seen in Figure 3.1, a further phonetic characteristic of SCE is a non-peripheral articulation of /ahr/, the START vowel. This vowel shows an allophonic pattern similar to Canadian Raising, in which a following voiceless consonant (*harp*, *start*, *dark*) causes shortening of the nucleus, thereby increasing its centralization, while /ahr/ in final position (*bar*, *star*, *car*) remains closer to the low-back periphery of the vowel space. In the eastern half of Canada, and particularly in the Atlantic region, /ahr/ retains a lower-mid-central quality that is closer to its historical origin, while in the western half it tends to be farther back, a regional divide that will be discussed in Chapter 5.

The last important phonetic characteristic of SCE is the allophonic distribution of /æ/, though this differs regionally, as will also be explored in Chapter 5. In the abstract national view of Figure 3.1, the main distribution of /æ/ is in low-front position, at [a], while the allophones before /g/ and

Table 3.14 *IPA notation of approximate phonetic values of Wells'*
(1982) lexical sets in SCE, based on data in Figure 3.1 (table format
adapted from Wells 1982: 493). Diacritics are used to indicate positions
of SCE vowels relative to the normal values of IPA vowel symbols.
Multiple values indicate allophonic and regional variation; following
consonants exemplify allophonic contexts.

Set	Value	Set	Value	Set	Value
KIT	ɪ	FLEECE	i	NEAR	iɹ, ɪɹ
DRESS	ɛ, æ	FACE	eʲ	SQUARE	ɛɹ
TRAP	a, æg, ɛᵊn	PALM	ɒ, ɑ	START	ɐɹ, ɐɹ
LOT	ɒ, ɑ	THOUGHT	ɒ, ɑ	NORTH	ɔɹ, oɹ
STRUT	ɐ	GOAT	oʷ, ʌʷ	FORCE	ɔɹ, oɹ
FOOT	ʊ	GOOSE	ʉʷ	CURE	ɝ, ʊɹ
BATH	a	PRICE	ɑʲ, ɐʲt	*happy*	i
CLOTH	ɒ, ɑ	VOICE	oʲ	*lett*ER	ɚ
NURSE	ɝ	MOUTH	aʷ, ɐʷt, æʷn	*comm*A	ə, ɐ

front nasals exhibit raising along the front periphery of the vowel space. The
position of /æg/, assessed with the words *bag*, *gag* and *tag*, approaches [æ],
often with a front upglide [æʲ]. For some speakers it is even higher and also
includes /æ/ before velar nasals, as in *bang* or *bank* (Orkin and Bickerstaff
respell *bank* as *beink* (1997: 27)). The position of /æN/, tested with *band*,
ham, *stamp* and *tan*, is raised as far as [ɛ], usually with anticipatory nasal-
ization and an inglide, [ɛ̃ᵊ]. The raising of /æg/ as well as /æN/ causes
SCE to be classified as a "continuous short-*a* system" by Labov, Ash and
Boberg (2006: 180), as opposed to a "nasal system" in which /æ/ is raised
only but always before nasals, with an abrupt break between the raised and
unraised allophones. In the *Atlas*, in fact, most of Canada is part of a territory
that also includes the north-central and northwestern regions of the United
States, from Wisconsin to Seattle to Alaska, in which /æ/ is higher and
fronter before /g/ than before /d/ (Labov, Ash and Boberg 2006: 182); in
most other regions of North America, /æg/ is one of the lower allophones
of /æ/. Nevertheless, Canadian raising of /æg/ does not generally approach
the level heard in the American Upper Midwest, especially Wisconsin and
Minnesota, where /æg/ can get as high as [eʲg]. Only two *PCE* participants,
one from Saskatchewan and one from southern Ontario, show an approximation of less than 50 Hz between the mean F_1 values of /æg/ and /ey/.
Beyond this statement, it is difficult to generalize about the phonetics of /æ/
in SCE; regional differences in the raising of /æg/ and /æN/ are analyzed
in Chapter 5.

In keeping with the practice of Wells (1982) and much subsequent British
work in sociophonetics, the foregoing discussion of the phonetics of SCE
is summarized in Table 3.14, which assigns IPA symbols to Wells' lexical
sets, indicating their usual pronunciation by most speakers of SCE. By way of

comparison, Wells' own version of this table may be consulted, with his values for Canadian English (1982: 493); corresponding tables for Newfoundland English are given by Wells (1982: 499) and Clarke (2004a: 369). Essentially, Table 3.14 represents a translation of the mean positions of the vowels in Figure 3.1 into IPA symbols. In cases where one of Wells' lexical sets involves an important allophonic distinction in SCE, or when SCE pronunciation varies along a range of phonetic values, two values are given; readers are referred to the foregoing discussion for clarification. Allophonic contexts are indicated by following consonants that exemplify them. Several of the values given in Table 3.14, particularly those for MOUTH and START, show important regional variation, which is discussed in Chapter 5.

Comparatively speaking, the phonetic values given in Table 3.14 are not far different from what would be found in many Midland and western varieties of American English, with a few exceptions: the lowered and retracted variants of DRESS and TRAP; the raised variants of PRICE and MOUTH; and the non-peripheral and centralized variants of START. As already mentioned, some of these features also occur in varieties of American English: Labov, Ash and Boberg (2006) show substantial frequencies of lowered /e/ (80), retracted /æ/ (83), Canadian Raising (114–115) and unretracted /ahr/ (110–111) in various regions of the United States, though in most cases these alternate with non-Canadian variants.

In order to assess more precisely the phonetic distance between SCE and various dialects of American English, a sample of twenty-two American students was interviewed along with the eighty-six Canadian *PCE* participants, representing six dialect regions established by Labov, Ash and Boberg (2006: 148): eastern New England; the north Mid-Atlantic (New York City) region; the south Mid-Atlantic (Philadelphia–Washington) region; the South; the Inland North; and the Midland-Midwest and West, which were combined as one. The American participants read the same word list as the Canadians and were analyzed in the same way. The mean formant measurements for the three regions bordering Canada are presented in Table 3.15, together with the equivalent values for the Canadians from Table 3.12. The table focuses on the two best-known, most consistent and most distinctive phonetic characteristics of SCE discussed above: the Canadian Shift, measured as the position of /e/, /æ/ and /o/; and Canadian Raising, measured here as the difference in Hz between the raised and unraised allophones of /aw/ and /ay/. The last line of the table shows the sum of all the absolute differences in formant values between Canada and each American region, giving a rough indication of the comparative phonetic distance at different positions along the international border.

The sums on the last line of Table 3.15 make it clear that the phonetic distance between Canadian and American English is greatest along the boundary between southern and eastern Ontario and the American Inland North. The sum of differences between Canadian and Inland Northern formant values

Table 3.15 *Comparison of phonetic values of Canadian and American PCE participants: mean formant values (in Hz) for the Canadian Shift and Canadian Raising, for Canada vs. the Midland–Midwest and West (MMW), the Inland North (IN) and eastern New England (ENE). Canadian Raising is measured as the difference between the mean F1 values of the raised and unraised allophones. Total diff. = sum of absolute differences between each American region and Canada.*

Measure	Canada (n = 86)	MMW (n = 4)	IN (n = 5)	ENE (n = 4)
F1 (e)	732	734	744	716
F2 (e)	1,891	1,952	1,782	1,942
F1 (æ)	885	896	733	837
F2 (æ)	1,727	1,806	1,943	1,906
F1 (o)	771	810	869	784
F2 (o)	1,214	1,230	1,400	1,188
F1 (aw) – F1 (awT)	142	25	46	110
F1 (ay) – F1 (ayT)	110	86	126	141
Total diff.		349	885	396

is more than twice as large as that between either the Midland/West or New England and Canada. This is just what would be expected, given what was said above about the opposite phonetic developments of the Canadian and Northern Cities Shifts. These differences are readily observable in Table 3.15: the biggest cross-border differences around the Great Lakes involve measures of the Canadian Shift. In particular, Canadian /æ/ is 150 Hz lower and 200 Hz farther back than the raised and fronted /æh/ of the Inland North, while Canadian /o-ah-oh/ is 100 Hz higher and almost 200 Hz farther back than the unmerged, low-central /o/ of the Inland North. Strikingly, however, the Northern Cities Shift produces even greater retraction of /e/ than the Canadian Shift: /e/ is about 100 Hz farther back for the Inland Northern students than for the Canadians.

The greatest difference between the Canadian and eastern New England participants also involves /æ/, which is much less retracted in New England; there is also less lowering and retraction of /e/ in eastern New England, indicating an absence of the Canadian Shift. Remarkably, the extension of the low-back merger to eastern New England produces very similar values for the F1 and F2 of /o/ in the two regions. This suggests that the extension of the Canadian Shift to eastern New England is prevented not by the position of /o-oh/ per se but by the presence of /ah/, which remains distinct from /o-oh/ in eastern New England, occupying a position between /æ/ and /o-oh/, where it blocks the retraction of /æ/. Where /ah/ is not distinct from /o-oh/, in the Midland/West, values for the F1 of /e/ and the F1 and F2 of /æ/ are closer to those of Canada, indicating a moderate version of the Canadian Shift, tempered by the somewhat lower and more central position of /ah-o-oh/. This suggests that the Canadian Shift is indeed an

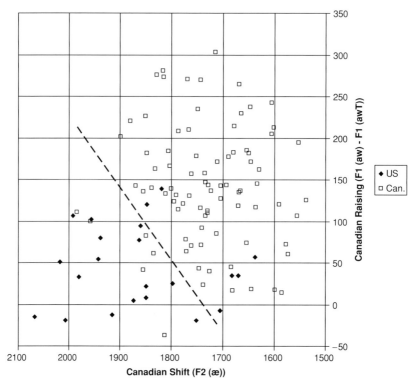

Figure 3.2 Two diagnostic phonetic characteristics of SCE: the Canadian Shift (F2 of /æ/) and Canadian Raising of /awT/ for 86 Canadian
and 22 American *PCE* participants. The dashed line separates 93% of
the Canadians from 73% of the Americans.

automatic response to the double low-back merger of /ah/, /o/ and /oh/,
which characterizes both Canada and the western United States.

By contrast, the biggest phonetic difference between Canada and the
Midland/Western region of the United States concerns not the Canadian
Shift but Canadian Raising of /awT/, which is negligible in the American
Midland and West. Raising of /awT/ is also comparatively rare in the Inland
North, but does occur in eastern New England, to a degree approaching that
in Canada. Despite this partial regional similarity, Table 3.15 makes it clear
that raising of /awT/ is generally diagnostic of SCE, while raising of /ayT/
is not. In fact, both the Inland North and eastern New England show greater
raising of /ayT/ than Canada. Only the Midland/Western region shows
less, though it occurs there as well.

The value of the Canadian Shift and Canadian Raising of /awT/ for
distinguishing SCE from American varieties of English is demonstrated by
Figure 3.2, which plots the retraction of /æ/ against the raising of /awT/

for the Canadian and American *PCE* participants, shown as white squares and black diamonds, respectively. The dashed line drawn across the graph, distinguishing retracted /æ/ and raised /awT/ from front /æ/ and unraised /awT/, separates 93 percent of the Canadian participants from 73 percent of the Americans. The individual exceptions to this division reflect the observations made above. Of the Canadians on the American side of the line, the one with no raising of /awT/ is from Newfoundland, while those with no retraction of /æ/ are from Edmonton and Cape Breton, rather than from the largest metropolitan regions, where the Canadian Shift is most advanced. Of the Americans on the Canadian side of the line, one of the two with strong raising of /awT/ is from New England and the other is from Virginia, an area of the United States well known for this feature (Kurath and McDavid 1961: map 29), while the two with the greatest retraction of /æ/ are both from the Midland/Western region (one from Los Angeles and one from Colorado).

3.2.5   Some remaining matters of pronunciation

As mentioned above, the *PCE* word list included 35 items in addition to the 145 that provided the basis for the general phonetic analysis just presented. Twenty of these were the tokens of foreign (a) presented in Table 3.10. Most of the remaining words were included in order to study some of the other variables discussed above: the merger of /hw/ and /w/; the conditioned merger of /iw/ and /uw/ after coronals; and the flapping of /t/. Since flapping is essentially invariable in its main environment, between vowels or between /r/ and a vowel immediately following primary word stress, most of the word list tokens were chosen to represent a more variable environment, between vowels but two syllables after primary word stress (*charity*, *monitor*, *relative* and *sanity*). Two more tokens of flapping represented other environments: *veto*, an atypical instance of post-tonic intervocalic /t/ because of its following /ow/, more characteristic of foreign than of native words; and *writer*, a more canonical context that was included as a token of /ayT/ but also contains a token of /VtV/. Data on these variables for 63 Canadian and 22 American participants, the result of impressionistic rather than acoustic analysis, are presented in Table 3.16.

The near completion of the merger of /hw/ and /w/ among young, university-educated North Americans can be seen in the low rate of [h] retention among both national groups. For at least 80 percent of this population, *whale*, *which* and *whine* sound like *wail*, *witch* and *wine*. The conditioned merger of /iw/ and /uw/ after coronals is similarly advanced in both groups, though slightly more advanced among the Americans. The flapping of /t/ presents a more complex picture. The canonical environment in *writer*, as would be expected, shows virtually categorical application of flapping, even in word list productions, a valuable benchmark for the less canonical

Table 3.16 *Data from 63 Canadian and 22 American* PCE
*participants on retention of [h] in /hw/, retention of [j] in /iw/, and
retention of [t] in /VtV/*

Retention of:	Can. (%)	Can. (n)	US (%)	US (n)
[h] in *whale*	3	2/63	0	0/22
[h] in *which*	11	7/63	14	3/22
[h] in *whine*	3	2/63	18	4/22
[j] in *due*	13	8/61	9	2/22
[j] in *new*	17	11/63	9	2/22
[j] in *student*	10	6/63	0	0/22
[j] in *tube*	16	10/63	18	4/22
[t] in *charity*	3	2/63	0	0/22
[t] in *monitor*	30	19/63	32	7/22
[t] in *relative*	89	56/63	91	20/22
[t] in *sanity*	24	15/63	23	5/22
[t] in *veto*	44	28/63	55	12/22
[t] in *writer*	10	6/63	5	1/22

environments. Flapping of non-stress-adjacent /t/ is also virtually categorical in *charity*, but less frequent in *monitor* and *sanity* and quite rare in *relative*,
where most participants retained [t]. The unusual following vowel in *veto*
produces a medial rate of flapping of around 50 percent. Though the frequency of flapping varies from one word to another, it is striking that the
constraints that determine its application work identically in Canadian and
American English, producing nearly identical shifts up and down. In fact,
all of the national frequencies in Table 3.16 are closely correlated: a Pearson
correlation test of the Canadian and American percentages returns a value
of $r = 0.97$, indicating an almost perfect correlation. In terms of the variables and populations featured in Table 3.16, SCE and SAE are virtually
indistinguishable.

Before concluding the discussion of phonetic patterns, reference should be
made to two further variables that have been widely studied in many varieties
of English, being two of the best-known variables in sociolinguistics generally: (-t/-d) and (ing). The first of these is a fast-speech rule in which /t/ and
/d/ are variably deleted in syllable-final consonant clusters when a consonant follows in the onset of the next syllable, as in *pos(t)card, fac(t)-finding,
lef(t) lane, passe(d) by, ol(d) man* or *gran(d)father* (Labov 1972: 216–226;
Guy 1980, 1991; Guy and Boberg 1997). Woods (1999: 98–100) examined
the deletion of /t/ in final /-st/ clusters in Ottawa English and found it
to be constrained by the same factors that have been identified in studies
of /t,d/-deletion in other dialects: [t]-retention occurs more frequently in
middle-class than in working-class speech and more frequently for all social
classes in more formal styles of speech, ranging from 10–40 percent in spontaneous speech to about 60 percent in word-list style. Since this variable has
been so thoroughly examined elsewhere and there is currently no reason to

believe it operates distinctly in Canadian English, it will not be discussed further.

The second standard variable, (ing), is sometimes treated as a morphological variable, since it involves alternation between two allomorphs of the verbal suffix <-ing>: one with a full vowel and a velar nasal, [ɪŋ], and one with a reduced vowel and an alveolar nasal, [ən], commonly identified in written representations of casual speech as <in'> (Labov 1972: 238–243; Trudgill 1974). In some dialects, including Canadian English, a third variant combines a full, usually tense vowel with the alveolar nasal, [in]. However, vowel reduction and the replacement of a velar with a coronal consonant are both phonetically natural processes of lenition, so (ing) will be treated here as a phonetic variable, as it is in both Gregg's survey of Vancouver English (2004: 43–46) and Woods' survey of Ottawa English (1999: 87–93). Unlike the case of (-t/-d), these Canadian studies of (ing) reveal somewhat different patterns from those observed in other dialects (e.g. Fischer 1958; Labov 1972: 238–239). In her comparison of the studies, De Wolf (1992: 83) suggests that "The investigation of (ing) in Canadian English may . . . not be so clear-cut as elsewhere . . . " First, there is a wide discrepancy between the two cities in the overall frequency of the standard velar variant, which reaches 84 percent in Vancouver, a surprisingly high level, but only 47 percent in Ottawa (De Wolf 2004: 233). Second, the data from both cities show less correlation with speech style and social class than has been observed elsewhere (Gregg 2004: 43; Woods 1999: 89). Finally, both studies found the third variant, with a full vowel but an alveolar nasal, to be much more common than the variant with a reduced vowel, which is assumed to be the normal non-standard variant in other studies (Gregg 2004: 43; Woods 1999: 91). However, further study of (ing) in Canada will be required before these patterns can be put forward with any confidence as generally characteristic of SCE.

The foregoing discussion of the pronunciation of SCE can be summarized by restating one of its recurring themes: that SCE, from the phonetic and phonological point of view, is a North American variety very similar to SAE. While there are many stark differences between SCE pronunciation and that of various regional American dialects, including the dialect spoken directly across from Ontario in the American Inland North, it is comparatively difficult to identify systematic variables that clearly distinguish SCE from the less overtly regional types of American English classified above as SAE. In terms of phonemic inventory, conditioned mergers and many purely phonetic patterns, SCE is largely indistinguishable from the speech of a large section of the United States, from Columbus, Ohio, to Seattle and Los Angeles, and increasingly from younger, middle-class speech in many areas outside this section. Nonetheless, two phonetic patterns – the Canadian Shift of /æ/ and Canadian Raising of /aw/ – do produce a subtle differentiation of most speakers of SCE from most speakers of SAE. While many features of SCE pronunciation are also shared with some northern and western dialects of British English, similarities with SBE are confined largely to matters of phonemic incidence – the pronunciation of individual words – though even at this level SCE shows a mixture of British and American forms.

3.3   Canadian English grammar

In the first substantial analysis of Canadian English grammar, Avis (1955) confined his discussion mostly to morphological variants and prepositional usage rather than examining variables of syntax proper, such as the rules or constraints governing the structure of sentences. This emphasis appears to have set the pattern for most future work on the subject: similar variables occur in the section on "grammatical usage" in the *Survey of Canadian English* (Scargill and Warentyne 1972: 72–85), in the "grammar and syntax" section of the report on the *Ottawa Survey of Canadian English* (Woods 1999: 185–199), among the "grammatical variables" of the *Survey of Vancouver English* (Gregg 2004: 82–103) and on Chambers' Dialect Topography questionnaire. A sample of these variables, with frequencies of variants from Scargill and Warentyne's survey, appears in Table 3.17.

As Table 3.17 suggests, many of the grammatical variables analyzed in past studies of SCE have a miscellaneous character; in fact, many of them are really lexical variables rather than systematic elements of grammar. A possible exception to this is the acceptability of positive *anymore*, which involves the syntactic concept of negative polarity. Positive *anymore* is the use of *anymore* to mean *nowadays* or *at present* in positive sentences, as in, *I spend a lot of time with my family anymore*, or, *anymore, I spend a lot of time with my family*, in addition to its standard use in negative sentences, as in, *I don't spend a lot of time with my family anymore*. Positive *anymore* is well known as a syntactic variant associated with the American Midland (Labov, Ash and Boberg 2006: 294). Its use by a minority of Canadian speakers, especially in Ontario, may be derived via Loyalist settlement from that region (Chambers 1993: 9–11; 2008: 9–11), but it is certainly not widespread in Canadian English.

A few other variables in Table 3.17 present morpho-syntactic issues of somewhat greater generality. The adverbial form of *real*, which often retains its adjectival form without *-ly* in vernacular American speech, is the most frequent of several similar variables, such as the adverbial forms of *awful* and *terrible*, used as adjectival or verbal modifiers: in *Anne of Green Gables*, Montgomery (1908) furnishes several examples, such as when Marilla proclaims, "I'll miss her terrible" (273). The form of the first-person singular pronoun in *between you and (I/me)* (see also Gregg 2004: 85–86; Woods 1999: 185–187) is one of many compound pronoun structures that show variation in grammatical case in contemporary vernacular Canadian English, perhaps as a confused reaction to schoolteachers' attempts to stigmatize and eradicate non-standard pronoun usage. For instance, in subject position many people now say *her and I went shopping* rather than *she and I*, while in object

Table 3.17 *A selection of grammatical variables from Scargill and Warkentyne (1972: 72–85), with nationwide frequencies (in percent) of each variant for male (M) and female (F) parents (P) and students (S)*

Variable	Variant	MP (%)	FP (%)	MS (%)	FS (%)
acceptability of positive	yes	9	8	11	8
anymore (*a lot of people are*	no	82	85	77	84
away anymore)	known but not used	7	7	10	7
adverbial form of *real*	*really*	51	58	37	45
(*it's _ hot*)	*real*	26	21	29	25
case of 1.sg. pronoun in	*I*	56	51	30	28
between you and _	*me*	36	41	56	60
objective case-marking on	*who*	73	69	80	83
who (*_ did you see?*)	*whom*	21	25	11	11
past participle of *drink* (*he has*	*drank*	63	59	63	59
_ 3 glasses of milk)	*drunk*	35	39	35	40
past subjunctive in	*was*	38	30	44	42
conditionals (*if he _ here,*	*were*	50	61	33	40
things would improve)					
past tense of *dive* (*he _ into*	*dove*	57	41	54	40
the pool)	*dived*	38	54	37	52
past tense of *sneak* (*he _ by*	*snuck*	31	29	61	66
...)	*sneaked*	60	64	22	23
preposition after *different*	*to*	5	3	4	2
(*my book is different _*	*than*	67	64	73	71
yours)	*from*	28	32	22	27

position many say *Mary saw John and I downtown* rather than *John and me*. Again, Montgomery provides an early example in the speech of Mrs. Lynde, who says "when Anne and them are together" (1908: 268). Similarly, the variable use of past subjunctive in conditionals, as in *if he were here*, is related to a larger set of variables arising from the expression of conditional mood. Many Canadians now use two conditionals rather than a past subjunctive and a conditional to indicate contingency, as in *if I would have known we were walking, I would have worn different shoes*, rather than *if I had known we were walking* or *had I known we were walking* (see also Gregg 2004: 92–93; Woods 1999: 192–193). By contrast, the objective form of *who*, while involving the syntactic issue of case-marking, nevertheless concerns only one word.

The remaining variables in Table 3.17 are similarly limited in their scope. The past tense forms of *dive*, *drink* and *sneak* involve variation in the membership of the historical class of strong verbs, or in the morphological paradigm of an individual strong verb, but are nonetheless essentially lexical variables: they involve a choice between two words with the same meaning, without systemic implications beyond each particular instance. The only systematic difference between the British and American patterns of verbal tense-marking, the past forms of a set of verbs with stems in /-m, -n, -l/, was not investigated by the major surveys of Canadian English. Verbs like *dream, burn, lean, kneel, spell* and *spill* tend to have past forms in /-t/, in some cases also with different stem vowels, in SBE, while they tend to have regular past forms in /-d/, without stem vowel changes, in SAE. In the absence of survey data on this set of verbs, the view of the *COD* that both forms are current in SCE, in varying proportions depending on the particular verb and other factors, will be accepted. Finally, the selection of prepositions after *different* in comparative statements might be better termed a matter of usage – in this case the incidence of particular words in particular contexts – rather than of grammar. There are many other variables of this type in the studies referred to above: *lend* vs. *loan*; *behind* vs. *in back of*; *fewer* vs. *less*; forms of the verb *lie*, etc. Since most of these constitute, in Avis' own words, a collection of "miscellaneous examples" (1955: 14), they have little to say about the general nature of SCE and will not be dealt with here.

In comparative terms, most grammatical variables, like most vocabulary and pronunciation variables, ally SCE more closely with SAE than with SBE. As Table 3.17 shows, there are cases of divided usage, though even these often show convergence with American grammar. While both past forms of *dive* and *sneak* occur in the United States, Chambers (1998c: 19–25) finds almost exclusive use of *dove* and *snuck* across the border from Ontario in western New York and the *Oxford Concise English Dictionary* labels these forms Americanisms. Apparent-time data from the Dialect Topography survey of Ontario's Golden Horseshoe region show a clear trend toward exclusive usage of these American forms among informants in their thirties and younger (Chambers 1998c: 21, 24), a shift that can also be seen with *snuck* in Table 3.17 and is further confirmed by data from the Ottawa and Vancouver surveys (De Wolf 1992: 117). Another American form on the rise, at least in Vancouver English, is *gotten* as the past participle of *get*, as opposed to the British *got* (Gregg 2004: 97–100; see also Avis 1955: 15).

Still another shift toward American grammar is the replacement of the inversion of lexical *have* in yes/no questions with *do*-support, as in *do you have any marmalade?* instead of *have you any marmalade?* (Avis: 1955: 16; see also Ayearst 1939: 232). Woods (1999: 191) finds the British *have you* form giving way to the American *do you have* among younger speakers of Ottawa English, though a third form, *have you got any marmalade?*, also enjoys some usage. For a related reason, lexical *have* undergoes contraction in SBE, as in *you've still a lot to read* and *we haven't any bread*, while North Americans would say *you still have a lot to read* and *we don't have any bread*. (There are, however, many examples of British *have*-usage in older Canadian fiction, as when a character in one of Munroe's stories says, "We haven't time to wait . . . " (1996: 400), or Sinclair Ross' diarist writes, "we've the woodshed converted into a stable already" (1941: 106), or Montgomery's Anne of Green Gables asks Marilla, "have I really a pretty nose?" (1908: 121), or one of MacLennan's characters in *Barometer Rising* remarks, "She's a lot more sense than we have" (1941: 72), while another enquires, "Have you enough money?" (111)).

Moreover, if we examine other, more systematic British–American grammatical differences beyond those studied in past Canadian usage surveys, we find that SCE aligns with American usage just as firmly as in the lexical examples of Table 3.1. Following are several examples of syntactic patterns from SBE that do not occur in North America (for similar lists, see Gramley and Pätzold 1992 or Trudgill and Hannah 1985).

- Collective nouns like *committee, council, government* and *team* take plural verbs in SBE but singular verbs in SAE and SCE, as in *the committee has/have met*, or *Canada is/are winning*.
- The indefinite pronoun *one* is commonly used in SBE and appears also in continued reference, as in *one should always look one's best*, whereas SAE and SCE tend to use *you* or *a person* in this sense, and often use *him, her* or *them* in continued reference when *one* is used, as in *one should always look his/their best*.
- To make up for the lack of a number distinction in the second person in modern English, colloquial British English uses *you lot* as a second-person plural pronoun, whereas colloquial SAE and SCE use *you guys*, the northern equivalent of southern *you all*, or *y'all*.
- The sensory verbs *appear, look, seem* and *sound* can take direct nominal complements in SBE but generally occur with *to be* or *like* in SAE and SCE, as in *you look (like) a fool in that hat*, or *that seems (like/to be) a large amount*, or *she sounds (like) a nice girl*.
- With double-object verbs like *give*, when both objects are pronouns, SBE can put the direct object before the indirect object without the use of *to*, as in *I gave it you yesterday* for *I gave you the book yesterday*, or *throw it me* for *throw me the ball*, whereas SAE and SCE have only *I gave you it yesterday* or *I gave it to you yesterday, throw me it* or *throw it to me*.
- There are many aspects of modal verb usage that differentiate SBE from both SAE and SCE. *Must, ought* and *shall* (with their contracted negatives, *mustn't, oughtn't* and *shan't*) are still common in SBE but rare in North America, where *have to, should* and *will* (or *shouldn't* and *won't*, in the negative) have largely replaced them (for *have to* vs. *must*, see Dollinger 2006: 295). *Dare* and *need* behave like modal verbs in SBE, undergoing inversion and contraction (*dare I make a suggestion?, he daren't say anything, need we bring anything?, you needn't bother with that*), but like lexical verbs in North America, requiring *do*-support (*do I dare to make a suggestion?, he doesn't dare to say anything, do we need to bring anything?, you don't need to bother with that*).

- SBE frequently copies a subject noun and auxiliary verb, in inverted order, at the end of a sentence, leaving a pronoun in subject position, as in *he's a good lad, is our John*, or *she's made a mess of this, has Mary*, or *he'll prove a brilliant leader, will Tom*. With lexical verbs, inversion is marked with *do*, as in *she cooks a delicious lunch, does Maggie*, or *he keeps a beautiful garden, does old Jim*. Sometimes, only the noun is moved, without the verb, as in *she's a charming girl, Jane*, or *they'll make a nice pie, those berries*. The last type of right-dislocation is much less common in SAE and SCE, while the first two are non-existent in North America.
- SBE uses pro-predicate *do* to stand in for main verbs and their complements that are either deleted or repeated in SAE and SCE when they follow auxiliary verbs and are understood from discourse. Asked *Will you be coming to the concert tonight?*, a British respondent could say, *I might do*, whereas the North American would say *I might* or *I might come*. If one person says *I've been thinking of writing him a letter*, a British interlocutor might answer, *you should do*, where the North American would say, *you should* or *you should write one*. (However, pro-predicate *do* does occur in Laurence's *The Diviners* (1974): "I don't understand you. I never have done" (88); and "Why not take a taxi? Anywhere else in the world, she would have done . . . " (393).)

It should be admitted that the alignment of SCE with SAE in regard to the foregoing syntactic variables is suggested here on the basis of casual observation rather than empirical study, since these variables have yet to attract much attention from analysts of Canadian English. As was said above, they were not examined in the major surveys of Canadian English published to date, nor have they figured in the author's own research. Some work has, however, been done on the syntax of Canadian English, which may prove to be a growing field in the future. For example, Tagliamonte (2006) and Tagliamonte and D'Arcy (2007a,b) examine changes in several aspects of the Canadian English verbal system, while Dollinger (2006), as already mentioned, focuses on changes in the use of the modal auxiliaries *have to* and *must*.

One reason that previous research on Canadian English has focused more on morphological variants – and on phonological and lexical variation – than on syntactic variables like those just discussed is that the latter are hard to investigate with traditional dialect surveys, being difficult to present succinctly to the general public on a survey form. They can also be hard to study in sociolinguistic interviews, to the extent that some of them do not occur frequently enough in spontaneous speech to be easily analyzed. Moreover, survey respondents' self-reports of grammatical usage can be more susceptible to self-conscious distortion than similar data on other types of variables, since "grammar" is strongly connected with notions of correctness in the public mind. This is particularly true of any variant that is perceived to be not an indicator of national differences in speech, like those listed above, but a marker of social status within national dialects.

Many syntactic variables do, in fact, mark social differences among speakers. While the lexical and phonological characteristics of SCE discussed in preceding sections can be assumed to be relatively uniform throughout the Canadian population, the syntax of Canadian English, like that of other varieties, displays considerable social variation. Avis suggests that this the principal dimension of syntactic variation: "In matters of grammar especially, cleavages are more commonly social than regional . . . " (1955: 14). Much of this variation, however, is not specific to Canadian English and is therefore of less interest in the comparative analysis of national varieties that is the subject of this chapter. Indeed, many of the non-standard variants found in working-class varieties of Canadian English are common to most if not all major national varieties of English and are correlated with social class in very similar if not identical ways. To that extent, they are the proper subject of a study of social variation in English generally, rather than of the distinctive characteristics of Canadian English. Nevertheless, their occurrence in Canadian English should at least be acknowledged here. Some of the most prominent, in the author's experience, are listed below, with examples.

- Double negatives or negative concord: *I didn't see no cars*; *he can't work no more*; *she couldn't prove nothing*; *there weren't hardly any left.*
- Non-standard person/number agreement: *he don't work there*; *it don't matter*; *they was gone*; *I says to her 'no'*; *we was all in it together.*
- Past participles for preterit: *I seen him there*; *he come by yesterday*; *we been there last week.*
- *Went* for *gone*: *she should have went yesterday*; *I knew he had went there before.*
- *Ain't* for negative of *be* and *have*: *he ain't afraid*; *she ain't coming*, *I ain't got the money*, *we ain't seen her.*
- *Them* for *those*, as a demonstrative determiner: *them guys were fighting*; *it's behind them trees.*
- Objective pronouns as conjoined subjects: *me and him were talking*; *John and them came for dinner.*
- *Youse* (pronounced like the verb *use*) as a second-person plural pronoun: *which of youse is coming?*; *youse are all wrong.*

All of the above are certainly well attested in vernacular varieties of American English and most also in Britain and/or Ireland; they are certainly not unique to Canadian English. While there is no shortage of distinctive morpho-syntactic patterns in vernacular Newfoundland English (Paddock 1981; Kirwin 2001; Clarke 2004b – though even many of these show similarities to vernacular Irish features, for obvious reasons discussed in Chapter 2), it is much more difficult to identify unique variants in the English of the rest of Canada. One possible candidate is the range of complements that *done* can take in its role as a synonym for *finished*, as in *I've finished talking* or *I'm finished talking*. Many speakers of colloquial SAE can say *I'm done talking*, or ask *are you done eating?*, as can many Canadians, with *done* taking a verbal complement. However, unlike most Americans, some Canadians can also use a nominal complement with *done*, as in *I'm done my breakfast*, or *are you done your homework?*. Most Americans would require *with* in these sentences: *I'm done with my breakfast*, or *are you done with your homework?*. Nonetheless, as interesting as this example may be, it hardly makes a strong case for the distinctive nature of Canadian English syntax.

In summary, the discussion in this section suggests that, if it is difficult to distinguish SCE from SAE in terms of vocabulary and pronunciation, it is even harder at the level of grammar. While a number of small differences in morphology and syntax do exist, few of them have the consistent and systematic character of the Canadian Shift, Canadian Raising or Canadian foreign (a) usage, and none of them has the iconic status of *zed* or *eh?*, or the diagnostic value of *bachelor apartment*, *bank machine* or *washroom*. This view receives support from popular characterizations of Canadian English. For instance, in Season 6, Episode 7, of the television series *Corner Gas* ("American Resolution"), when Brent's father is made to believe he is actually an American citizen, the comedy is supported by overt references to Canadian–American linguistic differences. These are not grammatical, but phonetic and lexical: in particular, Brent performs the American stereotype of Canadian Raising, tests his father's knowledge of Canadian acronyms like *CRTC*, and points out that Canadians say *pop* and *washroom* instead of *soda* and *restroom*. Of the grammatical differences that can be identified between American and Canadian English, most are in the domain of morphology, involving variables like alternate past forms of verbs, rather than of syntax proper. In morphology, as in phonemic incidence, some instances of surviving British influence can be found, though these often compete with American forms. In the structure of sentences and the syntactic properties of verbs, however, as to a large extent with vocabulary and pronunciation, where British and American English grammar differ, Canadian English grammar is generally aligned with the North American standard.

4   Variation and change in the vocabulary of Canadian English

In Chapter 3, the results of the *North American Regional Vocabulary Survey* (*NARVS*) were adduced to support the contention that, rather than being no more than a mixture of British and American words, the vocabulary of Canadian English features some uniquely Canadian words as well, even beyond the obvious category of words for things found only or mostly in Canada. For example, most Canadians say *bachelor apartment, bank machine, grade one, runners* or *running shoes* and *washroom* where most Britons say *studio flat* or *bed-sit, cash dispenser, first form, trainers* and *loo* and most Americans say *studio apartment, ATM, first grade, sneakers* and *restroom*; the Canadian terms, though referring to universal concepts, do not generally occur outside Canada. In this chapter, the *NARVS* data will again be referred to, in this instance to examine lexical variables that display regional differences within Canadian English, more than national differences between Canadian English and other dialects. Correlations between *NARVS* data and respondents' ages will also be analyzed in order to identify lexical changes in progress in Canadian English, measured in terms of apparent-time. A complementary view of change in real-time will be developed by comparing the *NARVS* data to data from earlier surveys.

4.1   The *North American Regional Vocabulary Survey* (*NARVS*)

Before turning to the *NARVS* data, however, some background information will be offered on the methods employed in their collection and analysis. *NARVS* began in 1999 as an exercise in data collection for undergraduate students in the introductory course in sociolinguistics at McGill University, taught by the author. A list of fifty-six lexical variables known to vary either within Canada or between Canadian and American English was prepared by the author in questionnaire format. These included both established variables from previous studies, for comparative purposes, and new variables whose diagnostic value as indicators of regional or national differences had yet to be tested. The questionnaire first solicited information on the sex, age, residential history, occupation and educational level of each respondent. It then presented the lexical variables in the form of a brief definition followed

167

by a list of variants in alphabetical order. For example, the first question took the form: "*the metal device over a sink or bath tub that controls the flow of water*: FAUCET / SPIGOT / TAP." Respondents were asked, "Please circle the word you would use MOST OFTEN IN YOUR EVERYDAY SPEECH. Circle more than one answer only if necessary. If the word you use is not listed, please write it in."

The questionnaire was initially circulated to the friends and family of the students in the class. Over several years (1999–2001), this generated an initial sample of about a thousand responses from a wide range of locations across the continent. The wide geographic coverage reflects the fact that McGill's undergraduate students are mostly non-local, coming from all across Canada as well as from many regions of the United States. The latter are concentrated especially along the northern Atlantic seaboard from New England down to Washington, DC, but also from Florida, the Midwest, California and elsewhere. Data from this initial sample were tabulated by nation and region and shared with a reporter from the *National Post*, a national newspaper based in Toronto, who put them on the paper's front page (Dubé 2002). The *Post* story touched off several weeks of continuous media attention that spread rapidly from newspapers to national radio and television, reflecting the interest of Canadians in anything that helps to define them relative to other Canadians and to Americans. In several of these articles and programs, the author included contact information for members of the public who wished to participate in the survey. This inspired requests for another one or two thousand survey forms from ordinary people all over Canada, well beyond the personal contacts of McGill's undergraduate population. Finally, for subsequent years of the sociolinguistics class, a new, electronic version of the questionnaire was put on the web, which encouraged yet another one or two thousand responses from an even wider range of people across the continent. Some of these were recruited or referred by McGill students, others were in classes at other universities and still others had no connection to universities but discovered the site by chance. In its current form, the *NARVS* sample is therefore both geographically and socially diverse.

By 2007, approximately 6,000 responses had been received. For purposes of the analysis presented below, these have been culled to a smaller set of approximately 2,400 responses by using the data on residential history to exclude respondents who either moved from one region to another during their childhood, or who now live in a different region from that in which they grew up. Thus, the data analyzed here represent only people who grew up entirely and still live in the region with which they are identified. This ensures that data from non-local respondents do not interfere with the regional analysis. Of this local group, approximately 1,900 are from Canada and 500 from the United States. They are further divided by region according to the dialect divisions established in the *Atlas of North American English* by Labov, Ash and Boberg (2006: 148), with the Canadians divided into even smaller regions that correspond to the traditional historical and cultural

Table 4.1 *Regional breakdown of NARVS respondents. Mean and standard deviation of number of responses per question per region and country*

Name	Territory	Mean n	S.D.
VV	Vancouver–Victoria (southwestern BC)	120	3
BC	Interior British Columbia	30	2
AB	Alberta	322	5
SK	Saskatchewan	102	2
MB	Manitoba	204	10
NO	Northwestern Ontario	112	1
SO	Southern Ontario	158	1
TO	Greater Toronto	75	6
EO	Eastern Ontario	58	3
MR	Greater Montreal	394	70
QC	Quebec outside Montreal	22	4
NB	New Brunswick	71	1
PE	Prince Edward Island	60	1
NS	Nova Scotia	77	5
CB	Cape Breton (northern NS)	24	0
NL	Newfoundland and Labrador	91	2
Canada	National total	1,920	105
WU	Western United States	124	9
IN	Inland North (incl. Upper Midwest)	97	8
MM	Midland Midwest (incl. W. Penna.)	37	2
SU	Southern United States (incl. Florida)	49	4
SM	South Mid-Atlantic (Phila. to DC)	30	3
NM	North Mid-Atlantic (NYC area)	32	2
NE	New England (incl. western NE)	94	9
US	National total	463	32

divisions of Canada. In some cases these follow provincial boundaries; in others, particularly in populous Ontario, they occur within provinces. The regional divisions are shown in Table 4.1, with the mean and standard deviation of the number of respondents per question per region. These sample data reflect only the forty-four questions that appeared on all versions of the questionnaire and therefore provide sufficient data for reliable regional analysis. Twelve questions, having been removed from or added to later versions of the questionnaire, were answered by only a portion of the sample and will therefore not be analyzed.

As suggested by the standard deviations in Table 4.1, the exact number of respondents per region varies slightly by question, mostly because not all respondents answered all questions, but the small size of the standard deviations indicates only minor variations from the mean. Since the mean gives a good indication of the number of respondents per question for each region, this number will not be repeated in the discussion that follows: regional and national frequencies of responses will be given as percentages, which are easier to interpret and compare.

The establishment of regional divisions was generally constrained by the requirement that there be at least twenty-five respondents in each region, in order to support reliable regional comparisons. As can be seen in Table 4.1, this threshold is more than satisfied in every case except for two regions, Quebec outside Montreal and Cape Breton, where the mean number of responses drops slightly below twenty-five. These were nevertheless maintained as separate regions for historical reasons, even if their regional frequencies are less reliable than those of regions with larger numbers of informants; moreover, the English-speaking populations of these regions are correspondingly small. In the analysis that follows, a minimal threshold was also established for the consideration of minority responses: those that did not account for at least 5 percent of the responses in at least one region were classified as "other" and not given further consideration. The "other" category also includes multiple responses, in which respondents indicated more than one answer for a given question. The analysis presented below is therefore based on the most frequent single responses to each question.

4.2   Regional variation

Of the forty-four questions that appeared on all versions of the *NARVS* questionnaire, some reveal substantial regional variation within Canada, others feature mainly national differences between Canada and the United States (or other countries), and still others involve very little variation of any kind. In order to identify the most useful variables for an analysis of regional variation, the standard deviation of the variation in Canadian regional frequencies was calculated for each variant. The resulting figures for all of the variants of each variable, including the "other" category, were then added together. This produced a global measure of the amount of variation displayed by a set of competing words, which will be referred to as *total variation*. Since the frequencies it is based on are percentages, this measure is expressed as a percentage. It can be used to rank the variables in order of their regional diagnostic power. Total variation comprises three dimensions of regional lexical variation: the number of variants of a variable; the number of important regional differences in the frequencies of those variants; and the relative size of the differences. Variables that display several large regional differences in the frequencies of several variants produce maximal total variation, while those with smaller differences in the frequencies of only two variants across only one regional boundary produce minimal total variation. The resulting values range from 4 percent, indicating a virtual absence of regional variation, to 110 percent, indicating several major regional differences. Table 4.2 shows the ten *NARVS* variables that produced total variation values of over 65 percent: of the variables on the questionnaire, these ten involve the greatest amount of regional variation within Canada.

Table 4.2 NARVS *variables that produced total regional variation of more than 65 percent (the sum of the standard deviations of the regional frequencies of each variant of each variable), ranked in descending order of total variation*

Variable	Variants	Total var. %
standard set of pizza toppings	the works, all-dressed, deluxe, everything on it, supreme, loaded	110
house in country for summer weekends	cottage, cabin, camp, chalet, the lake	107
athletic shoes worn as casual attire	running shoes, sneakers, runners	98
standard set of hamburger or hotdog toppings	the works, everything on it, all-dressed, deluxe, supreme, loaded	96
book of lined paper for schoolwork	notebook, scribbler, exercise book, copybook, cahier	88
multi-storey building for parking cars	(parking) garage, parkade, parking lot, indoor parking, car park	85
small store open late that sells snacks, beverages, tobacco, lottery tickets, newspapers, etc.	convenience store, depanneur/dep, corner store, [brand name], variety store, general store	85
bag with shoulder straps for student's books, etc.	backpack, schoolbag, knapsack, book bag	83
place where you pay for something in a store	cashier, check-out, cash, (cash) register, till	72
non-alcoholic carbonated beverage	pop, soft drink, coke, soda	68

Among the variables included in the *NARVS* questionnaire, that with the greatest Canadian regional diagnostic power is the set of words for the standard set of toppings on pizza. This is a prime example of variation in a lexical domain that, unlike some of those featured in older dialectological studies, is relevant to the lives of most contemporary Canadians. Pizza is among the most popular foods in modern Canada, as in the United States: it is consumed in vast quantities by millions of people across the country in shopping mall food courts, at children's birthday parties, during late-night work sessions at the office, or after moving furniture into a new apartment. Its popularity is partly due to the variety of toppings with which it can be made, suiting a wide array of tastes and diets. This variety has forced pizza providers to come up with ways of simplifying the ordering process, by assigning names to popular combinations of toppings. The standard set of toppings at Canadian pizzerias includes pepperoni sausage, mushrooms and green pepper, in addition to tomato sauce and cheese. This combination is known as *the works* in Atlantic Canada (over 80 percent of responses in New Brunswick, Prince Edward Island and southern Nova Scotia) and as *all-dressed* in Quebec (over 90 percent both in and outside Montreal, where its French equivalent is *toute garnie*). West of Montreal, a greater variety of terms is found. *All-dressed* retains some strength as the leading term just over the Quebec border in eastern Ontario (41 percent) and, more surprisingly, much further away in Saskatchewan (63 percent). In Toronto, the leading term among several is *everything-on-it* (38 percent), which is also the main response in most of the northern United States (the American South prefers *supreme*). From southern Ontario to Vancouver, the most common response by varying margins is *deluxe*, which reaches a peak of 48 percent in Alberta: the exceptions are Saskatchewan, already mentioned, and interior British Columbia, where the Maritime term *the works* edges out *deluxe* by a small margin.

Another regional variable in Table 4.2 is the closely related set of equivalent terms for the standard set of toppings on a hamburger or hotdog, foods of similar popularity across most of Canada, served in fast-food restaurants, at sporting events or at backyard barbecues. On hamburgers, the standard toppings usually include lettuce, tomato, ketchup, mustard and relish or a slice of pickle; on a hotdog they normally include ketchup, mustard and either relish or shredded cabbage, and perhaps also diced onions. Though the regional distribution of terms for these combinations is closely parallel to those for pizza, there are subtle differences between the sets. In Atlantic Canada, *the works* is still dominant, but it cedes some ground to *everything-on-it* in the Maritimes, while gaining strength in Cape Breton and Newfoundland. *Everything-on-it* also erodes a small portion of the almost unanimous support for *all-dressed* in Quebec. The biggest difference in the sets of terms, however, occurs west of Montreal, where the people in eastern Ontario and Saskatchewan who said *all-dressed* for pizza switch to other terms for burgers. In eastern Ontario, most of them join the 61 percent of Torontonians who say *everything-on-it*, while in Saskatchewan they fall in with their Alberta and British Columbia neighbors who say *deluxe*. In this case, it is interior British Columbia that registers the highest frequency of *deluxe* (63 percent), while Manitoba and southern Ontario lean more toward *everything-on-it*. The last term also gains frequency in the United States relative to its use with pizza, especially in the South, where it largely replaces *supreme*, though a small minority of southerners use *dressed*, a term with a remarkable similarity to the Montreal variant.

While many adults would consume their pizza or burgers with beer, some children might enjoy a non-alcoholic carbonated beverage instead, the generic terms for which constitute one of the best-known regional lexical variables across North America (Labov, Ash and Boberg 2006: 290). As already mentioned in Chapter 3, the dominant term in Canada is *pop*, which is shared with much (though not all) of the American Midwest and Northwest. The frequency of *pop* reaches 100 percent in interior British Columbia, over 90 percent across the Maritimes (despite its absence across the border in New England), and over 85 percent in southern Ontario, Alberta and Vancouver–Victoria. The only important competitor to *pop* in Canada is *soft drink*, a term that is certainly known and used in most places but is the principal generic term for carbonated beverages only in Quebec, both in and outside Montreal (73 percent), where *pop* is very rare (4 percent). *Soft drink* also intrudes on the dominion of *pop* in Manitoba (32 percent), eastern Ontario (38 percent) and Newfoundland (27 percent), though *pop* is somewhat stronger in all of these regions. In Quebec, *soft drink* has two French equivalents, only one of which, *liqueur douce*, is a direct parallel, *doux* meaning 'soft.' The more common expression, *boisson gazeuse*, is closer to the usual British term, *fizzy drink*. *Soda*, the main term in the northeastern and southwestern United States, and *coke*, the main variant in the American South, enjoy virtually no currency in Canada.

Pop or soft drinks would be among the staples on offer at a small store, open beyond normal hours, that sells snacks, beverages, tobacco products, lottery tickets, newspapers and the like. An establishment of this type is most often called a *convenience store* in Canada, as in the United States, reflecting its being available closer to people's homes than full-sized grocery stores and/or after larger stores are closed. This is its most common name from interior British Columbia to Saskatchewan and across most of Ontario and Atlantic Canada. In Vancouver–Victoria and northwestern Ontario, location takes precedence over opening hours and the term *corner store* prevails (46 and 47 percent, respectively). In Manitoba, the most frequent response is a brand name (44 percent), as many of these stores belong to chains that dominate regional markets. In southern Ontario, the second-most common term after *convenience store* is *variety store* (29 percent), stressing the diversified nature of the goods on offer. The main Canadian competitor to *convenience store*, however, is another Quebec term, in this case borrowed from French: *dépanneur*. In France, this word suggests emergency repairs, or *dépannage*: a *dépanneur* is a breakdown mechanic. The Quebec usage retains the emergency connotation but transfers it to groceries and related items. As such, it has been enthusiastically adopted by Montreal anglophones (77 percent), many of whom shorten it to *dep*. Until recently, deps were the only places in Quebec other than provincial government liquor stores (and restaurants) licensed to sell wine and beer. In order to prevent competition with the provincial monopoly and support local industry, the selection of wine in the deps was limited to cheaper, blended varieties that were imported in bulk and bottled in Quebec: this is known sarcastically in local parlance as *château dépanneur*. It can serve in a pinch for unanticipated dinners at restaurants whose policy is *apportez (votre vin)*, known outside Quebec as *BYO(B)*, or *bring your own (booze/bottle)*.

When paying for the things one buys in a convenience store or other commercial establishment, Canadians use different terms for the place where the cashier tallies purchases and accepts payment. The most common are *cashier* and *check-out*: the former is the most frequent term in western Canada and Toronto, while the latter is more common in southern Ontario and Atlantic Canada. Quebec is once again distinct in this respect: in Montreal, 78 percent of respondents chose the term *cash*, directly parallel to French *la caisse*. Bilingual Montreal store clerks are commonly heard to call, *s'il vous plaît passer à la prochaine caisse, please pass to the next cash. Cash*, which in the rest of Canada means money in the physical sense as opposed to cheques or credit cards, is also the majority term in Quebec outside Montreal (60 percent) and the leading term in neighboring eastern Ontario (32 percent). Additional terms are the *register* and the *till*, the latter accounting for a quarter of responses in the less urban regions of Saskatchewan and northwestern Ontario. American usage is dominated by *register* on both coasts, joined by *check-out* in middle America.

While paying at the cashier or check-out, especially in a downtown store, one might have left one's car in a multi-storey parking structure, perhaps attached to a shopping mall, department store or office tower. The terms for this structure are one of three lexical variables that clearly differentiate western from central and eastern Canada, as discussed in Chapter 3. All across western Canada, from Vancouver–Victoria to northwestern Ontario, the dominant term is *parkade*, reaching 82 percent of responses in the latter region; only in Manitoba does *parking lot* (30 percent) challenge it. *Parking lot*, which implies not a structure but an open space without a structure for most Canadians, is also the leading term in Quebec outside Montreal (50 percent) and a common response (28 percent) in Montreal itself. While mainly a western word, *parkade* also has some support in the Maritimes: it is the leading term on Prince Edward Island (61 percent) and the second-most common choice in the main part of Nova Scotia (35 percent). Apart from these exceptions, however, Ontario and Atlantic Canada are dominated by the standard American term, *parking garage*, which accounts for a solid two-thirds of Toronto and three-quarters of southern Ontario responses (65 percent and 75 percent respectively), even though signs in the downtown Toronto Eaton Centre direct customers to the *parkade*; very few Ontarians south of Sudbury chose this essentially western term. As suggested in Chapter 3, it may have its roots in use by the Hudson's Bay Company to designate the parking structures attached to its department stores, which were originally limited to western Canadian cities, before the company expanded its retail operations across the country. A third variant that enjoys minority support from eastern Ontario to Quebec is *indoor parking*, while the normal British term, *car park*, is the second choice in New Brunswick (15 percent). American usage is strongly dominated by *parking garage* (82 percent nationally); this term is challenged only by *parking ramp* in the Inland North (22 percent) and by *parking deck* in the South (11 percent).

Another major east–west divide appears in words for a house in the country where people go on weekends (or longer periods), especially during the summer. The term *cottage* dominates eastern Canada, from southern Ontario to Nova Scotia; it peaks at 91 percent in Toronto, where the rural region north of the city is known as *cottage country*. In western Canada, the territory from Vancouver to Saskatchewan is equally dominated by *cabin*, though the highest frequency of this otherwise western variant actually occurs on the other side of *cottage* territory in Newfoundland (85 percent). *Cabin* is also the leading American term, being the most frequent response in all regions except New England, where *cottage* has a slight advantage, and the north-Mid-Atlantic New York City region, where *summer house* is twice as popular. The most important competitor to *cottage* and *cabin* in Canada is *camp*, which is the majority term in northwestern Ontario (77 percent) and a strong second-place choice to *cottage* in New Brunswick (28 percent); it is also another alternative to *cabin* and *cottage* in New England (19 percent). Other regional minority variants include *chalet*, throughout Quebec, and *the lake* in Manitoba (15 percent), the latter reflecting the usual location of cabins: many western Canadians simply say, "we went to the lake this weekend," implying a cabin on the shore of a nearby lake. In Montreal, use of *chalet* (20 percent) might be encouraged not only by contact with French, but by the local use of *cottage* to mean a two-storey house in the city, in contrast to a one-storey bungalow. Outside Quebec, of course, *chalet* refers mostly to a ski lodge.

Another variable in Table 4.2 clearly divides Canada into three rather than two regions: western, central and eastern. This is the use of *runners* or *running shoes* to refer to athletic shoes worn as casual attire, for example with jeans. Like *parkade*, *runners* dominates western Canada from Vancouver to north-western Ontario, while *running shoes* prevails in central Canada from southern Ontario to Quebec, each term consistently accounting for over 50 percent of the responses in its respective domain. Throughout Atlantic Canada, however, the most popular American term, *sneakers*, virtually excludes the Canadian variants, reaching 95 percent of responses in Nova Scotia. West of New Brunswick, use of *sneakers* drops off sharply, taking a distant second-place to *running shoes*. There is a parallel if less dramatic shift south of the border, as the basically eastern term *sneakers*, strongly dominant along the Atlantic seaboard, gives way to *tennis shoes* in the American Midwest and West.

The two remaining variables in Table 4.2 involve terms connected with school life, another lexical domain that is rich in regional variation. The first of these involves words for a book of blank, lined paper in which students make notes during class. As already discussed in Chapter 3, the American term for this is *notebook*, which accounts for 97 percent of American responses. This is also the most frequent Canadian term, exercising less exclusive dominance (over 50 percent) from Vancouver to Montreal, peaking at 85 percent in Toronto. In the Maritimes, however, a Canadianism takes over: *scribbler* (apparently a book in which you scribble notes) garners over 80 percent of responses in Prince Edward Island and Nova Scotia, including Cape Breton, and a smaller majority (57 percent) in New Brunswick. Further east in Newfoundland yet a third variant dominates, the normal British term *exercise book* (73 percent). The latter is also in second place to *notebook* in Vancouver–Victoria (22 percent) and Montreal (15 percent), where it has a direct parallel in French *cahier d'exercises*. The Maritime word *scribbler* also has a secondary territory: on the Prairies. It runs a strong second to *notebook* in Alberta (37 percent) and Saskatchewan (25 percent) and equals *notebook* in Manitoba (38 percent). Because the frequency of *scribbler* drops below 10 percent all across Ontario (reaching a low of 4 percent in Toronto), its distribution is strangely split into two discontinuous regions, west and east. Finally, a fourth term, *copybook*, appears only as the third choice (12 percent) in Montreal.

The other school-based variable in Figure 4.2 is the item in which a student might carry a notebook or scribbler: a bag suspended on the back by two straps over the shoulders. This has a remarkable variety of names across the English-speaking world, including the mainly British *rucksack*, borrowed from German. North American usage is dominated by *backpack*, which accounts for 70 percent of American and over half of Canadian *NARVS* responses. It is particularly strong west of Toronto, where it peaks at 87 percent in Vancouver–Victoria and was chosen by four fifths of respondents across the Prairies. In Toronto itself, while just over half of respondents chose *backpack*, the peak in usage of another term, *knapsack* (23 percent), is also found, which is relatively rare elsewhere. East of Ontario, the frequency of *backpack* drops below 50 percent and three further terms compete with it. One is *schoolbag*, which is equal to *backpack* in Montreal (33 percent) and also strong in Quebec outside Montreal and Cape Breton (29 percent each), but is the majority choice only on Prince Edward Island (60 percent). Another is *book bag*, which is the leading choice in New Brunswick (56 percent), Cape Breton (46 percent) and Newfoundland (65 percent). It is also the second choice after *backpack* in Nova Scotia (26 percent), making it the leading term in Atlantic Canada generally. The third alternative is *kit bag*, a rarity found only on Prince Edward Island (13 percent), which is elsewhere restricted mainly to military use. A final term, *packsack*, is similarly rare, being a distant second choice in two non-urban areas dominated by *backpack*, interior British Columbia (9 percent) and northwestern Ontario (10 percent).

Many other *NARVS* questions revealed regional variation that was somewhat less dramatic than that displayed by the top ten variables in Table 4.2 but nonetheless tied to equally interesting regional patterns. For instance, the Canadianism *eavestroughs*, discussed in Chapter 3, was found to unite the Prairie West (67 percent in Alberta and 88 percent in Saskatchewan) with Ontario (from 78 percent in Toronto to 88 percent in southern Ontario), while the two coasts inclined toward its American competitor, *gutters*, which peaks at 80 percent in Vancouver, also reaching 65 percent in Montreal. Newfoundland, however, shares *eavestroughs* with Ontario and the Prairies (71 percent). By contrast, Newfoundland joins Montreal and Quebec outside Montreal as the only regions of Canada where *see-saw* is the normal word for the tilting board on which children play in a park or schoolyard. Its frequency peaks at 91 percent in Montreal. Everywhere else, *teeter-totter* is the majority term, peaking at 90 percent in Saskatchewan; Nova Scotia comes closest to an even split (57 percent *teeter-totter*). The Canadian proportions of these terms, strongly favoring *teeter-totter*, are opposite those in the United States: the whole American East and South are totally dominated by *see-saw* (up to 97 percent in the south Mid-Atlantic region), while the two terms are evenly matched in the Inland North and West; only in the Midland-Midwest does *teeter-totter* prevail (59 percent; see also Kurath 1949: figs. 13, 79).

The variables discussed so far are summarized in Table 4.3, which, at the risk of oversimplifying, presents an overview of the regional distribution of the main variants of the variables of Table 4.2 and of the two others just discussed. In the interest of clarifying an otherwise complex picture, minor variants are ignored and each region is characterized by its most common variant, thereby making regional divisions easier to perceive, while the number of regions has been reduced to six, corresponding to the main non-linguistic regions of Canada: British Columbia, the Prairies, Ontario, Quebec, the Maritimes and Newfoundland. The actual percentages and detailed regional breakdown that underlie Table 4.3 are given in Table 4.4. It is already evident in Table 4.3 that some regional divisions are more important than others: there are fewer differences between British Columbia and the Prairies, for instance, than between Quebec and the Maritimes. This issue is examined in greater detail below.

Beyond the regional variables already considered, two others appear to be aligned with an urban–rural dimension as well as with region in the stricter sense. These are also shown in detail in Table 4.4. One of them is a classic variable of American dialectology (Kurath 1949: figs. 59, 66): the words people use for a container in which they might put water for washing the floor or the car (or, in the old days, for watering horses, or a container in which to collect milk from cows). A large majority of Americans (89 percent) and a smaller majority of Canadians (69 percent) call this a *bucket*, originally a Midland and southern word. *Pail*, once the northern equivalent, is now used by only 26 percent of Canadians. In less urban western regions, however, it still survives as the majority term: it was chosen by 50 percent of respondents from northwestern Ontario and by 70 percent from Saskatchewan. By comparison, only 9 percent of Vancouver–Victoria respondents chose *pail*; 89 percent chose *bucket*. On the other hand, equally non-urban areas of eastern Canada are even more dominated by *bucket*, which rises to 95 percent in Newfoundland and 98 percent on Prince Edward Island, so the split is not simply along the urban–rural divide.

A less complicated example of alignment with the urban–rural dimension is afforded by words for the main evening meal. Again, there are only two, both of which are originally French: *dinner* and *supper*. The variation between them – essentially involving when one *dines*, or has *dinner*, one's main meal of the day – is still tied to the traditional difference in eating habits between rural society, with its extension into the urban working class, and

Table 4.3 *A simplified view of regional lexical variation among six Canadian regions: the most common NARVS lexical variants in British Columbia (BC), the Prairies (PR), Ontario (ON), Quebec (QC), the Maritimes (MT) and Newfoundland (NL)*

Variable	BC	PR	ON	QC	MT	NL
standard pizza toppings	deluxe	deluxe	everything-on-it	all-dressed	the works	the works
house in country	cabin	cabin	cottage	cottage	cottage	cabin
athletic shoes	runners	runners	running shoes	running shoes	sneakers	sneakers
book of lined paper	notebook	notebook	notebook	notebook	scribbler	exer. book
parking structure	parkade	parkade	pkg garage	pkg garage	pkg garage	pkg garage
small store open late	corner store	conv. store	conv. store	dépanneur	conv. store	conv. store
bag with 2 shoulder straps	backpack	backpack	backpack	backpack	book bag	book bag
place where you pay	cashier	cashier	cashier	cash	check-out	check-out
carbonated beverage	pop	pop	pop	soft drink	pop	pop
tilting-board	teeter-totter	teeter-totter	teeter-totter	see-saw	teeter-totter	see-saw
structures along roof	gutters	eavestroughs	eavestroughs	gutters	gutters	eavestroughs

middle-class urban society. In the former, *dinner* came quite appropriately in the middle of a long day of hard physical work, a usage still reflected in the modern urban expressions *Thanksgiving Dinner* and *Christmas Dinner*, which are normally afternoon rather than evening meals; in traditional middle-class homes, *Sunday dinner*, at which a roast was served, awaited the family on its return from morning church services. In this regime, the evening meal is

Table 4.4 *Regional frequencies (in percent) of major lexical variants in NARVS data. See Table 4.1 for region key and mean n per region. (All-dressed, etc., refer to pizza, not burgers and hotdogs.) Part A: West and Ontario*

Variant	VV	BC	AB	SK	MB	NO	SO	TO	EO
bucket	89	61	59	26	52	44	57	64	55
pail	9	29	37	70	36	50	40	27	40
eavestroughs	18	44	67	88	58	86	88	78	84
gutters	80	53	32	12	40	13	11	20	11
pop	87	100	86	73	40	85	85	67	41
soft drink	5	0	3	10	32	3	5	12	38
all-dressed	2	0	3	63	2	2	3	8	41
the works	27	32	10	8	23	24	28	14	11
deluxe	30	29	48	12	35	28	37	30	13
everything-on-it	23	13	16	5	28	28	23	38	20
supper	29	59	60	79	52	74	52	16	58
dinner	68	37	26	15	32	19	39	74	29
running shoes	26	16	26	26	8	20	65	57	64
runners	56	63	55	54	61	66	16	15	8
sneakers	9	19	11	9	14	9	10	16	15
teeter-totter	70	81	64	90	53	87	76	58	59
see-saw	28	19	28	10	32	13	18	35	31
notebook	65	59	50	62	37	77	83	85	74
scribbler	7	19	37	25	38	4	9	4	8
exercise book	22	19	2	4	1	13	5	6	8
backpack	87	81	83	79	80	79	70	52	59
schoolbag	2	0	2	4	4	3	4	4	7
knapsack	8	6	6	6	4	5	15	23	10
bookbag	0	0	3	8	0	2	1	3	7
cottage	16	11	12	18	25	7	85	91	88
cabin	72	78	66	57	28	7	4	0	0
camp	2	4	3	4	3	77	1	0	0
conv. store	18	38	43	38	26	26	36	50	32
brand name	24	13	32	26	44	12	8	6	10
corner store	46	34	12	16	12	47	9	13	25
dep(anneur)	0	0	0	0	1	0	0	0	3
parkade	72	50	79	81	45	82	1	4	0
pkg garage	7	19	5	5	8	6	75	65	68
parking lot	13	19	9	6	30	6	11	17	8
indoor pkg	0	3	0	1	4	0	5	4	14
cashier	36	45	45	32	39	30	30	31	27
check-out	23	32	14	24	20	23	38	15	14
cash	1	0	0	1	3	1	4	19	32

Part B: Quebec, Atlantic and national (interregional) mean

Variant	MR	QC	NB	PE	NS	CB	NL	Mean
bucket	72	81	67	98	86	100	95	69
pail	23	15	29	2	12	0	4	26
eavestroughs	30	38	39	23	46	33	71	56
gutters	65	62	58	70	51	63	29	42
pop	4	8	94	90	90	92	38	68
soft drink	73	73	1	2	6	0	27	18
all-dressed	96	92	0	0	3	0	5	20
the works	1	0	97	84	87	63	66	36
deluxe	1	4	0	8	3	4	12	18
everything-on-it	1	0	1	3	3	0	9	13
supper	53	76	82	92	83	88	90	65
dinner	33	18	15	7	14	13	9	28
running shoes	65	60	6	0	2	0	0	28
runners	4	4	1	3	0	8	4	26
sneakers	20	12	92	93	95	92	86	38
teeter-totter	6	32	82	75	57	71	24	62
see-saw	91	64	13	22	42	29	75	34
notebook	59	56	33	8	6	0	10	48
scribbler	2	16	57	83	88	96	8	31
exercise book	15	16	0	0	1	0	73	12
backpack	36	46	21	18	49	13	13	54
schoolbag	33	29	10	60	11	29	4	13
knapsack	18	0	6	2	5	4	7	8
bookbag	0	13	56	0	26	46	65	14
cottage	43	56	51	67	76	38	5	43
cabin	3	13	1	16	10	25	85	29
camp	0	6	28	3	7	0	1	9
conv. store	5	8	76	38	51	50	70	38
brand name	1	4	1	28	9	17	4	15
corner store	3	8	11	26	25	25	10	20
dep(anneur)	77	67	0	0	0	0	0	9
parkade	2	0	1	61	35	13	10	33
pkg garage	38	25	65	18	48	75	43	36
parking lot	28	50	8	16	9	4	26	16
indoor pkg	19	21	8	2	4	8	10	6
cashier	11	15	19	20	22	17	13	27
check-out	2	0	39	43	47	67	66	29
cash	78	60	26	18	8	8	4	16

relatively light, often little more than a snack, which is called *tea* in British working-class circles and *supper* in Canada.

In urban bourgeois society both in England and Canada, by contrast, the upper-class habit of dressing elegantly for a grand *dinner* in the evening, eaten in a *dining room* rather than at the kitchen table, was thought an admirable model to imitate. This reduced the midday meal to lighter fare, which was called *luncheon* or *lunch*. Strikingly, Canadian French, with its strong rural roots, displays the same contrast. In France, reflecting Parisian bourgeois usage, *dîner* is an evening meal, preceded by *déjeuner* ('lunch') and *petit déjeuner* ('breakfast'). In Quebec, following French rural tradition, *dîner* is the midday meal, preceded by *déjeuner* ('breakfast') and followed by *souper*, which might consist, as the name suggests, mostly of soup and bread. Thus, traditional rural usage of *dinner* and *supper* in Canadian English and French is exactly parallel.

While the midday use of *dinner* has given way in most of English Canada to *lunch*, the evening use of *supper* hangs on in a solid belt between the two biggest metropolitan regions: from interior British Columbia (59 percent) to southern Ontario (52 percent), peaking at 74 percent in northwestern Ontario and 79 percent in Saskatchewan (Nylvek 1993: 221 shows that it responds to the urban–rural dimension even within Saskatchewan). Unlike in the case of *pail*, however, the rural east is also included in the domain of *supper*, which extends from Quebec outside Montreal (76 percent) to Newfoundland (90 percent), peaking on Prince Edward Island (92 percent). Of the metropolitan regions, only Montreal shows a preference for supper (53 percent, against 33 percent for *dinner*), which may show the influence of French, or perhaps simply of British working-class immigration. In Vancouver–Victoria and Toronto, by contrast, *dinner* is strongly dominant (68 and 74 percent respectively; see Gregg (2004: 78) for a more detailed analysis of Vancouver usage). This urban–rural difference is well-evidenced in Canadian novels: while Atwood's *Edible Woman*, set in Toronto, refers to the evening meal as *dinner* (1969: 22, 29, 30, 110, apart from one reference to *supper dishes*, 8), novels with rural settings, like Ross' *As for Me and My House* (1941: 12–15, 27, 42, 63, 89, 91, 130), set in Saskatchewan, or Leacock's *Sunshine Sketches of a Little Town* (1912: 29, 33, 35, 41, 87–88, 100), set in rural Ontario, or Montgomery's *Anne of Green Gables* (1908: 10, 17, 34, 80, 135, 285, 293), set on Prince Edward Island, regularly use *supper* instead, reserving *dinner* for the midday meal (Ross 1941: 19, 27; Leacock 1912: 65, 119; Montgomery 1908: 42, 61, 80, 112, 117, 119, 160, 278).

The lexical variables discussed so far have been national in nature, either separating large sections of the country from one another or distinguishing several regions. There are several other regional variables in the *NARVS* data that are not as national in scope, distinguishing instead a single region or pair of neighboring regions from the rest of the country. A few examples of purely local variants have already arisen in the discussion of nationwide variables, such as the identification of *corner store* with British Columbia, of *camp* with northwestern Ontario, of *dépanneur* with Quebec, both in and outside Montreal, or of *exercise book* with Newfoundland. There are many other such variants in the *NARVS* data, like *bunnyhug*, a term for a hooded sweatshirt in Saskatchewan, or *public school*, a term for elementary school in Ontario, or *bar*, the shortened form of *chocolate bar* that is usual in Newfoundland.

The largest number of such variants, however, is associated with Quebec, both in and outside Montreal. While this partly reflects the origins of the *NARVS* questionnaire at McGill University, it also reflects the unique status of Quebec's English-speaking community as a minority group that has been insulated from the rest of English-speaking Canada, both by the local dominance of French and by physical distance, particularly to the east. When this present status is combined with the distinct settlement history discussed in Chapter 2, in which Loyalist settlement played a smaller part than to the west or east and settlement from overseas a proportionally larger part, it is not difficult to understand why Quebec English should prove to be so different. Every region of Canada – particularly the older settlements of Atlantic Canada but also the regional cultures of Ontario and the West – has its body of unique local vocabulary: this has been well documented elsewhere, particularly for Newfoundland and Prince Edward Island, as discussed in Chapter 1. The unique circumstances of Quebec English, however, have caused it to be highly differentiated from other regions in terms of the national, indeed universal, lexical variables examined by the *NARVS* questionnaire.

Apart from the foregoing examples of *all-dressed*, *cash*, *chalet*, *dépanneur* and *soft drink*, some of which appear with lower frequency in other regions, the *NARVS* data supply several other instances of unique Quebec usage. One is another food term, from the same fast-food domain as pizza, burgers and soft drinks: this is the word used by restaurants to describe the standard combination of a sandwich or other main item, French fries and a drink, offered at a special price. In most of Canada, this is known as a *combo*, though over a quarter of people in interior British Columbia call it a *special*. In Quebec, it is known as a *trio*, a word that works in both English and French, though in other forms of English it tends to connote a musical group. While many Quebec respondents also chose *combo*, 47 percent of those in Montreal and 29 percent outside Montreal circled *trio*, the term that appears on many local fast-food menu boards. This sense of *trio* is unknown outside Quebec, its frequency dropping to zero across the border in eastern Ontario and New Brunswick. Another completely unique variant is a translation from French, which classifies apartments by the number of separate rooms they contain, the bathroom counting for half. Thus, the Canadianism *bachelor apartment*, which describes what Americans would call a *studio*, without a separate bedroom, would be a *one-* or *two-and-a-half* in Montreal, depending on whether it had a separate kitchen. A one-bedroom apartment would be a *three-and-a-half*, and so on. Of Quebec respondents, 34 percent in Montreal and 29 percent outside chose this nomenclature, frequencies that drop to near zero outside the province.

Many Quebec English terms are adopted directly from French, rather than translated, though their pronunciation undergoes varying degrees of anglicization. Apart from the well-known *dépanneur*, these include the following:

- *abri-tempo* ('snow shelter for driveway,' often shortened to *tempo*, a trade name)
- *allongé* ('diluted espresso coffee,' literally 'lengthened')
- *biologique* ('organic,' of agricultural produce)
- *cabanon* ('garden shed')
- *caisse populaire* ('credit union')
- *CÉGEP* ('junior college,' an acronym for *Collège d'enseignement général et professionnel*)
- *cinq-à-sept* (literally 'five-to-seven' [o'clock], the time when bars offer special prices on drinks, elsewhere called 'happy hour')
- *fripperie* ('used clothing store')
- *garderie* ('daycare')
- *métro* ('subway' or 'underground' [train])
- *péquiste* ('Parti Québécois supporter')
- *pure laine* ('Quebecker of pure French-Canadian origin,' literally 'pure wool')
- *SAQ* ('liquor store,' an initialism for *Société des alcools du Québec*)
- *suce* ('baby's pacifier/dummy')
- *terrasse* ('sidewalk café')
- *tisane* ('herbal tea')
- *vernissage* ('private view' or 'opening night' of an exhibit)

For others, see Fee (2008). Still other terms represent semantic shifts of English words influenced by the meanings of their French counterparts: for instance, a *delay* can be a deadline and *formation* can mean 'training'; for others, see McArthur (1989).

The *NARVS* questionnaire could not examine all of these words, given their irrelevance to most of the continent outside Quebec, but several examples of Quebec English gallicisms do emerge from *NARVS* variables that also involve variation among other terms. That with the highest frequency of occurrence is *stage*, pronounced as in French, meaning a period of supervised work as part of a professional training program, elsewhere called an apprenticeship, internship or practicum. *Stage* is the leading term across Quebec, making up 39 percent of Montreal and 53 percent of non-Montreal responses, but with virtually no usage outside Quebec. Several other gallicisms were used by only a minority of Quebec respondents, nonetheless attesting to the influence of French on Quebec English. With their frequencies in Montreal and Quebec outside Montreal, these include *autoroute* for 'highway' (8%, 25%), *guichet* for 'bank machine' (11%, 21%) and *library* for 'bookcase' (6%, 16%), the latter a translation reflecting the French use of *bibliothèque* to mean the article of furniture as well as the room or institution containing books. It is perhaps not coincidental that the frequency of gallicisms is generally greater outside Montreal, given the smaller size of

Table 4.5 *Strength of lexical boundaries within Canada: mean variant frequency difference (averaged over forty-four variables) and number of frequency differences of greater than 50 percent between neighboring Canadian regions, ranked in descending order of latter*

Comparison	Mean freq. diff. (%)	n (diff. > 50%)
MR–NB	12	17
EO–MR	10	9
NS–NL	8	8
CB–NL	8	5
NO–SO	6	5
NB–PE	7	3
MB–NO	7	1
SK–MB	7	1
AB–SK	5	1
PE–NS	7	0
MR–QC	6	0
NS–CB	6	0
VV–BC	6	0
SO–TO	5	0
TO–EO	5	0
NB–NS	5	0
VV–AB	4	0

the non-Montreal anglophone population and its necessarily more intensive immersion in francophone society.

The combined effect of this large set of distinct Quebec vocabulary is to make the regional border between Quebec and New Brunswick the most important regional lexical division in Canada, at least with respect to the data gathered by the *NARVS* questionnaire. It is possible to measure the relative linguistic importance of regional borders by calculating the mean difference in variant frequencies between each pair of adjacent regions, averaged over forty-four variables. Another approach, which focuses on major differences and ignores minor ones, is to count the number of frequency differences of greater than 50 percent between each pair of adjacent regions. A difference of 50 percent implies a contrast either between a minority of responses in one region and a majority in another, or between divided usage in one region and almost categorical usage (presence or absence) in another. Differences of this magnitude have more than merely quantitative status: they indicate qualitative shifts in usage from minority to split to majority to categorical. The result of both approaches to measurement is shown in Table 4.5, which ranks the borders first by the number of major differences, then by the mean frequency difference. Montreal's eastern border with New Brunswick comes out on top by either method, while its western border with eastern Ontario is in second place. The eastern border accounts for more than twice as many major lexical isoglosses as any other regional division in the country.

Before further examining the rankings of Table 4.5, a few methodological comments are in order. In general, given the distribution of most of Canada's population in a narrow band along the northern border of the United States, the regions that underlie the *NARVS* analysis are aligned horizontally, each with a western and an eastern neighbor, except of course for those on either coast. The major exception to this is Prince Edward Island, which lies north of the border between New Brunswick and Nova Scotia, though its capital, Charlottetown, is slightly east of Halifax, the capital of Nova Scotia. New Brunswick and Nova Scotia are therefore compared both to each other and to Prince Edward Island. Three other modifications of strict horizontal adjacency were made to avoid excessive reliance on less populous regions that produced smaller samples. One is that Alberta is compared with Vancouver–Victoria rather than with the intervening territory of interior British Columbia, which is compared only with southwestern British Columbia (Vancouver–Victoria). The second is that New Brunswick is compared with Montreal rather than with Quebec outside Montreal, which is compared only with Montreal. The third is that (southern) Nova Scotia is compared both with Cape Breton, its northern half, and with Newfoundland, which is also compared with Cape Breton, its closest neighbor.

Beyond the clearly distinct status of Montreal English, the next most important regional borders isolate Newfoundland from both Nova Scotia and Cape Breton, the former more than the latter. This is a reflection in the *NARVS* data of the unique properties of Newfoundland English, so well documented elsewhere (see Chapter 1). It is perhaps more surprising that a similarly important division emerges between northwestern and southern Ontario. This has a geographic explanation: much of the distance between Thunder Bay, the largest city in northwestern Ontario, and the more densely populated region of southern Ontario is a vast, sparsely inhabited expanse of rocks, trees and water that takes two days to drive across. The original English-speaking settlement of southern Ontario did not extend into northwestern Ontario and even today much of the latter region is comparatively remote and inaccessible, limiting its contact with the main population center in the south. For two of the three variables that clearly distinguish western from eastern Canada, northwestern Ontario patterns with the Prairies rather than with the rest of Ontario: *runners* and *parkade* are just as frequent in Thunder Bay as in Alberta. For the third, northwestern Ontario has its own variant, *camp*, splitting the western territory of *cabin* from the eastern domain of *cottage*. The last regional division of considerable lexical significance is another water boundary, in recent years traversed by the Confederation Bridge: that between New Brunswick and Prince Edward Island.

The remaining boundaries are aligned with no more than one major lexical isogloss and relatively low mean frequency differences, indicating subtle, quantitative shifts in lexical usage rather than sharp, qualitative shifts. Not surprisingly, these tend to occur within the larger traditional regions of Canada: British Columbia, the Prairies, western Canada as a whole, Ontario, Quebec and the Maritimes. At the lexical level, the speech of Vancouver is virtually indistinguishable from that of Calgary; that of Toronto from that of Ottawa; and that of Saint John from that of Halifax, at least in terms of the variables examined here. This is hardly surprising, given the artificiality of many of these borders, which traverse regions of more or less continuous population and common history and culture.

A final aspect of regional variation to be examined before passing on to other matters is the question of American influence, which so excites the attention of Canadians concerned with their cultural independence from the United States. The preceding discussion, as well as that in Chapter 3, indicated that many American terms, like *couch, faucet, notebook, parking garage, silverware, sneakers* and *zee*, are found in Canada beside their more uniquely Canadian or British-Canadian equivalents, *chesterfield, tap, scribbler, parkade, cutlery, runners* and *zed*. The question to be addressed here is whether these tend to occur, as a whole, with greater frequency in certain regions of Canada, making other regions, in a lexical sense, more Canadian. If asked to speculate on this question, members of the Canadian public would most likely point fingers at two regions as probable centers of American influence. One would be southern Ontario, which is in close geographic and economic contact with large centers of American population directly across the border, as discussed in Chapter 1. The other would be Alberta. That province, even among people who know nothing of the history of western settlement discussed in Chapter 2, is often perceived by easterners to be a Canadian version of Texas, with its vast cattle ranches and oil wealth and its annual Calgary Stampede, a summer rodeo and festival during which many locals deck themselves out in western gear. Using the same quantitative methods as were employed for Table 4.5, it is possible to move beyond these stereotypes and derive a more objective measurement of the relative lexical importance of the border between each Canadian region and the adjacent region of the United States. This analysis is shown in Table 4.6; for the key to American regions, see Table 4.1.

Table 4.6 shows that the stereotype of Alberta as the most American place in Canada is completely unfounded, at least with respect to its vocabulary. The border between that province and the western United States, along with those between every other western Canadian province and the American West, appears near the top of the table, indicating a comparatively large number of major lexical differences. In this respect, the West is the most Canadian part of Canada. On the other hand, the stereotype of southern Ontario – indeed, Ontario in general – as the greatest recipient of American influence is strongly supported by Table 4.6. The three regions of southern and eastern Ontario are at the bottom of the table, with only two-thirds as many major lexical isoglosses dividing them from the American Inland North

Table 4.6 *Strength of lexical boundaries between the US and Canada: mean variant frequency difference (averaged over forty-four variables) and number of frequency differences of greater than 50 percent between neighboring Canadian and US regions, ranked in descending order of latter*

Comparison	Mean freq. diff. (%)	n (diff. > 50%)
SK–WU	17	30
BC–WU	16	29
MB–WU	15	28
PE–NE	17	27
AB–WU	15	27
NL–NE	16	26
VV–WU	15	26
QC–NE	17	25
CB–NE	16	25
NO–IN	16	24
MR–NE	16	23
NB–NE	16	23
NS–NE	15	23
EO–IN	15	22
TO–IN	14	21
SO–IN	15	20

as divide Canadian from American regions farther west. Whether this reflects historical settlement patterns or the effects of more recent contact is not clear, but the comparatively American status of Ontario is remarkable. It presents exactly the opposite picture of variation in the regional linguistic strength of the international border from the picture that emerged from the phonetic data considered in Chapter 3 (Table 3.15). The phonetic analysis showed the border to be strongest between the Inland North, home of the Northern Cities Shift, and Ontario, home of the Canadian Shift, while phonetic differences between the two western varieties of North American English were more difficult to establish.

The ranking of various segments of the international border in terms of lexical variation can only be established with major differences in frequency of over 50 percent; unlike in Table 4.5, the mean frequency differences in Table 4.6 do not decline in tandem with the number of major differences. This reflects the fact that, beyond the major differences that can be identified, individual American terms that occur to some extent in most regions of Canada show their maximal frequencies in different regions, so that a relatively high frequency of one American term in a given Canadian region is canceled out by a relatively low frequency of another. For instance, of the American variants mentioned above, *couch* displays its highest frequency on Prince Edward Island (93 percent), *faucet* in Montreal (40 percent), *notebook* in Toronto (85 percent), *parking garage* in southern Ontario and Cape Breton (75 percent), *silverware* on Prince Edward Island (58 percent), *sneakers* in Nova Scotia (95 percent) and *zee* in Cape Breton (50 percent). Few people would think of any of these places as particularly Americanized in comparison with other regions of Canada. Perhaps the most remarkable fact to emerge from Table 4.6 is that all of the numbers it displays are larger than all of the numbers in Table 4.5. This indicates that, whatever the relative importance of lexical differences between each Canadian region and the adjacent region of the United States, Canada's regions have more in common with each other than any of them has with the United States. At the lexical level, at least in terms of the *NARVS* data, Canadian English is a unified dialect that can be distinguished from American varieties of English by a substantial set of major lexical isoglosses.

4.3   Changes in progress

In addition to the regional variation discussed in the foregoing section, the vocabulary of Canadian English displays variation correlated with participants' ages. According to the apparent-time hypothesis, variation of this type can generally be assumed to reflect changes in progress. This hypothesis, by which age-based differences in variant frequencies are interpreted as the synchronic manifestation of diachronic processes, is a standard construct in sociolinguistic theory (e.g. Labov 1972: 163, 1994: 43–72; Chambers 1995a: 185–206). Because most aspects of a person's grammar are thought to stabilize once they have been acquired, showing little or no change over the adult lifespan, the adult grammar is assumed to represent the state of the language at the time it was acquired. By comparing the usage of different generations, it is therefore possible to obtain a view of linguistic change as it is happening: 80-year-olds represent the language seventy years ago, while 20-year-olds represent the language ten years ago, and so on.

Though there is little reason to doubt that the apparent-time hypothesis is largely valid for phonology and syntax, the most highly structured aspects of grammar, there may be reason to question its application to the lexicon, which is less systematic and therefore less impervious to post-acquisition change. Boberg (2004d), for instance, found that some lexical variables in Montreal English displayed patterns that implied the late adoption of innovative forms by some older speakers (see also Tagliamonte and D'Arcy 2007a: 213). This calls into question the validity of the apparent-time hypothesis for lexical variables: if the assumption of post-acquisition stability does not hold, data from older generations of speakers are less useful in assessing previous synchronic stages of the language, while those from younger speakers are no guarantee of the future state of the language, since younger speakers may change the way they speak as they grow older. The only way to confirm an apparent-time analysis beyond doubt is with real-time data from earlier studies, which are often not available. In the absence of comparable data from an earlier study on most of the *NARVS* variables, the apparent-time hypothesis will therefore be adopted here by necessity. That said, in the few cases where real-time comparisons are possible, it will be seen that they generally support more than contradict the apparent-time analysis, suggesting that it is at least not entirely invalid in the case at hand.

With this important caveat, then, an apparent-time analysis of the Canadian *NARVS* data will be undertaken here, adducing real-time data in support of the analysis where possible. To this end, the Canadian *NARVS* participants have been divided into four generational groups by birth year: a first generation of participants born in or before 1945; a second born between 1946 and 1965; a third born between 1966 and 1985; and a fourth born in or after 1986. This division is similar to that of Howe and Strauss (1993: 42), who analyze attitudinal and behavioral changes underway in modern American culture, in particular the major cleft between the post-war baby-boom generation, roughly the second of the *NARVS* groups just listed, and the baby-boomers' children, the third group. The younger half of this third group would have included people who were undergraduate students during the years the survey was implemented; it is therefore not surprising that this group is represented by the largest number of *NARVS* participants. As in the regional analysis of the previous section, the age analysis presented below will involve only the forty-four questions that were included in all versions of the survey, which were answered by a maximal number of respondents. The exact number of respondents varies again by question, but the mean number per question for each of the four generational groups just identified is 333, 665, 1,385 and 545, respectively, for a mean total of 2,928 Canadian respondents per question. This is larger than the sample for the regional analysis shown in Table 4.1, because it includes Canadians who moved from one region to another within Canada while growing up or who now live in a different Canadian region from the one in which they grew up, which disqualified them from the regional sample.

Tables 4.7 and 4.8 present ranked lists of the most dramatic changes in word frequency evident among the forty-four variables included on all versions of the *NARVS* questionnaire. Table 4.7 shows the largest increases in word frequency, while Table 4.8 displays the largest decreases. Both rankings are produced by adding the difference in frequency between each pair of successive generations for each variant of each variable. A word that shows a substantial and linear increase or decrease through all four groups will therefore produce a large percentage value, either positive or negative, while one that shows only small or contradictory changes – up in one generation then down again in the next – will produce a small value. Consequently, the words in Tables 4.7 and 4.8 mostly show unidirectional developments across all four generations involving constant increase or decrease, if at differing rates from one generation to the next: some changes start only in the middle groups while others level off before the youngest group. In the tables, the percentage frequency is given for each of the four generations, followed by the intergenerational mean for the whole Canadian sample,

Table 4.7 *Lexical change in progress: largest increases in word frequency in Canadian NARVS data (in percent; sum of generational increases ≥ 25%). Comparison of four generations: participants born in or before 1945; 1946–1965; 1966–1985; and in or after 1986; with Canadian intergenerational mean and US interregional mean*

Q no.	Q1	1st	2nd	3rd	4th	Mean	Change	US
Q25	couch	24	54	72	78	57	55	61
Q31	stroller	31	59	76	80	61	49	73
Q29	cupboard	14	11	37	61	31	47	17
Q27	closet	36	40	58	84	55	47	39
Q4	bucket	30	46	83	76	59	47	90
Q5	gutters	23	21	40	62	36	40	95
Q49	highway	42	58	81	81	66	39	44
Q46	loft	1	1	11	37	13	35	7
Q30	bookshelves	15	26	49	50	35	35	29
Q2	water fountain	57	78	85	90	78	33	58
Q39	notebook	26	42	67	54	47	28	97
Q38	zee	7	12	28	34	20	27	99
Q36	internship	16	16	35	42	27	25	71
Q48	parking lot	3	7	19	28	14	25	3
Q22	bathroom	9	13	27	33	20	25	30

Table 4.8 *Lexical change in progress: largest decreases in word frequency in Canadian NARVS data (in percent; sum of generational decreases ≥ 25%); comparisons as in Table 4.7*

Q no.	Q1	1st	2nd	3rd	4th	Mean	Change	US
Q4	pail	66	49	13	16	36	−50	7
Q30	bookcase	83	70	43	41	59	−43	60
Q25	chesterfield	43	20	4	2	17	−41	0
Q5	eaves(troughs)	75	77	57	35	61	−40	2
Q29	buffet	46	54	22	7	32	−39	22
Q46	bachelor	70	73	49	32	56	−38	3
Q27	wardrobe	41	27	20	7	24	−34	31
Q45	(summer) cottage	59	47	46	27	45	−32	11
Q2	drinking fountain	38	17	10	7	18	−31	30
Q38	zed	92	88	70	61	78	−31	1
Q31	baby carriage	39	22	14	12	21	−28	13
Q36	apprenticeship	60	47	28	33	42	−26	12
Q39	scribbler	49	29	13	23	28	−26	0

followed by the frequency in the American sample. Comparison with the American data allows an assessment of whether the change in Canadian usage represents convergence with or divergence from American usage or an unrelated development.

Many of the words in Table 4.7 are the competitors, so to speak, of words in Table 4.8, belonging to the same variable. This is only natural, as an increase

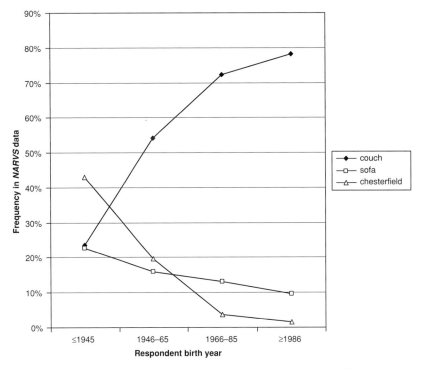

Figure 4.1 The replacement of *chesterfield* and *sofa* with *couch* in the Canadian *NARVS* data

in one variant normally implies a corresponding decrease in another. These relationships are made explicit by the question numbers given in the first column of the tables, which are from the current form of *NARVS*. They are exemplified by the competition between *couch*, *sofa* and *chesterfield*, charted in Figure 4.1, and between *bucket* and *pail*, charted in Figure 4.2. These forms have altered their status from majority to minority usage over the course of the four generations represented in the *NARVS* sample.

One of the main preoccupations of linguists studying Canadian English, as discussed in the previous section, has been the extent to which it exhibits growing American influence. Chambers (1995b), Clarke (1993b), Nylvek (1992) and Woods (1993) have all characterized some of their research in these terms and many others have engaged the subject less explicitly. This is a natural concern, given what was said in Chapter 1 about the ample opportunities for such influence arising from Canada's close contact with the United States. It is therefore not surprising that the convergence of Canadian with American English is exemplified by several of the developments portrayed in Tables 4.7 and 4.8. The most dramatic example is the rise of *couch* and corresponding decline of *chesterfield*, already discussed in Chapter 3 and shown

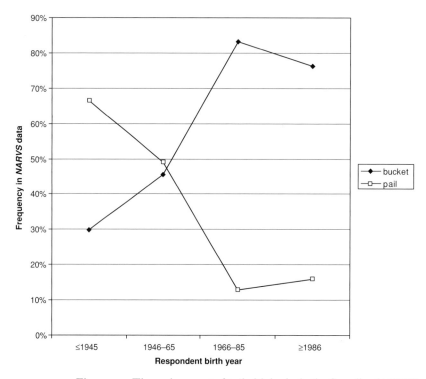

Figure 4.2 The replacement of *pail* with *bucket* in the Canadian *NARVS* data

in Figure 4.1. Among the youngest *NARVS* participants, the most common American term, *couch*, has become the dominant choice (78 percent), while the Canadianism, *chesterfield*, has all but disappeared (2 percent); *sofa*, less common than *chesterfield* to begin with, is also declining. Other waning Canadianisms in Table 4.8 are *eavestroughs* and *scribbler*: both are now minority terms among young *NARVS* respondents, though the decline of *scribbler* appears to have been halted, with a slight rise in frequency from the second-youngest to the youngest group and a corresponding drop in the frequency of the most common American term, *notebook*. The tenacity of *scribbler* is all the more surprising given that the Hilroy company, a leading manufacturer of school supplies in Canada, labels its products not *scribbler* but *notebook* and *exercise book*.

   Not all instances of Americanization involve the loss of distinctive Canadianisms. The rise of *stroller*, *bucket* and *internship* to replace *baby carriage*, *pail* and *apprenticeship*, respectively, while bringing Canadian usage closer to American, involves the continental generalization of certain terms at the expense of others more than the eclipse of specifically Canadian vocabulary: all of these words also occur in the United States. Finally, the rise

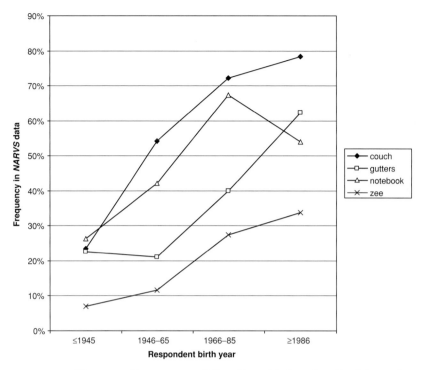

Figure 4.3 Convergence of Canadian with American English vocabulary in the *NARVS* data: the rise of four Americanisms in Canadian English (replacing *chesterfield*, *eavestroughs*, *scribbler* and *zed*)

of *zee*, though still a minority choice even among the youngest *NARVS* respondents, involves the expansion of a specifically American form, but it competes in Canada with an international rather than a Canadian form. To illustrate growing American influence on Canadian vocabulary, Figure 4.3 charts the rise of *couch*, *gutters*, *notebook* and *zee* in apparent time, based on the data in Table 4.7.

In several of these cases of Americanization, real-time data are available for comparison with the apparent-time data from *NARVS*. Data from Scargill and Warkentyne's *Survey of Canadian English* (*SCE*, 1972) on *zed/zee* and *tap/faucet* were already featured in Table 3.2 of Chapter 3. The *SCE* data are particularly useful, because they are based on a national sample and also include an apparent-time component of their own: the parents of 1972, most of whom would probably have been born in the 1930s, would be grandparents (or great grandparents) today, while the grade 9 students of 1972, born in about 1958, would be parents of grade 9 students themselves today, in their forties. Thus, we can compare the two generations of the *SCE* with the two oldest groups of *NARVS* respondents: though not actually the same people,

Table 4.9 *Real-time comparison of data (in percent) from Avis' study of speech differences along the Ontario–United States border (1954: 18; 1956: 50), Scargill and Warkentyne's Survey of Canadian English (SCE, 1972: 54, 86, 87, 99) and the four generations of NARVS respondents (from oldest to youngest). The SCE data show frequencies for males and females*

Variant	Avis (Ont.)	SCE parents	SCE students	NARVS ≤1945	NARVS 1946–1965	NARVS 1966–1985	NARVS ≥1986
chesterfield	76	82/84	67/65	43	20	4	2
eavestroughs	n/a	68/69	48/48	75	77	57	35
gutters	n/a	26/23	29/22	23	21	40	62
zed	93	79/75	72/76	92	88	70	61
zee	7	13/15	14/11	7	12	28	34
tap	90	89/89	89/93	80	72	65	75
faucet	6	9/9	7/6	15	23	30	20

the older *NARVS* respondents represent the hypothetical development of the *SCE* respondents in real time, thereby allowing the stability of lexical variables over the adult lifespan to be evaluated. Scargill and Warkentyne's age groups can also be compared in real time with the second-oldest and youngest groups of *NARVS* respondents, who are at about the same stage of life today: those born after 1985 would include today's grade 9 students, while those born between 1946 and 1965 would include their parents; the second-youngest *NARVS* group is a transitional group, too old to be in grade 9 but too young to have children in grade 9. The real-time comparison allows lexical change in Canadian English to be measured while age is held constant. In three cases, the time-depth of the comparison can be increased by appealing also to Avis' data from the 1950s: though these represent only Ontario rather than the whole country, they extend the data back another generation in real time before the *SCE*. Data from these three surveys for three of the variables just discussed, plus *tap* versus *faucet*, a fourth variable that does not appear to show Americanization in apparent time in the *NARVS* data (or in Chambers 2008: 17), are presented in Table 4.9.

The picture of lexical change and variation that emerges from Table 4.9 is far from clear. Each variable appears to demonstrate a different pattern. The apparent-time decline of *chesterfield* in *NARVS* is confirmed by the real-time data showing higher frequencies in earlier surveys: a majority of grade 9 students still chose *chesterfield* in 1972 compared to only 2 percent today. However, the change appears to have been accelerated by late adoption of the innovative form *couch* (or late rejection of the conservative *chesterfield*) by speakers as they get older: the frequency of *chesterfield* for 1972 parents has fallen from 82/84 percent to only 43 percent today, while that of 1972 grade 9 students has fallen from 67/65 percent to only 20 percent today. As discussed in Boberg (2004d), this suggests that older speakers do, in some cases, adopt newer forms that they did not learn as children, perhaps when they hear them from their own children, or from other younger speakers in the community. Unfortunately, corresponding data on *couch* are not available, because the earlier studies identified only *sofa* as a competing form.

A real-time confirmation of apparent-time change can also be seen in the rise of *gutters*. The frequency of this term remains stable over the lifetimes of the 1972 speakers but rises sharply in the speech of the youngest generation of *NARVS* speakers, who show more than double the frequency of their 1972 age-peers. The complementary data on the decline of *eavestroughs* are not so clear: they show a decline in real time from 48 percent among 1972 grade 9 students to 35 percent in the analogous group today, but they also show a dramatic increase in the use of *eavestroughs* over the lifetime of the 1972 grade 9 students, who register a frequency of 77 percent as today's parents. This suggests that part of the decline in apparent-time evident in the *NARVS* data may really be a stable pattern of age-grading, whereby speakers increase their use of *eavestroughs* as they get older (though why this should be so is far from clear; it may be an artifact of irregularities in the sample).

A similar mix of age-grading and real-time change is seen in the case of *zee* and *zed*. The real-time comparison of 1972 students with today's students shows a drop in *zed* of 11–15 percent and an increase in *zee* of over 20 percent; this is confirmed for earlier generations by the real-time comparison of Avis with Scargill and Warkentyne, allowing for Avis' more restricted sample. However, the extrapolation of the 1972 groups forward in time suggests that some people increase their use of *zed* and decrease their use of *zee* as they age, as suggested by Chambers (1995a: 189). This implies that today's rate of 61 percent *zed* and 34 percent *zee* among the youngest speakers may change somewhat in favor of *zed* as these speakers grow older, thereby moderating the real degree of shift toward the American form. Finally, in the case of *tap* and *faucet*, the real-time data clarify an uncertain picture in the apparent-time data from *NARVS*, which essentially suggest diachronically stable usage of about 75 percent *tap* and about 25 percent *faucet*. The earlier surveys make it clear that these levels represent a slight shift away from the British term toward the American term in both real time and over people's lifespans, the latter perhaps reflecting once again the late adoption of the incoming form among older speakers: with respect to this variable, Canadian usage was once more solidly British than it now is.

In light of the complex interplay of age-grading, late adoption and real-time change evident in Table 4.9, the picture of Americanization suggested by the data in Figure 4.3 is perhaps not as convincing as it may originally have seemed. Notwithstanding these complexities, there is no doubt that some lexical changes in Canadian English do offer evidence of Americanization. Nevertheless, the pattern of convergence they suggest is not the only direction of lexical change in Canada. As Chambers (1998c: 31) has pointed out, the true picture involves a variety of developments. If examples of convergence are numerous, there are also many counterexamples of non–convergence and even of divergence, while still other developments cannot be clearly classified in these terms. Instances of non-convergence are particularly easy to identify. Of the American equivalents of Canadianisms listed in Table 3.4 of Chapter 3, those that, according to the apparent-time analysis of *NARVS* data, are not increasing in frequency in Canada include *studio apartment*, *ATM*, *first grade*, *parking garage*, *sneakers*, *tennis shoes* and *restroom*. Other Americanisms that show no rise in Canadian usage are *trash*, *soda*, *grilling out*, *candy bar*, *frosting*, *silverware* and *pocketbook*: all of these remain minority forms among the youngest Canadian *NARVS* respondents, most of them quite rare. It must therefore be concluded that there is no evidence for a general, ongoing Americanization of Canadian vocabulary, beyond its already-established North American character. Evidence of American influence does exist, but instances of non-convergence, or resistance to American influence, are at least equally common. This may reflect the largely anti-American and pro-British or pro-Canadian views of young Canadians about the relative correctness and esthetic qualities of national varieties of English, reported in Chapter 1.

Instances of actual divergence are harder to find, but they would include the rise of *parking lot* shown in Table 4.7. This comes at the expense not of the Canadianism *parkade*, which is holding its own, but of the most common American term, *parking garage*. Another, not included in Table 4.7 because of its more gradual progress, is the rise of *utensils* as a general word for knives, forks and spoons. This is a rare response among Americans (10 percent) but almost three times as frequent among the youngest Canadians (27 percent). By contrast, the American equivalent *silverware* (78 percent of US responses) enjoys little use in Canada except in Cape Breton (50 percent) and Prince Edward Island (58 percent), the British term *cutlery* remaining the most common choice among all generations of Canadians (55 percent). Similarly, if the Canadianism *bachelor apartment* is declining in Table 4.8, its replacement in Table 4.7 is not the American term *studio apartment* but a new Canadian term, *loft apartment*, which is very rare among American respondents (7 percent). A final example is the rise of *water fountain* at the expense of *drinking fountain* portrayed in Tables 4.7 and 4.8: while both these terms occur in American English, the Canadian trend in favor of the former is driving Canadian usage away from American rather than toward it.

Several developments in the vocabulary of Canadian English cannot be classified clearly in relation to American English. For instance, the decline of *cottage* in Table 4.8 reflects an increase in "other" responses, particularly multiple responses (*cottage* and *cabin*, or *cottage* and *the lake*), rather than convergence with American usage, which is itself divided on this matter. The rise of *highway* in Table 4.7 represents the generalization of this term at the expense of several minority forms, *freeway*, *expressway* and *autoroute*, perhaps as a result of the adoption of *highway* by the federal Ministry of Transport to designate the *Trans-Canada Highway*, a Canadian equivalent of the American Interstate highway system. In any case, though the rise

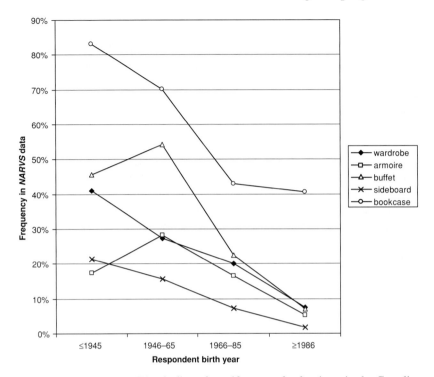

Figure 4.4 The decline of specific terms for furniture in the Canadian *NARVS* data: the replacement of *wardrobe* and *armoire* with *closet*; of *buffet* and *sideboard* with *cupboard*; and of *bookcase* with *bookshelves*

of *highway* cannot be seen as a divergence from American English, since it is also the most popular term in the United States, the more characteristically American terms *expressway* and *freeway*, associated with the eastern and western United States respectively, are declining rather than rising in Canadian usage. Finally, three diachronic developments in the *NARVS* data seem to represent a generalization of generic vocabulary in the semantic domain of household furniture. The three instances of this in Tables 4.7 and 4.8 are: the substitution of *closet* for *wardrobe*, to designate 'a tall piece of furniture in your bedroom with hanging space for suits and dresses' (another specialized word for this, *armoire*, was less frequent to begin with but is also declining); of *cupboard* for *buffet*, to designate 'a long, low piece of furniture with sliding doors or drawers, for storing dishes, etc.' (another specialized word for this, *sideboard*, was less frequent to begin with but is also declining); and of *bookshelves* for *bookcase*, to designate 'a piece of furniture with shelves for storing books.' These developments are charted in Figure 4.4.

The foregoing tables and figures indicate that lexical change in Canadian English is not a unidirectional process that can be easily characterized in simple terms. Rather, it displays a number of contradictory developments. Some lexical variables show convergence with American usage but others show an absence of such convergence, exemplifying instead the survival of Canadianisms despite close contact with the United States and American English. Still other variables reveal patterns of change related to cultural developments that cannot be understood in terms of cross-border influence. Yet more patterns can be found among the large set of variables examined in other studies. Scargill and Warkentyne's presentation of vocabulary data from the *Survey of Canadian English* (1972: 86–100) facilitates apparent-time analysis of nationwide data, while De Wolf (1996) examines the effect of speaker age, among other social factors, on the vocabulary variables that were included in the sociolinguistic surveys of Vancouver and Ottawa, which include several of those discussed here (see also Gregg 2004: 77–82 and Woods 1999: 244–251). As with so many aspects of lexical variation, the overall direction of lexical change in Canadian English resists intuitively tempting generalizations.

5 Variation and change in the phonetics of Canadian English

In Chapter 3, acoustic phonetic data from the *Phonetics of Canadian English* (*PCE*) project were used to establish the general phonetic characteristics of Canadian English and to demonstrate how Canadian English differs phonetically from neighboring American dialects. In this chapter, data from the same source will be used to examine phonetic variation within Canadian English. To these will be added data from an allied project, also carried out by the author, called the *Phonetics of Montreal English* (*PME*), as well as data from other studies, where these are able to add to the picture that emerges from the author's own research. Methodological details of the *PCE* project were already presented in Chapter 3 and will therefore not be repeated here; they can also be found in other publications (Boberg 2005a, 2008a). The following discussion will also make reference to many of the phonological and phonetic patterns introduced in Chapter 3, without repeating the basic descriptive information contained in that chapter: for explanations of patterns like the Canadian Shift and Canadian Raising and the phonemic and phonetic transcription of the vowels they involve, readers are referred to Chapter 3.

Regional variation in the phonetics of Canadian English will be discussed below in Section 5.1, while social and ethnic variation and changes in progress will be handled in Sections 5.2, 5.3 and 5.4, respectively. As in Chapter 3, the focus here will be on Standard Canadian English (SCE): essentially, the speech of middle-class people from Vancouver to Halifax. To the extent that it differs substantially from SCE, the speech of working-class people, particularly in traditional enclaves such as Newfoundland and Cape Breton, as well as the speech of other distinct groups, like Aboriginal communities, will be set aside as the proper subject for research with a different focus. The one exception to this will be the ethnic communities that make up the English-speaking community of Montreal, which were the subject of the author's own *PME* project.

5.1 Regional variation

The main purpose of the *PCE* project was to investigate regional variation in the phonetics of Canadian English in a more focused way than was possible in the *Atlas of North American English* (Labov, Ash and Boberg 2006). With only thirty-three Canadian participants from a broad social range, the *Atlas* sample was sufficient for establishing the main phonological and phonetic differences between Canadian English and neighboring American dialects, which was the main goal of the *Atlas*, but not for investigating variation within Canadian English. While small to begin with, the *Atlas* sample was also socially diverse, meaning that the analysis of regional differences within Canada was hampered by potential interference from social factors. The reliance of the *Atlas* on spontaneous speech as its main source of data presented a further problem: while this brought the analysis closer to the ultimate object of description (vernacular speech), it made it difficult to ensure that the representation of crucial allophonic environments, like those involved in Canadian Raising, was comparable for all speakers. These methodological issues were addressed in the *PCE* project by drawing the sample of participants from the undergraduate student population at McGill University, in which age and education are largely controlled for, leaving sex as the main social factor; and by relying on a word list as the main source of data, thereby ensuring a uniform set of data from each participant. While it has some corresponding disadvantages, this approach, along with a larger sample of eighty-six speakers, allows the *PCE* analysis to focus with greater confidence on speakers' regional origins as the independent variable of interest.

The regional breakdown of the *PCE* sample was designed to test both the intra-Canadian dialect boundaries established by the *Atlas* and the internal homogeneity of the regions created by those boundaries. Essentially, the *Atlas* divided Canada into two regions. "Inland Canada" extends from Edmonton to Toronto or, in respect of the Canadian Shift, from Vancouver to Montreal; the latter is also the extent of the territory labeled "Canada" in the overall view of North American dialects of map 11.5 (148). The eastern remainder of the country is classified as the "Atlantic Provinces," comprising the Maritime provinces and Newfoundland (148), which lie outside the territory of the Canadian Shift. Though the internal dialect geography of Canada was not a focus of the *Atlas*, which was concerned more with structural dialectology and sound change on a continental scale, its map of Canada (map 15.7, 224) indicates two important dialect boundaries. One divides British Columbia from the Prairies, marking the western edge of Inland Canada; the other divides central Canada from the Maritimes, marking its eastern edge, though the eastern edge is really more a transition zone of several isoglosses. These separate individual cities across the main population belt of central Canada, from Windsor, Ontario, to Montreal. In the *PCE* sample, therefore, distinctions parallel to those of the *Atlas* were made between British Columbia, Atlantic Canada and the territory between them, but several smaller regions within Inland and Atlantic Canada were also distinguished. These reflect the traditional historical and cultural divisions of Canada, as well as the settlement patterns discussed in Chapter 2. The full

Table 5.1 Phonetics of Canadian English *(PCE) participants by region and sex*

Symbol	Region	Female	Male	Total
BC	British Columbia	8	4	12
PR	Prairies (Alberta, Saskatchewan, Manitoba and northwestern Ontario)	8	7	15
SO	Southern Ontario	4	3	7
TO	Greater Toronto	4	4	8
EO	Eastern Ontario	5	4	9
QC	Quebec (mostly Greater Montreal)	8	5	13
MT	Maritimes (New Brunswick and Nova Scotia)	9	7	16
NL	Newfoundland	5	1	6
	Total	51	35	86

set of *PCE* regions, with the number of female and male participants from each, is shown in Table 5.1.

In order to qualify as *PCE* participants, students had to have grown up entirely in the region they were to represent, and to have had both parents from the same region. The *PCE* participants are therefore good representatives of regional speech, at least for their age and social level. Their social characteristics, as young, mostly middle-class speakers, imply that they represent the extent of regional variation within Standard Canadian English, which is likely to be minimal, rather than among local working-class vernaculars, which would hypothetically be greater. At a broader social level, any regional differences identified in the following analysis can generally be assumed to be even sharper than they appear here. As in Chapter 3, the analysis here will be confined to data from the word list, which was read by all of the participants. This eliminates the potentially confounding effects of phonetic, prosodic and lexical factors such as word stress and the nature of neighboring segments, except insofar as these are deliberately controlled, for purposes of allophonic analysis. For example, there is no possibility that the degree to which subjects appear to participate in Canadian Raising will be affected by the number of tokens of unraised /aw/ that happen to be available for analysis from their spontaneous speech. Of the items on the word list, 145 were included to represent the normal phonetic range of all of the vowel phonemes of English, with extra representation of allophonic contexts of particular interest. The mean F1 and F2 values of these phonemes and allophones from the word list productions of the national sample of participants were presented in Table 3.12 and Figure 3.1 of Chapter 3. The following analysis will identify the most important regional differences in these values.

The analysis of regional differences was carried out on the mean formant values of each vowel for each participant. The mean values were grouped according to the phonetic processes in which they are involved: those involved in the Canadian Shift, in Canadian Raising, in the laxing of the nuclei of tense upgliding vowels, in the raising of /æ/, etc. Each functional set of measurements was then subjected to a MANCOVA, run in SPSS, which examined the effect of region, city size and sex on the formant values. The regional categories were those of Table 5.1. Northwestern Ontario was included in the Prairie region on the basis of initial observations that its speech is more similar to that of the Prairie provinces than to that of southern Ontario, as demonstrated with lexical data in Chapter 4 (Section 4.2); the exclusion of Prince Edward Island from the Maritime region reflects a lack of data rather than a matter of classification.

The city size variable involved the relative size of the communities in which participants had grown up, divided into three categories: towns of less than 100,000 people (n = 40); cities of 100,000 to one million people (n = 20); and major metropolitan areas of over one million people (Vancouver, Toronto and Montreal; n = 26). However, city size was not found to have a significant overall effect on any of the sets of dependent measures, either on its own or in combination with region. It will therefore not be further discussed.

Following the main multivariate analysis, tests of between-subjects effects were run in SPSS to determine which of the dependent measures in each set were significantly influenced by each independent variable. Finally, for the regional analysis, pairwise comparisons were run to determine which of the regional divisions had a significant effect on the dependent measure. The between-subjects effects and pairwise comparisons are reported only where the MANCOVA found an overall significant effect of the independent variable ($p \leq 0.05$ by Wilks' Lambda), or a marginally significant effect ($p \leq 0.10$). The significant effects of region and sex identified in the MANCOVA are listed in Table 5.2. The results of the tests of between-subjects effects and the pairwise comparisons for the regional analysis are shown in Table 5.3, while the regional means for the measures that show significant regional differences are given in Table 5.4. The effects of region will be examined in this section; those of sex will be examined in the next.

The first phonetic characteristic of Canadian English discussed in Chapter 3, and the main defining feature of Inland Canada in the *Atlas of North American English*, was the Canadian Shift, first identified by Clarke, Elms and Youssef (1995). There have been several studies of the shift in particular regions: Esling and Warkentyne (1993) first noticed the retraction of /æ/ in Vancouver English; Clarke, Elms and Youssef's original study of the shift examined mostly Ontario speakers; Boberg (2005a) analyzed the shift in Montreal English; D'Arcy (2005) studied it in St. John's, Newfoundland; and Hagiwara (2006) added data from Winnipeg. Partly because of methodological differences that hamper direct comparison and partly because of the lack of a national data set other than that of the *Atlas*, a clear view of whether the shift operates in the same way in all regions of Canada has yet to emerge. The *PCE* data provide an opportunity for direct comparison of socially similar young Canadians from coast to coast. If the shift does not

Table 5.2 *Effects of region and sex on sets of phonetic measures in data from* PCE *project: results of MANCOVA. "Dist." = distance in Hertz*

Process/set	Dependent measures	Effect of region	Effect of sex
Canadian Shift	F1/F2 of short vowels	NO: F = 0.939 (84 df); n.s.	MARGINAL: F = 1.771 (12 df); p = 0.082
Canadian Raising	F1/F2 of /ayT, awT/; dist. from /ay, aw/	YES: F = 1.625 (49 df); p = 0.009	NO: F = 1.209 (7 df); n.s.
Fronting of /uw/	F1/F2 of /uw/; F2 dist. from /æ/	MARGINAL: F = 1.503 (21 df); p = 0.083	YES: F = 3.981 (3 df); p = 0.012
Position of /ey/ and /ow/	F1/F2 of /ey, ow/	YES: F = 1.192 (28 df); p = 0.006	YES: F = 4.554 (4 df); p = 0.003
Position of /ay/ and /aw/	F1/F2 of /ay, aw/	NO: F = 1.182 (28 df); n.s.	NO: F = 1.356 (4 df); n.s.
Position of /ahr/	F1/F2 of /ahr/	YES: F = 3.941 (14 df); p = 0.000	YES: F = 3.153 (2 df); p = 0.050
Raising of /æN/ and /æg/	F1/F2 of /æN, æg/, Cartesian dist. from /æ/	YES: F = 2.184 (42 df); p = 0.000	YES: F = 2.361 (6 df); p = 0.043

Table 5.3 *Significant effects of region on* PCE *phonetic measures (p ≤ 0.05): results of tests of between-subjects effects*

Measure	F	df	Sig.
F1(awT)	2.435	7	0.030
F2(awT)	3.555	7	0.003
F2(uw)	2.485	7	0.027
F2(æ)-F2(uw)	2.491	7	0.026
F2(ow)	2.363	7	0.034
F2(ahr)	7.328	7	0.000
F1(æg)	2.508	7	0.026
F1(æN)	4.209	7	0.001
F2(æg)	4.438	7	0.001
Cart. dist.(æ-æN)	3.699	7	0.002
Cart. dist.(æ-æg)	5.439	7	0.000
Diff.(æ/æN-æ/æg)	3.858	7	0.002

operate in some regions, or operates in a different way, we would expect to see regional differences in the mean positions of the shifting vowels in the *PCE* data set. The result of the MANCOVA reported in Table 5.2, together with the absence of Canadian Shift vowels from Tables 5.3 and 5.4, indicates that we do not see such differences: region had no significant effect on the mean position of /i/, /e/ or /æ/. As suggested by Figure 3.2 in Chapter 3, a relatively retracted /æ/ is displayed by the large majority of *PCE* participants, irrespective of region, serving to distinguish them from the

Table 5.4 *Regional means (in Hz) for* PCE *phonetic measures showing significant effect of region (from Table 5.3)*

Measure	BC	PR	SO	TO	EO	QC	MT	NL
F1(awT)	736	732	716	685	691	776	718	826
F2(awT)	1,636	1,612	1,770	1,784	1,757	1,705	1,702	1,750
F2(uw)	1,804	1,657	1,895	1,827	1,769	1,751	1,652	1,546
F2(æ)-F2(uw)	−100	113	−241	−110	−95	−22	99	230
F2(ow)	1,337	1,227	1,258	1,352	1,350	1,288	1,269	1,226
F2(ahr)	1,298	1,313	1,396	1,428	1,443	1,339	1,509	1,524
F1(æg)	746	746	750	741	739	832	771	832
F1(æN)	741	742	693	670	653	761	696	806
F2(æg)	2,008	2,103	1,927	1,912	1,972	1,862	1,978	1,896
Cart. dist.(æ-æN)	382	358	582	463	552	356	415	286
Cart. dist.(æ-æg)	335	370	311	243	329	166	257	147
Diff.(æ/æN-æ/æg)	47	−12	271	220	222	190	158	139

large majority of their American peers. The Canadian Shift, then, appears to be a pan-Canadian pattern, at least among young, middle-class Canadians. An analysis of the progress of the shift in apparent time will be presented below in Section 5.4.

In connection with the analysis of the Canadian Shift, the mean positions of /o/ and /ʌ/ were tested for regional effects, since they are part of the short vowel system on which the shift operates. While there was no overall effect of region on these vowels, among Newfoundland participants they did exhibit patterns characteristic of Newfoundland English, whereby /ʌ/ is articulated farther back and /o/ lower and farther forward than in the rest of Canada (Clarke 2004a: 371; 2008: 95–97). However, differences between Newfoundland and other regions for the F2 of /ʌ/ and the F1 and F2 of /o/ attained significance in only some cases, and then often only marginal significance, preventing their inclusion in Tables 5.3 and 5.4. The social characteristics of the *PCE* sample are likely to blame for this result: these phonetic patterns are more pronounced in vernacular Newfoundland English than in the more formal, middle-class variety elicited in the *PCE* interviews.

Canadian Raising, by contrast, does show clear regional differences, in terms of both its application and its phonetic output. However, this is true only of /awT/, the more distinctively Canadian domain of raising: no significant regional differences appeared in the raising of /ayT/. The application of /awT/-raising is reflected in the F1, or height, of /awT/: the lower its F1, the higher the vowel and the more pronounced the pattern of raising. The pairwise comparisons performed in SPSS indicate significant differences in the F1 of (awT) between Quebec and surrounding regions, particularly the Maritimes, eastern Ontario and Toronto, and between Newfoundland and every other region of Canada except Quebec. These differences confirm the regional exceptions to Canadian Raising mentioned in Chapter 3: a significantly higher F1 of /awT/ in Quebec and Newfoundland (776 and 826

Hz, respectively, as shown in Table 5.4) reflects the variable application of the raising of /awT/ in those regions. Ethnic effects on raising in Montreal English will be considered below.

Among those areas where raising of /awT/ does apply consistently, we find regional variation in the relative advancement of the raised vowel, reflected in its F2. The highest F2 values, indicating the most advanced nuclei, are found across Ontario, from southern Ontario through Toronto to eastern Ontario. In these regions, the mean F2 of /awT/ is above 1,750 Hz, a quality closer to the mean F2 value of /e/ (1,891 Hz) than to that of /ʌ/ (1,504 Hz), as given in Table 3.12 in Chapter 3. The F2 means of all of these regions are significantly higher than those of the Prairies and British Columbia, where we find the lowest mean F2 values for /awT/. In western Canada, the F2 of /awT/ is below 1650 Hz, indicating a nuclear quality much closer to that of /ʌ/. The Inland Canada region of the *Atlas*, then, is bisected by an important isogloss in the F2 of /awT/, amounting to a 100-Hz difference between western Canada and Ontario: east of this isogloss, *house* is pronounced something like [hɐ̈ʊs]; west of it, we hear instead something like [hʌʊs].

In the Maritimes, where Emeneau (1935: 143) reported a merger of *couch* and *coach* in Lunenburg, implying a very low value for the F2 of /awT/, the *PCE* data show a medial mean value (1,702 Hz), which is significantly different from the lowest value on the Prairies and from the highest value in Toronto but not from those of other regions. It certainly does not indicate a merger of /awT/ with /ow/, which has a mean F2 of 1,269 Hz in the Maritimes. In fact, within the Maritime region, the lower values for the F2 of /awT/ tend to occur in New Brunswick more than in Nova Scotia: several of the Nova Scotia participants, including the single speaker from Lunenburg itself, produced values in the range of those of Ontario.

The next phonetic process discussed in Chapter 3, the movement of /uw/ away from the high-back corner of the vowel space, shows only a marginally significant effect of region. This reflects the fact that the effect is limited to the F2 or advancement of /uw/, its height being relatively uniform across the country. Table 5.3 shows that region has a significant effect both on the absolute position of /uw/ and on its position relative to /æ/, which moves in the opposite direction in the Canadian Shift. The latter provides an index of phonetic innovation in Canadian English, uniting two of its most important developments. For the most innovative speakers in these respects, /uw/ is now farther front than /æ/, the vowels having reversed their relative orientation; for more conservative speakers, /uw/ remains behind /æ/. The fronting of /uw/ is most advanced in British Columbia, southern Ontario and Toronto, where its F2 is over 1,800 Hz. It is least advanced on the Prairies and in Atlantic Canada, where F2 values drop below 1,700 Hz (as low as 1,546 Hz in Newfoundland). The mean F2 values of all of the advanced regions are significantly higher than those of all of the conservative regions; eastern

Ontario and Quebec show medial values that are not significantly different from either extreme. Strikingly, then, an important isogloss in the F2 of /uw/ appears within western Canada, between British Columbia and the Prairies. While this western isogloss corresponds to the western edge of the Inland Canada region of the *Atlas*, a second isogloss, between the Prairies and Ontario, once again bisects Inland Canada. Turning to the relative positions of /uw/ and /æ/, we find exactly the same set of significant differences: /uw/ and /æ/ have reversed their relative positions in British Columbia, southern Ontario and Toronto, with /uw/ 100 Hz or more farther front than /æ/, while they maintain their traditional relative positions on the Prairies and in Atlantic Canada, with /æ/ 100 or more Hz farther forward than /uw/.

A parallel development to the movement of /uw/ away from the rear periphery of the vowel space is the corresponding shift of /ow/ toward mid-central position, which is much less advanced in Canada than in many American regions. Also unlike the centralization of /ow/ in the American Midland and South, the Canadian version has no front counterpart in the retraction and lowering of the nucleus of /ey/. Despite its comparatively limited extent, the centralization of /ow/ does exhibit significant regional differences in Canada, which are broadly similar to the patterns observed with /uw/, emphasizing the systematic connection between these developments. The F2 of /ow/ is significantly lower on the Prairies than in either British Columbia or Toronto and eastern Ontario, and the contrast between the lower values of Atlantic Canada and the higher values of Toronto and eastern Ontario is marginally significant: the division between advanced and conservative regions occurs at about 1,300 Hz. The main difference in the regional profile of the fronting of /uw/ and /ow/ is southern Ontario, which participates in the former to the same extent as the rest of Ontario, but which joins the Prairies and Atlantic Canada in the conservative camp when it comes to the latter. This introduces an isogloss within Ontario, in addition to a second isogloss dividing British Columbia from the Prairies.

In regard to the next phonetic variable, the phonetic character of /ahr/, British Columbia and the Prairies are once again united as a western region where /ahr/ has a comparatively back articulation, as shown by the F2 vales of about 1,300 Hz in Table 5.4. These are significantly lower than the mean values for Ontario (the contrast with southern Ontario is marginally significant). The Ontario values are in turn lower than those for Atlantic Canada, which rise to over 1,500 Hz, a central quality, though in this case the statistical significance is in the marginal range of $p = 0.05$–0.10. Quebec is an island of lower values, similar to those of western Canada, between the unretracted vowels on either side of it: its mean is significantly lower than those of either eastern Ontario or the Maritimes. As the range of means in Table 5.4 suggests, regional differences in the relative advancement of /ahr/ are highly salient and easily perceived: to a western ear, an easterner's pronunciation of *bar* and *dark* as [bɐɹ] and [dɐɹk] rather than [bɑɹ] and [dɑɹk] is quite striking.

The remaining measures in Tables 5.3 and 5.4 all concern the allophonic configuration of /æ/: in particular, the raising of /æ/ before front nasals and /g/. In Chapter 3, it was observed that Canadian English as a whole exhibits a "continuous" short-*a* pattern, in which /æ/ is raised more before nasals than before /g/, but that this pattern displays regional variation. Table 5.3 shows that this variation involves both the absolute position of the /æN/ and /æg/ allophones and their relative proximity to the main, unraised distribution of /æ/. The latter is measured as Cartesian distance in Hz, since raising occurs along a diagonal trajectory that follows the front periphery of the vowel space, involving the F1 and F2 dimensions simultaneously. However, because the position of unraised /æ/ may be affected by the relative advancement of the Canadian Shift, the absolute position of the raised allophones may be a more reliable indication of the extent of raising. The last measure in Tables 5.3 and 5.4 is the difference between the two Cartesian distances, indicating the degree of approximation in Hz between the two allophones along the diagonal dimension: the smaller the value, the closer their positions.

In Table 5.4, the most obvious divergences from the general pattern are in Quebec and Newfoundland, which show less raising than other regions; and in western Canada, particularly the Prairies, where a close approximation between the two raised allophones appears, reflecting less extreme pre-nasal raising and more fronting of /æg/ than is found in Ontario. Maximal raising of /æN/ is heard in Toronto, eastern Ontario and the Maritimes, where the F1 of /æN/ is significantly lower than in western Canada, Quebec or Newfoundland (the western–Maritimes contrast attains marginal significance). The raising of /æg/ shows slightly different variation in each dimension. In the F1 dimension, it is the comparative lack of /æg/-raising in Quebec and Newfoundland that stands out, more than advanced raising in any particular place: the F1 of /æg/ is significantly higher in Quebec than anywhere except Newfoundland. In the F2 dimension, however, while Quebec again shows a lower value than most other regions, it is the maximal value on the Prairies that is most striking.

The fronting of /æg/ is significantly more advanced on the Prairies than in any other region, including neighboring British Columbia, with the result that the Prairies are the only region to show a negative value for the difference between the two Cartesian distances, with /æg/ apparently higher and tenser than /æN/. Actually, a paired *t*-test of the two Cartesian distances for the Prairie speakers reveals that the two means are not significantly different, suggesting that raising of /æg/ is equivalent to, rather than greater than, raising of /æN/. A similar test of the British Columbia data also reveals no significant difference. Nevertheless, though this measure is not significantly different from that of British Columbia, which is similarly small, it is significantly smaller than those in the rest of Canada and is remarkable in continental terms. While the dialect geography of short-*a* systems presented by Labov, Ash and Boberg (2006: 182) shows many locations where raising of /æg/ is greater than raising of /æ/ before /d/, including the Canadian Prairies, the *Atlas* gives no indication of the western Canadian pattern found here, in which /æg/ raising is equivalent to the raising of /æN/.

While most of Canada shows raising of /æ/ only before nasals and /g/, Labov, Ash and Boberg identified a distinct pattern in the Maritimes, best exemplified by a young woman from Halifax, in which /æ/ is also raised before voiced stops (2006: 223). Tokens of /æ/ before /b, d, g/ occupied an intermediate zone between the fully raised pre-nasal tokens and the unraised tokens before voiceless stops and in other "elsewhere" environments. This system is still a continuous system in that it does not appear to involve a split into two phonemes, but its phonetic output has more in common with Mid-Atlantic American /æ/ patterns than with those in the rest of Canada. Though evidence from the young participants in the *PCE* project suggests that this pattern is recessive, an example of it can be seen in the vowel system of an older speaker from Nova Scotia in Section 5.5, below.

In the foregoing analysis of regional phonetic patterns, several significant differences emerged. These constitute isoglosses that can be used to establish a division of Canadian English – even at the middle-class level analyzed here – into several regional types. In general, it must be said, little evidence was found to support the bipartite division of Canada into Inland and Atlantic regions proposed by Labov, Ash and Boberg. In fact, while *PCE* data on the fronting of /uw/ match the *Atlas* view of Atlantic Canada as a relatively conservative region in this respect, not a single feature discussed above exhibits a regional distribution coterminous with the Inland Canada region of the *Atlas*. On the contrary, where isoglosses aligned with its western edge were found to divide British Columbia from the Prairies in the advancement of /uw/ and /ow/, these same variables revealed additional isoglosses splitting the Prairies from Ontario within Inland Canada. Further divisions of Inland Canada into western and eastern regions arose from the advancement of raised /awT/ and /ahr/ and the relative positions of /æN/ and /æg/, which in fact unite the Prairies and British Columbia into a western region opposed to Ontario. Together, these six isoglosses constitute the most substantial set in the *PCE* data, suggesting that the separation of the Prairies from Ontario within Inland Canada is a more important division than the separation of the Prairies from British Columbia.

On the other side of Inland Canada, Atlantic Canada as a whole is distinguished from Ontario by three isoglosses, involving the advancement of /uw/, /ow/ and /awT/, but united with Ontario by the raising of /æN/ and the advancement of /ahr/, suggesting that the eastern edge of Inland Canada is also problematic. This is not surprising, given the joint heritage of Loyalist settlement in the Maritimes and Ontario, discussed in Chapter 2. Lower-mid-central /ahr/ and raised /æN/, which together distinguish

Table 5.5 *Establishment of six dialect regions of Canada using seven phonetic variables, based on regional divisions in* PCE *data*

Variable	BC	PR	ON	QC	MT	NL
Canadian Raising: F_1 (awT) < 750 Hz	+	+	+	−	+	−
Canadian Raising: F_2 (awT) > 1,750 Hz	−	−	+	−	−	−
Fronting of /uw/: F_2 (uw) > 1,800 Hz	+	−	+	−	−	−
Fronting of /ow/: F_2 (ow) > 1,300 Hz	+	−	+	−	−	−
Unretracted /ahr/: F_2 (ahr) > 1,350 Hz	−	−	+	−	+	+
Raising of /æN/: F_1 (æN) < 700 Hz	−	−	+	−	+	−
Raising of /æg/: F_2 (æg) > 2,000 Hz	+	+	−	−	−	−

the Maritimes and Ontario from the West, may be a legacy of this settlement history: they also occur throughout the northern United States, from Boston through Detroit and Chicago to Minneapolis (Labov, Ash and Boberg 2006: 84–85, 111). Quebec, which did not receive permanent Loyalist settlement to the same degree, usually appears as an interstitial region of uncertain status between Ontario and the Maritimes, with only variable occurrence of typical Canadian features, including Canadian Raising itself. The ethnic variation that to some extent underlies this uncertain status will be explored below in Section 5.3. As for Newfoundland, while some of the most characteristic phonetic patterns of Newfoundland English were not as evident in the *PCE* data as they might have been in a different sample, the traditionally distinct status of Newfoundland English, even from that of the Maritimes, let alone the rest of Canada, leaves little doubt as to the linguistic importance of the Gulf of St. Lawrence and the Cabot Strait.

In summary, the isoglosses identified above motivate the division of Canadian English into six regions at the phonetic level: British Columbia, the Prairies, Ontario, Quebec, the Maritimes and Newfoundland. In some respects, British Columbia and the Prairies unite to form a western super-region, reducing the number to five. In its general outlines, this model corresponds well to the dialect divisions established with lexical data in Chapter 4, shown in Table 4.3. As a corresponding overview, Table 5.5 demonstrates how the regional differentiation of Canadian English can be established using the phonetic variables analyzed here.

5.2   Social variation: sex and social class

In its broadest sense, social variation in language comprises the co-variation of linguistic variables with any aspect of the social identity of a speaker, including age, sex, socio-economic status, ethnicity, attitude, status on the urban–rural dimension, etc. This section will focus on two of the most important and often studied social variables – sex and socio-economic status (SES) – reserving the analysis of ethnicity and age for subsequent sections. As shown in Table 5.1, the *PCE* sample included 51 women and 35 men,

Table 5.6 *Significant effects of speaker sex on* PCE *phonetic measures (p ≤ 0.10 @ 1 d.f.): results of tests of between-subjects effects, with female (F) and male (M) means and standard deviations (s.d.) and sex difference (all in in Hz)*

Measure	F	Sig.	F mean	F s.d.	M mean	M s.d.	Diff.
F1(e)	7.090	0.010	745	44	714	37	31
F2(e)	4.295	0.043	1,871	86	1,920	87	49
F1(æ)	5.247	0.026	903	61	860	63	43
F2(æ)	9.339	0.003	1,701	95	1,766	86	65
F1(u)	3.146	0.081	586	41	574	54	12
F2(uw)	6.165	0.016	1,760	180	1,662	210	98
F2(æ)-F2(uw)	10.212	0.002	−59	227	104	257	163
F2(ey)	3.201	0.079	2,211	94	2,178	106	33
F2(ahr)	5.857	0.019	1,377	110	1,423	130	46
Cart. dist.(æ-æg)	3.938	0.052	291	142	239	105	52

which allows for an analysis of the effect of sex on the phonetic measures discussed above. The design of the *PCE* sample did not, however, control for SES and does not include enough of a social range to permit an analysis of the effect of SES on phonetic variation, the entire sample having, by definition, a university education. The discussion of SES will therefore rely on data from other studies.

The analysis of sex as a social factor in the *PCE* study proceeded in the same way as the analysis of region, described above, except that it was simplified by there being only two categories in the independent variable – male and female – which obviates the final step of pairwise comparisons. The effects of sex on the sets of phonetic measures as revealed by the MANCOVA were listed above in Table 5.2. The individual phonetic measures that show a significant correlation with sex are listed in Table 5.6, with female and male means and standard deviations and the difference between the means.

There is a striking contrast in the roles of region and sex in conditioning phonetic variation in the *PCE* data: region has no effect on the Canadian Shift but does affect Canadian Raising, while sex has no effect on Canadian Raising but does affect the Canadian Shift. The first five rows of Table 5.6 are measures of the quality of the short vowels; the first four of these – the height and advancement of /e/ and /æ/ – have been shown to be involved in the Canadian Shift, as discussed above and in Chapter 3. The effect of sex on measures of the Canadian Shift is absolutely consistent: women are more shifted than men in every respect. Female values for the F1 of both /e/ and /æ/ are higher than male values, indicating lower vowels, while female values for the F2 of both /e/ and /æ/ are lower than male values, indicating more retracted vowels. This difference is consistent with general observations of the leading role of women in language change (Labov 1990). The fifth short-vowel measure, the F1 of /u/, shows a marginally significant effect of sex that is parallel to those operating on the front vowels: /u/ is slightly lower among females than among males. The relation of this variable to the Canadian Shift is not clear: it was also studied by Clarke, Elms and Youssef (1995: 222), but they examined fronting rather than lowering.

The leading role of women in sound change is also exemplified by the next two lines of Table 5.6, which concern the fronting of /uw/. The female mean for the F2 of /uw/ is 98 Hz farther forward than the male mean, by far the largest sex difference in the *PCE* data. Together with the more retracted female mean for the F2 of /æ/, this produces a remarkable sex difference in the combined measure of phonetic innovation discussed above. Just as British Columbia and Ontario were seen to be innovative in having /uw/ farther front than /æ/, while the Prairies and Atlantic Canada were seen to be conservative in preserving the traditional orientation of these vowels, so women have a strongly positive mean for this measure, indicating the advance of /uw/ beyond /æ/, while men have a negative mean, indicating the traditional orientation. Sound change in Canadian English, then, appears to be led by women in British Columbia and Ontario, while Prairie and Atlantic men represent older, conservative norms. The leading role of women in the Canadian Shift and the fronting of /uw/ is displayed graphically in Figure 5.1.

Table 5.6 indicates three further sex differences in the *PCE* data. The position of /ey/ is less clearly related to ongoing sound change than variables involved in the Canadian Shift or the fronting of /uw/. Here again there is a contrast between the roles of region and sex: region affects /ow/ but not /ey/, with the conservative regions of the country – the Prairies and Atlantic Canada – showing less centralization of /ow/, while sex affects /ey/ but not /ow/, with women showing more peripheral values of /ey/ than men. While only marginally significant, this is the opposite effect from what might be expected if /ey/ were moving away from the front periphery in a parallel shift to that affecting /ow/. Its broader importance is not yet clear. The F2 of /ahr/ was shown above to be an important regional indicator, with low values in western Canada and Quebec, medial values in Ontario and high values in Atlantic Canada; it was suggested that this pattern may reflect historic settlement patterns. Table 5.6 shows that this traditional regional feature is associated more strongly with male than with female speech. By contrast, another regional feature, the raising of /æ/ before /g/, is favored by women.

The role of sex in conditioning phonetic variation has also been examined in other studies. While the *PCE* data show no effect of sex on Canadian Raising, Woods (1993: 161; 1999: 111, 119) reveals a shift away from raising in Ottawa led by young women. Gregg (2004: 42–43), on the other hand, finds no effect of sex on the frequency of raising in Vancouver, which is uniformly high, as in the *PCE* data. As for the quality of the raised nuclei, the more retracted value of raised /awT/ in western Canada that is displayed above in Table 5.4 was noted as "rounding" in Vancouver English by Chambers and Hardwick (1986: 37–41), who found it to be associated with male speech in

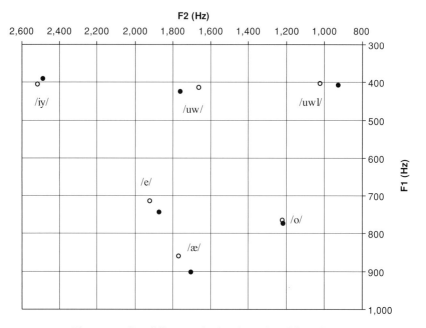

Figure 5.1 Sex differences in the phonetics of Canadian English: means
for six vowels for female and male *PCE* participants. Female means are
black circles (n = 50); male means are white circles (n = 36). Women
lead in the fronting of /uw/ and in lowering and retraction of /e/ and
/æ/ in the Canadian Shift. Means for /iy/, /o/ and /uwl/ are given
to establish the perimeter of the vowel space.

particular. Chambers and Hardwick also observed another change affecting
/aw/ in both Vancouver and Toronto: a fronting of the unraised allophone,
which was led by women (1986: 32). Turning to the Canadian Shift, the leading role of women revealed in the *PCE* data replicates the pattern identified
by Clarke, Elms and Youssef (1995: 216–217), though they note it only with
respect to lowering, not retraction. Esling and Warkentyne (1993: 240) also
note that women lead the retraction of /æ/, presumably the first phase of the
shift, while Boberg (2005a) finds that women lead the retraction of both /æ/
and /i/ in Montreal. The convergence of these data from several separate
studies leaves little doubt that the Canadian Shift fits the typical model of a
sound change led by women.

   These other studies also reveal some effects of socio-economic status
(SES) on phonetic variables. For instance, in the sociolinguistic survey of
Ottawa, Woods (1999: 107, 115) found that the shift away from Canadian
Raising observable among young female speakers was also associated with
the lower-middle-class SES group, while retention of raising was associated
with the lower-upper-class SES group. Lower-middle-class speakers were

also found to lead the conditioned merger of /iw/ and /uw/ after coronals (94). These data suggest curvilinear SES correlations similar to that associated by Labov (1990) with changes in progress, in which change is led by the interior or medial social classes, rather than by the groups on either end of the social scale. On the other hand, Esling and Warkentyne (1993: 242) report that retraction of /æ/ in Vancouver English is most advanced among the highest SES group, which contradicts the curvilinear model. This is especially noteworthy, given that Esling (1991, 2004) finds that, in a global sense, middle-class Vancouver English vowels tend to be relatively fronted and nasalized, whereas working-class vowels tend to be relatively retracted. Where the sociolinguistic surveys of Vancouver and Ottawa examined phonetic variables that are linked to formality of speech, like (VtV), (ing) and (-t,-d), SES correlations tend to match the monotonic pattern associated by Labov (1990) with stable variation. For example, Woods (1999: 79) shows the frequency of flapped /t/ to be inversely correlated with SES, with the most flapping in the lowest group and the least in the highest, while the coronal variant of (ing) and (-t,-d) deletion are also most frequent among working-class speakers in spontaneous speech (89, 99). These patterns, then, are not particularly Canadian, but are merely Canadian instantiations of general patterns that occur across the English-speaking world.

5.3   Ethnic variation

The discussion in Chapter 1 of the linguistic demography of urban Canada made it clear that modern urban Canadian English exists in contact with many other languages, some of which are spoken by substantial populations of immigrants. Moreover, as these immigrant groups learn English, they add second-language varieties of English, with their distinctive phonetic and syntactic properties, to the mix of native varieties heard in Canada's cities. The discussion of settlement history in Chapter 2 demonstrated that this is not a new situation: rather, Canadian English has existed in a multilingual context for several generations, particularly in the cities of western Canada, which attracted large numbers of non-English-speaking immigrants in the land boom of the early twentieth century. In the second half of the twentieth century, eastern cities likewise filled with speakers of non-official languages, or *allophones*. Where the proportion of immigrants to native-English-speaking Canadians is greatest, the possibility arises that second-language varieties might have some influence on the local native variety, or at least that certain features of the second-language English of immigrants might survive in the native English of their children, thereby creating an *ethnolect*, a distinctive variety associated with a particular ethnic group (Carlock and Wölck 1981; Wölck 2002).

   Ethnic variation within speech communities has long been a standard subject for sociolinguistic analysis, beginning with Labov's identification of ethnic differences on Martha's Vineyard (1963), through the many studies of African American English as a distinct variety in most American cities (e.g., Labov 1972: 216–237), to studies of Latino English in the United States (Eckert 2008; Fought 2003, 2006: 70–88; Poplack 1978). Another set of studies has examined subtler types of ethnolectal variation that differentiate native from recent immigrant populations and their children, in locations ranging from Sydney, Australia (Horvath 1985) to Buffalo, New York (Carlock and Wölck 1981; Wölck 2002), to London, England (Kerswill, Torgersen and Fox 2008; Torgersen, Kerswill and Fox 2006).

One Canadian city, Montreal, has been particularly affected by this subtler type of ethnolectal variation because of both the relative size of its native English-speaking population – half a million in a metropolitan area of over 3 million (see Table 1.2) – and the legal, social and practical status of English as a minority language relative to French. Unlike in Vancouver, Edmonton, Winnipeg or Toronto, where even large groups of allophones can generally be assimilated into the dominant anglophone speech community within one or two generations, in Montreal the dominant speech community is not anglophone but francophone. As a result of the language-planning measures discussed in Chapter 1, French is not only the majority language in Montreal, but also the major language of public life – indeed the sole official language – and a required language in most workplaces. Immigrant and allophone groups therefore have to spend at least part of their linguistic assimilatory energy learning French and often receive their formal education mostly or entirely in that language.

Despite this situation, many Montrealers of non-British origin do speak English. For some, this reflects the former dominant position of English in Montreal, still in force at the time they arrived or sent their children to school. For others, arrived more recently, it reflects the continued socio-economic vitality of English as the dominant official language of Canada and the leading global lingua franca, a status that Quebec's language-planning regime has been unable to eliminate entirely. As mentioned in Chapter 1, Montreal's originally Yiddish-speaking Ashkenazi Jewish community, which began arriving in large numbers before World War II, is now almost entirely anglophone: with the exception of the small Hassidic minority, few speak Yiddish and most speak only second-language French. The city's Italian and Greek communities, which mostly came after the war, still tend to retain their heritage languages and often speak native or near-native French as well, but are nevertheless also largely English-oriented. The Chinese, South Asian and Anglo-Caribbean communities are, not surprisingly, mostly anglophone. Even the large and growing Arabic-speaking population, favored as immigrants by the Quebec government because of their origin in francophone countries like Lebanon, Algeria and Morocco, now includes many people fluent in English, some with native or near-native ability. This transfer of immigrant groups to the anglophone community, seen as a dangerous problem by those committed to preserving the local dominance of French, has had the secondary effect of creating the potential for ethnolectal variation in Montreal English, first investigated by Boberg (2004c).

The perpetuation of ethnolects among post-immigrant generations of Montreal allophones is encouraged not only by the need to learn French but by limited access to Montreal's native anglophone speech community, which has been marginalized since the 1970s. Following the introduction of legal measures designed to promote the vitality of French by suppressing the public use of English, a third of the anglophone community left Quebec and the remainder is now socially and geographically fragmented. Its small elite lives in isolated splendor, attended by nannies and gardeners, in the mountainside mansions of Westmount, just northwest of downtown. Its working class is dispersed among a number of southwestern districts where it mingles with equally disadvantaged francophones and allophones. A substantial portion of its middle-class majority, apart from wealthier pockets in central districts like Notre-Dame-de-Grâce and the Town of Mount Royal, occupies the suburban sprawl of the "West Island," a chain of largely English-speaking municipalities that extends along the northern shore of Lac St-Louis, from Dorval through Pointe Claire and Beaconsfield to Baie d'Urfé. These communities, which remain administratively separate from the City of Montreal, are distant from downtown (6–12 miles; 10–20 km) and comparatively ill-served by public transit, effectively cutting them off from the urban majority of central and eastern Montreal. The role that the long-established, native anglophone community plays in other cities as an assimilatory target for immigrants and allophones is therefore comparatively restricted in Montreal: potential contact with British-origin anglophones is mainly limited to downtown vocational contexts.

The isolation of Montreal's non-British ethnic groups from West Island anglophones is increased by their own tendency to segregate themselves in certain neighborhoods, where they enjoy the company of their ethnic kin (Lieberson 1981). The Jewish community, for example, moved from its original "ghetto" along St-Laurent Boulevard, the setting for Mordecai Richler's novels, to post-war suburban homes on the city's west side. There is now a heavily Jewish corridor that extends along Décarie Boulevard from Côte-St-Luc and Hampstead up to southwestern Ville St-Laurent: Boberg (2004c: 561) reports Statistics Canada data on ethnic origin showing that one census tract in Côte-St-Luc is over 80 percent Jewish. While the Jewish corridor is at least partly contiguous with the anglophone West Island, having spread into Dollard-des-Ormeaux, the Italian community installed itself instead among francophones on the opposite side of town, in parts of St-Léonard and later Rivière-des-Prairies, where they live in almost complete isolation from British-origin native speakers of English (Boissevain (1967) offers a detailed social and linguistic portrait of the Montreal Italian community, now somewhat out of date). Montreal's Greeks started out in Park-Extension, a poor area of cramped apartments north of downtown that is now occupied by newer immigrants from South Asia. As their situation improved they moved to better and more expansive homes in parts of Ville St-Laurent and western Laval, on the island directly north of Montreal, where people of British origin are equally scarce.

In many of these areas, immigrants and their children exist in largely homogeneous communities, marrying, worshipping, socializing, going to school and often also working with other members of their own groups. Many Jewish children, for instance, apart from growing up in Jewish homes and worshipping at synagogues, also attend Jewish schools, where they develop largely or entirely Jewish social networks. This is also true of Greeks and Armenians: in an effort to encourage the children of these communities to learn French, the provincial government agreed to subsidize private Greek and Armenian schools, where the heritage language would be taught but a large proportion of the instruction would be in French rather than English. While having little effect on the generally pro-English inclinations of these groups (Jedwab (1996: 71) reports that 76 percent of Canadian-born Armenians and 98 percent of Canadian-born Greeks have transferred to English rather than French), this measure allowed their children to isolate themselves from people outside their own communities, thereby incubating ethnic subvarieties of English, as well as the linguistic and cultural traditions that the parents hoped to preserve.

Of Montreal's largest non-Anglo-Scottish ethnic groups, only the Irish, who came earliest, have largely lost their distinct identity in the larger anglophone community, dispersing to the West Island and other areas and inter-marrying with other groups. While pockets of working-class Irish remain in a few places, the main historic Irish community of Griffintown, on the southwestern edge of downtown, has all but disappeared, its slum housing now replaced by new commercial and industrial developments. As Roman Catholics, some Irish intermarried with French Canadians, thereby producing francophones with last names like Kelly, O'Connor, O'Reilly and Sullivan, some of whom can speak little or no English. Most, however, are now a largely undifferentiated part of the greater British-origin anglophone community, along with other, smaller northwestern European groups.

Given the special circumstances of its English-speaking community, Montreal provides an ideal site for a study of ethnolectal variation. The initial results of such a study, called the *Phonetics of Montreal English* (*PME*), were presented by Boberg (2004c); an analysis of the complete set of *PME* data is presented below. Like the *PCE* project discussed in the previous sections, the *PME* project was primarily an acoustic phonetic study, focusing on sociophonetic variation within Montreal rather than on regional variation across Canada. Its sample was therefore divided according to ethnicity, age, sex and education. The distribution of the 93 *PME* participants among the

Table 5.7 Phonetics of Montreal English *(PME) participants by ethnic origin, age (birth year) and sex (F = female; M = male)*

Ethnicity	Born before 1946		Born 1946–1965		Born after 1965		Total
	F	M	F	M	F	M	
British	8	5	5	1	7	3	29
Italian	3	1	6	3	8	9	30
Jewish	8	8	5	3	5	5	34
Total		33		23		37	93

first three of these categories is shown in Table 5.7. As for education, there were equal numbers of participants with and without a university degree: 46 in each category, with one who could not be classified; some university degrees were still in progress at the time of the interview.

Rather than attempting to sample the full range of ethnic groups in the English-speaking community, the project focused on its three largest groups: people of British origin, including Irish origin, who form a kind of control group representing the local variety of Standard Canadian English; and people of Jewish and Italian origins, who are compared to the British group. (Jews and Italians were also the ethnic groups examined by Labov (1972) in New York City and by Laferrière (1979) in Boston, being, along with the Irish, the largest European immigrant groups in most northeastern North American cities. Along with French Canadians, they are the two main non-British groups included in Rudin's discussion of the ethnic make-up of Quebec's English-speaking population (1985: 165–172).) All of the *PME* participants are native speakers of English who grew up entirely in Montreal, whether or not they also speak other languages: this is a study of ethnic patterns in native Montreal English, not of the second-language English of immigrants. In order to qualify, a participant's parents must both have belonged to the same ethnic group and either grown up entirely in Montreal or immigrated to Montreal from a non-English-speaking country; people with parents who had had significant exposure to non-Montreal English were excluded from the sample.

Methods of data elicitation and analysis for the *PME* project closely followed those of the *PCE* project, as described above and in Chapter 3. Interviewers were McGill undergraduate students, usually but not always of the same ethnic group as the participants. During the interview, participants gave demographic information about themselves, read a word list and engaged in free conversation; the analysis here is based on the word list, which was identical to that used in the *PCE* project, in order to ensure a uniform set of data from each participant. Interviews were recorded on analog cassette tape and later digitized for acoustic analysis using linear predictive coding in the CSL program; formant values were then normalized by the additive

Table 5.8 *Effects of ethnic origin on sets of phonetic measures in data from* PME *project: results of MANCOVA. "Dist." = distance in Hertz*

Process/set	Dependent measures	Effect of ethnicity
Canadian Shift	F1/F2 of short vowels	NO: F = 1.051 (24 df); n.s.
Canadian Raising	F1/F2 of /ayT, awT/; dist. from /ay, aw/	YES: F = 2.592 (14 df); p = 0.003
Position of front-upgliding vowels /Vy/	F1/F2 of /iy, ey, ay, oy/	YES: F = 2.360 (16 df); p = 0.005
Position of back-upgliding vowels /Vw/	F1/F2 of /uw, ow, aw, awn/	YES: F = 2.938 (16 df); p = 0.000
Position of /ahr/	F1/F2 of /ahr/	YES: F = 4.657 (4 df); p = 0.002
Raising of /æN/	F1/F2 of /æN/, Cartesian dist. from /æ/	YES: F = 1.851 (6 df); p = 0.095

point system of Nearey (1978). Finally, a MANCOVA was run in SPSS to determine which of the social factors used in constructing the sample had an effect on each of the sets of phonetic variables analyzed above for the *PCE* project. The results of the MANCOVA are shown in Table 5.8. Since the focus of this section is ethnic variation, in the interest of concision the analysis here will be confined to effects of ethnic origin (effects of age are examined in the next section). As a comparison with Table 5.2 will show, there are only minor differences between the sets of dependent measures in the *PCE* and *PME* analyses: in the *PME* analysis, the long upgliding vowels are grouped according to the direction of the glide into front- and back-upgliding sets, rather than according to height, while the analysis of allophones of /æ/ examines only the pre-nasal allophone, not /æg/ (which, as discussed above, does not exhibit substantial raising in Montreal). A list of effects of ethnic origin on individual phonetic measures from the sets listed in Table 5.8, established by tests of between-subjects effects in SPSS, is presented in Table 5.9, along with mean formant values for each ethnic group and the results of pairwise comparisons among the groups.

While British-, Italian- and Jewish-origin speakers of Montreal English are not differentiated in terms of the Canadian Shift or the short vowels on which it operates, they do show ethnic differences in every other set of phonetic measures in Table 5.8. The most remarkable difference is in the application of Canadian Raising, reflected in the first five lines of Table 5.9. Essentially, while Jewish raising of /awT/ matches that of British-origin speakers, Montreal Italians do not consistently raise /awT/. The British and Jewish values for the F1 of /awT/ are similar to those of western Canada and Ontario in Table 5.4, whereas the Italian value is closer to that of Newfoundland, where raising is also inconsistent. Measured another way, the distance between raised and unraised allophones of /aw/ is much smaller for Italians (81 Hz) than for speakers of British or Jewish origin, who are virtually identical in this respect (132–133 Hz). Contrary to the suggestion

Table 5.9 *Significant effects of ethnic origin on* PME *phonetic measures (p ≤ 0.10 @ 2 d.f.): results of tests of between-subjects effects, means (in Hz) and standard deviations (in parentheses) for each ethnic group, and results of pairwise comparisons testing significance of each ethnic contrast. BR = British origin; IT = Italian; JW = Jewish*

Measure	F	Sig.	BR	IT	JW	Diffs.
F1 (awT)	9.351	0.000	717 (14)	801 (14)	734 (12)	(BR, JW) ≠ IT
F1 (ayT)	3.041	0.055	729 (11)	765 (11)	752 (10)	BR ≠ IT
F1 (awT)–F1 (aw)	3.360	0.041	132 (16)	81 (16)	133 (14)	(BR, JW) ≠ IT
F1 (ayT)–F1 (ay)	3.547	0.035	82 (11)	79 (11)	45 (10)	(BR, IT) ≠ JW
F2 (ayT)–F2 (ay)	2.644	0.079	204 (28)	216 (27)	262 (25)	n/s
F1 (iy)	3.916	0.025	389 (8)	382 (7)	400 (7)	IT ≠ JW
F1 (ey)	3.847	0.027	545 (9)	538 (9)	570 (8)	(BR, IT) ≠ JW
F1 (ay)	6.335	0.003	811 (12)	851 (11)	797 (11)	(BR, JW) ≠ IT
F2 (ay)	7.500	0.001	1,373 (22)	1,397 (21)	1,295 (20)	(BR, IT) ≠ JW
F1 (awn)	6.731	0.002	855 (17)	899 (16)	807 (15)	BR ≠ IT ≠ JW
F1 (ow)	2.970	0.059	577 (14)	549 (13)	612 (12)	(BR, IT) ≠ JW
F2 (aw)	12.814	0.000	1,560 (18)	1,527 (17)	1,617 (16)	(BR, IT) ≠ JW
F2 (awn)	7.589	0.001	1,759 (32)	1,689 (30)	1,809 (28)	IT ≠ JW
F2 (ow)	7.541	0.001	1,090 (26)	1,070 (25)	1,204 (23)	(BR, IT) ≠ JW
F2 (uw)	9.206	0.000	1,461 (40)	1,301 (37)	1,527 (35)	(BR, JW) ≠ IT
F1 (ahr)	4.100	0.021	718 (11)	747 (10)	718 (10)	(BR, JW) ≠ IT
F2 (ahr)	5.846	0.005	1,298 (17)	1,274 (16)	1,238 (15)	BR ≠ JW
F2 (æN)	3.758	0.029	1,987 (28)	1,900 (26)	1,851 (25)	BR ≠ (IT, JW)
Cart. dist. /æ-æN/	4.522	0.015	288 (27)	184 (25)	157 (24)	BR ≠ (IT, JW)

of Hung, Davison and Chambers (1993: 265) that "Montreal never had as its standard the raised back vowel in words like *house*," the *PME* data indicate that raising of /awT/ is a native Canadian feature in Montreal as much as anywhere else in Canada. It is clearly evident in British Montreal English and has been faithfully acquired by the well-established Jewish group, but not by the more recently arrived Italians. Since Hung, Davison and Chambers do not discuss the ethnic origins of their thirteen Montreal subjects, calling them only "English-speaking, born and bred Montrealers" (257), it is not possible to know whether the instances of non-raising they observed among younger Montrealers are related to ethnic variation of the type documented here, but it is clear that any analysis of Canadian Raising in Montreal English must take ethnicity into account.

Turning to the Canadian Raising of /ayT/, it is Jewish participants who show a distinct pattern. They have a smaller F1 distance than British and Italian speakers between raised and unraised allophones, but a larger F2 distance, suggesting that Jewish speakers mainly front rather than raise /ayT/, though the latter differences failed to attain significance in pairwise comparisons. In fact, since there are no significant ethnic differences in the F2 of /ayT/, the larger F2 distance for Jews mostly reflects the more retracted position (lower F2) of Jewish unraised /ay/, shown farther down in the table. One of the more impressionistically salient aspects of Montreal Jewish English is its pronunciation of words like *tie, line* and *time* with a vowel that sounds closer to /oy/ than the vowel used by non-Jews and by Canadians outside Montreal. As shown in Table 5.9, Jewish /ay/ is almost 100 Hz farther back than those of the other groups, a difference significant at $p = 0.001$.

Indeed, it is in the articulation of the long, upgliding vowels more generally that Jewish Montreal English distinguishes itself from other varieties. Table 5.9 indicates that Jewish speakers have a significantly more open nucleus of /iy/ than Italians and a more open /ey/, a more open and centralized /ow/ and a fronter /aw/ than either British or Italian speakers. The last of these, fronted /aw/, was also noted in the study of Canadian Raising in Montreal by Hung, Davison and Chambers (1993: 261), who speculate that "the standard in Montreal may never have been the back variant" (262). In the *PME* data, it is only the Jewish mean for the F2 of /aw/ that is farther front than the general Canadian mean of 1,604 Hz shown in Table 3.12 of Chapter 3; the British and Italian means are in fact farther back. This suggests that, if Montreal English does indeed show fronting of /aw/, it is mostly to be found among Jewish speakers. Again, it is impossible to know whether Hung, Davison and Chambers' fronted tokens came from Jewish subjects, but their comment that variation in the fronting of /aw/ in Montreal "appears to be between individuals, regardless of gender and age" (262) may be a reflection of ethnic variation that was not controlled for in their study and therefore not detected.

Another difficulty in comparison with previous studies of (aw) is the treatment of /aw/ before /n/, as in *pound*, *town* or *gown* (/aw/ does not normally occur before non-coronal nasals). Since /awn/ tends to be raised and fronted relative to /aw/ before oral voiced consonants or in final position, it was treated as a separate allophone in the *PCE* and *PME* studies (as shown in Chapter 3, Section 3.2, Figure 3.1). For the sample of eighty-six Canadians in the *PCE* data, /awn/ was 234 Hz farther front and 57 Hz higher than /aw/ ($p = 0.000$ for both comparisons in a paired t-test). The inclusion of pre-nasal tokens among other tokens of /aw/ would therefore considerably increase the observed degree of fronting, yet there is no mention of this aspect of phonetic conditioning in either Chambers and Hardwick (1986) or Hung, Davison and Chambers (1993), who take only the voicing of the following consonant into consideration. In the *PME* data, the ethnic differences observed in the fronting of /aw/ also apply to the fronting of /awn/, though the higher F2 for Jewish participants is significantly different only from the lower Italian value, not from the intermediate British value. In the F1 dimension, however, an ethnic difference appears before nasals that was not evident before oral consonants: raising of /awn/ is strongest among Jews, less advanced among British speakers and absent among Italians, who retain a low-central vowel for /awn/, with significant differences among all three groups.

Viewed in combination, the distinct aspects of the Jewish Montreal long vowel system involve less peripheral long-vowel nuclei than are produced by the other groups. While these non-peripheral nuclei have not shifted downward to the extent observed in most truly southern dialects, they do display a greater affinity with what Labov (1991: 25) identifies as the Southern Shift than the vowels of non-Jewish Montreal English. Why this should be is not clear.

The most striking aspect of Italian Montreal English, aside from the lesser degree of Canadian Raising already noted, is the relative failure of Italian speakers to participate in the fronting of /uw/, which characterizes much of North American English. At only 1,301 Hz, the F2 of Italian-Montreal /uw/ indicates a vowel still firmly in the high-back quadrant of the vowel space, compared to the much higher means for the other groups, which indicate more centralized vowels. The less centralized quality of the Italian vowel may reflect the influence of the /u/ of Italian, which has the high-back phonetic value of cardinal [u]. The same influence may account for a third distinctive characteristic of Italian Montreal English, a more open articulation of unraised /ay/, and for the more open articulation of /awn/ mentioned above (for further discussion of the English of Italian-English bilinguals in Canada, see Piske 2008).

There are also ethnic differences in the articulation of /ahr/, shown above to be an important regional indicator across Canada. In Montreal, Italian /ahr/ has a more open quality than those of the other groups, while Jewish /ahr/ is more retracted than the British vowel. Finally, while raising of /æN/ is much less evident in Montreal English than in Ontario or the Maritimes, it is more pronounced in the speech of British-origin Montrealers than in the speech of Italians or Jews. The absence of /æN/-raising in Italian and Jewish Montreal English is quite striking to North American ears that do not expect to hear unraised [æ] in pre-nasal contexts. Its quality is similar to the lax /æ/ of two-phoneme short-*a* systems, like those found in New York and Philadelphia, in which *banner* and *hammer* have lax, low-front /æ/ but *band* and *ham* have tense, mid-front and ingliding /æh/. In the one-phoneme Montreal system, however, non-British speakers have the phonetic quality of lax /æ/ in all of these words. Ethnic differences in the raising of /æN/, together with a selection of the other differences examined above, are displayed graphically in Figure 5.2.

The phonetic variables examined so far are not the only ones that differentiate Italian and Jewish from British-origin Montreal English. Others concern consonantal variables. For instance, both non-British groups tend to pronounce the velar nasal with an oral stop release, so that *singer* rhymes with *finger* and *hanger* with *anger*; even final /-ŋ/, as in *bang* or *wrong*, can be realized as [-ŋg]. This pattern is variable among Italians but almost categorical among Jews: in auditory coding of the PME word list data, it emerged that a [g] was produced in *hanger* by 100 percent of Jews (n = 25) and 73 percent of Italians (n = 26) but by only 11 percent of British-origin participants (n = 19); a [g] was produced in *strong* by 36 percent of Jews and

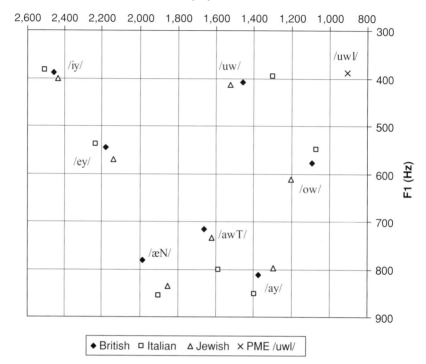

Figure 5.2. Ethnic differences in the phonetics of Montreal English:
mean formant values for *PME* participants of British, Italian and Jewish
ethnic origin, from Table 5.9. Note Italian resistance to fronting of /uw/
and failure to raise /awT/; Jewish backing of /ay/ and less peripheral
/ey/ and /ow/; and British raising of /æN/.

35 percent of Italians but by not a single person of British origin. Non-British
speakers also release final stops, particularly /-t/, much more emphatically
than British-origin speakers, who produce unreleased allophones except in
particularly emphatic contexts. The aspirated release of final stops in Montreal ethnolects might encourage some phonologists to analyze them not as
coda consonants but as the onsets of empty-headed syllables, reflecting, at
least in the Italian case, a heritage-language constraint on coda consonants;
the lack of a parallel constraint in Yiddish, of course, argues against such an
analysis. Another consonantal ethnic variable is the place of articulation of
coronal stops, which is alveolar in British-origin speech, as in most native
dialects of English, but tends to be more dental in Italian and Jewish speech.
Yet another, much more characteristic of Italian than of Jewish speech, is the
substitution of dental stops for interdental fricatives, producing *that*, *them*,
this and *those* with initial [d], as in many non-standard varieties elsewhere.

Though this chapter is concerned with phonetic analysis, it is important to add that ethnolinguistic differentiation in Montreal English is not restricted to phonetic variables. Both Italian- and Jewish-origin speakers exhibit distinctive characteristics at other levels, as well. Yiddish vocabulary and Yiddish-influenced syntax, for instance, which has been widely documented in the English of American Jewish communities, can also be observed in Montreal. A wealth of examples can be found in Mordecai Richler's best-known novel, *The Apprenticeship of Duddy Kravitz* (1959), which recounts the adventures of a young man from Montreal's Jewish ghetto trying to succeed in real estate speculation. Here we find words like *gevalt!* ('woe, alas!', 101), *goniff* ('thief, swindler,' 24), *goy* ('non-Jew, gentile,' 73, 169, 171, 198, 245, 267, 268, 296), *latkas* ('potato pancakes,' 43, 71, 129), *mazel tov!* ('good luck!, congratulations!', 185), *mensh* ('decent person of worth and dignity,' 280), *narishkeit* ('nonsense,' 44), *shiksa* ('non-Jewish woman,' 79, 107, 191, 214, 232, 315), *shmo* ('fool, stupid person,' 23, 284), *shnook* ('meek, naive, gullible person,' 71, 75, 115, 136), *ver geharget!* ('drop dead!', 94, 167, 178, 203, 207, 229, 240, 276) and *zeyda* ('grandfather,' 106, 130, 172). Richler's Jewish characters also exhibit Yiddish-influenced sentence structure, such as the use of post-phrasal *but* (25, 106, 161, 171, 174, 182, 196, 234, 238, 243, 251, 290, 315), as in, "He brought me round some radishes last week and they were so bitter you could die. I had to eat them but" (106), or "There's no news yet. I'm seeing more people tonight but" (171). The pattern known as Yiddish left-dislocation (fronting the verbal object in non-contrastive contexts) is also well attested (49, 60, 64, 138, 172, 284), as in "Of your father I won't even speak" ('I won't even speak of your father,' 49), or "A Yiddish song they couldn't sing?" ('Couldn't they sing a Yiddish song?', 64). Another Jewish English pattern might be called *should*-exclamations (13, 26, 123, 132, 214), which are often protestations or curses, as in, "I should drop down dead it wasn't me" ('I swear it wasn't me,' 13), or "He should live so long I'd make him such a price" ('He'll never find a lower price than what I'm offering him,' 123).

Italian influence on the speech of Italian-origin English-speakers is less widely documented in scholarly work than Jewish English, though the stereotype of the Brooklyn Italian is certainly as common in popular culture as that of the New York Jew, each having linguistic elements. Truly syntactic variants that are specifically Italian are harder to identify than the Jewish examples above, though one pattern that characterizes Montreal allophone English in general, including Italian-origin English, is the use of the present tense instead of the perfect past in sentences like, "This is the first time I see him since he came back" (instead of '. . . I've seen him . . .'), or "We're living here three years already" ('We've been living here . . .'). Though he does not comment on this variable, Trivisonno (1998) gives an example of it in his *Official St. Leonard Dictionary* while illustrating an Italian lexical variant: "It's three days I can't find parking! When . . . are they gonna come and clean the snow?" Trivisonno is interested in the substitution of *clean* for *clear* or *shovel*, but the syntax is also Italian: standard English would have, "It's been three days that I haven't been able to find parking," or something similar. A syntactic variable that Trivisonno does comment on is word order in embedded questions, which follows the pattern of main-clause questions, which he calls "St. Leonard Reversal": his example is, "Do you know what time is it?" Italian lexical variants are easier to identify than syntactic patterns and Trivisonno's dictionary is full of them. Aside from *clean the snow* for *clear the snow*, he cites *close the lights* for *turn off the lights*; *or* for *either* ("or this, or that", as in Italian); use of phrase-initial *ma* ('but'), from Italian, as in "Ma what are you doing?" or "Ma you're crazy!", and the use of *me* before *I* in subject position even where explicit contrast is not required, as in, "Me, I like to shop downtown," or "Me, I never take the bus." Less frequent is the plural, "Us, we always eat out on Friday", or the second person, "You, you need to find a better job." The last pattern would seem to reflect influence from Canadian French, which uses *moi, je*... ('me, I...') as well as *nous, on*... ('we, one...') and *toi, tu*... ('you, you...') in a parallel way, but Italian-English use of *me, I*... appears to have become more frequent and general than its French counterpart.

The large number of ethnophonetic differences discussed above demonstrates that, where communities of new Canadians face barriers to their integration into the life of the larger Canadian community – whether these are self-imposed or arise through prejudice or unequal opportunity – the perpetuation of distinct ethnic identities beyond the initial population of immigrants can be reflected in sociolinguistic variation. In Montreal, it was said above, the minority status of English and the residential and social self-segregation of many ethnic groups have impeded the access of these groups to models of native Canadian English that might otherwise serve as targets for assimilation. As a result, speech patterns characteristic of particular ethnic groups are preserved even in the speech of children born in Canada who speak English with native fluency. If those children continue to live primarily within their own ethnic communities and marry and have children with members of the same group, as do many in Montreal, the differences may persist for yet another generation. The extent to which these differences have their origin in substrate effects imposed by the native languages of the original generation of immigrants, as was suggested in the case of Italian /uw/, is a subject beyond the scope of the present analysis. It is furthermore not possible to say with any certainty whether the ethnic differences observed here exist to the same degree in other Canadian cities, where English is the majority language and where ethnic self-segregation may be less extreme than in Montreal: these are questions for future research. Whatever their resolution, ethnic differences certainly contribute greatly to the distinctive character of Montreal English, making it possible to guess people's ethnic identities based purely on the way they speak.

Table 5.10 *Sample for analysis of age differences:* PCE *participants from Vancouver and Halifax and British-origin* PME *participants from Montreal, by age (birth year) and sex (F = female; M = male)*

City	Older (≤1965)		Younger (>1965)		Total
	F	M	F	M	
Vancouver	4	2	4	4	14
Montreal	13	6	8	5	32
Halifax	6	2	3	3	14
Total	23	10	15	12	60

5.4   Changes in progress

The description of several phonetic characteristics of Canadian English – the Canadian Shift, the fronting of /uw/, etc. – implies that these are dynamic processes rather than static features, yet no data on correlations between phonetic measures and speakers' ages have so far been presented. In order to assess the degree to which these characteristics really do involve changes in progress, a small sample of older speakers was recruited in two cities that could complement the sample of older participants in the *PME* study. The cities chosen were Vancouver and Halifax, representing the western and eastern extremes of the region identified above and in Chapter 3 as the domain of Standard Canadian English. The older Vancouver and Halifax participants were interviewed and analyzed in exactly the same way as the younger PCE participants from those regions, with whom they were compared. Table 5.10 shows the breakdown of the sample of older and younger speakers in the three cities that will serve as the basis for the following analysis of change in progress in the phonetics of Canadian English. The generational division was made at the year 1965, coinciding approximately with the end of the post-war "baby boom": participants born in or before 1965 were considered "older," while those born after 1965 were classified as younger. For this analysis, the Montreal sample was restricted to British-origin speakers in order to provide a set of data more comparable with that of the other cities.

As in the foregoing analyses, a MANCOVA was performed in SPSS in order to determine which sets of phonetic measures exhibited a significant effect of age. The results of this analysis are shown in Table 5.11, which also indicates whether each set of measures also showed co-variation between age and region. When a main effect of age was identified, the results of tests of between-subjects effects were examined in order to determine which individual phonetic measures were significantly affected by age: these are listed in Table 5.12, along with the means and standard deviations for each age group and the difference between the means, in Hz.

Table 5.11 *Effects of age (birth year) on sets of phonetic measures from Vancouver, Montreal and Halifax: results of MANCOVA. "Dist." = distance in Hertz*

Process/set	Dependent measures	Effect of age	Co-variation with region?
Canadian Shift	F1/F2 of short vowels	YES: F = 3.183 (12 df); p = 0.003	YES: F = 1.658 (24 df) p = 0.052
Canadian Raising	F1/F2 of /ayT, awT/; dist. from /ay, aw/	YES: F = 2.171 (7 df); p = 0.057	NO: F = 1.194 (14 df); n.s.
Position of front-upgliding vowels /Vy/	F1/F2 of /iy, ey, ay, oy/	NO: F = 0.638 (8 df); n.s.	NO: F = 1.391 (16df); n.s.
Position of back-upgliding vowels /Vw/	F1/F2 of /uw, ow, aw/	YES: F = 3.392 (6 df); p = 0.008	YES: F = 1.875 (12 df) p = 0.049
Position of /ahr/	F1/F2 of /ahr/	NO: F = 0.526 (2 df); n.s.	NO: F = 0.281 (4 df); n.s.
Raising of /æN/	F1/F2 of /æN/, Cartesian dist. from /æ/	YES: F = 1.955 (6 df); p = 0.093	NO: F = 0.440 (12 df); n.s.

Table 5.12 *Significant effects of age (birth year) on phonetic measures from Vancouver, Montreal and Halifax (p ≤ 0.10 @ 1 d.f.): results of tests of between-subjects effects, with means and standard deviations for each age group and age difference (all in Hz). Older (O) group born in or before 1965; younger (Y) born after 1965*

Measure	F	Sig.	O mean	O s.d.	Y mean	Y s.d.	Diff.
F1 (i)	3.527	0.066	539	9	563	9	24
F1 (e)	9.845	0.003	694	10	735	9	41
F1 (æ)	2.871	0.097	838	18	879	17	41
F1 (u)	7.471	0.009	546	10	582	9	36
F2 (e)	7.987	0.007	1,969	22	1,885	20	84
F2 (æ)	13.423	0.001	1,802	18	1,710	17	92
F2 (u)	7.490	0.009	1,233	20	1,308	19	75
F2 (ayT)	3.073	0.086	1,613	19	1,660	18	47
F2 (ayT-ay)	3.034	0.088	200	23	257	22	57
F1 (ow)	7.987	0.007	571	9	607	9	36
F2 (ow)	13.633	0.001	1,173	22	1,286	21	113
F2 (uw)	7.348	0.009	1,606	34	1,732	32	126
F1 (æg)	5.296	0.026	736	15	784	14	48
F2 (æg)	4.193	0.046	2,004	24	1,935	23	69

The first report of the Canadian Shift, Clarke, Elms and Youssef (1995), though implying that the Shift was a change in progress underway in contemporary Canadian English, was unable to address its diachronic aspect directly because the sample it was based on was drawn entirely from younger speakers; according to the authors' own estimation, six older speakers analyzed for purposes of comparison were not sufficient to support a reliable apparent-time analysis (217). The *Atlas of North American English* (Labov, Ash and Boberg 2006) did include age as one of the independent variables in its analysis of the Canadian Shift, though its small sample and large territory cast some doubt on the reliability of this analysis, as well. Nevertheless, the multivariate analysis of the *Atlas* did find the Canadian Shift to be a change in progress, allowing Labov, Ash and Boberg to conclude that "/e/ is moving backward and downward in apparent time, and /æ/ is moving backward" (220). Prior to this, Esling and Warkentyne (1993: 242) demonstrated that "/æ/ appears to be acquiring a more retracted quality in Vancouver English," which is likely to be the first phase of the shift, if it is understood to be a response to the low-back merger of /o/ and /oh/, while Boberg (2005a) found apparent-time evidence for the advance of the shift in Montreal English.

The analysis of the three-city sample in Table 5.10 reveals significant effects of age on all three of the vowels previously believed to be involved in the Canadian Shift (analysis of the shift in the Vancouver and Halifax data was first presented by Sadlier-Brown and Tamminga (2008), who collected the data on older speakers in those cities). As shown in the first seven lines of Table 5.12, age is correlated with the F_1 of /i/ and with the F_1 and F_2 of /e/ and /æ/ in ways that are consistent with the established view of the shift: all three vowels are moving downward in apparent time, while /e/ and /æ/ are also retracting, creating diagonal trajectories. That /e/ is moving both down and inward suggests that the systematic relation among the individual developments of the front vowels involves parallel shifts rather than a classic chain shift, in which each vowel moves into the space vacated by the one in front of it. There was no age effect for /o/, suggesting that the phonetic quality of the low-back merger acts as a diachronically stable initiating condition for the lowering and retraction of the front vowels. Table 5.11 indicates that the shift also involves co-variation between age and region. This is true only for the F_1 of /e/, which shows a more dramatic increase in Montreal than in Vancouver. However, this difference reflects lower F_1 values for older Montreal speakers rather than higher values for younger Montreal speakers: there is virtually no regional difference in the mean F_1 of /e/ for younger participants.

In their diagram of the Canadian Shift, Clarke, Elms and Youssef (1995: 212) include a lowering and/or fronting of /ʌ/, which appears to be approaching the phonetic space occupied by shifted allophones of /e/ and /æ/, though the systematic relation of this development to other parts of the shift is not clear. The analysis of the three-city sample of Table 5.10 identified no such development of /ʌ/, which appeared to be relatively stable in apparent time. There was, however, strong evidence of an equivalent shift of /u/, also mentioned by Clarke, Elms and Youssef (1995: 213) as an ancillary development. Table 5.12 indicates that /u/ is moving downward and inward in apparent time, a shift that mirrors those affecting the front vowels, though the functional basis of this development is not clear.

Age also has a significant effect on Canadian Raising, but not in ways that relate to previous reports on this variable. For (awT), there was some indication in the Vancouver subsample of the recession of raising and the backing of raised nuclei that were observed by Chambers and Hardwick (1986: 40), but neither pattern attained statistical significance. While the lack of a stronger trend in Vancouver may simply reflect the relatively small sample size, the larger, nationwide sample also failed to show a significant degree of recession: though the F1 of /awT/ was slightly higher for younger participants, suggesting less extreme raising, the generational difference was just shy of being significant (p = 0.104). Furthermore, there was virtually no generational difference in the distance between raised and unraised nuclei, which was 152 Hz for the older group and 143 Hz for the younger. It must therefore be concluded from the evidence of the sample analyzed here that Canadian Raising of /awT/ is diachronically stable, though there are indications of a slight recessive trend that may prove stronger in the future, or with a larger sample from a wider range of cities. The only generational change identified by the MANCOVA of Canadian Raising concerned the F2 of raised /ayT/, which is higher for younger speakers, indicating a fronting of the nucleus; Table 5.12 shows that this forward shift is causing an increase in the mean F2 distance between the raised and unraised allophones of /ay/.

Apart from the Canadian Shift, the major phonetic change currently underway in Canadian English is a shift of the mid and high back-upgliding vowels, /ow/ and /uw/, away from their initial positions along the rear periphery of the vowel space. Table 5.12 indicates that /uw/ is shifting forward into the high-front quadrant of the vowel space, while /ow/ is shifting both inward and downward along a very similar trajectory to that of /u/, discussed above. The co-variation with region reported in Table 5.10 involves the F2 of /ow/, which again shows a more dramatic shift in Montreal, where the mean F2 of older participants is below those of their age peers in the other cities; younger Montreal speakers have caught up with younger speakers in Vancouver and Halifax. Montreal also shows a fronting of /aw/ in apparent time amounting to 55 Hz difference between the age groups, but no such trend appears in the Vancouver data, contrary to the observations of Chambers and Hardwick (1986: 31). In fact, the mean F2 of /aw/ is lower for the younger Vancouver speakers than for the older, suggesting retraction rather than fronting, but the MANCOVA did not identify a significant effect of age on the F2 of /aw/. The apparently opposite trends affecting the F2 of /aw/ in Montreal and Vancouver contributed to a marginally significant co-variation of age and region at $p = 0.086$.

The last phonetic measure to show a significant correlation with age is the position of /æg/, shown above to be an important regional indicator, with raising equivalent to that affecting the pre-nasal allophone of /æ/ in western Canada but an absence of such raising in Quebec and Newfoundland. Ontario and the Maritimes showed intermediate levels of /æg/-raising. The data in Table 5.12 suggest that this regional difference may be receding: in the three-city sample, which includes participants from regions with advanced, moderate and minimal raising, younger speakers have a higher F1 and a lower F2 of /æg/ than older speakers, implying a reversal of raising. However, the fact that there was no generational difference in the Cartesian distance between /æg/ and /æ/ indicates that what is happening is not so much a reversal of raising as an inclusion of the /æg/ allophone in the more general lowering and retraction of /æ/ in the Canadian Shift. This explains why there is no co-variation with region indicated in Table 5.12: the regions that used to raise /æg/ still do so, but the whole distribution of /æ/ is shifting downward and inward. This analysis is further supported by a shift of /æN/ parallel to that affecting /æg/ (40 Hz in F1 and 57 Hz in F2) without a consequent reduction of the Cartesian distance between /æ/ and /æN/, though the pre-nasal shift was not strong enough to attain statistical significance.

In the analyses of region and sex presented above, the relative advancement of /uw/ and /æ/ was proposed as a global measure of phonetic innovation: for conservative speakers, like men on the Prairies and in the Maritimes, these vowels retain their traditional orientation, with /æ/ farther front than /uw/; for innovative speakers, like women in British Columbia and Ontario, the vowels change places, /uw/ being farther front than /æ/. That this measure, which reflects the combined effect of back-vowel fronting and the Canadian Shift, is indeed associated with change in progress is confirmed by the data in Table 5.12: for older speakers, the F2 of /æ/ is 196 Hz farther forward than the F2 of /uw/, while for younger speakers this relation is reversed, with /uw/ 22 Hz farther forward than /æ/. Of the three cities in the sample, only Vancouver shows a complete reversal, with /uw/ almost 100 Hz farther forward than /æ/, but both Montreal and Halifax, in more conservative regions, show a dramatic reduction in the F2 distance between /uw/ and /æ/, which are more or less aligned in F2 space for younger speakers. This change, together with others discussed in this section, is displayed graphically in Figure 5.3, which plots a selection of the older and younger formant means from Table 5.12 in F1/F2 space. The operation of the Canadian Shift, the fronting of /uw/ and the fronting and lowering of /ow/ and /u/ can be clearly seen in the different positions of the clear diamonds and black squares, which represent the two generations of speakers.

As in the interpretation of apparent-time data on lexical changes in the previous chapter, the generational changes indicated in Figure 5.3 must be

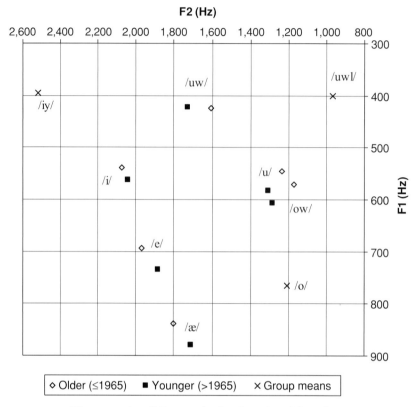

Figure 5.3 Age differences in the phonetics of Canadian English: mean formant values for older and younger speakers from Vancouver, Montreal and Halifax, from Table 5.12. Note advance of Canadian Shift and fronting of /uw/, /ow/ and /u/ in apparent time. Group means for /iy/, /uwl/ and /o/ are also given to show outline of vowel space.

interpreted with caution. While it is generally accepted that phonological and phonetic patterns are more stable over adult lifetimes than lexical patterns, there is nevertheless a possibility that some of the shifts that can be deduced from the generational comparison are illusory, being instead examples of age-related variation that are diachronically stable in the community as a whole. There is nothing to prevent younger speakers from reversing the Canadian Shift as they get older: perhaps they will come to consider excessively retracted /æ/ or lowered /e/ to be inappropriate once they reach middle age and will revert to pronunciations more like those used by their parents' generation today. Given the well-documented history of linguistic change, however, this is unlikely: the fact that languages do undergo dramatic changes over their histories suggests that most generational differences in language are indeed the synchronic manifestation of diachronic change in progress. Future studies will be able to confirm which analysis is correct in the case of the putative changes examined here.

To the extent that the patterns in Figure 5.3 do represent real changes, they present a complex picture of the general direction of change in the phonetics of Canadian English. On one hand, the Canadian Shift appears to be a local, Canadian development, triggered by the low-back merger, that serves to differentiate Canadian English from neighboring American varieties, particularly in Ontario, as discussed in Chapter 3. On the other hand, the fronting of /uw/ and /ow/ is a continental development, which responds to natural phonetic pressures on back vowels: not only is this trend widely attested in English dialects, but it has occurred in other languages, like French and Swedish, where earlier /u/ is now a high-front or high-mid vowel, respectively. Given its wide application outside Canada, the young Canadians who participate in this change are diminishing the degree of difference between their own English and that of other regions.

Two further examples of possible phonetic convergence were not included among the dependent variables examined by the *PCE* project, but anecdotal evidence suggests they can be heard in the speech of many younger speakers of Canadian English today, indicating that they may be changes in progress. One is the palatalization of /s/ in /str-/ onset clusters, in words like *street*, *string*, *destroy*, *distract*, *construction* and *demonstrate*, a trend previously noticed in American English by Shapiro (1995), among others. The apparent cause of the retraction is the tongue constriction required for the /r/. Many English varieties, including Canadian English, have a palatalized /t/ in initial /tr-/ clusters like *train*, *trip* or *true*, but palatalization was traditionally blocked, or reduced, by a preceding /s/ (*strain*, *strip*, *construe*). The current development, then, involves the elimination of this constraint, with anticipatory spreading of the palatalization to the preceding /s/. Though it has a clear phonetic motivation, it seems most likely that this change is diffusing into Canada from the United States via popular culture, such as television and popular music.

The other case of potential convergence is the loss of the distinction between the preconsonantal and prevocalic allomorphs of *the* and *to*, so that in contexts like *the apple* or *to Anne* they have the same reduced vowel, [ə], as in *the pear* or *to Bill*. This, too, can be heard in some varieties of American English, which are a possible source of its diffusion into Canadian English, though the cross-linguistic frequency of changes of this type – the elimination of morpho-phonemic alternations in the interest of grammatical simplicity – suggests that it may just as well have arisen independently in Canada.

The combination of divergent and convergent patterns discussed above is emblematic of the evolution of Canadian English at a broader level: as seen above and in previous chapters, it is not possible to identify a simple, unitary trajectory of change in Canadian English. While some developments suggest convergence with other varieties, particularly with varieties of American English, others indicate non-convergence or even divergence, thereby adding to the distinctive character of English in Canada.

5.5   Examples of individual vowel systems

So far, the foregoing analysis of the phonetics of Canadian English has relied entirely on comparisons among groups of speakers classified by region, sex, ethnic group and age, rather than among individual speakers. While individuals cannot give the same evidence of systematic variation as groups, the vowel systems of individual speakers nevertheless merit examination as concrete illustrations of the patterns identified by group comparison. In order to exemplify some of the most important phonetic and phonological features of different varieties of Canadian English, six *PCE* participants were selected for individual analysis in this section. Examples were chosen in order to represent as broad a range of varieties as possible: one from each of British Columbia, the Prairies, Ontario, Quebec, the Maritimes and Newfoundland, with a mix of ages and sexes. Since vowel charts displaying all of the vowels in a given system tend to lose focus, only the most notable features of each vowel system have been selected for display, along with enough of the remaining formant means to give a sense of the general outline of the vowel space. In the charts, vowels of particular interest are listed in the legend, while the remaining means are marked with 'x' symbols and labeled directly on the chart. Where it is not possible to compare the individual systems with each other, because they focus on different features, they can all be compared with the interregional mean system displayed in Chapter 3, Section 3.2 (Figure 3.1).

Beginning on the west coast and moving eastward, the first vowel system is that of a man from Vancouver, born in 1958, presented in Figure 5.4. This participant grew up in the mainly middle-class suburb of North Vancouver and has an undergraduate university degree; his parents, both of British ethnic background, are also native Vancouverites. As can be seen in this system, Vancouver English exemplifies most of the features of Standard Canadian English discussed in Chapter 3. The low-back merger is evident in the near-overlap of the black and white squares representing the mean F_1-F_2 measurements of /o/ and /oh/. The fronting of /uw/ (mean F_2 = 1,661 Hz) is quite advanced, especially considering the speaker's age (one token, *do*, being directly behind /iy/). It far exceeds the fronting of /ow/, which has moved only slightly inward from the rear periphery. Canadian Raising of /awT/ is clearly shown in the mean position of that allophone well above the low vowels, though it is not as retracted as for other western speakers, having a central F_2 value. This speaker's raising of /awT/ is illustrated in greater detail in Figure 5.5, which clearly shows the complete separation of

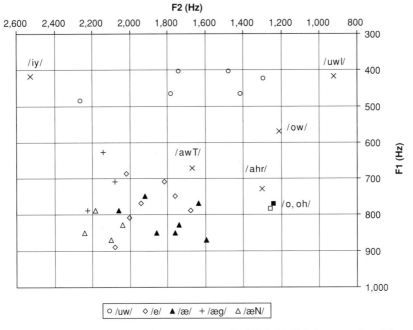

Figure 5.4 Vowel measurements for PCE2 VVM58: a man from Vancouver, BC, born in 1958

the two allophones in F1/F2 space: though each allophone has a wide field of
dispersion reflecting the influence of other phonetic factors, all four tokens
of /awT/ are higher than all five tokens of /aw/, the division between raised
and unraised vowels occurring at around 750 Hz. The pre-nasal allophone, by
contrast, is in low-front position, generally in front of the main distribution
of /aw/. Returning to the previous figure, the effect of the Canadian Shift
is visible in the encroachment of lowered and retracted /e/ (mean F1 = 772
Hz; mean F2 = 1,900 Hz) on the low-front to low-central field of dispersion
of /æ/ (mean F1 = 814 Hz; mean F2 = 1796 Hz); the tokens of *deck* and
sad, for instance, are directly adjacent. However, the speaker's age and sex
are reflected in the fact that the Canadian Shift and the fronting of /uw/
have not yet combined to reverse the orientation of /æ/ and /uw/: the mean
F2 of /æ/ remains 135 Hz higher than the mean F2 of /uw/, making this a
relatively conservative system that retains a conventional trapezoidal shape.
Beyond these general Canadian features, the western origin of the speaker is
evident in the comparatively retracted position of /ahr/, which occurs just
inside the low-back corner of the vowel space. Another western feature is the
raising of /æg/, two tokens of which are well above the distribution of both
/æ/ and /æN/; the pre-nasal allophone shows fronting more than raising.

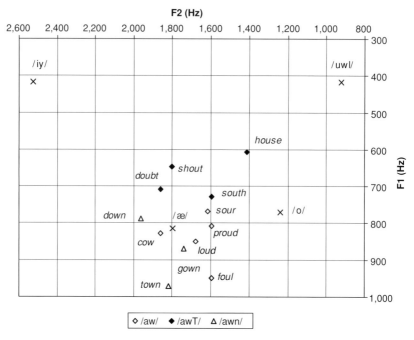

Figure 5.5 Canadian Raising of /awT/ in the vowel system of PCE2
VVM58 (figure 5.4)

Figure 5.6 shows another western system, in this case that of a young
woman from Swift Current, a town in southwestern Saskatchewan, west
of Regina. Though a science student at McGill at the time she was interviewed, the woman grew up entirely in Swift Current. Her parents are
both from small towns in Saskatchewan: her mother a teacher of German ethnic background; her father a farmer and lawyer of British ethnic background. This participant's means for /o/ and /oh/ appear to be
slightly separate, but their relative positions are reversed; in fact, the difference between them is not significant in either dimension ($p > 0.10$).
She shows even more advanced fronting of /uw/ than the older man
from Vancouver, with no tokens remaining in the high-back quadrant
(mean $F2 = 1{,}974$ Hz), indicating that this is not an exclusively urban feature
but is associated generally with young women. By contrast, she exhibits less
fronting of /ow/, which remains fully back, its characteristic position on the
Prairies. Her Canadian Raising appears somewhat weaker than that of the
Vancouver man, but the mean F_I of /awT/ is nevertheless 135 Hz lower
than that of unraised /aw/. An advanced stage of the Canadian Shift has
produced an essentially triangular configuration of the vowel space, with /æ/
in low-central position like the /a/ of other languages (mean $F_I = 857$; mean

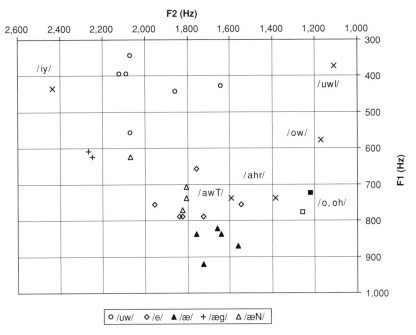

Figure 5.6 Vowel measurements for PPC PRF79: a woman from Swift Current, SK, born in 1979

F2 = 1,669). The shift of /e/ is also evident, though it has not produced the same overlap with /æ/ as was seen in the Vancouver system (mean F1 = 756; mean F2 = 1,774). Nevertheless, the contrast between the basically triangular system of this young woman and the trapezoidal system of the older man from Vancouver is clear. The woman's comparatively innovative status is also seen in the fact that the fronting of /uw/ and the Canadian Shift have combined to reverse the orientation of /uw/ and /æ/: the mean F2 of /uw/ is 305 Hz higher than that of /æ/. Like her fellow westerner, this woman produces /ahr/ well to the back and shows more advanced raising and fronting of /æg/ than of /æN/.

The vowel system in Figure 5.7 is from another young woman from another smaller center, in this case Woodstock, a large town between London and Hamilton in southwestern Ontario. The woman grew up entirely in Woodstock but was a student at McGill University when interviewed; her parents, of middle-class socio-economic status and mixed British and European ethnic background, also grew up in southwestern Ontario. The Swift Current and Woodstock speakers are quite similar socially and their vowel systems have many innovative features of Standard Canadian English in common. The low-back merger is complete; /uw/ is fully fronted (mean

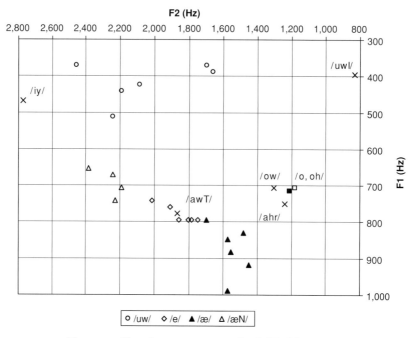

Figure 5.7 Vowel measurements for PCE SOF83: a woman from Woodstock, ON, born in 1983

F2 = 2055 Hz); and the Canadian Shift is advanced, with /e/ retracted and lowered (mean F1 = 780 Hz; mean F2 = 1,852 Hz) and /æ/ in low-central to almost low-back position as the bottom corner of an inverted triangle (mean F1 = 878 Hz; mean F2 = 1,555 Hz). The mean F2 of /uw/ is 500 Hz higher than that of /æ/, a strongly innovative orientation. Beyond these similarities, the regional difference between the Prairies and Ontario is most evident in the position of raised /awT/ (mean F1 106 Hz lower than that of unraised /aw/), which is 275 Hz farther forward for the Ontario woman. The Ontario system also shows more centralization of /ow/ and strong raising of /æN/, which is well separated from the main distribution of /æ/ (mean F1 = 693 Hz; mean F2 = 2,262 Hz). Though not shown for sake of clarity, /æg/ (mean F1 = 795 Hz; mean F2 = 1,796 Hz) occupies a range much closer to /æ/.

Since the discussion of Montreal English in this chapter has mostly concerned ethnic variation, the speaker selected to represent that city is a member of one of the ethnic groups analyzed in Section 5.3, the city's large Jewish community. The speaker has a high-school education and has lived his whole life in Montreal. His parents, who were bilingual English-Yiddish speakers,

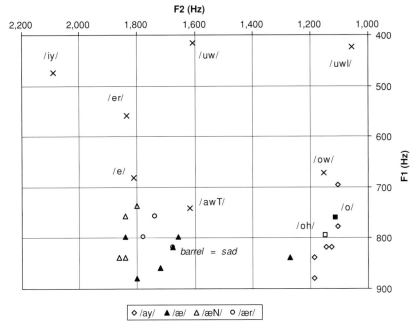

Figure 5.8. Vowel measurements for PME JWM49N: a Jewish man from Montreal, QC, born in 1949

grew up near St. Urban Street, in the Jewish ghetto of Richler's novels; their parents immigrated from Russia and Romania in the early 1900s. Several of the distinctive qualities of Jewish Montreal English discussed above are discernible in Figure 5.8. The most remarkable is the retracted position of /ay/ (mean F2 = 1,166 Hz): the nucleus of this diphthong has the same quality as the low-back vowels /o/ and /oh/. As in Figure 5.6, though the latter vowels appear to be slightly separated and reversed in orientation, the difference between the means is not significant in either dimension ($p >$ 0.10), indicating a completed low-back merger. The failure to raise /æN/ significantly beyond the main distribution of /æ/ is also typically Jewish: two of the four tokens of /æN/ are not raised at all. Less specifically Jewish but distinctly characteristic of Montreal English as a whole is the wide separation between /er/ and /ær/ (*berry* and *carry*), the latter remaining firmly in low-front position (mean F1 = 791 Hz), with the main distribution of /æ/; by contrast, /er/ is well above the main distribution of /e/. The association of /ær/ with /æ/ rather than /e/ is best illustrated by the word *barrel*, which overlaps exactly with *sad*, one of the /æ/ tokens. Despite these local characteristics, this speaker does share some pan-Canadian features, such as the

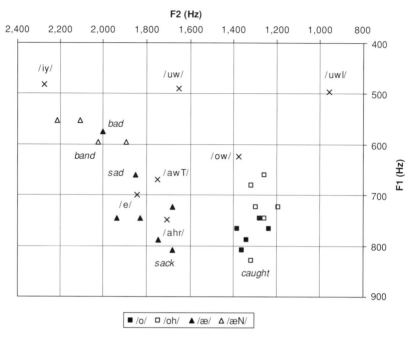

Figure 5.9 Vowel measurements for PCE2 NSM46: a man from Liverpool, NS, born in 1946

fronting of /uw/ and the Canadian Raising of /awT/ (which has a mean F1 109 Hz lower than that of /aw/). The Canadian Shift is much less advanced than among the preceding speakers, /e/ remaining in mid-front and /æ/ in low-front position (mean F1 = 832 Hz; mean F2 = 1,661 Hz), but this may have more to do with the speaker's age than with his regional or ethnic origin. Like the man from Vancouver, this Montreal speaker preserves the traditional trapezoidal shape of the vowel space and retains the conventional orientation of /æ/ and /uw/, with the former farther front than the latter, if only by 55 Hz.

There is no space here for a detailed treatment of the many subvarieties of English to be heard in Canada's Maritime provinces, but broadly representative of some of the main features of Maritime English identified above is the vowel system shown in Figure 5.9. It belongs to a middle-aged man from Liverpool, a small town on the south shore of Nova Scotia, down the coast from Halifax. The speaker, who now lives in Halifax, has no university education; his parents, also from Liverpool, came from families of German–Dutch ethnic background who arrived in Nova Scotia in the eighteenth century. This Nova Scotian shows fronting of /uw/ (mean F2 = 1,652 Hz) and Canadian Raising of /awT/ (mean F1 is 104 Hz lower than that of /aw/), which is front of center as in Ontario, but in most other respects he differs strikingly from the speakers from central and western Canada. To begin with, the low-back merger is clearly incomplete: one token of /oh/, *caught*, is very open, appearing at the bottom of the field of dispersion of /o/, but otherwise the ranges of the low-back vowels are largely separate, with /oh/ higher and backer than /o/, the conventional orientation. A *t*-test reveals a significant difference in both dimensions ($p = 0.03$ for F1; $p = 0.06$ for F2). In the low-front space, there is strong raising of /æN/ (mean F1 = 574 Hz; mean F2 = 2,058 Hz), as in Ontario, but /æ/ is also raised before /d/, with *bad* as high as any pre-nasal token (the unraised tokens are *cast*, *sack*, *sat*, *tap* and *tally*; see also Labov, Ash and Boberg 2006: 223). This pattern has more in common with Mid-Atlantic American English than with other varieties of Canadian English, at least in terms of phonetic output. While there is no evidence of a Mid-Atlantic phonemic split of /æ/ into tense and lax classes, and while some words, like *cast*, that would be raised in the Mid-Atlantic region are not raised here, the raising of /æ/ in *bad* and *sad* above the mean position of /e/ suggests a historical connection with New York City, most likely established by Loyalist refugees during the English-speaking settlement of Nova Scotia in the eighteenth century. The trapezoidal shape of this speaker's vowel space reflects the relative absence of the Canadian Shift, for which the initiating condition of the low-back merger is not present. The phonetic position of /ahr/ also presents a striking contrast with the previous speakers, occupying a position in the low-front quadrant amid the upper range of the main distribution of /æ/. A final distinctive feature of this system is the strongly centralized position of /ow/, considerably more advanced than among the previous speakers.

The final individual vowel system is that of a young woman from St. John's, the largest city and capital of Newfoundland. It need hardly be said that representing the wide variety of regional and social dialects of Newfoundland English with a single exemplar is even more unsatisfactory than in the Maritime case just discussed, but as with the previous speaker, the one displayed in Figure 5.10 is at least representative of some of the main characteristics of Newfoundland English discussed above and in Chapter 3. This speaker is from a middle-class social background: her parents are both Newfoundlanders but she has traveled widely in North America and was a student at McGill when interviewed. She therefore represents a weaker variety of Newfoundland speech than might be heard from someone of lower socio-economic status. Nevertheless, like the man from Nova Scotia, she shows an incomplete merger of the low-back vowels. While there is some overlap in the fields of dispersion, /o/ is again generally lower and fronter than /oh/ and the means are again significantly different in both dimensions ($p = 0.01$ for F1, 0.02 for F2). As in the Nova Scotia system, this residual distinction has prevented the full development of the Canadian Shift and maintained a trapezoidal vowel space, though there is much less

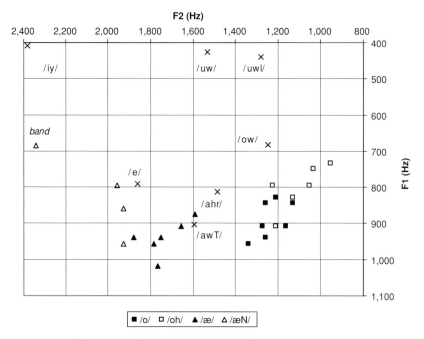

Figure 5.10. Vowel measurements for PCE NLF812: a woman from St. John's, NL, born in 1981

raising of /æN/ than in Nova Scotia (except in one word, *band*) and no raising of /æ/ before /d/. There is also less Canadian Raising of /awT/: the difference between the mean F1 values of the raised and unraised allophones of /aw/ is in fact not statistically significant, indicating the absence of this mainland Canadian feature. While /ahr/ is more central than in the Ontario or western systems, as would be expected from an Atlantic Canadian speaker, it is not as advanced as in the Nova Scotia system, perhaps reflecting the sex difference identified above rather than a regional difference. One feature that this Newfoundlander shares with her Canadian compatriots is the fronting of /uw/, though this is somewhat less advanced than in central or western regions; moreover, the separation of the main distribution of /uw/ from its allophone before /l/ is considerably reduced by a moderate fronting of the latter, not observed in other regions.

The six vowel systems displayed in Figures 5.4–5.10 show that it is difficult to identify phonetic features that are truly representative of Canada from coast to coast: even the low-back merger, the Canadian Shift and Canadian Raising of /awT/ are not characteristic of every Canadian speaker or community. In this sense, a unified national type of Canadian English cannot be put forward at the phonetic level. Nevertheless, as was suggested in Chapter 1, what is Canadian about the enclave varieties represented by the speakers from Nova Scotia and Newfoundland (and to some extent also the speaker from Montreal) is their ongoing convergence with the variety represented by the speakers from Ontario and western Canada, rather than with non-Canadian varieties. Though many speakers with distinct phonetic patterns remain in these and other communities, younger, middle-class speakers, who tend to represent the leading edge of change in progress, now display many of the characteristics of Standard Canadian English. It may be that a truly unified national variety of Canadian English has yet to emerge, but is now in the making.

6 Summary and future directions

In the five preceding chapters of this book, three aspects of Canadian English have been emphasized: its current status as one of many languages spoken in Canada; its historical roots in settlement patterns; and its principal modern characteristics, viewed from both comparative and variationist perspectives. In this final chapter, the main outlines of these analyses will be briefly summarized and tentative projections will be made into the future, in terms of both research on Canadian English and the possible future development of the language itself. The analysis of Canadian English presented here is based on both the author's own research and the work of others, especially Avis, Chambers, Clarke, De Wolf, Gregg, Scargill, Warkentyne and Woods, as well as Labov, Ash and Boberg (2006) and data from Statistics Canada. Citations of this research are made throughout the foregoing chapters; in the interest of concision, they will not be repeated here.

6.1 The status, history and comparative analysis of English in Canada: a summary

In Chapter 1, English was seen to be the most widely spoken of many Canadian languages, being the mother tongue of about 18 million Canadians (57 percent of the national population). Of the other languages, the most important is French, Canada's other official language. Speakers of French are concentrated almost entirely in Quebec, where English is a minority language, and in neighboring regions of Ontario and New Brunswick. Canadians also speak a wide variety of non-official languages. These include the languages brought from overseas by more recent immigrants, such as Chinese, Italian, German, Panjabi, Spanish and Arabic, which are spoken by more than a quarter of a million people each; their speakers are concentrated particularly in Canada's major cities. Canada's non-official languages also include Aboriginal languages, spoken by smaller populations (the largest, Cree, has only 73,000 speakers); some of these reside in remote areas or on reservations set aside for Aboriginal groups.

English is particularly dominant in Atlantic Canada east of New Brunswick and in smaller towns and rural areas of Ontario and western Canada, regions that have attracted comparatively little recent immigration. While English flourishes across most of Canada, in Quebec its vitality is threatened by provincial language legislation that seeks to sustain the vitality of French partly by suppressing the public and institutional use of English. A substantial decline of the local English-speaking population that followed the introduction of this legislation in the 1970s has only recently been halted. Outside its main base in central and western Montreal, Quebec's historic anglophone population – established in the eighteenth century – has suffered a particularly sharp decline, similar to the fate of minority francophone populations outside Quebec. Many areas that historically had significant anglophone populations – in some cases anglophone majorities – are now overwhelmingly francophone.

In Canada's major cities, and particularly in Vancouver and Toronto, English is in contact with the languages of large groups of recent immigrants, who represent varying stages in the acquisition of Canadian English and in assimilation to Canadian culture. Just under half of the populations of greater Toronto and Vancouver are native speakers of non-official languages. In Montreal, the smaller population of English-speakers is actually outnumbered by speakers of non-official languages, as well as by the French-speaking majority. In some cities with large non-official-language populations, distinct ethnic varieties of English have arisen. This is only one of the several dimensions along which Canadian English varies, like most dialects of most languages. Others are region (Newfoundland and several areas of the Maritime provinces being notably distinct from the main variety of central and western Canada), social class, sex and age. Age differences often reflect diachronic changes in progress.

More important than its contact with immigrant languages or French is the intensive exposure of Canadian English to influence from American English, which arises from the geographic situation of Canada in the top half of North America and from the many historical, cultural and economic ties between Canada and the United States. A combination of historical American settlement and more recent cross-border influence has caused Canadian English to develop a generally North American character. This contrasts notably with the standard varieties of English spoken in Britain and the southern hemisphere, despite Canada's former status as a British colony and member of the British Commonwealth.

Chapter 1 also examined of the status of Canadian English as a literary language and as the medium of English-Canadian culture. This culture has often had difficulty maintaining its independence from American culture but has nevertheless generated noteworthy achievements in literature, music, film and programming for radio and television, from the novels of Margaret Atwood, Robertson Davies and Margaret Laurence to the rock band Rush to the television series *Corner Gas*. The chapter ended with a review of previous research on six aspects of Canadian English, which has now produced a substantial body of work in several scientific traditions. These include: (1) lexicographic work on Canadian and regional Canadian English; (2) the alternation in Canada among American, British and Canadian words, pronunciations and usage, with an accompanying discussion of the historical origins and development of Canadian English; (3) the documentation of traditional regional speech enclaves; (4) microsociolinguistic studies of variation in urban Canadian English; (5) sociophonetic research on regional and social variation in the articulation of the vowels of Canadian English; and (6) macrosociolinguistic studies of the use of English and other languages in various regions of Canada, particularly Quebec.

Chapter 2 explored Canada's settlement history, with a view to identifying the regional origin of potential sources of influence on the formation of Canadian English in different parts of the country. The very existence of Canadian English was seen to have resulted from three important historical forces: (1) Britain's victory in the Seven Years' War, which solidified the achievements of its colonial and commercial activities in North America and established Canada as a British colony; (2) the American Revolution, which drove many of the colonists who opposed it northward into Canada, thereby establishing the country's first substantial English-speaking population; and (3) the Industrial Revolution, which, among other things, produced a surplus population in Britain that sought better opportunities in emigration, thereby greatly increasing Canada's English-speaking population and settling most of the territory that would form the Dominion of Canada in 1867. Finally, the need for new agricultural land and for economic growth, coupled at the end of the nineteenth century with the building of a transcontinental railroad, opened the western half of Canada to non-Aboriginal settlement, which came from four sources: the older Canadian provinces, the United States, Britain and Europe.

Given the important role of Canadians from other provinces, particularly Ontario, in settling the West, western Canadian English can be seen historically as a modified form of Ontario English, though not without influences from other sources. It is therefore in the origins of Ontario and Maritime English that the origins of Canadian English as a whole must be sought (Newfoundland English has a separate, though in some respects similar, history that has been well studied in a separate body of scholarship). Ontario and Maritime English have their roots in the northward migration of Loyalist refugees from the United States, but it was shown in Chapter 2 that it is difficult to determine with any certainty what specific features the varieties of English spoken by this group would have displayed. It is easier to characterize the speech of the immigrants who came in the first half of the nineteenth century and in far greater numbers directly from the British Isles. They would have spoken regional varieties from all over Great Britain and Ireland, with northern and western (especially Irish) varieties better represented than the southeastern varieties on which modern Standard British English is based.

Significantly, all of the characteristic features of modern Canadian English can be traced, at least theoretically, to one or more of these British varieties, just as well as to the speech of the earlier Loyalist group. Indeed, the Loyalist group itself would have had at least some historical inputs from these British dialects. This casts doubt on attempts to identify the origins of Canadian English exclusively with the speech of former American colonists. It seems most likely that the formative period of Canadian English, during the late eighteenth and early nineteenth centuries, was characterized by a mixture and leveling of regional varieties of English from Ireland, Scotland, England and the northeastern American colonies. Furthermore, it is difficult to know to what degree the current characteristics of Canadian English reflect more recent influence from the emerging standard south of the border. The growing prestige and power of American English, with its inevitable spillover into Canada, may have selected some features from among the earlier mixture for promotion while causing others to fade and disappear.

In Chapter 3, the main characteristics of Standard Canadian English were presented in comparison to the corresponding features of Standard American and British English (the former designation excluding the older, identifiable regional varieties of the Inland North, the Atlantic seaboard and the South). With respect to lexical variation, or vocabulary, Canadian English was shown to be much closer to American than to British English where those varieties differ, though a small set of unique Canadian words was also identified, showing that Canadian English is not simply a mixture of British and American forms. Canadianisms like *bachelor apartment*, *bank machine*, *chesterfield*, *eavestroughs*, *grade one*, *parkade*, *runners* or *running shoes*, *scribbler* and *washroom* are not merely words for things found only or mostly in Canada, but Canadian words for universal concepts that have other names outside Canada (compare American *studio apartment*, *ATM*, *couch*, *gutters*, *first grade*, *parking garage*, *sneakers* or *tennis shoes*, *notebook* and *restroom*; or British *studio flat* or *bed-sit*, *cash dispenser*, *settee*, *gutters*, *first form*, *car park*, *trainers*, *exercise book* and *lavatory* or *loo*).

In phonological and phonetic terms, Standard Canadian English is also much more similar to Standard American than to Standard British English; in fact, it was shown that, with respect to major variables of phonemic inventory, Standard Canadian and American English are largely indistinguishable. While all three varieties share the merger of /hw/ and /w/ (e.g. *which* and *witch*) and the split of FOOT and STRUT, the Standard North American varieties are jointly distinguished from Standard British English by the retention of a single short-*a* class (the same vowel, /æ/, in TRAP and BATH) and by the double-merger of the LOT, THOUGHT and PALM classes as a single, low-back-to-low-central vowel quality. They also share several other important phonological characteristics: the retention of non-prevocalic /r/, with a consequent reduction of the number of phonemic vowel contrasts before intervocalic /r/; the neutralization of the contrast between /iw/ and /uw/ after coronal stops through loss of palatal glides (*due* = *do*); and the conditioned merger of /t/ and /d/ in post-tonic, intervocalic position (*shutter* = *shudder*), also known as *flapping*. One distinctive feature of Canadian English phonemic incidence is the comparatively frequent nativization of the foreign vowel [a] as English /æ/ rather than /ah/: Canadian English shares British assignment to /æ/ where Americans use /ah/, as in *pasta*, but also assigns many words to /æ/ that have /ah/ in both British and American English, like *drama*, *lava* or *saga*.

Apart from this difference, Standard Canadian and American English are most easily distinguished in phonetic rather than phonological terms, though even at this level many of the differences tend to be subtle and gradient. Ontario English is sharply distinguished from that of the American Inland North not only by the low-back merger, which has not occurred south of the border, but by the consequences of that merger for the short front vowels, especially /e/ and /æ/ (TRAP and DRESS), which have moved inward and downward in the Canadian Shift. This shift has produced a striking contrast in the pronunciations of TRAP and LOT on either side of the border, with Canadian TRAP having the same vowel quality as American LOT. Farther west, where the Canadian Shift is less distinctive, the contrast with American English is more clearly seen in the absence of Canadian Raising in the western United States, the pattern by which the low diphthongs /ay/ and /aw/ have non-low nuclei before voiceless consonants (PRICE and MOUTH).

It is even more difficult to distinguish Standard Canadian from Standard American English in grammatical terms than at other levels. Apart from a small residue of British morphological variants, very little separates the two North American varieties, while both diverge from standard British syntactic patterns in similar ways.

Chapter 4 examined regional differences and changes in progress in the vocabulary of Canadian English, using data from the *North American Regional Vocabulary Survey*. Several lexical variables displayed clear regional differentiation across Canada. These included words for the standard set of pizza toppings (*the works, all-dressed, deluxe, everything on it*); a house in the country for summer weekends (*cottage, cabin, camp*); athletic shoes worn as casual attire (*running shoes, sneakers, runners*); a book of lined paper for schoolwork (*notebook, scribbler, exercise book*); a multi-storey building for parking cars (*parking garage, parkade*); a small store open late that sells a variety of goods (*convenience store, dépanneur/dep, corner store*); a bag with shoulder straps for a student's books (*backpack, book bag*); the place where you pay for something in a store (*cashier, check-out, cash*); the generic term for non-alcoholic carbonated beverages (*pop, soft drink*); the tilting board in a playground (*teeter-totter, see-saw*); and the structures along the edge of a roof for catching rainwater (*eavestroughs, gutters*). Based on this set of data, the most important regional divisions within Canada were shown to isolate Montreal (and Quebec) from its neighbors to the east and west and to divide Newfoundland from the Maritimes; the regions of central and western Canada were less strongly differentiated in lexical terms. However, while lexical isoglosses do occur within Canada, the regions of Canada were shown to have more in common with one another than any of them has with American English, even if trans-border lexical differences are somewhat stronger in western than in central or eastern Canada. The primacy of the international border as a lexical division suggests that Canadian English can be seen as a distinct national variety of English at the lexical level, despite its regional divisions.

The analysis of lexical changes in the second half of Chapter 4, based on a comparison of successive generations of questionnaire respondents, iden-tified some examples of convergence with American English, which many people imagine must be taking place for purely intuitive reasons. These include the replacement of *chesterfield* with *couch*, of *eavestroughs* with *gut-ters*, of *scribbler* with *notebook*, and of *zed* with *zee* (though most Canadians still say *zed*). However, the *NARVS* data displayed even more examples of non-convergence: no generational increase was observed in Canadian use of Americanisms like *ATM*, *candy bar*, *first grade*, *frosting*, *grilling out*, *parking garage*, *pocketbook*, *restroom*, *silverware*, *sneakers*, *soda*, *studio apartment*, *tennis shoes* or *trash*. There were even a few instances of divergence, with Canadian and American usage becoming less similar over time. Altogether, these devel-opments indicate that there is no evidence for a general Americanization of Canadian vocabulary beyond its already North American character, and that it is not possible to characterize lexical change in Canadian English in simple terms as a unidirectional process.

Finally, Chapter 5 examined variation and change in the phonetics of Canadian English. The analysis began with regional variation. Statistically significant regional differences were identified for several regional variables: in the application and phonetic output of the Canadian Raising of /awT/, wherein raising applies only variably in Newfoundland and Montreal and raised /awT/ is produced farther back in western Canada than in Ontario; in the fronting of /uw/ (GOOSE), which is less advanced on the Prairies and in Newfoundland than elsewhere; in the fronting of /ow/ (GOAT), which is more advanced in British Columbia and Ontario than elsewhere; in the non-back articulation of /ahr/ (START), which distinguishes Ontario and particularly Atlantic Canada from Quebec and western Canada; and in the allophonic distribution of /æ/, which shows more raising before front nasals in Ontario and the Maritimes than elsewhere and more raising before /g/ in western than in central or eastern Canada. These differences motivated a division of Canadian English into six regions at the phonetic level: British Columbia, the Prairies, Ontario, Quebec, the Maritimes and Newfoundland.

Chapter 5 also examined social variation in the phonetics of Canadian English. Significant sex differences were identified for several variables, with women ahead of men in the Canadian Shift, the fronting of /uw/

and the retraction of /ahr/. Along another social dimension, ethnic differences were found among speakers of British, Italian and Jewish ethnic origin in Montreal. Italians showed resistance to the fronting of /uw/ and only variable Canadian Raising of /awT/; Jews showed backing of /ay/ and less peripheral /ey/ and /ow/ (FACE and GOAT); and both groups showed less raising of pre-nasal /æ/ than people of British origin. Ethnic differences in consonant production and at other levels of grammar (lexicon and syntax) were also briefly discussed. In the last section of Chapter 5, phonetic differences between younger and older speakers in three Canadian cities (Vancouver, Montreal and Halifax) were examined in order to identify ongoing changes in the pronunciation of Canadian English. This analysis confirmed the progress of the Canadian Shift, with /e/ and /æ/ moving inward and down in apparent time, and of the simultaneous shift of three back vowels, /uw/, /ow/ and /u/ (FOOT), which are all moving forward (/ow/ is also moving down). Canadian Raising, by contrast, was found to be diachronically stable, at least in the small sample considered here.

6.2   Future directions for research

Though a great deal is now known about Canadian English, there are certainly aspects of the subject that could be usefully explored in future research. For instance, while the broad outlines of Canadian English phonetics have been sketched on a national level, detailed regional studies have yet to be done in many locations. The results of major sociolinguistic surveys of Vancouver and Ottawa have been published, but no comparable data have been published on any other speech community, apart from analyses of individual variables, and even the Vancouver and Ottawa studies do not include acoustic phonetic analysis. It may be that the Canadian Shift and Canadian Raising, for example, reveal unique characteristics in each major city when examined in sufficient detail. Variation above the phonetic level has been better studied on a national basis because of its amenability to investigation with written questionnaires, but the last general, nationwide survey of variation in phonemic incidence, morpho-syntax, lexicon and spelling to be fully published was done in 1972 and is now considerably out of date; subsequent surveys have not yet attained national coverage or have dealt with only lexical variation. Moreover, the English of some regions of Canada has never been adequately studied. This is particularly true of the North, which presents many obstacles to conventional survey methods and a different population from those that have been studied in the past, but is nonetheless worthy of investigation. Some social groups have also been largely omitted from studies of Canadian English, such as Aboriginal groups and communities of recent immigrants from Asia and their children.

  One of the persistent interests of researchers working on Canadian English has understandably been its relationship to American English and the extent to which it maintains its independence in this continental context. While the basic differences between these varieties are now well known, the cross-border contrast is both spatially and diachronically variable. The border was shown in foregoing chapters to be aligned with different linguistic contrasts at different locations and the societies and linguistic varieties spoken on either side continue to evolve. This raises the question of whether Canadian and American English are becoming more similar or more different over time, or whether this depends on which features one examines, in which locations. The social mechanisms of cross-border influence might also be examined in greater detail, particularly the role of sources of influence that sociolinguists have traditionally set aside as less important, like travel and the mass media. Canada's southern border presents an ideal opportunity to study the linguistic effects of political boundaries.

While the analyses of sociolinguists and dialectologists normally concentrate on production, perception is of course equally important to communication; many of the subjects discussed in the foregoing chapters could also be examined from this angle. Perceptual studies could assess which features Canadians themselves recognize in their own speech and take to be most associated with Canadian English, which they associate with American English, and which they acknowledge as constituting regional divisions within Canada. Indeed, it would be interesting to know to what degree the homogeneity that linguists have attributed to Canadian English between Vancouver and Ottawa is also perceived by ordinary Canadians: if the average person can in fact judge another speaker to be from Alberta rather than from Ontario, on which linguistic variables does this judgment depend?

Finally, while the preceding chapters cited a few efforts to trace the origins of Canadian English in more than a speculative way by working with historical and archival materials, much more could be done in this line of research. To a great extent, the nature of even early twentieth- and nineteenth-century Canadian English, let alone of its historical inputs in the eighteenth century, is still only vaguely known, especially with respect to phonetic and phonological properties not preserved in written texts. Some aspects of this history may indeed be beyond the reach of most investigations, but the archival materials held by the National Archives of Canada, the Canadian Broadcasting Corporation and other institutions or individuals at the national, provincial and local levels might prove to be a valuable resource in this regard, if access to them could be obtained at a reasonable cost for scholarly purposes. Future research on early Canadian English might make some progress in identifying more precisely the linguistic contributions of the various groups that settled English-speaking Canada and in resolving the question of the relative importance of Loyalist and direct British settlement in establishing the main patterns of modern Canadian English.

6.3　Future directions for Canadian English

One consequence of obtaining more information about earlier stages of Canadian English would be the development of a deeper understanding of the diachronic trajectory of its current and future evolution. The trajectories identified by the apparent-time analyses of the preceding chapters – the change from a trapezoidal to a triangular vowel system, or the resistance to further general Americanization of Canadian vocabulary – are limited by the age-depth of their samples, which reach back to the beginning of the twentieth century at the earliest. Projecting these or other changes beyond their present stages is of course a matter of guesswork, but current indications are that Canadian English is not on the verge of disappearance in a continental blend dominated by American speech patterns. Despite the massive influence of American English over the last half-century, exercised through increasingly powerful channels like television and the internet, regional linguistic variation remains one of the few ways in which Canadians can still be reliably distinguished from Americans, at least in most parts of the continent. Except in the event of some disastrous disintegration of the Canadian state, this state of affairs seems likely to persist for the foreseeable future.

The influence of momentous future events or trends cannot, however, be ruled out when considering the future of Canadian English. Just as the very origins of Canadian English lie in major world events that caused thousands of people to move to Canada, so its future may be shaped by another world-changing episode. Possible candidates, apart from a nuclear military confrontation, which now seems less likely than it once did, or catastrophic terrorist activity, which seems perhaps more likely, include global competition over Canada's natural resources, especially its minerals, forests, fresh water and open spaces. The prospect of significant climate change, which threatens to make some of the world's most densely populated and economically productive places increasingly uninhabitable while warming heretofore cold and barren stretches of Canada's wilderness, adds another possible dimension to this competition, as the rest of the world may strive to gain access not only to Canadian resources but to Canadian land for resettlement. Global problems of over-population, environmental pollution and waste management may have similar future consequences.

Canada's comparatively high standard of living, pluralistic society and stable tradition of liberal democracy attracted millions of immigrants during the twentieth century and continue to do so today, like those of other "rich" countries. Even current levels of dissatisfaction in many parts of the world, without being intensified by climate change, are sufficient to fill Canada with many more immigrants than most Canadians think they can reasonably accommodate: only Canada's immigration laws and border security now hold back this potential human tide. Those laws might prove ineffective in some future emergency, or Canadians may themselves decide to change them, thereby introducing populations so large as to prevent their full (or even partial) assimilation to the distinctive features of Canadian English (not to speak of non-linguistic matters). The present immigrant populations of Canada's major cities, some of which are already very large, may be the leading edge of this future trend; studies of their linguistic assimilation and adoption of Canadian English features (or of their failure to assimilate) will give some sense of how Canadian English might be affected by even bigger international migrations in the future.

Of course, Canadian English has successfully absorbed large groups of new speakers in the past without much altering its character, as discussed in Chapter 2. Even where unassimilated pockets have remained distinct for several generations, most of them have eventually succumbed to assimilation, a process that continues today. If sounding Canadian retains social prestige, at least in Canada, future immigrants and their children will no doubt make their best efforts to assimilate. Nevertheless, as the changes now underway in Canadian English suggest, sounding Canadian in one or two centuries, or even in one or two generations, may be quite a different thing from sounding Canadian today.

References

Ahrend, Evelyn R. 1934. Ontario speech. *American Speech* 9/2: 136–139.

Algeo, John. 2006. *British or American English? A Handbook of Word and Grammar Patterns*. Cambridge: Cambridge University Press.

Allen, Harold B. 1959. Canadian–American speech differences along the middle border. *Journal of the Canadian Linguistic Association* 5/1: 17–24.

1976. *The Linguistic Atlas of the Upper Midwest in Three Volumes*. Minneapolis: University of Minnesota Press.

1989. Canadian Raising in the Upper Midwest. *American Speech* 64/1: 74–75.

Arnopoulos, Sheila McLeod and Dominique Clift. 1984. *The English Fact in Quebec*, 2nd edn. Montreal: McGill-Queen's University Press.

Ash, Russell. 2003. *The Top 10 of Everything 2004*. Toronto: Dorling Kindersley / International Book Productions.

Atwood, Margaret. 1969. *The Edible Woman*. Toronto: Seal Books.

Avis, Walter S. 1954. Speech differences along the Ontario–United States border. I. Vocabulary. *Journal of the Canadian Linguistic Association* 1/1: 13–18.

1955. Speech differences along the Ontario–United States border. II. Grammar and syntax. *Journal of the Canadian Linguistic Association* 1/1 (Regular Series): 14–19.

1956. Speech differences along the Ontario–United States border. III. Pronunciation. *Journal of the Canadian Linguistic Association* 2/2: 41–59.

1972. The phonemic segments of an Edmonton idiolect. In L. M. Davis (ed.), *Studies in Honor of Raven I. McDavid, Jr*. Tuscaloosa, AL: University of Alabama Press, 239–250.

1973. The English language in Canada. In T. A. Sebeok (ed.), *Current Trends in Linguistics*, vol. 10: *Linguistics in North America*. The Hague: Mouton, 40–74.

1983. Canadian English in its North American context. *Canadian Journal of Linguistics* 28: 3–15.

1986. The contemporary context of Canadian English. In Harold B. Allen and Michael D. Linn (eds.), *Dialect and Language Variation*. San Diego: Academic Press, 212–216.

Avis, Walter S., C. Crate, P. Drysdale, D. Leechman and M. H. Scargill (eds.). 1967. *A Dictionary of Canadianisms on Historical Principles*. Toronto: W. J. Gage.

Avis, Walter S. and A. Murray Kinloch. 1978. *Writings on Canadian English 1792–1975: An Annotated Bibliography*. Toronto: Fitzhenry & Whiteside.

Ayearst, Morley. 1939. A note on Canadian speech. *American Speech* 14/3: 231–233.

Babiak, Todd. 2006. *The Garneau Block*. Toronto: McClelland & Stewart.

Baeyer, C. V. 1980. *The Ancestry of Canadian English*. Hull, QC: Minister of Supply & Services Canada.

Bähr, Dieter. 1981. *Die Englische Sprache in Kanada: Eine Analyse des "Survey of Canadian English"*. Tübingen: Gunter Narr Verlag.

Bailey, Richard W. 1982. The English language in Canada. In Richard W. Bailey and Manfred Görlach (eds.), *English as a World Language*. Ann Arbor, MI: University of Michigan Press, 134–176.

Baillie, Ray and Diana Baillie. 2001. *Imprints: Discovering the Historic Face of English Quebec*. Montreal: Price-Patterson.

Barbaud, Philippe. 1998. French in Quebec. In Edwards (ed.), 177–201.

Barber, Katherine (ed.). 1998. *The Canadian Oxford Dictionary*. Toronto: Oxford University Press.

2008. *Only in Canada You Say: A Treasury of Canadian Language*. Toronto: Oxford University Press.

Barris, Alex and Ted Barris. 2001. *Making Music: Profiles from a Century of Canadian Music*. Toronto: HarperCollins.

Beal, Joan. 2004. English dialects in the North of England: Phonology. In Kortmann and Schneider (eds.), 113–133.

Belcher, Major E. A. 1924. *Migration within the Empire*. London: W. Collins Sons & Co.

Bloomfield, Morton. 1948. Canadian English and its relation to eighteenth century American speech. *Journal of English and Germanic Philology* 47: 59–67.

Boberg, Charles. 1997. Variation and change in the nativization of foreign (a) in English. PhD dissertation, University of Pennsylvania.

2000. Geolinguistic diffusion and the US–Canada border. *Language Variation and Change* 12: 1–24.

2004a. Canadian English. In Kortmann and Schneider (eds.), 351–365.

2004b. The dialect topography of Montreal. *English World-Wide* 25/2: 171–198.

2004c. Ethnic patterns in the phonetics of Montreal English. *Journal of Sociolinguistics* 8/4: 538–568.

2004d. Real and apparent time in language change: Late adoption of changes in Montreal English. *American Speech* 79/4: 250–269.

2005a. The Canadian Shift in Montreal. *Language Variation and Change* 17/2: 133–154.

2005b. The North American Regional Vocabulary Survey: New variables and methods in the study of North American English. *American Speech* 80/1: 22–60.

2008a. Regional phonetic differentiation in Standard Canadian English. *Journal of English Linguistics* 36/2: 129–154.

2008b. Canadian English vocabulary: National and regional variants. *Anglistik* 19/2: 65–79.

2009. The emergence of a new phoneme: Foreign (a) in Canadian English. *Language Variation and Change* 21/3: 355–380.

Boissevain, Jeremy. 1967. *The Italians of Montreal: Social Adjustment in a Plural Society*. Studies of the Royal Commission on Bilingualism and Biculturalism, vol. 7. Ottawa.

Bourhis, Richard Y. (ed.). 1984a. *Conflict and Language Planning in Quebec*. Clevedon: Multilingual Matters.

1984b. The Charter of the French Language and cross-cultural communication in Montreal. In Bourhis (ed.), 174–204.

2001. Reversing language shift in Quebec. In Joshua A. Fishman (ed.), *Can Threatened Languages Be Saved?* Clevedon: Multilingual Matters, 101–141.

Bradley, A. G. 1932. *The United Empire Loyalists: Founders of British Canada*. London: Thornton Butterworth.

Brinton, Laurel J. and Margery Fee. 2001. Canadian English. In John Algeo (ed.), *The Cambridge History of the English Language*, vol. VI: *English in North America*. Cambridge: Cambridge University Press, 422–440.

Britain, David. 1997. Dialect contact and phonological reallocation: "Canadian Raising" in the English Fens. *Language in Society* 26: 15–46.

Brown, Wallace and Hereward Senior. 1984. *Victorious in Defeat: The Loyalists in Canada*. Toronto: Methuen.

Burnett, Wendy. 2006. Linguistic resistance on the Maine–New Brunswick border. *Canadian Journal of Linguistics* 51/2–3: 161–176.

Caldwell, Gary. 1974. *A Demographic Profile of the English-speaking Population of Quebec 1921–1971*. Publication B-51. Quebec City: International Center for Research on Bilingualism.

1982. People and society. In Gary Caldwell and Eric Waddell (eds.), *The English of Quebec: From Majority to Minority*. Montreal: Institut québécois de la recherché, 57–70.

1984. Anglo-Quebec: Demographic realities and options for the future. In Bourhis (ed.), 205–221.

1998. English Quebec. In Edwards (ed.), 273–292.

Caldwell, Gary and Eric Waddell. 1982. *The English of Quebec: From Majority to Minority*. Montreal: Institut québécois de la recherche.

Campey, Lucille H. 2003. *The Silver Chief: Lord Selkirk and the Scottish Pioneers of Belfast, Baldoon and Red River*. Toronto: Natural Heritage Books.

2004. *After the Hector: The Scottish Pioneers of Nova Scotia and Cape Breton*. Toronto: Natural Heritage Books.

2005. *The Scottish Pioneers of Upper Canada, 1784–1855: Glengarry and Beyond*. Toronto: Natural Heritage Books.

Canada. Department of Justice. 1983. *A Consolidation of the Constitution Acts, 1867 to 1982*. Ottawa: Minister of Supply and Services.

Canada. Dominion Bureau of Statistics, General Statistics Branch. 1933. *The Canada Year Book 1933*. Ottawa: King's Printer.

Canadian Press Stylebook: A Guide for Writers and Editors, The. 1992. Toronto: The Canadian Press.

Carlock, Elizabeth and Wolfgang Wölck. 1981. A method for isolating diagnostic linguistic variables: The Buffalo ethnolects experiment. In David Sankoff and Henrietta Cedergren (eds.), *Variation Omnibus*. Edmonton, AB: Linguistic Research, 17–24.

Carrothers, W. A. 1929/1969. *Emigration from the British Isles*. New York: Augustus M. Kelley.

Casselman, Bill. 1995. *Casselman's Canadian Words: A Comic Browse through Words and Folk Sayings Invented by Canadians*. Toronto: McArthur & Company.

1999–2004. *Canadian Sayings*, vols. 1–3. Toronto: McArthur & Company.

Castonguay, Charles. 1998. The fading Canadian duality. In Edwards (ed.), 36–60.

Chambers, J. K. 1973. Canadian raising. *Canadian Journal of Linguistics* 18/2: 113–135.

(ed.). 1975a. *Canadian English: Origins and Structures.* Toronto: Methuen.

1975b. The Ottawa Valley "twang." In Chambers (ed.), 55–59.

(ed.). 1979a. *The Languages of Canada.* Montreal: Didier.

1979b. Canadian English. In Chambers (ed.), 168–204.

1989. Canadian raising: Blocking, fronting, etc. *American Speech* 64: 75–88.

1991. Canada. In Cheshire (ed.), 89–107.

1993. "Lawless and vulgar innovations": Victorian views of Canadian English. In Clarke (ed.), 1–26.

1994. An introduction to dialect topography. *English World-Wide* 15/1: 35–53.

1995a. *Sociolinguistic Theory.* Oxford: Blackwell.

1995b. The Canada–US border as a vanishing isogloss: The evidence of *chesterfield*. *Journal of English Linguistics* 23/1–2: 155–166.

1998a. English: Canadian varieties. In Edwards (ed.), 252–272.

1998b. Inferring dialect from a postal questionnaire. *Journal of English Linguistics* 26/3: 222–246.

1998c. Social embedding of changes in progress. *Journal of English Linguistics* 26/1: 5–36.

2000. Region and language variation. *English World-Wide* 21/2: 169–199.

2006a. The development of Canadian English. In Kingsley Bolton and Braj B. Kachru (eds.), *World Englishes: Critical Concepts in Linguistics.* London: Routledge, 383–395.

2006b. Canadian Raising: retrospect and prospect. *Canadian Journal of Linguistics* 51/2–3: 105–118.

2008. The tangled garden: Relics and vestiges in Canadian English. *Anglistik* 19/2: 7–21

Chambers, J. K. and Margaret Hardwick. 1986. Comparative sociolinguistics of a sound change in Canadian English. *English World-Wide* 7: 23–46.

Chambers, J. K. and Troy Heisler. 1999. Dialect topography of Québec City English. *Canadian Journal of Linguistics* 44/1: 23–48.

Charbonneau, Hubert, Bertrand Desjardins, Jacques Légaré and Hubert Denis. 2000. The population of the St. Lawrence Valley, 1608–1760. In Haines and Steckel (ed.), 99–142.

Charbonneau, Hubert, Jacques Henripin and Jacques Légaré. 1970. L'avenir démographique des francophones au Québec et à Montréal en l'absence de politiques adéquates. *Revue de Géographie de Montréal* 24/2: 199–202.

Charbonneau, Hubert and Robert Maheu. 1973. *Les aspects démographiques de la question linguistique.* Synthèse S3. Quebec City: Commission d'enquête sur la situation de la langue française et sur les droits linguistiques au Québec.

Cheshire, Jenny (ed.). 1991. *English around the World: Sociolinguistic Perspectives.* Cambridge: Cambridge University Press.

Clarke, Sandra. 1991. Phonological variation and recent language change in St. John's English. In Cheshire (ed.), 109–122.

(ed.). 1993a. *Focus on Canada.* Amsterdam: John Benjamins.

1993b. The Americanization of Canadian pronunciation: A survey of palatal glide usage. In Clarke (ed.), 85–108.

2004a. Newfoundland English: Phonology. In Kortmann and Schneider (eds.), 366–382.

2004b. Newfoundland English: Morphology and syntax. In Kortmann and Schneider (eds.), 303–318.

2004c. The legacy of British and Irish English in Newfoundland. In Raymond Hickey (ed.), *Legacies of Colonial English*. Cambridge: Cambridge University Press, 242–261.

2006. Nooz or nyooz?: The complex construction of Canadian identity. *Canadian Journal of Linguistics* 51/2–3: 225–246.

2008. Newfoundland and Labrador English: Phonology and phonetic variation. *Anglistik* 19/2: 93–106.

Clarke, Sandra, Ford Elms and Amani Youssef. 1995. The third dialect of English: Some Canadian evidence. *Language Variation and Change* 7: 209–228.

Coupland, Douglas. 2002. *Souvenir of Canada*. Vancouver: Douglas & McIntyre.

Cowan, Helen I. 1961. *British emigration to British North America*. Toronto: University of Toronto Press.

Crystal, David. 1997. *English as a Global Language*. Cambridge: Cambridge University Press.

Dailey-O'Cain, Jennifer. 1997. Canadian raising in a midwestern US city. *Language Variation and Change* 9/1: 107–120.

D'Anglejan, Alison. 1984. Language planning in Quebec: An historical overview and future trends. In Bourhis (ed.), 29–52.

D'Arcy, Alexandra. 2004. Contextualizing St. John's Youth English within the Canadian quotative system. *Journal of English Linguistics* 32/4: 323–345.

2005. The development of linguistic constraints: Phonological innovations in St. John's. *Language Variation and Change* 17/3: 327–355.

2008. Canadian English as a window to the rise of *like* in discourse. *Anglistik* 19/2: 125–140.

De Wolf, Gaelan Dodds. 1983. A comparison of phonetically-ordered phonological variables in two major Canadian urban surveys. *Journal of the International Phonetic Association* 13: 90–96.

1988. On phonological variability in Canadian English in Ottawa and Vancouver. *Journal of the International Phonetic Association* 18/2: 110–124.

1989. Analytical methods in a Labovian framework: A mainframe comparison of Canadian urban sociodialect data. *Journal of English Linguistics* 22/1: 119–128.

1990. Patterns of usage in urban Canadian English. *English World-Wide* 11/1: 1–31.

1992. *Social and Regional Factors in Canadian English*. Toronto: Canadian Scholar's Press.

1993. Local patterns and markers of speech in Vancouver English. In Clarke (ed.), 269–293.

1996. Word choice: Lexical variation in two Canadian surveys. *Journal of English Linguistics* 24/2: 131–155.

2004. Evidence for linguistic change in urban Canadian English. In De Wolf, Fee and McAlpine (ed.): 229–252.

De Wolf, Gaelan Dodds, Margery Fee and Janice McAlpine (eds.). 2004. *The Survey of Vancouver English: A Sociolinguistic Study of Urban Canadian English.* Kingston, ON: Strathy Language Unit, Queen's University.

De Wolf, Gaelan Dodds, Robert J. Gregg, Barbara P. Harris and Matthew H. Scargill (eds.). 1997. *Gage Canadian Dictionary, Revised and Expanded.* Vancouver: Gage Educational Publishing.

Dollinger, Stefan. 2006. The modal auxiliaries *have to* and *must* in the Corpus of Early Ontario English. *Canadian Journal of Linguistics* 51/2–3: 287–308.

2008. *New-Dialect Formation in Canada: Evidence from the English Modal Auxiliaries.* Amsterdam: John Benjamins.

Forthcoming. Written sources for Canadian English: Phonetic reconstruction and the low-back vowel merger in the nineteenth century. In Raymond Hickey (ed.), *Varieties in Writing: The Written Word as Linguistic Evidence.* Amsterdam: John Benjamins.

Dollinger, Stefan and Laurel J. Brinton. 2008. Canadian English lexis: Historical and variationist perspectives. *Anglistik* 19/2: 43–64.

Drysdale, P. D. 1959. A first approach to Newfoundland phonemics. *Journal of the Canadian Linguistic Association* 5/1: 25–34.

Dubé, Francine. 2002. The region where you live affects the words you use. *National Post*, Nov. 27: 1.

Eckert, Penelope. 1989. The whole woman: Sex and gender differences in variation. *Language Variation and Change* 1: 245–267.

2008. Where do ethnolects stop? *International Journal of Bilingualism* 12/1: 25–42.

Edwards, J. (ed.). 1998. *Language in Canada.* Cambridge: Cambridge University Press.

Elliott, Bruce S. 1988. *Irish Migrants in the Canadas: A New Approach.* Montreal: McGill-Queen's University Press.

2004. Regional patterns of English immigration and settlement in Upper Canada. In Barbara J. Messamore (ed.), *Canadian Migration Patterns From Britain and North America.* Ottawa: University of Ottawa Press, 51–90.

Emeneau, M. B. 1935. The dialect of Lunenburg, Nova Scotia. *Language* 11: 140–147.

Esling, John H. 1991. Sociophonetic variation in Vancouver. In Cheshire (ed.), 123–133.

2004. Vowel systems and voice setting in the Survey of Vancouver English. In De Wolf, Fee and McAlpine (eds.): 253–288.

Esling, John H. and Henry J. Warkentyne. 1993. Retracting of /æ/ in Vancouver English. In Clarke (ed.), 229–246.

Falk, Lilian and Margaret Harry (eds.). 1999. *The English Language in Nova Scotia.* Lockeport, NS: Roseway Publishing.

Fee, Margery. 2008. French borrowing in Quebec English. *Anglistik* 19/2: 173–188.

Fee, Margery and Janice McAlpine. 1997. *Guide to Canadian English Usage.* Toronto: Oxford University Press.

Findley, Timothy. 1977. *The Wars.* Toronto: Penguin.

Fischer, John L. 1958. Social influences on the choice of a linguistic variant. *Word* 14: 47–56.

Fishman, Joshua A. 1991. *Reversing Language Shift*. Clevedon: Multilingual Matters.

Fought, Carmen. 2003. *Chicano English in Context*. New York: Palgrave MacMillan.

2006. *Language and Ethnicity*. Cambridge: Cambridge University Press.

Fraser, Graham. 2006. *Sorry, I Don't Speak French: Confronting the Canadian Crisis that Won't Go Away*. Toronto: McClelland & Stewart.

Freelance Editors' Association of Canada. 1987. *Editing Canadian English*. Vancouver: Douglas & McIntyre.

Gemery, Henry A. 2000. The white population of the Colonial United States, 1607–1790. In Haines and Steckel (eds.), 143–190.

Giles, Howard, Donald M. Taylor and Richard Bourhis. 1973. Toward a theory of inter-personal accommodation through speech: Some Canadian data. *Language in Society* 2: 177–192.

Gold, Elaine. 2008. Canadian eh?: From eh to zed. *Anglistik* 19/2: 141–156.

Gold, Elaine and Mireille Tremblay. 2006. Eh? and Hein?: Discourse particles or national icons? *Canadian Journal of Linguistics* 51/2–3: 247–264.

Görlach, Manfred. 1991. The identity of Canadian English. In Manfred Görlach (ed.), *Englishes: Studies in Varieties of English 1984–1988*. Amsterdam: John Benjamins, 108–121.

Government of Canada. 1912. *The Canada Year Book 1911, Second Series*. Ottawa: King's Printer.

1914. *The Canada Year Book 1914*. Ottawa: King's Printer.

1974. *Perspective Canada: A Compendium of Social Statistics*. Ottawa: Minister of Industry, Trade and Commerce.

Government of Quebec. 1972. *Report of the Commission of Enquiry on the Position of the French Language and on Linguistic Rights in Quebec* [the Gendron Commission]. Quebec City: Éditeur Officiel du Québec.

Gramley, Stephan and Kurt-Michael Pätzold. 1992. *A Survey of Modern English*. London: Routledge.

Gregg, R. J. 1957a. Notes on the pronunciation of Canadian English as spoken in Vancouver, B.C. *Journal of the Canadian Linguistic Association* 3/1: 20–26.

1957b. Neutralisation and fusion of vocalic phonemes in Canadian English as spoken in the Vancouver area. *Journal of the Canadian Linguistic Association* 3/2: 78–83.

1973. The diphthongs əi and aɪ in Scottish, Scotch-Irish and Canadian English. *Canadian Journal of Linguistics* 18: 136–145.

1983. Local lexical items in the Sociodialectal Survey of Vancouver English. *Canadian Journal of Linguistics* 28/1: 17–23.

1984. *Final Report to the Social Sciences and Humanities Research Council of Canada on "An Urban Dialect Survey of the English Spoken in Vancouver."* Vancouver: University of British Columbia Linguistics Department.

1992. The Survey of Vancouver English. *American Speech* 67/3: 250–267.

1993. Canadian English lexicography. In Clarke (ed.), 27–44.

1995. The survival of local lexical items as specific markers in Vancouver English. *Journal of English Linguistics* 23/1–2: 184–194.

2004. The survey of Vancouver English, 1976–1984: Methodology, planning, implementation and analysis. In De Wolf, Fee and McAlpine (ed.), 1–138.

Guy, Gregory. 1980. Variation in the group and the individual. In William Labov (ed.), *Locating Language in Time and Space*. New York: Academic Press, 1–36.

1991. Explanation in variable phonology: An exponential model of morphological constraints. *Language Variation and Change* 3: 1–22.

Guy, Gregory and Charles Boberg. 1997. Inherent variability and the Obligatory Contour Principle. *Language Variation and Change* 9: 149–164.

Hagiwara, Robert. 2006. Vowel production in Winnipeg. *Canadian Journal of Linguistics* 51/2–3: 127–142.

Haines, Michael R. 2000. The white population of the United States, 1790–1920. In Haines and Steckel (eds.), 305–369.

Haines, Michael R. and Richard H. Steckel (eds.). 2000. *A Population History of North America*. Cambridge: Cambridge University Press.

Hamilton, Donald E. 1958. Notes on Montreal English. *Journal of the Canadian Linguistic Association* 4/2: 70–79.

Handcock, W. Gordon. 1977. English migration to Newfoundland. In Mannion (ed.), 15–48.

Hansen, Marcus Lee. 1940. *The Mingling of the Canadian and American Peoples*, vol. I: *Historical*. Completed and prepared for publication by John Bartlet Brebner. New Haven: Yale University Press.

Harris, Barbara P. 1983. Handsaw or harlot? Some problem etymologies in the lexicon of Chinook Jargon. *Canadian Journal of Linguistics* 28/1: 25–32.

Harris, R. Cole and John Warkentin. 1974. *Canada Before Confederation: A Study in Historical Geography*. New York: Oxford University Press.

Harvey, David D. 1991. *Americans in Canada: Migration and Settlement since 1840*. Lewiston, NY: The Edwin Mellen Press.

Heller, Monica S. 1982. Negotiations of language choice in Montreal. In John J. Gumperz (ed.), *Language and Social Identity*. Cambridge: Cambridge University Press, 108–118.

Henripin, Jacques. 1973. Quebec and the demographic dilemma of French Canadian society. In Dale C. Thomson (ed.), *Quebec Society and Politics: Views from the Inside*. Toronto: McClelland & Stewart, 155–166.

1989. *Naître ou ne pas être*. Quebec City: Institut québécois de recherche sur la culture.

Hickey, Raymond. 2002. The Atlantic edge: The relationship between Irish English and Newfoundland English. *English World-Wide* 23/2: 283–316.

2004. Irish English: phonology. In Kortmann and Schneider (eds.), 68–97.

2007. *Irish English: History and Present-Day Forms*. Cambridge: Cambridge University Press.

Higinbotham, John D. 1962. Western vernacular. *Alberta Historical Review* 10/4: 9–17.

Hillenbrand, James, Laura A. Getty, Michael J. Clark and Kimberlee Wheeler. 1995. Acoustic characteristics of American English vowels. *Journal of the Acoustical Society of America* 95/5: 3099–3111.

Hollett, Pauline. 2006. Investigating St. John's English: Real- and apparent-time perspectives. *Canadian Journal of Linguistics* 51/2–3: 143–160.

Hollingshead, Greg. 1995. *The Roaring Girl.* Toronto: Somerville House Publishing.

Horvath, Barbara. 1985. *Variation in Australian English: The Sociolects of Sydney.* Cambridge: Cambridge University Press.

Houston, Cecil J. and William J. Smyth. 1990. *Irish Emigration and Canadian Settlement: Patterns, Links, & Letters.* Toronto: University of Toronto Press.

Howe, Neil and Bill Strauss. 1993. *13th Gen: Abort, Retry, Ignore, Fail?* New York: Vintage Books.

Hultin, Neil C. 1967. Canadian views of American English. *American Speech* 42/4: 243–260.

Hung, Henrietta, John Davison and J. K. Chambers. 1993. Comparative sociolinguistics of (aw)-fronting. In Clarke (ed.), 247–267.

Idsardi, William J. 2006. Canadian raising, opacity, and rephonemicization. *Canadian Journal of Linguistics* 51/2–3: 119–126.

Jackson, Rick. 1994. *Encyclopedia of Canadian Rock, Pop & Folk Music.* Kingston, ON: Quarry Press.

Jedwab, Jack. 1996. *English in Montreal: A Layman's Look at the Current Situation.* Montreal: Les Éditions Images.

2000. *Ethnic Identification and Heritage Languages in Canada.* Montreal: Les Éditions Images.

2004. *Going Forward: The Evolution of Quebec's English-speaking Community.* Ottawa: Department of Public Works and Government Services Canada.

Johnson, Stanley C. 1913. *A History of Emigration from the United Kingdom to North America, 1763–1912.* London: George Routledge & Sons.

Johnson, William. 1991. *Anglophobie Made in Quebec.* Montreal: Stanké.

Joos, Martin. 1942. A phonological dilemma in Canadian English. *Language* 18: 141–144.

Kachru, Braj B. 1985. Standards, codification and sociolinguistic realism: The English language in the Outer Circle. In Randolph Quirk and Henry G. Widdowson (eds.), *English in the World: Teaching and Learning the Language and Literatures.* Cambridge: Cambridge University Press, 11–30.

Kachru, Braj B., Yamuna Kachru and Cecil L. Nelson. 2006. *The Handbook of World Englishes.* Oxford: Blackwell.

Kerswill, Paul. 2003. Dialect levelling and geographical diffusion in British English. In David Britain and Jenny Cheshire (eds.), *Social Dialectology: In Honour of Peter Trudgill.* Amsterdam: John Benjamins, 223–243.

Kerswill, Paul, Eivind Nessa Torgersen and Susan Fox. 2008. Reversing "drift": Innovation and diffusion in the London diphthong system. *Language Variation and Change* 20/3: 451–491.

Kerswill, Paul and Ann Williams. 2000. Creating a new town koine: Children and language change in Milton Keynes. *Language in Society* 29: 65–115.

Kinloch, A. M. 1983. The phonology of Central/Prairie Canadian English. *American Speech* 58/1: 31–35.

1995. The significance for the study of Canadian English of the work of Harold B. Allen. *Journal of English Linguistics* 23/1–2: 167–183.

Kinloch, A. M. and Walter S. Avis. 1989. Central Canadian English and Received Standard English: A comparison of pronunciation. In Ofelia García and Ricardo Otheguy (eds.), *English Across Cultures, Cultures Across English: A Reader in Cross-cultural Communication.* Berlin: Mouton de Gruyter, 403–420.

Kirwin, William J. 1960. LABRADOR, ST. JOHN'S and NEWFOUNDLAND: Some pronunciations. *Journal of the Canadian Linguistic Association* 6/2: 115–116.

1993. The planting of Anglo-Irish in Newfoundland. In Clarke (ed.), 65–84.

2001. Newfoundland English. In John Algeo (ed.), *The Cambridge History of the English Language*, vol. VI: *English in North America*. Cambridge: Cambridge University Press, 441–455.

Kortmann, Bernd and Edgar W. Schneider (eds.). 2004. *A Handbook of Varieties of English*, vol. 1: Phonology. Berlin: Mouton de Gruyter.

Kurath, Hans. 1949. *A Word Geography of the Eastern United States*. Ann Arbor, MI: University of Michigan Press.

Kurath, Hans and Raven I. McDavid. 1961. *The Pronunciation of English in the Atlantic States*. Tuscaloosa, AL: University of Alabama Press.

Labov, William. 1963. The social motivation of a sound change. *Word* 19: 273–309.

1972. *Sociolinguistic Patterns*. Philadelphia: University of Pennsylvania Press.

1990. The intersection of sex and social class in the course of linguistic change. *Language Variation and Change* 2: 205–254.

1991. The three dialects of English. In Penelope Eckert (ed.), *New Ways of Analyzing Sound Change*. New York: Academic Press, 1–44.

1994. *Principles of Linguistic Change: Internal Factors*. Oxford: Blackwell.

Labov, William, Sharon Ash and Charles Boberg. 2006. *The Atlas of North American English: Phonetics, Phonology and Sound Change*. Berlin: Mouton de Gruyter.

Labov, William, Malcah Yaeger and Richard Steiner. 1972. *A Quantitative Study of Sound Change in Progress*. Philadelphia: US Regional Survey.

Laferrière, Martha. 1979. Ethnicity in phonological variation and change. *Language* 55: 603–617.

Lambert, Wallace E. 1967. A social psychology of bilingualism. *Journal of Social Issues* 23: 91–109.

Laporte, Pierre E. 1984. Status planning in Quebec: An evaluation. In Bourhis (ed.), 53–80.

Lass, Roger. 2006. Phonology and morphology. In Richard Hogg and David Denison (eds.), *A History of the English Language*. Cambridge: Cambridge University Press, 43–108.

Laurence, Margaret. 1974. *The Diviners*. Toronto: McClelland & Stewart.

Laurin, Camille. 1980. Préface. In Michel Amyot (ed.), *La Situation démolinguistique au Québec et la Charte de la Langue Française*. Quebec City: Conseil de la langue française, 9–11.

Leacock, Stephen. 1912. *Sunshine Sketches of a Little Town*. Toronto: McClelland & Stewart, 1982.

Legault, Josée. 1992. *L'invention d'une minorité: Les Anglo-québécois*. Montreal: Boréal.

Lehn, Walter. 1959. Vowel contrasts in a Saskatchewan dialect. *Canadian Journal of Linguistics* 5/2: 90–98.

Léon, Pierre R. and Philippe J. Martin (eds.). 1979. *Toronto English: Studies in Phonetics*. Ottawa: Marcel Didier (Canada).

Levine, Marc V. 1990. *The Reconquest of Montreal: Language Policy and Social Change in a Bilingual City*. Philadelphia: Temple University Press.

Libman, Robert. 2009. 20 years later. *Montreal Gazette*, Sept. 22: A15.

Lieberson, Stanley. 1970. *Language and Ethnic Relations in Canada*. New York: Wiley.

　1981. Linguistic and ethnic segregation in Montreal. In Anwar S. Dil (ed.), *Language Diversity and Language Contact: Essays by Stanley Lieberson*. Palo Alto, CA: Stanford University Press, 218–248.

Lindsey, Geoff. 1990. Quantity and quality in British and American vowel systems. In Susan Ramsaran (ed.), *Studies in the Pronunciation of English*. London: Routledge, 106–118.

Lipset, Seymour Martin. 1990. *Continental Divide: The Values and Institutions of the United States and Canada*. New York: Routledge.

Locher, Uli. 1988. *Les Anglophones de Montréal; émigration et évolution des attitudes 1978–1983*. Quebec City: Conseil de la Langue Française.

　1992. *Intentions to Leave Quebec among Students in English High Schools and Colleges*. Working papers in Social Behaviour 92–05. Montreal: Department of Sociology, McGill University.

Lougheed, W. C. (ed.). 1986. *In Search of the Standard in Canadian English*. Kingston, ON: Strathy Language Unit, Queen's University.

　1988. *Writings on Canadian English 1976–1987: A Selective, Annotated Bibliography*. Kingston, ON: Strathy Language Unit, Queen's University.

Lovell, Charles J. 1955. Whys and hows of collecting for the Dictionary of Canadian English. Part I: Scope and source material. *Journal of the Canadian Linguistic Association* 1/2: 3–8.

　1956. Whys and hows of collecting for the Dictionary of Canadian English. Part II: Excerption of quotations. *Journal of the Canadian Linguistic Association* 2/1: 23–32.

　1958. A sampling of materials for a dictionary of Canadian English based on historical principles. *Journal of the Canadian Linguistic Association* 4/1: 7–33.

MacGregor, James G. 1972. *A History of Alberta*. Edmonton, AB: Hurtig Publishers.

MacLennan, Hugh. 1941. *Barometer Rising*. Toronto: McClelland & Stewart, 1982.

MacMillan, Michael C. 1998. *The Practice of Language Rights in Canada*. Toronto: University of Toronto Press.

MacNutt, W. Stewart. 1965. *The Atlantic Provinces: The Emergence of Colonial Society 1712–1857*. Toronto: McClelland & Stewart.

Mallea, John. 1984. Minority language education in Quebec and anglophone Canada. In Bourhis (ed.), 222–261.

Mannion, John J. 1977a. *The Peopling of Newfoundland: Essays in Historical Geography*. St. John's, NL: Institute of Social and Economic Research, Memorial University of Newfoundland.

　1977b. Introduction. In Mannion (ed.), 1–13.

McArthur Tom. 1989. *The English Language as Used in Quebec: A Survey*. Kingston, ON: Strathy Language Unit, Queen's University.

McConnell, R. E. 1979. *Our Own Voice*. Toronto: Gage Educational Publishing.

McGillis, Ian. 2002. *A Tourist's Guide to Glengarry*. Erin, ON: The Porcupine's Quill.

McInnis, Marvin. 2000a. The population of Canada in the nineteenth century. In Haines and Steckel (eds.), 371–432.

2000b. Canada's population in the twentieth century. In Haines and Steckel (eds.), 529–599.

McLay, W. S. W. 1930. A note on Canadian English. *American Speech* 5/4: 328–329.

McRae, Kenneth. 1998. Official bilingualism: From the 1960s to the 1990s. In Edwards (ed.), 61–83.

Meechan, Marjory. 1998. I guess we have Mormon language: American English in a Canadian setting. *Cahiers linguistiques d'Ottawa* 26: 39–54.

1999. The Mormon drawl: Religious ethnicity and phonological variation in southern Alberta. PhD dissertation, University of Ottawa.

Meechan, Marjory and Michele Foley. 1994. On resolving disagreement: Linguistic theory and variation – "There's bridges." *Language Variation and Change* 6/1: 63–85.

Meyer, Matthias L.G., ed. 2008. Focus on Canadian English. *Anglistik* 19/2.

Miller, Jeffrey. 1986. *Street Talk: The Language of Coronation Street*. Toronto: CBC Enterprises.

Miller, Roger. 1984. The response of business firms to the francization process. In Bourhis (ed.), 114–129.

Mitchell, W. O. 1947. *Who Has Seen the Wind*. Toronto: McClelland & Stewart, 1998.

Montgomery, Lucy Maud. 1908. *Anne of Green Gables*. Toronto: McClelland & Stewart, 1992.

Moore, Christopher. 1984. *The Loyalists: Revolution, Exile, Settlement*. Toronto: Macmillan of Canada.

Moore, Margaret E. 1989. *Understanding British English: Bridging the Gap Between the English Language and Its American Counterpart*. New York: Citadel Press.

Morgan, Kenneth O. (ed). 1984. *The Oxford History of Britain*. Oxford: Oxford University Press.

Morrison, Val, Bill Reimer and Frances M. Shaver. 1991. English speakers in the Eastern Townships of Quebec. *English World-Wide* 12/1: 63–74.

Munro, Alice. 1996. *Selected Stories*. Harmondsworth: Penguin, 1998.

Munroe, Helen C. 1929. Montreal English. *American Speech* 5/1: 21.

Murdoch, Margaret M. 2004. Are the traditional Canadian diphthongs on the move? In De Wolf, Fee and McAlpine (eds.), 221–228.

Nearey, Terrance Michael. 1978. *Phonetic Feature Systems for Vowels*. Bloomington, IN: Indiana University Linguistics Club.

Niedzielski, Nancy. 1999. The effect of social information on the perception of sociolinguistic variables. *Journal of Language and Social Psychology* 18/1: 62–85.

Noad, Algy Smillie. 1932. *A Canadian Handbook of English*. Toronto: Sir Isaac Pitman & Sons (Canada).

Nylvek, Judith. 1993. A sociolinguistic analysis of Canadian English in Saskatchewan: A look at urban versus rural speakers. In Clarke (ed.), 201–228.

Nylvek, Judith. 1992. Is Canadian English in Saskatchewan becoming more American? *American Speech* 67/3: 268–78.

Oakes, Leigh and Jane Warren. 2007. *Language, Citizenship and Identity in Quebec*. Basingstoke, Hants: Palgrave Macmillan.

Orkin, Mark M. 1970. *Speaking Canadian English: An Informal Account of the English Language in Canada*. Toronto: General Publishing.

Orkin, Mark M. and Bickerstaff [Don Evans]. 1997. *Canajan, eh?* (3rd rev. edn.) Toronto: Stoddart.

Owens, Thompson W. and Paul M. Baker. 1984. Linguistic insecurity in Winnipeg: Validation of a Canadian Index of Insecurity. *Language in Society* 13/3: 337–350.

Paddock, Harold J. 1981. *A Dialect Survey of Carbonear, Newfoundland*. Publications of the American Dialect Society 68. Tuscaloosa, AL: University of Alabama Press.

(ed.). 1982. *Languages in Newfoundland and Labrador*. St. John's, NL: Memorial University Press.

Paillé, Michel. 1985. *Contribution à la démolinguistique du Québec*. Quebec City: Conseil de la Langue Française.

1989. *Nouvelles tendances démolinguistiques dans l'Île de Montréal 1981–1996*. Quebec City: Conseil de la Langue Française.

Palmer, Howard. 1990. *Alberta: A New History*. Edmonton, AB: Hurtig Publishers.

Paradis, C. 1980. La règle de Canadian raising et l'analyse en structure syllabique. *Canadian Journal of Linguistics* 25: 35–45.

Parenteau, Philippe, Marie-Odile Magnan and Caroline V. Thibault. 2008. *Portrait socio-économique de la communauté anglophone au Québec et dans ses régions*. Montreal: Institut national de la recherche scientifique.

Parkin, Tom. 1989. *Wet Coast Words: A Dictionary of British Columbia Words and Phrases*. Victoria, BC: Orca Book Publishers.

Peterson, Gordon E. and Harold L. Barney. 1952. Control methods used in a study of the vowels. *Journal of the Acoustical Society of America* 24: 175–184.

Picard, Marc. 1977. Canadian raising: The case against reordering. *Canadian Journal of Linguistics* 22: 144–55.

Piske, Thorsten. 2008. Italian-English bilinguals in Canada: Age and L1 use effects on their perception and production of L2 and L1 speech. *Anglistik* 19/2: 215–228

Poplack, Shana. 1978. Dialect acquisition among Puerto Rican bilinguals. *Language in Society* 7:89–103.

2008. French influence on Canadian English: Issues of code-switching and borrowing. *Anglistik* 19/2: 189–200.

Poplack, Shana and Sali Tagliamonte. 1991. African American English in the diaspora: Evidence from old-line Nova Scotians. *Language Variation and Change* 3/3: 301–339. (Also in Clarke 1993a: 109–150.)

Poplack, Shana, James A. Walker and Rebecca Malcolmson. 2006. An English "like no other"? Language contact and change in Quebec. *Canadian Journal of Linguistics* 51/2: 185–213.

Porter, Bernard H. 1966. Some Newfoundland phrases, sayings, and figures of speech. *American Speech* 41: 294–297.

Poteet, Lewis J. 1988. *The South Shore Phrase Book*. Hantsport, NS: Lancelot Press.

1992. *Talking Country: The Eastern Townships Phrase Book*. Ayers Cliff, QC: Pigwidgeon Press.

Pratley, Gerald. 2003. *A Century of Canadian Cinema*. Toronto: Lynx Images.

Pratt, T. K. (ed.). 1988. *Dictionary of Prince Edward Island English*. Toronto: University of Toronto Press.

1993. The hobgoblin of Canadian English spelling. In Clarke (ed.), 45–64.

Pratt, T. K. and Scott Burke (eds.). 1998. *Prince Edward Island Sayings*. Toronto: University of Toronto Press.

Priestly, F. E. L. 1951. Canadian English. In E. Partridge and J. W. Clark (eds.), *British and American English since 1900*. New York: Greenwood Press, 72–79.

Pringle, Ian. 1983. The concept of dialect and the study of Canadian English. *Queen's Quarterly* 90: 100–21.

Pringle, Ian, C. Stanley Jones and Enoch Padolsky. 1981. The misapprehension of Ottawa standards in an adjacent rural area. *English World-Wide* 2/2: 165–180.

Pringle, Ian and Enoch Padolsky. 1983. The linguistic survey of the Ottawa Valley. *American Speech* 58/4: 325–344.

Provost, Honorius. 1984. *Les Premiers Anglo-Canadiens à Québec*. Quebec City: Institut québécois de recherche sur la culture.

Quebec Ministry of Education. 1992. *Task Force on English-Language Education in Quebec: Report to the Minister of Education in Quebec* [the *Chambers Report*].

Richards, D. J. 2004. The *Survey of Vancouver English*: Attitudes and awareness. In De Wolf, Fee and McAlpine (eds.), 178–199.

Richler, Mordecai. 1959. *The Apprenticeship of Duddy Kravitz*. Toronto: McClelland & Stewart, 1983.

Roberts, Julie. 2007. Vermont lowering? Raising some questions about /ai/ and /au/ south of the Canadian border. *Language Variation and Change* 19/2: 181–197.

Rodman, Lilita. 1974. Characteristics of BC English. *English Quarterly* 7: 49–82.

Ross, Sinclair. 1941. *As for Me and My House*. Toronto: McClelland & Stewart, 1982.

Rothney, G. O. 1973. *Newfoundland: A History*. Ottawa: The Canadian Historical Association.

Rudin, Ronald. 1985. *The Forgotten Quebecers: A History of English-Speaking Quebec, 1759–1980*. Quebec: Institut québécois de recherche sur la culture.

Sadlier-Brown, Emily and Meredith Tamminga. 2008. The Canadian Shift: Coast to coast. In Susie Jones (ed.), *Proceedings of the 2008 Annual Conference of the Canadian Linguistic Association*, 1–14.

Sandilands, John (ed.). 1912. *Western Canadian Dictionary and Phrase Book*. Edmonton: University of Alberta Press.

Scargill, Matthew Henry. 1954. A pilot study of Alberta speech: Vocabulary. *Journal of the Canadian Linguistic Association* 1/1: 21–22.

1955. Canadian English and Canadian culture in Alberta. *Journal of the Canadian Linguistic Association* 1/1 (Regular Series): 26–29.

1956. Eighteenth century English in Nova Scotia. *Journal of the Canadian Linguistic Association* 2/1: 3.

1957. Sources of Canadian English. *Journal of English and Germanic Philology* 56: 610–614.

1974. *Modern Canadian English Usage*. Toronto: McClelland & Stewart.

1977. *A Short History of Canadian English*. Victoria, BC: Sono Nis Press.

Scargill, Matthew Henry and Henry J. Warkentyne. 1972. The Survey of Canadian English: a report. *English Quarterly* 5/3: 47–104.

Schur, Norman W. 1987. *British English A to Zed*. New York: Harper Perennial.

Scollon, Ronald and Suzanne B. K. Scollon. 1979. *Linguistic Convergence: An Ethnography of Speaking at Fort Chipewyan, Alberta*. New York: Academic Press.

Scott, N. C. 1939. Canadian caught and cot. *Maître Phonétique* 66: 22.

Scowen, Reed. 1991. *A Different Vision: The English in Quebec in the 1990s*. Toronto: Maxwell Macmillan.

Shapiro, Michael. 1995. A case of distant assimilation: /str/ → /štr/. *American Speech* 70: 101–107.

1997. Broad and flat *A* in marked words. *American Speech* 72/4: 437–439.

Shaw, Matthew. 2003. *Great Scots!: How the Scots Created Canada*. Winnipeg: Heartland Associates.

Siemund, Peter and Alexander Haselow. 2008. Newfoundland English morpho-syntax: Universal aspects and trends. *Anglistik* 19/2: 201–213.

Staveley, Michael. 1977. Population dynamics in Newfoundland: The Regional patterns. In Mannion (ed.), 49–76.

Stevenson, Garth. 1999. *A Community Besieged: The Anglophone Minority and the Politics of Quebec*. Montreal: McGill-Queen's University Press.

Story, G. M. 1982. The dialects of Newfoundland English. In Paddock (ed.), 62–70.

Story, G. M., W. J. Kirwin and J. D. A. Widdowson (eds.). 1990. *Dictionary of Newfoundland English, Second Edition with Supplement*. Toronto: University of Toronto Press.

Stroinska, Magda and Vikki Cecchetto. 1999. Canada – the winter half of North America. In Eddie Ronowicz and Colin Yallop (eds.), *English: One Language, Different Cultures*. London: Cassell, 136–178.

Stuart-Smith, Jane. 2004. Scottish English: Phonology. In Kortmann and Schneider (eds.), 47–67.

Tagliamonte, Sali A. 2006. "So cool, right?": Canadian English entering the 21st century. *Canadian Journal of Linguistics* 51/2–3: 309–332.

Tagliamonte, Sali A. and Alexandra D'Arcy. 2004. He's like, she's like: The quotative system in Canadian youth. *Journal of Sociolinguistics* 8/4: 493–514.

2007a. Frequency and variation in the community grammar: Tracking a new change through the generations. *Language Variation and Change* 19/2: 199–217.

2007b. The modals of obligation/necessity in Canadian perspective. *English World-Wide* 28/1: 47–87.

Tagliamonte, Sali A. and Rachel Hudson. 1999. Be like et al. beyond America: the quotative system in British and Canadian youth. *Journal of Sociolinguistics* 3/2: 147–172.

Taylor, Donald M. and Lise Dubé-Simard. 1984. Language planning and intergroup relations: Anglophone and francophone attitudes toward the Charter of the French Language. In Bourhis (ed.), 130–147.

Termote, M. and D. Gauvreau. 1988. *La situation démolinguistique du Québec*. Quebec City: Conseil de la Langue Française.

Thain, Chris. 1987. *Cold as a Bay Street Banker's Heart: The Ultimate Prairie Phrase Book*. Saskatoon: Western Producer Prairie Books.

Thomas, Erik R. 1991. The origin of Canadian raising in Ontario. *Canadian Journal of Linguistics* 36: 147–70.

2001. *An Acoustic Analysis of Vowel Variation in New World English.* Publication of the American Dialect Society no. 85. Durham, NC: Duke University Press.

Toohey, Kelleen. 1985. English as a second language for Native Canadians. *Canadian Journal of Education* 10/3: 275–293.

Torgersen, Eivind, Paul Kerswill and Sue Fox. 2006. Ethnicity as a source of changes in the London vowel system. In Frans Hinskens (ed.), *Language Variation – European Perspectives.* Amsterdam: John Benjamins, 249–263.

Trivisonno, John. 1998. *The Official St. Leonard Dictionary, Revised and Updated.* Montreal: Chapter 11 Productions.

Trudgill, Peter. 1974. *The Social Differentiation of English in Norwich.* Cambridge: Cambridge University Press.

1986. *Dialects in Contact.* Oxford: Blackwell.

2004. *New-Dialect Formation: The Inevitability of Colonial Englishes.* New York: Oxford University Press.

Trudgill, Peter and Jean Hannah. 1985. *International English: A Guide to Standard Varieties of English,* 2nd edn. London: Edward Arnold.

Underhill, Doug. 1996. *Miramichi Dictionary.* Rothesay, NB: Neptune Publishing Company.

Urquhart, M. C. and K. A. H. Buckley (eds.) 1965. *Historical Statistics of Canada.* Toronto: Macmillan (Canada).

Vance, Timothy J. 1987. "Canadian Raising" in some dialects of the northern United States. *American Speech* 62: 195–210.

Vancouver Public Library. 1999. *Great Canadian Books of the Century.* Vancouver: Douglas & McIntyre.

Veltman, Calvin. 1996. The English language in Quebec 1940–1990. In Joshua A. Fishman, Andrew W. Conrad and Alma Rubal-Lopez (eds.), *Post-Imperial English: Status Change in Former British and American Colonies, 1940–1990.* Berlin: Mouton de Gruyter, 205–237.

Wallace, W. Stewart. 1964. *The United Empire Loyalists: A Chronicle of the Great Migration.* Toronto: University of Toronto Press.

Walker, Douglas C. 1975. Another Edmonton idiolect: Comments on an article by Professor Avis. In Chambers (ed.), 129–132.

Walker, James A. 2001. Using the past to explain the present: Tense and temporal reference in Early African American English. *Language Variation and Change* 13/1: 1–35.

2005. The ain't constraint: Not-contraction in Early African American English. *Language Variation and Change* 17/1: 1–17.

2007. "There's bears back there": Plural existentials and vernacular universals in Quebec English. *English World-Wide* 28/2: 147–166.

Warkentyne, Henry J. 1973. Contemporary Canadian English: A report of the Survey of Canadian English. *American Speech* 46/3–4: 193–199.

1983. Attitudes and language behavior. *Canadian Journal of Linguistics* 28/1: 71–76.

Watson, Sheila. 1959. *The Double Hook.* Toronto: McClelland & Stewart.

Wells, J. C. 1982. *Accents of English.* Cambridge: Cambridge University Press.

Wiebe, Armin. 1984. *The Salvation of Yasch Siemens.* Winnipeg: Turnstone Press.

Willis, Clodius. 1972. Perception of vowel phonemes in Fort Erie, Ontario, Canada, and Buffalo, New York: An application of synthetic vowel categorization tests to dialectology. *Journal of Speech and Hearing Research* 15: 246–255.

Wölck, Wolfgang. 2002. Ethnolects – between bilingualism and urban dialect. In Li Wei, Jean-Marc Dewaele and Alex Housen (eds.), *Opportunities and Challenges of Bilingualism*. Berlin: Mouton de Gruyter, 157–170.

Woods, Howard B. 1991. Social differentiation in Ottawa English. In Cheshire (ed.), 134–149.

  1993. A synchronic study of English spoken in Ottawa: Is Canadian English becoming more American? In Clarke (ed.), 151–178.

  1999. *The Ottawa Survey of Canadian English*. Kingston, ON: Strathy Language Unit, Queen's University.

Wyld, Henry Cecil. 1925. *A History of Modern Colloquial English*, 3rd edn. Oxford: Blackwell.

Zelinsky, Wilbur. 1973. *The Cultural Geography of the United States*. Englewood Cliffs, NJ: Prentice-Hall.

Zeller, Christine. 1993. Linguistic symmetries, asymmetries, and border effects within a Canadian/American sample. In Clarke (ed.), 179–200.

Index